CUTTING
THE VINES OF
THE PAST

CUTTING THE VINES OF THE PAST

Environmental Histories of the Central African Rain Forest

Tamara Giles-Vernick

University Press of Virginia   *Charlottesville and London*

THE UNIVERSITY PRESS OF VIRGINIA
© 2002 by the Rector and Visitors of the University of Virginia
All rights reserved
Printed in the United States of America on acid-free paper

First published 2002

9 8 7 6 5 4 3 2 1

Library of Congress Cataloging-in-Publication Data

Giles-Vernick, Tamara, 1962–
    Cutting the vines of the past : environmental histories of the
Central African rain forest / Tamara Giles-Vernick.
        p.   cm.
    Includes bibliographical references and index.
    ISBN 0-8139-2102-3 (cloth : alk. paper) — ISBN 0-8139-2103-1
(pbk. : alk. paper)
    1. Mpiemo (African people) —History. 2. Nature—Effect of human
beings on —Central African Republic. 3. Geographical perception—
Case studies. 4. Human ecology—Philosophy—Case studies. I. Title.

DT546.345 .M67 G55 2002
967.41—dc21
                                                              2002016708

For Ken

CONTENTS

ILLUSTRATIONS

ACKNOWLEDGMENTS

This book began as a dissertation about memory, place, environment, and changing land-use patterns among Mpiemu people in the Sangha basin rain forests. But after I had completed it, I was so dissatisfied with the slippery, nebulous concept of memory that I chucked the entire work and rewrote it. This book, a historical study of a category of knowledge and way of seeing, is thus an effort to elucidate the changing ways that one group of people imagines and characterizes human relations with the forest and the past.

Innumerable people contributed to the original project, as well as the process of dismantling and rebuilding it as a book. My heartfelt thanks go first to Sara Berry, who supervised an unruly dissertation and whose keen insights and criticisms shaped my understandings of how people invest in, use, and imagine property over time and of how to do interdisciplinary historical research.

Funds for the dissertation research and subsequent research trips came from several sources, for which I am most grateful. Under the rubric of the Social Science Research Council and the American Council of Learned Societies, the Rockefeller Foundation supplied training and research monies, as did a Fulbright dissertation grant. The University of Virginia financed multiple research trips and generously gave me leave time to write. The Yale Agrarian Studies program provided me with a generous fellowship in 1998–99 and a stimulating intellectual home for a year. Fellows, faculty, and students associated with Agrarian Studies challenged me to think in more sophisticated and grounded ways about environmental relations, particularly Bob Harms, Kathy Cooke, Jim McCann, and Jin Sato.

In the Central African Republic, I received assistance from and had valuable conversations with many people. Rebecca Hardin, David Harris, Anna Kretsinger, Justina Ray, Andrea Turkalo, David Wilkie, and Zana Henri helped me to understand the diverse ways of thinking about relations between people and environment in the Sangha basin forest. Professor Amaye Maurice of the University of Bangui was helpful at a time when the university was not even functioning. I am also indebted to the wisdom and patience of research assistants, friends, and acquaintances with whom I had the privilege of working in Central Africa. My sincere thanks go to the

Amions family for sharing their stories, meat, and love. Mabessimo Florent, Biloue Raymond, and Wan-Mbissa Samuel proved to be patient and dedicated research assistants. Lindjombo chief Lindjombo Etienne welcomed me into his village and shared freely his impressions of the region's history. Kadele Charles, Gondo Jeanne, Satuba Omer, Bongolo Elisabeth, Dinoramibali Martine, Mabessimo-Angoula Levi, Yodjala Philippe, Alouba Clotere, Mpeng Patrice, and countless others put up with endless and sometimes rude questions with more good humor and genuine interest than I probably deserved.

People associated with conservation efforts in the Dzanga-Ndoki National Park and the Dzanga-Sangha Special Reserve remained ever gracious and generous during my stay and after. I thank Allard Blom and Ngatoua Urbain for logistical support and their careful insights into the politics of conservation. Doungoumbe Gustave offered some very helpful perspectives on conservation debates in the Central African Republic. Danyelle O'Hara and Richard Carroll of the World Wildlife Fund in Washington, D.C., kindly gave me access to relevant project documents.

I thank archivists at the Centre des Archives d'Outre-mer, the Musée de l'Homme, and the Muséum National de l'Histoire Naturelle in Paris for their assistance. At the Archives de la Congrégation des Pères du Saint-Esprit in Chevilly-la-Rue, Père Ghislain de Banville actively helped me to locate a cache of wonderful writings and photographs. Pères Simon Légasse and Francis Betemps of the Archives des Capucins in Toulouse and Annecy, respectively, helped to make my visits enormously productive, and our afternoon coffee and conversations remain an enjoyable memory. I am especially indebted to Karin Sjostedt and Olle Bergstrom, who took a genuine interest in my research on Örebromission activities in equatorial Africa. Karin Sjostedt, Björn Ljungström, and Lena Råberg provided excellent translations and summaries of Swedish documents, and I am truly grateful for their efforts. I also thank Christof Morrissey for his assistance in the Bundesarchiv in Berlin.

In the United States, Great Britain, and France, I benefited from the wisdom and generosity of many people whom I wish to thank. Philip Burnham and Elisabeth Copet-Rougier took time to orient me in the literature and major historical questions in this part of equatorial Africa. Philip Curtin sparked my interest in environmental history, and Gillian Feeley-Harnik had an uncanny ability to ask creative, provocative questions that years later I am still struggling to answer. At the Oxford Forestry Institute, Peter Kanowski, Peter Savil, and Nicholas Brown guided me through the rudiments of tropical rain-forest ecology and forestry. I also found much value in interactions with Misty Bastian, John Cinnamon, Dennis Cordell, Kandioura Dramé, Bob Geraci, Peter Geschiere, Michelle Kisliuk, Kairn Klieman, Greg

Maddox, Phyllis Martin, Allan Megill, Olivier Ouassongo, Dylan Penningroth, Sophie Rosenfeld, Stephanie Rupp, Anne Schutte, Ajay Skaria, Nancy Leys Stepan, and Dave Waldner. Thanks also go to David Cohen, Stephan Miescher, Luise White, and participants of the "Words and Voices" Bellagio conference, who galvanized me to think differently about historical evidence, interpretation, performance, and writing.

My eternal gratitude goes to the astute readers who slogged through all or parts of the rewritten manuscript and generously produced a wealth of stimulating comments: Sara Berry, Alon Confino, Michelle Kisliuk, Joe Miller, Elizabeth Meyer, Paul Richards, Jonathan Sadowsky, Carol Summers, Libby Thompson, and Monica van Beusekom. Very special thanks go to the University Press of Virginia's readers, Phyllis Martin and Rod Neumann, whose careful reading, insights, and criticisms helped to make this book a much better one than it would have been otherwise. All misconceptions, errors, and oversights, of course, are my own. Thanks, too, to Dick Holway, who enthusiastically took on this project and guided it through the review and editing processes and to other staff at the Press for their efforts in transforming the manuscript into a book.

Chapter 2 appeared in a slightly different version as "*Doli*: Translating an Environmental History of Loss in the Sangha River Basin of Equatorial Africa," *Journal of African History* 41:3 (2000): 373–94, and is reprinted by permission of the publisher. Portions of chapters 3 and 4 appeared in "Leaving a Person Behind: History, Personhood, and Struggles over Forest Resources in the Sangha Basin of Equatorial Africa," *International Journal of African Historical Studies* 32: 2–3 (1999): 311–38, and are reprinted by permission of the editors.

And finally, family and dear friends have remained unceasingly supportive when they no doubt wondered why this book was taking so long to finish. My daughter Marina learned at a much earlier age than a toddler should to tolerate a distracted mother hunched over the computer. I thank her for simply being the delightful person-in-the making that she is. Most of all, I thank Ken Vernick, with whom I have shared a rich life for more than a decade. I still think he's the funniest person I know, and I am ever grateful for the innumerable ways that his wit and incomparable good sense have sustained me in the many homes we have created together.

ABBREVIATIONS

AEF	French Equatorial Africa (Afrique Équatoriale Française)
CAR	Central African Republic
CFSO	Compagnie Forestière de la Sangha-Oubangui
CPS	Compagnie des Produits de la Sangha
GTZ	Gesellschaft für Technische Zusammenarbeit
WCS	Wildlife Conservation Society
WWF	World Wildlife Fund (U.S.)

Archival Sources

ACS	Archives des Capucins de Savoie, Annecy, France
ACT	Archives des Capucins de Toulouse, Toulouse, France
AGCS	Archives Générales de la Congrégation du Saint-Esprit, Chevilly-la-Rue. France
CAOM	Centre des Archives d'Outre-mer, Aix-en-Provence, France
FAIO/AO	Folksrorelsernas Arkiv I Örebro, Arkivbildaire Örebromissionen, Örebro, Sweden

CUTTING
THE VINES OF
THE PAST

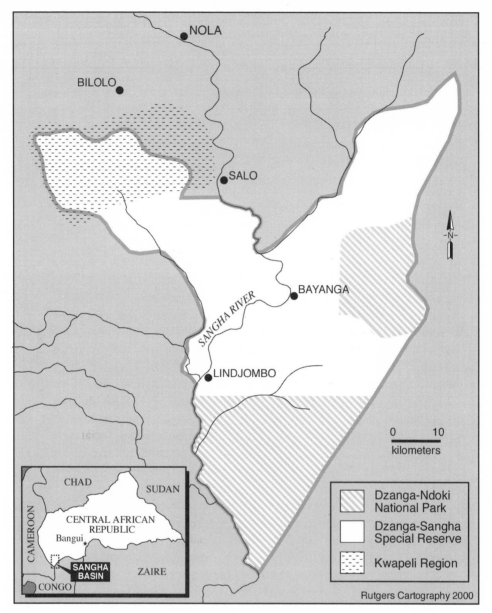

Fig. 1. The Sangha River basin. (Reprinted by permission from Tamara Giles-Vernick, "Rethinking Migration and Indigeneity in the Sangha River Basin of Equatorial Africa," in *Producing Nature and Poverty in Africa,* ed. Vignis Broch-Due and Richard Schroeder [Uppsala: The Nordic Africa Institute, 2000], 296).

INTRODUCTION

THIS BOOK is about how a group of equatorial Africans understands environmental change. *Cutting the Vines of the Past* examines the changing intellectual tools and content of environmental and historical perception and knowledge among Mpiemu people who lived in the middle and upper Sangha River basin of the Central African Republic during the twentieth century (fig. 1). It focuses on the environmental and historical category called *doli,* through which Mpiemu have expressed, debated, and made claims of truth about the past and present. *Doli* is a process—a way of perceiving, characterizing, and interpreting the past and present. Fundamentally shaped by visions of the past, *doli* is intimately tied up with ways of thinking about spaces and particular places in the equatorial rain forest. But *doli* is also a body of knowledge about the past through which Mpiemu people have highlighted and debated people, events, places, and natural-resource exploitation, as well as the social and political relations, social categories and self-definitions, and environmental interventions that have been important to them. Thus, as a broad category of knowledge, it can include advice about past relations between generational, kin, and gender groups that guide social relations in the present. It consists of didactic tales of mythical deities, as well as historical narratives concerning past people and events. But *doli* also incorporates the processes of evaluating forest landscapes and knowledge about farming, hunting, trapping, gathering, and fishing in the forest—ways of perceiving and knowing the forest that ancestors discovered long ago. In practicing, debating, and teaching *doli,* Mpiemu seek to "leave a person behind"—to reproduce themselves biologically, socially, and historically.

Exploring the interrelations between Mpiemu historical consciousness and their understandings of environmental change, this book argues that *doli* as a process and as a body of knowledge changed over the twentieth century. Mpiemu conceptions of their past and present environments altered as they encountered other Africans, concessionary companies, colonial officials, Christian missionaries, the postcolonial state, and a major international conservation project. This book also shows that Mpiemu understand twentieth-century environmental interventions through the prism of *doli*. These insights do more than reveal an alternative view of colonial and postcolonial environmental interventions: they shed critical light on how local people have engaged with and responded to some environmental interventions—including conservation efforts—and why these interventions have failed to achieve their aims.

This study of *doli* was inspired by African responses to a contemporary environmental intervention in the Sangha basin forest of the Central African Republic: the 1990 creation of the Dzanga-Ndoki National Park and its buffer zone, the Dzanga-Sangha Special Reserve. In 1993, when I conducted the bulk of the field research for this book, the park and reserve restrictions on hunting, trapping, gathering, and mining that the Central African Republic had imposed, and that World Wildlife Fund (WWF-US) personnel upheld, were a major concern of reserve inhabitants. Many Africans whom I encountered found these limitations onerous, complaining of a legion of deprivations and losses that the park's establishment had precipitated. Unlike previous European company bosses who had cleared vast tracts of forest in the Sangha during the twentieth century, the conservation project administering the park and reserve hired too few Africans, provided too few transportation and medical services, placed too many restrictions on forest-resource exploitation, and curtailed human mobility in the forest too stringently.[1] Because Africans interpreted this forest-conservation intervention through the lens of the past, it made sense to examine past environmental interventions from the perspective of people who participated in and recollected them. And thus I began to explore how one people, the Mpiemu, who had worked extensively for the European plantation and logging bosses during the twentieth century, understood their changing knowledge of and relationships with their environments (the sites, objects, and spaces that shape and are shaped by, interpreted, and acted upon by human beings).[2] It became clear that *doli* was a complex and variegated process and body of knowledge whose purposes extended well beyond the frequently oppositional but also supplicating responses to conservation interventions.[3] The severed vines (lianas, features of some forest formations) in this book's title refer in part to the forest clearings undertaken during the time of the European bosses. But these vines, it turns out, served as objects to "think with," creating and evoking connections between past and present people, environmental and historical knowledge, and particular places in the forest. The cut vines of this book's title thus also allude to the perceptions of loss and disconnection with a past time when Mpiemu prospered from intensive environmental exploitation.

The book poses three questions about African environmental and historical perception and knowledge. How has one group of Africans organized their perceptions and knowledge around the environments that they have inhabited in the past and the present?[4] How did their ways of seeing and interpreting forest environments and their knowledge of the forest and its resources change over the twentieth century, in the context of colonial and postcolonial environmental interventions? And how have Mpiemu used their ways of perceiving the forest and its resources and their knowledge of their past and the forest to contend with environmental interventions, including recent biodiversity conservation efforts? This study of *doli* shows that Mpiemu people organized their perceptions, interpretations, and knowledge of the forest and the past around a deeply human-centered ecology, onto which they grafted colonial, Christian, and commercial perceptions of the person and environment. And it reveals that they used these accumulated ways of perceiving, exploiting, and talking about the forest and its resources as a means of both opposing and supplicating contemporary conservationists and government agents involved in protecting the forest.

Illuminating contemporary forest conflicts from an environmental history perspective, and specifically through the environmental perceptions and knowledge that contributed to and developed in response to colonial and postcolonial environmental interventions, this book is part of a growing literature that explores the relations between colonialism, environmental interventions, and environmental visions.[5] A major aim of this literature has been to show how historical inquiry can shed light on contemporary environmental conflicts and, in some cases, the causes of environmental degradation. Many works illuminate how past environmental interventions fit into the politics of colonial rule around the world, and how present interventions have colonial origins and thus galvanize conflicts reminiscent of the colonial era. Environmental historians have linked interventions into forest, game, and agricultural exploitation to colonial states' priorities of establishing control over unruly subjects and extracting valued resources from colonized lands. "Scientific forestry," game management, and soil-erosion policies, then, were technologies of colonial control, and the struggles ensuing from these interventions were of a distinctly colonial nature. And in some cases these interventions contributed to, rather than remedied, ecological destruction.[6]

In exploring how colonial environmental interventions have shaped contemporary environmental conflicts in the upper and middle Sangha basin forest, *Cutting the Vines* builds on this literature. But it also diverges from it: onto a history of environmental interventions and its relation to struggles over contemporary conservation policy and practice, this book grafts an analysis of one people's changing intellectual tools and knowledge about the past and the environment. Without an understanding of people's historical and environmental consciousness, we can have little insight into why they act with and upon natural resources as they do.

Such an effort presents an additional challenge. *Doli,* as the changing intellectual tools and knowledge about the past and forest environments, is unique to Mpiemu people, but it does have its rough equivalents elsewhere.[7] But such intellectual tools and knowledge have no easy translations and thus require description and interpretation for readers unfamiliar with them. *Doli* is not history (a modern discipline that locates origins and places people and events temporally in relation to past, present, and future), but it is historical.[8] One genre of *doli,* for instance, recounts narratives of past encounters with outsiders that have shaped present environmental, political, and economic relations. Nor can *doli* be consigned to the treacherous, overly broad terrain of memory, for it is a specific and changing method of evaluating, interpreting, and making claims of truth about the past and the Sangha forest environment.[9] But certainly remembering (tales, sites, narratives, and practices) is an act in which elderly tellers of *doli* engage. This book thus translates how Mpiemu people, as they encountered twentieth-century outsiders who intervened in their environmental relations, altered *doli's* processes and content, later invoking it in their contemporary engagements with Sangha basin forest conservation.

Though scholars have not conducted much research into the middle and upper Sangha basin, which includes the present-day Central African Republic where this study takes place, it is an apt setting for exploring such questions about knowledge of environment and history.[10] For well over a century, the Sangha basin has been the subject of Western mythmaking about tropical forests. Popular depictions of this rain forest today paint it as a veritable Eden, a luxuriant green home to forest elephants, lowland gorillas, chimpanzees, leopards, and other endangered forest mammals, not to mention the so-called pygmies, isolated forest dwellers who exist solely on the forest's gathered, hunted, and trapped foods.[11] For the most part these popular portrayals show the forest as unpeopled and unchanging, though they hint at recent threats to its biodiversity. The Hall of Biodiversity at New York City's American Museum of Natural History describes the forest as mostly unaffected by human beings until the twentieth century. Similarly, the World Wildlife Fund has identified the central goal of its project in the Dzanga-Ndoki National Park and Dzanga-Sangha Special Reserve as "conserv[ing] . . . the last remaining undisturbed tropical lowland forest in the Central African Republic."[12]

Nothing, however, could be further from the truth. In the first place, to suggest that this forest is "undisturbed" contradicts what scientists understand about Guinea-Congolian forests. Storms, flooding, and forest elephants can inflict significant disturbances in the forest; elephants, for instance, knock down trees, trample understories, compact soils, and consume soil minerals, preventing vegetation from growing. And more important, the upper and middle Sangha basin forest has been the focus of intensive environmental exploitation for at least two centuries. During the twentieth century it has been a subject of policy making and extraction that shaped the fates of forest peoples and resources. Moreover, as diverse African peoples and outsiders have moved in and out of this forest basin over the previous centuries, it has also been a crucible for diverse ideas about environment and the past.

BODIES, PERSONS, ENVIRONMENTS, AND PASTS

This work seeks to contribute to a literature concerning the historical struggles over forest spaces, places, and resources by focusing on the diverse and mutually influencing perceptions and meanings of these sites and objects. *Doli* as a way of seeing can be understood partly in terms of the "imaginative intuition" involved in perceiving things and places.[13] For Merleau-Ponty, the "bodily experience . . . provides us with a way of access to the world and the object" and is an integral part of becoming a person and of "historical processes of meaning-making"; this process in turn contributes to the creation of groups of people who share a sense of connection and commonality (and vice versa).[14] Although environmental historians have not drawn explicitly on this approach to explore changing environmental perceptions, such interactions between bodies, persons, things, and places are at the very heart of environmental relations. As people interact with flora, fauna, spaces, places, and other social groups, they help to constitute an environment just as environments constitute persons.[15]

Perception alone, however, does not guide how environments, persons, and social relations constitute one another. Nyerges has argued convincingly that both social purposes and "cultural goals and values behind them" shape how people use and modify natural resources to meet their needs. Hence, *doli* as a process not only is related to how persons see and use the things that make up their environments. It is also a way of perceiving and interpreting that must be understood in terms of social relations and practices: persons and gender, generational, ethnic, and regional groups use environments as sites of social reproduction, getting food and other materials but also working out their respective aims and differences. These processes also shape how persons perceive, think about, and use resources in fields, forests, and villages. Thus, in exploring *doli* as a process of characterizing and interpreting environmental interventions and change, this book examines how Mpiemu people have viewed, moved through, inhabited, exploited, and imagined the Sangha River basin forest's ecological zones and their resources.[16]

Doli as a way of seeing and a body of knowledge also bears a relation to a literature on landscape as a "thing and a social 'process'" of perception, a perspective from which environmental historians are increasingly drawing.[17] European scholarship has revealed that landscape as a process of perception had its roots in seventeenth-century Europe, but this way of seeing is neither static nor confined to Europeans. Scholars of African environmental history have paid careful attention to African perceptions of the landscapes that Africans have created and inhabited. These environmental historians have made important contributions to our understanding of how Africans have exploited and managed their environments in the past and have struggled with one another for access to and control over valued resources. This book expands on those efforts by exploring the diverse ways that Mpiemu perceive, characterize, interpret, and act upon past environmental relations to illuminate, in Luise White's terms, "categories and constructs with which people make their worlds and articulate and debate their understandings of those worlds."[18]

But this study of *doli* provides a commentary on the literature of landscape in another way. Some scholars have examined how landscape as a process of perception has translated into inappropriate assignations of blame for forest and woodland degradation. Articulated by colonial administrators, scientists, development workers, conservationists, and state agents, degradation narratives have shaped external interventions into the relations between African people and their environments, transforming both livelihoods and lands, often for the worse. These scholars take as their primary objective to counter influential degradation narratives, by showing how African farmers, hunters, gatherers, and fishing folk have deployed "indigenous knowledge" (IK) to shape their environments.[19]

Though they provide a powerful corrective to erroneous assumptions, counternarratives—and the conceptions of indigenous knowledge that support them—have their limitations. Characterizations of IK can be problematic, and for this reason I avoid defining *doli* (as knowledge of the forest and its uses) as "indigenous knowledge." Lauded as "practical" knowledge that ensures the wise use of environments and resources, IK has been portrayed at times as static, hermetically sealed from external influences. But this historical analysis of *doli* reveals that its content changes. And not all farmers, hunters, gatherers, and fishing folk use their knowledge to improve their natural resources or the environments that they inhabit.[20] In the Sangha basin, for instance, many young and old farmers fallow their fields for only two years, a period that is insufficient to replenish the soil's nutrients, particularly when farmers have no access to fertilizers, compost, or manure. Moreover, most trappers set cable snare traps that capture all game, including pregnant mammals and threatened species, and harvests from snares are greater than game populations can support.[21] Neither of these practices is ecologically sound. Although some environmental practices in which Sangha people engage do make ecological sense, all of these practices are part of a porous, changing body of knowledge that cannot be uncritically embraced as a fail-safe solution guaranteeing the success of environmental interventions. Even when some scholars have acknowledged that the content of IK changes, they still argue that the intellectual tools by which people conceive of themselves, their past and present worlds, and their relations with their environments do not change. On the contrary, this book shows that *doli* is a historically and regionally specific way of seeing, characterizing, and interpreting the past and the Sangha forest environment, and that this process has changed over the twentieth century.[22]

Finally, this book argues for another way of interpreting the environmental and historical knowledge that ordinary people produce. Recent literature that harnesses IK to counter powerful degradation stories can misconstrue the changing significance of "indigenous knowledge," because it neglects to account for the underlying cognitive processes and intellectual tools that people use to perceive, characterize, and interpret their environments. What does it mean, for instance, when someone observes, "There were once few trees here, but now there are many"? A literal interpretation of that claim in support of a narrative of forest growth or enrichment misses many other possible meanings of trees: increased tree cover might be an idiom for accumulated or unexploited wealth, or it could suggest increased isolation. In the Sangha basin trees and forests have acquired both of these meanings at different historical moments. Reducing such complex remembrances of environmental practices and landscapes to support a single argument can cause us to overlook the myriad meanings that such claims can acquire.[23]

The Sangha basin people and past simply do not lend themselves to a single narrative depiction of the forest and its changes. Various linguistic and ethnic African groups, colonial administrators, missionaries, commercial agents, state agents, and conservationists have sought to control both the resources in those environments and Mpiemu themselves. These struggles have altered Mpiemu conceptions of themselves, their past, and their environmental relations. Mpiemu have responded to attempts to reshape and expropriate their places, persons, and resources in the name of God, civilization, profit, patronage, and biodiversity by appropriating the historical visions of interveners.[24] But they did not borrow these visions wholesale. Instead, they filtered them through their own distinctive intellectual tools for interpreting their pasts and their relations with their environments.[25] At the same time Mpiemu appropriations also forced interveners to accommodate local conceptions of relations with their environments, persons, and the past.

The study, then, investigates the multiplicity of ways that people tell, enact, embody, and locate conceptions of past relations between people and their environment. It treats Mpiemu environmental knowledge as one of several quests for historical truth that have interlocked with, influenced, and appropriated from one another in the Sangha River basin. Following Johannes Fabian, I confront these diverse visions not as representations but as *"realities . . . as practices"* which confronted "my own ethnographic practice (of representing realities) . . . on the same level."[26] These diverse visions of past relations with environments constitute alternative, mutable "searches for truth and reality."[27] This search entails exploring Mpiemu productions about the past in myriad forms. Mpiemu articulate *doli* not only in narrative forms but also through bodily and spatial practices that organize and recollect their pasts. Past people, events, people-environment relations, and historical and social processes may be embodied in various bodily sites and places—a field, a tree, a document, a person's stomach, or a corner of an elderly woman's kitchen. Although these bodily and spatial sites of recollection do not fit easily within conventions of historical writing, they reflect powerful ways of invoking and recalling the past people and events and processes of creating gendered, generational, ethnic, and familial persons.[28]

The Mpiemu appropriation of outsiders' notions of persons, history, and environments had crucial effects on *doli*. First, *doli* both shaped and was shaped over time by Mpiemu people's engagement with colonial administrators, concessionaires, missionaries, conservationists, and functionaries of the state. And second, over the twentieth century Mpiemu appropriated and reshaped colonial and missionary discourses of dearth, insufficiency, lost opportunities, and in the case of missionaries, charity and redemption, transforming them into their own powerful discourses of dearth, hunger, loss, and disconnection.[29] *Dearth* is an old word in English, but it richly evokes the senses of deprivation, scarcity, and mourning that Mpiemu conveyed. Though the phrase has been used all too frequently without rigor, I invoke "colonial discourse," borrowing appreciatively from Frederick Cooper, who has shown how African labor protests in late colonial Africa stimulated colonial officials to attempt to imagine, create, and stabilize an African working class. Cooper elaborates the complex "imaginative project" among colonial officials, trade union leaders, and other African elites that created an African working class and shows how this project was forged through a "range of acts—laden with power" whose meanings shifted according to the contexts in which they took place.[30] Yet because Cooper neglected to elucidate what African workers themselves thought about their work, his depiction of colonial discourse seems incomplete. Colonial discourse must include how ordinary Africans thought about and acted upon the environments that they inhabited, and how they contributed to Europeans' conceptions of and actions within the middle and upper Sangha basin forest.

There was no single "imaginative project" animating colonial administrators, explorers, company agents, missionaries, state agents, and conservationists in the twentieth-century Sangha basin. Each group of outsiders brought their own aims to the Sangha basin, helping to shape the process and content of *doli*. This book traces, in Mpiemu sites of organizing and recollecting the past, the effects of these encounters on *doli*. Simultaneously, it shows how Mpiemu speakers interpreted the interventions of these outsiders through the prism of *doli*. In the process of engagement, Mpiemu refashioned *doli* as a historical body of knowledge, concerned with questions of origin, temporal placement, and dearth and loss. How this transformation came about and how Mpiemu came to understand their pasts as stories and sites invoking dearth, loss, and disconnection are crucial questions for exploring how people interpret their pasts. The discourse of dearth, loss, and disconnection that permeated *doli* came to mean many things in different contexts. In the villages it came to signify depopulation, death, and the loss of senior male authority. In agricultural spaces Mpiemu spoke of hunger and disconnection from networks of authority. In the forest, however, they rejected administrative, state, and conservationist discourses about depleted forests, opting instead to mourn their hunger and squandered opportunities for accumulating wealth in people and objects.[31]

The multiple meanings of dearth, loss, and deprivation illustrate that debates over the forest and its resources extend beyond pursuing strategies of accumulation and leveling when people seek access to and control over forest resources. Some scholars have argued that "custom, power and property" shape resource struggles in Africa. Others add that culture helps to define the contours of such struggles. This study of Mpiemu *doli* in the upper and middle Sangha basin contends that such struggles are also deeply historical. Invoking *doli* in their contemporary disputes with a powerful conservation project over access to and control over forest resources, Mpiemu have demonstrated that they perceive themselves as historical actors, entangled in life-and-death struggles to reproduce themselves as historical beings in places and to uproot other claimants from those places. This study thus seeks to add a crucial dimension to understanding how people use, struggle over, alienate, and transform the forest and its resources.[32]

SOURCES

In documenting the changing processes and content of *doli,* this book draws from several kinds of sources. First, it is based upon field research in the Central African Republic and the Republic of Congo conducted primarily in 1993 but also during short trips in 1991 and 1994. The very nature of *doli* fundamentally shaped how I pursued this research. I began to understand *doli* as both a process and a body of knowledge about the forest, its uses, and the past by asking elderly and middle-aged Mpiemu to teach me *bi san bi doli* (the things of *doli*). Their responses to this request ranged widely, but eventually I became familiar with a standard repertoire of processes, practices, and knowledge that constituted *doli*: didactic tales, proverbs, specific narratives of the twentieth-century past, particular practices, objects, and sites in houses, fields, and the forest, and the processes of learning about (and knowledge itself of) the forest's game and medicinal plants. What bound together *doli*'s varied knowledge, practices, behaviors, and processes was a preoccupation with the past (recent, but also distant and unchanging) and with places and spaces through which Mpiemu people had once moved and which they had exploited to pursue livelihoods and to accumulate wealth in the form of persons, valued social relations, material goods, and knowledge.

Twentieth-century Mpiemu mobility also influenced the geographical coverage of this research and the regional comparisons of *doli* that cut across the chapters of this book. I began field research among Mpiemu workers and their families in the village of Lindjombo (see fig. 1), where they, their parents, or their grandparents had moved to work for rubber-exploiting companies, coffee plantations, and later logging companies during the twentieth century. I had arrived in the Central African Republic speaking the national language Sango comfortably, because I had learned it as a Peace Corps volunteer in the late 1980s and had used it elsewhere in the country for historical research. Over time, however, as I worked more closely with Mpiemu workers and their families, I learned enough of the Mpiemu language to understand conversations, to learn about environmental practices, and with the aid of a research assistant, to engage in dialogues about their pasts.

In the course of their explications of *doli,* these Mpiemu invoked a poignant discourse of loss, claiming that they were a "dead people," disconnected from the places, practices, knowledge, and powerful networks of people that they associated with the past. In contrast, they contended, their kin in the *metego Mpiemu* (Mpiemu soil) of Kwapeli and Bilolo in the northern forest (where they and their forebears had originated earlier in the twentieth century) retained the knowledge and practices of *doli* and were fully connected to networks of power and prosperity. To explore whether other Mpiemu expressed these distinctions and the historical etiologies of this notion of loss and disconnection, I followed kin and affinal networks farther north to loci of Mpiemu settlement in Bayanga, Salo, Kwapeli, and to a limited extent, Bangui.

Because Mpiemu have produced *doli* over the twentieth century as they engaged with various other historical agents, I also conducted limited research among people who belonged to other linguistic and ethnic groups in the middle Sangha, including Gbaya, Aka, "Sangha Sangha," and Kako (Kaka) peoples. And in order to detail outsiders' environmental interventions and their interactions with Mpiemu and other Sangha basin inhabitants, this study also makes use of written reports, letters, photographs, and maps from the Spiritan and Savoy and Toulouse Capuchin archives in France, the Örebromission archives in Sweden, and various colonial archives in France and the Central African Republic. Finally, it relies upon ecological studies conducted in the upper and middle Sangha basin and elsewhere in the equatorial rain forest.

Conducting historical research in the upper and middle Sangha presents some significant challenges, for there is a real dearth of historical sources documenting Mpiemu and other Sangha basin inhabitants for much of the twentieth century. Thus, exploring how Mpiemu perceived and exploited different kinds of sites (villages, fields, and forests), particularly earlier in the century, requires examining not only the frequently contradictory claims of contemporary Africans about past environmental perceptions and practices but the writings of administrators, missionaries, and others. Generally, I try to avoid privileging one kind of source (written or oral) over the other in a search for absolute historical truth and instead examine how these sources shed light on past worlds that people create and inhabit.[33] In the following chapters, too, I have adopted two different interpretive strategies in an effort to get at how various people may have exploited and perceived the Sangha basin forests. First, I read through a range of available sources (descriptions and photographs by early explorers, colonial administrators, and missionaries) to trace particular practices of Mpiemu speakers to exploit different environments in the early twentieth century. I use documentary evidence, as well as interviews with missionaries, company agents, administrators, and conservationists, to trace outsiders' environmental visions and interventions over the twentieth century. But I then juxtapose these reconstructive efforts with two kinds of informed speculations. Grounding my interpretations in both early twentieth-century descriptions and photographs and the oral accounts of contemporary Mpiemu, I elaborate Mpiemu environmental perceptions and knowledge embedded in *doli*. At times, this interpretive strategy admittedly has the disadvantage of employing "documentary material to flesh out, contextualize, and even explain the words of . . . informants."[34] But I also seek to turn this strategy on its head and to use *doli* in order to flesh out and contextualize the documentary evidence. I attempt to show how Mpiemu filtered twentieth-century environmental interventions through *doli* as a process and a body of knowledge and to trace how Mpiemu relations with their environments, conceptions of the person, and *doli* changed.

To some readers this speculative exercise may raise some questions. How can I know, for instance, what Mpiemu speakers were doing or thinking in the late nineteenth century? And more critically, how do I know that people filtered past environmental interventions through *doli* but also altered it in their engagement with outsiders?

These are crucial questions, but ones that Africanist historians have been tackling for decades. *Doli* is, of course, not simply a production of contemporary concerns and circumstances but contains aims, idioms, sites, and practices accumulated over time. Thus my speculations are interpretations drawn from these elements in conjunction with available written and photographic interpretations of turn-of-the-century observers. Historical, environmental, and ethnographic material in contiguous areas of the forest in the present-day Central African Republic, Cameroon, Congo, and Gabon usefully supplements these sources and provides valuable comparisons. Historians and anthropologists working in the equatorial forest—and more important, equatorial Africans themselves—agree that forest inhabitants share a broad repertoire of social, political, and cultural relations and practices.[35] Hence this study interprets changing Mpiemu beliefs and practices around *doli* as part of a broader equatorial African repertoire but also accounts for the differences that distinguish them from neighboring peoples.

Concerning the task of tracing how people filtered past environmental interventions through *doli* and simultaneously altered it in their engagement with outsiders, I would contend that this exercise fits squarely into the enterprise of "doing history." Direct "proof" of the precise moments and mechanisms of these changes, of course, does not exist. And at times I use correlations between discourses of dearth and loss in *doli* and those in colonial and missionary perceptions of human-environment relations to speculate that Mpiemu appropriated and transformed these outsiders' visions. But "evidence," as Luise White has argued, is itself far "messier" and more complex than positivists demanding explicit proof suggest: it can emerge from multiple sources—including interpretations—and be interpreted in a multitude of ways.[36] Moreover, *doli*, itself a process and a body of interpretations of the past, contains the indelible marks of these past changes. The very work of the historian is to interpret these aims, idioms, sites, and practices and to try to show the processes by which they emerged and changed.

THE LANDSCAPE OF THIS BOOK

Although it is a historical work, this book is organized around the sites that allow people to organize and recollect *doli*. As an ongoing engagement between language and practice, *doli* centers on particular sites (open shelters, villages, fields, and forest) where people enact the most important activities and relationships within their daily lives. It is in these sites, then, that they experienced the environmental, social, economic, and intellectual transformations of the twentieth century. Hence the book's organization reflects the ways in which Mpiemu lived, interpreted, and reworked these encounters with colonial and postcolonial interventions in their relations with their environments, as well as in their social and economic relations. Paying careful attention to villages, fields, and forests reflects better than a chronologically organized narrative the way people organize their own environmental perceptions of the world and avoids importing tired assumptions about divisions between "people" and "environment," between "humanized" and "natural" spaces.[37]

The sites of the *panjo* (an open shelter where male kin of different houses gather), villages, fields, and forests are also interconnected in important ways. Over time, through the intersection of human and ecological processes, villages could be transformed into fields, fields into forests, and forests into fields and villages. In their engagement with colonial and postcolonial economies, Mpiemu people exploited these different zones for food, building materials, and valued commodities, and the effects of human habitation and exploitation persisted long after people abandoned their villages and fields.[38] Mpiemu perceived the interconnections of villages, fields, and forests not only in material terms but also in symbolic ones. These sites served as "tool[s] for thought" that "mediate[d] and synthesize[d] the natural symbols of both the body and the landscape . . . [and] provide[d] the environment and context for social life."[39] Idioms of domesticated, cut, and overgrown forest vines and of the circulation of fats between human bodies, agricultural soils, and forest game pervaded Mpiemu expressions about these past and present environments.

Chapter 1 describes the different actors participating in the Sangha basin's historical dynamics over the twentieth century. Drawing from secondary historical, anthropological, linguistic, and archaeological literature, as well as archival evidence, it also provides an overview of the major historical changes that took place in the middle and upper Sangha basin. Chapter 2 is primarily an effort to translate *doli* as a process of describing and interpreting the forest and the past, but also as a changing category of knowledge about the forest and its resources and about past persons and events. The chapter traces *doli*'s aims and genres, introducing readers to some differing Mpiemu interpretations of twentieth-century environmental interventions in the Sangha basin.

Chapters organized around sites of *doli* follow: the domesticated spaces of the *panjo* and the village (chapters 3–4), the field (chapter 5), and the forest (chapter 6). These chapters also move chronologically, from late nineteenth-century social arrangements within domesticated spaces and their relations to fields and forests, to the interventions that transformed those sites and Mpiemu people's activities and relationships within them during the twentieth century, to contemporary conservationist efforts that contravene older, accumulated notions of relations between people and their environments.

Generally, Mpiemu added to the environmental knowledge, practices, and visions of *doli*, though in some cases they discarded older visions and practices in favor of new ones. For instance, Mpiemu men and women in the early twentieth century perceived and interpreted the forest's diverse ecology in human-centered terms, defining forest types in terms of past human interventions or by their capacities for future human use. From the 1930s Mpiemu grafted onto this human-centered ecology the value that commercial agents put on intensive forest exploitation and clearing for creating new wealth and promoting its accumulation. Older and accreted visions of the forest ran counter to the kind of unpeopled, "pristine" forest that the World Wildlife Fund and the CAR state hoped to create in the Dzanga-Ndoki park in the 1990s. In other contexts some Mpiemu simply rejected past knowledge and practices. To be sure, many Mpiemu in the upper Sangha continued to construct particular settlement patterns and to organize resource distribution and political relations around these places. But in the late 1920s and 1930s, some workers and their families who moved to the coffee plantations of the middle Sangha abandoned older settlement patterns altogether and created new built environments that contained none of the hallmarks of older senior male authority. Settlement patterns reflected and reinforced new patterns of resource sharing among friends rather than kin and promoted new forms of individual accumulation based on forest clearing.

Chapter 3 elaborates the spatial organization and the social and cultural significance of the built environments of the Mpiemu *panjo* and village in the late nineteenth and early twentieth centuries, before the middle Sangha basin's effective colonization by the French and Germans. Chapter 4 illustrates how these domesticated environments changed during the twentieth century, as Mpiemu people encountered a changing forest environment, colonial administrators, concessionaires and plantation owners, and Catholic and Baptist missionaries. Labor recruitment, village *regroupement,* and repeated epidemics of sleeping sickness did more than reshape the spatial arrangements by which Mpiemu lived; they also helped to reformulate how Mpiemu understood authority, the person (*mori*), and agency. It appears that Mpiemu reworked a colonial discourse of depopulation and depletion and a missionary discourse of hunger and charity to mourn population losses and the depletion of elders' authority. Mpiemu responses to a new state and WWF map of settlement and forest exploitation drew from these accumulated notions about built environments, dearth, depletion, and charity. Chapter 5 explores how various agents sought to alter Mpiemu environmental relations in fields, changing agricultural practices, labor-allocation decisions, and the geography of the upper and middle Sangha basin forests. These interventions shaped how Mpiemu came to understand the person and gender, generational, and interethnic relations, as well as how they came to value productive humanized landscapes, cleared of obstructions. Explorers and colonial officials all depicted the Sangha basin farmlands and Mpiemu agriculture as insufficient. Mpiemu reinterpreted and transformed colonial discourses of poor agricultural productivity and lost economic opportunities to develop the Sangha basin's agricultural potential and a missionary discourse of hunger and charity. They later would invoke claims of hunger, deprivation, and charity in their historically informed responses to perceived limits on farming and marketing of alcohol (distilled from maize and cassava). They drew unflattering comparisons between conservationists and state agents on the one hand and generous company bosses of the past on the other.

Finally, chapter 6 focuses on the forest as a site of *doli* and illuminates how the interventions of European colonizers, missionaries, and commercial agents intensified forest-resource use but also built upon Mpiemu visions of the forest and its past, present, and future. Outsiders who promoted new ways of using the forest worried over the depletion of its resources or expressed anxieties over lost economic and political opportunities that had materialized through intensive environmental exploitation. Mpiemu speakers living in the middle and upper Sangha basin of this rain forest appropriated and reshaped these twin discourses of dearth and loss over the twentieth century. In particular, they integrated the anxieties over squandered economic opportunities into *doli*. In response to 1990s restrictions on hunting, trapping, and other forms of forest exploitation, they invoked these anxieties in claims of hunger and invisibility, lamenting their present sense of deprivation.

THE SOURCES AND CONTEXTS OF *DOLI*

MPIEMU HAVE have constituted *doli* both as a way of interpreting the past and environments and as a composite historical category, a set of spatial and bodily sites and objects, practices, didactic tales, and narratives that articulate and debate claims of truth about the past and sustain claims to authority. Although Mpiemu knowledge of the past is not temporally deep, often dating only to the First World War, the sites, objects, practices, and narratives of *doli* betray crucial influences of participants of the Sangha basin's twentieth-century historical dynamics. Administrators, company agents, missionaries, and other outsiders introduced new interventions to gain access to and control over valued forest resources and offered Mpiemu new ways of perceiving and exploiting their environments, but also new models of authority and new ways of thinking about the past. This chapter sets out those participating groups and the historical contexts in which they contributed to *doli*.

THE SANGHA BASIN FOREST ENVIRONMENT

The Sangha River basin forest was a critical source of *doli* and the context within which Mpiemu created *doli*. Treating environment as an actor is a major theme within environmental history, though one that raises crucial questions about how environment may function as both an agent of change and a slate onto which people map out their visions and fantasies of ideal landscapes. This book follows David Demeritt's efforts to resolve debates between environmental historians and cultural geographers by invoking metaphors of nature that frame it "as both a real material actor and a socially constructed object."[1] One of the major aims of this book is to disaggregate the category "environmental relations" in order to understand how people engage with the material objects that can constitute an environment. And because the production of *doli* relies so heavily on environment, we need to understand something about its spaces, sites, objects, other life-forms, and their complex interactions with human historical actors in the twentieth-century Sangha forest.

These spaces, sites, nonhuman life-forms, and their interactions that make up the upper and middle Sangha basin forest are part of the Congo River basin's vast equatorial rain forest. Ecologists, however, disagree over the boundaries of this forest, the range of forest forms, and the taxonomies of its flowering plants. Some have delineated the equatorial forest as extending from coastal West Africa through much of the Congo River basin, sustaining rainfall of more than 1,200 millimeters each year. Others perceive the Congo basin forest as distinct, extending over a 2-million-square-kilometer expanse and containing over 7,000 species of flowering plants. In the Sangha basin forest, French and American ecologists have measured yearly rains averaging between 1,350 and 1,500 millimeters, falling between March and November, punctuated by a short dry season in June and July and a longer one lingering between December and February.[2] Other studies have documented a varied topography in the basin. Farther south, it remains very flat, with localized outcroppings of clayey schist, a coarse-grained metamorphic rock yielding a highly fertile soil, well suited for cultivation. And to the north, in the forests more distant from the Sangha River, the undulating hills of the Kwapeli forests give way to steeper ones near Bilolo. The soils are more varied, containing boulders, conglomerates, quartzites, and clayey schists. They, too, have supported small-scale agriculture. This steep terrain, as well as its distance from the Sangha River, isolated forest dwellers from the early European forays into the Sangha basin and later provided a haven for people to escape from onerous colonial demands for labor and taxes.[3]

The Sangha River and its tributaries are central ecological features of the region. Located in the northern equatorial forest, the Sangha itself is one of several tributaries of the Congo River. Formed by the confluence of the Kadei and Mambere Rivers on the forest's northern limits, it is a broad river flowing 785 kilometers south to join the Congo. Navigable by canoe throughout the year, the Sangha is wide and deep enough during the rainy season to be passable by steamers. During the dry season water levels decline, and sandbars emerge, blocking the passage of large steamers. The numerous smaller tributaries of the Sangha, including the Nyoue, Kadei, and others, are passable only by canoe. The river and its tributaries contain a wealth of fish, including Nile perch and assorted catfish, providing a valuable source of protein for many people in the middle and upper Sangha.

To observe that the Central African Republic contains 8,330 square kilometers of rain forest reveals little of that forest's striking diversity of forms and species. Both French and American ecologists have identified six to eight forest types, which bear some resemblance to Mpiemu forest typologies. For these ecologists, though, the dominant forest type is a mixed, semideciduous one on well-drained soil; its physiognomy and composition can vary greatly, with densities of *Khaya* and *Entandrophragma* species (prized mahogany woods) or Irvingiaceae (some of which produce *Irvingia excelsa,* the edible bush mango, a widely consumed food). Other forest types that ecologists have identified include dense forest on marshy soil; raffia-palm forest in flooded areas; *Guibourtia demeusii* forest, which grows in dense concentrations along large rivers; and the rare *Gilbertiodendron dewevrei* forest, a monodominant (single-species) forest populated by a very large deciduous tree. Interspersed in this mosaic of forest forms are patches of savanna, fallowed fields, and herbaceous marshy clearings.[4]

Wildlife biologists and ecologists also have observed high wildlife diversity. Elephants (*Loxodonta africana cyclotis*), bongo antelope (*Tragelaphus eurycerus*), sitatunga (*T. spekei*), forest buffalo (*Syncerus caffer nanus*), and western lowland gorillas (*Gorilla gorilla gorilla*) are among the impressive larger wildlife. But there are also chimpanzees (*Pan troglodytes*) and several monkey species, as well as populations of bushpigs (*Potamochoerus porcus*), giant forest hogs (*Hylochoerus meinertzhageni*), leopards (*Panthera pardus*), golden cats (*Profelis aurata*), several mongoose and genet species (*Herpestidae* and *Viverridae*), various rodents, and seven species of duiker antelope (*Cephalophus* spp.). And while ecologists and wildlife biologists have identified spectacular reptiles and at least 254 bird species, they are only beginning to examine the complex interrelations between different species and the forest.[5]

Just what has caused such variability in this forest also appears to be in dispute, because ecologists assign different weight to nonhuman and human interventions. In theory, storms, tree fall, high winds, and landslides can help to create gaps in the forest, to disperse seeds, and therefore to sustain the forest's high plant and animal biodiversity, though standard texts on tropical rain-forest ecology tend to assign less importance to nonhuman interventions. And the forests adjacent to the Sangha riverbanks reveal that seasonal shifts have considerable effects on the forests. Trees growing in these locations must be able to tolerate flooding, because at the peak of the rainy season, the river floods its banks, spilling into the forests. Trees adapt to these marshy conditions, forming stilt roots for support and peg roots (pneumorrhizae) for respiration in poorly aerated, waterlogged soils.[6]

According to rain-forest ecologists, people and forest animals also can affect the structure and composition of the forest, but they disagree about their relative importance in creating such disturbances. For some, marshy clearings provide water, minerals, and food to several forest mammals, including bongo, forest buffalo, and forest elephants, and in turn, these animals help to maintain clearings. Elephants feed in already exploited spaces, and the forest once occupying these spaces does not have a chance to grow again. But others have argued that elephants are "bulldozer herbivores," dramatically altering dense forest by knocking down trees in search of fruit and creating "light gaps," openings in the forest canopy, where smaller, light-seeking plants emerge.[7]

Other ecologists, as well as conservationists and the popular press, have argued that human beings are primarily responsible for forest disturbance.[8] But despite contemporary conservationist and popular media claims that this forest is "pristine" but "threatened" by human encroachment, the story is much more complex. For centuries the forest has shaped and been shaped by human beings. It has long provided human inhabitants with resources to live by means of some combination of hunting, gathering, and farming.[9] During the later nineteenth century, according to Elisabeth Copet-Rougier, the upper Sangha forest was densely populated, a magnet for mobile peoples who were attracted to its ample game, fertile soils, and valuable trees. Copet-Rougier does not explicitly cite the evidence on which she relies, though some descriptive sources lend credence to her claims. Some descriptions of Mpiemu villages in the late nineteenth and early twentieth centuries mentioned (but did not count) large village populations. By 1915 several demographic factors would have already begun to precipitate village population losses, though explorers and missionaries, new to the region, may have had little basis for comparison. Jean Maley's recent paleobotanical analyses provide indirect support for Copet-Rougier's claims, because he has found localized evidence of forest expansion in the twentieth century in the Kadei basin, a Sangha River tributary where many Mpiemu speakers have concentrated their settlements since the late nineteenth century.[10] It is possible, then, that increasing nineteenth-century populations cleared more forests to accommodate their farming needs, but that demographic factors accompanying colonization in the twentieth century reduced these population pressures, leading to forest regrowth.[11]

That populations diminished in the Sangha during the twentieth century is likely, and this demographic change may have increased forest cover in some places, though certainly not in others. Although demographic evidence is notoriously unreliable, reduced population densities after 1900 probably resulted from several factors. The expansion of venereal diseases such as syphilis, spread by European explorers and administrators and African troops, may have reduced fertility and population growth.[12] Sleeping-sickness mortality certainly contributed to population declines. The forests around Nola and Bilolo, where Mpiemu settlements were concentrated, were particularly unhealthy, probably a long-standing focus for sleeping sickness, and the French anti-sleeping-sickness campaign did not begin in earnest in the Haute-Sangha sectors (where Nola and Bilolo were situated) until 1930. Labor recruitment and mobility out of sleeping-sickness foci to centers of employment also probably helped to diminish population densities in this part of the Sangha. All of these factors, in turn, may have helped to increase forest cover in the Kadei, as Maley has described.[13]

Nonetheless, these changes probably were highly localized. Although Kadei basin forest cover may have grown in response to twentieth-century population declines, forest cover certainly declined around the villages of Berbérati, Bania, Salo, and Lindjombo, because of the development of large-scale coffee plantations. These plantations attracted hundreds of workers, who cleared their own fields from the forests to feed their families. Subsequently, logging and diamond-mining enterprises substantially altered forest cover in parts of the middle and upper Sangha, with mining and logging sites, worker settlements, and worker fields.

The ebb and regrowth of the Sangha forests, changing populations of mammals, seasonal fluctuations in rivers and streams, all shaped Mpiemu perceptions and activities in the twentieth century. The forest and changes within it provided both a context and the material objects and places for the creation and practice of *doli*.

MPIEMU AND EQUATORIAL AFRICANS

The Mpiemu, who understand themselves as sharing a language, knowledge, beliefs, and practices, have been part of a complex multiethnic society in the Sangha River basin for at least the past century and a half. One of several linguistic groups moving into the Sangha basin during the late nineteenth century, Mpiemu have participated in Sangha residents' dense social interactions and cultural and economic exchanges, as well as in the widespread borrowing of words, foods, cultivation methods, and other practices.

None of these movements or exchanges took place on a grand, organized scale, and it is difficult to identify a single linguistic and ethnic group called Mpiemu during the nineteenth century. The movements and exchanges resulted, however, from two major changes sweeping equatorial Africa in the nineteenth century. During that century this area found itself increasingly incorporated into a global economy. Historians have detailed this process, identifying several compelling reasons for it, including favorable terms of trade for Africans selling their tropical oils, ivory, and rubber overseas and an industrializing Europe with a seemingly insatiable hunger for African exports. As a result, Africans in the Congo River basin began to form their own trading networks, exchanging cassava, palm oil and wine, slaves, and ivory for such imports as firearms, beads, and cloth.[14]

In the upper Sangha, though, the influence of this trade was probably indirect, in contrast to the lower Sangha and adjacent areas of the Congo basin, where Nunu, Bobangi, Beembe, and Tio participated extensively in it. In their descriptions of late nineteenth-century life, Mpiemu tellers of *doli,* as well as those from other groups of the middle and upper Sangha— Pande, Ngundi, and Kako (or Kaka)—mention none of the hallmarks of this trade: firearms, ivory trades, and long-distance voyages. And in 1891 the explorer Gaillard was astonished to discover that "European merchandise is unknown in the middle Sangha." By all accounts the Sangha basin trade was a dynamic but short-distance trade.[15]

At this juncture it makes sense to ask what these names—Mpiemu, Pande, Ngundi, Kako—mean. They are, first of all, diverse language groups that form some of the western Bantu languages. The upper and middle Sangha was the locus of different language families and groups, both Bantu (A and C groups) and languages like Gbaya and Ngundi of the Ubanguian family. Mpiemu is a western Bantu (A.80) language spoken by 29,000 speakers in the present-day Central African Republic and Cameroon. It is closely related to other Bantu A languages—Kako, Konzimé, and Bajwe—spoken in eastern Cameroon. But some of the other language groups in the Sangha, including Pande and Aka, are Bantu C languages, not mutually intelligible with Mpiemu; and the Ubanguian languages like Gbaya and Ngundi have different vocabularies and structures.[16]

Presently, some of these groups are ethnicities, one of several possible ways that people conceive of their relationships to broader collectivities.[17] At times, however, regional ("southern") and ecological ("forest-dwelling") senses of commonality subsumed notions of ethnic similarity and difference during the Central African Republic's political turmoil in the 1990s. But the process of becoming an ethnic group was dynamic, ever changing, and complex. What, for instance, did these names signify to Sangha basin inhabitants in the nineteenth century? The few Africanist scholars working in this particular region have not fully analyzed this question, primarily because of the dearth of nineteenth-century sources. But some scholars have identified flexible social categories that could incorporate or exclude "outsiders" elsewhere in the equatorial forest. Harms, for instance, detailed the expansion and contraction of Bobangi ethnicity in the lower Sangha during the rapid growth and subsequent decline of Congo basin trading houses and networks. In the same vein Vansina described the equatorial African political tradition based on the House (a basic social unit centered on one big man and his accumulated wives, friends, clients, and slaves), a building block for broader, district-wide war and trading alliances that developed into ethnic identities. Alternatively, Burnham, focusing on Gbaya-Fulbé-Mbororo interactions in northern Cameroon, traced nineteenth-century processes that momentarily centralized and then fragmented Gbaya clan territories, which were dispersed hamlets that allied during warfare or trade. Clans, which shared patrilineal descent, a clan name, food taboos, and a rule of exogamous marriages, were not "supra-lineage" groupings but rather "sub-ethnicities."[18]

Based on what we know about contiguous areas of equatorial Africa in the nineteenth century, subethnic identities among upper and middle Sangha basin people probably existed. No evidence exists for a Mpiemu ethnicity during the nineteenth century, and it remains likely that the broadest category of social connectedness among Mpiemu speakers was the *kuli ajing* ("cord family," which contained members with putative but untraceable kin ties). Members of an *ajing* shared a food taboo and were not permitted to marry one another. Frequently identified in early twentieth-century explorers' descriptions and maps, these groups had names that most often contained the prefix *Pi-* (Piantimo, Piani) or *Pe-* (Pejalo, Petombo, Pekwaro), but also *Bi-* (Bikie, Bikaboulo) or *Bo-* (Bowong). A few tellers of *doli* identified the first *kuli ajing* as Piakombo, founded by Likagoulo and Ligagoura, and Bijuki, whose first member was Mentounge. Defining nineteenth-century *kuli ajing* remains a complex task, because contemporary Mpiemu now use the term to refer to ethnicity, to territories, and to kin groups. *Ajing* probably acquired these diverse meanings under colonial interventions, which carved the forests in which Mpiemu resided into administrative divisions called *terres, cantons,* and *circonscriptions,* so that some Mpiemu eventually could argue that *ajing* were associated with particular lands. In the nineteenth century, however, a *kuli ajing* did not lay explicit claims to land. Like its Gbaya and Beembe counterparts, the *kuli ajing* seems to have been highly flexible, fluid in its membership, continuously engaged in the process of segmentation because of personal, political, and economic tensions.[19]

What form *kuli ajing* took remains open to question. Harms and Vansina, on the one hand, and Burnham and Copet-Rougier on the other, present different models of nineteenth-century social organization and ethnicity in equatorial Africa. Mpiemu descriptions of how they organized their past mobility and settlement combine aspects of both models. Like Gbaya clans,

Mpiemu spoke of nineteenth-century *kuli ajing* as geographically scattered collectivities made up of several spatially scattered *panjo,* open shelters where male kin shared food from a constellation of their wives' separate kitchens, allocated labor for kin-group activities, and adjudicated kin-group disputes. Simultaneously, like Harms's and Vansina's models, these *panjo* also could include wives; clients, such as Ngombe and Aka (so-called pygmies); slaves (*mpala*); and pawns (*shumbo*), given in exchange for a debt.[20] Nevertheless, the Mpiemu descriptions of these *panjo* and *kuli ajing* bear little resemblance to the trading Houses, Villages, and Districts of Harms and Vansina, perhaps because Mpiemu did not participate in the sort of long-distance trade that Bobangi or lower Congo basin peoples did. Mpiemu social groups seemed far smaller, and their residential organization more geographically scattered, than Vansina's House-Village-District model describes.

Oral accounts about the nineteenth century mentioned other groups with whom contemporary Mpiemu now recognize linguistic and cultural similarities, including the Mpompo, Kunabembe, Vunvu, and Bajwe.[21] They also mentioned contacts with Aka and Ngombe, Ngundi, Gbaya, and Kako, among others. Both oral accounts from Mpiemu and other groups in the Sangha and linguistic evidence attest to a complex ethnic mosaic in the nineteenth-century Sangha basin that sustained intensive cultural interactions. Before the mid-nineteenth century most interactions were peaceful, entailing intermarriage and trade. Frequently, upper and middle Sangha peoples engaged in a much smaller-scale trade, concluded blood brotherhoods and marriages, and exchanged different varieties of maize, cassava, yams, and similar forms of cultural expressions. Mpiemu actively participated in these exchanges, although numerous genealogies that I collected among elderly people suggest that in the late nineteenth century, intermarriage with different linguistic groups occurred less frequently than among other peoples. Nevertheless, the expansion of equatorial Africa's trade with Europe and intensified migration of various peoples into the upper Sangha basin increased competition for forest resources and labor but also opportunities for social, cultural, and linguistic exchanges.[22]

Increased enslavement was another related trend in the northern forest and bordering savanna that encouraged movement and interaction of different language and ethnic groups. The development of Fulbé kingdoms in Ngaoundere (present-day Cameroon) indirectly touched off movement among forest populations in and near the Sangha. In the 1830s the Fulbé conquered Adamawa (in the northwestern highlands of Cameroon) as an offshoot of Usuman dan Fodio's early nineteenth-century jihads in West Africa. The conquest of Adamawa had enormous consequences for northern savanna dwellers, inspiring some of them to centralize political control among various clans. But Fulbé raids also precipitated flight among Mbum, Banda, Gbaya, and Kako speakers, who created pressures among neighboring Mpiemu, Pande, Ndzimou, and Pomo speakers and others residing in or around the Sangha basin. Indeed, by the 1840s and 1850s, the Sangha basin was in a permanent state of warfare. Oral accounts from widespread sources attest to warfare, shifting alliances, and mutual enslavement among Mpiemu and Bakwele, Gbaya, Bangando, and Kako speakers of the northern forest. Explorers of the Sangha basin in the late nineteenth and early twentieth centuries found themselves caught in these ongoing conflicts and sought to exploit them.[23]

Thus, Mpiemu groups who made their way to the middle and upper Sangha forests near the Kadei River by the mid-nineteenth century did so in a broader context of dynamic economic accumulation, political and social upheaval, cultural and economic exchange, and political alliance and competition. They did not arrive in these forests en masse. Rather, men, women, and children organized themselves in *panjo*. Members of different *panjo*, sometimes related by *kuli ajing*, putative kin ties, moved short distances along the northern Congo basin's major and minor rivers and streams, such as the Dja (Ngoko), Sangha, and Boumba. In response to new opportunities, intravillage conflicts over resources, and raids, villages would split and move again. With each group led by a *wani* (leader) or a *pendo* (war leader) and their warriors, Mpiemu *kuli ajing* and *panjo* fought among themselves but also encountered and battled with Kako, Ngundi, Pande, and Gbaya peoples, and they ultimately resettled in new, small forest villages near the Kadei River.

Speakers of Mpiemu found that they shared with other Sangha basin inhabitants (including Pomo, Bomassa, Kako, Maka, Gbaya, and Bangando peoples) some common language structures and ways of organizing themselves spatially and socially.[24] But they also borrowed words, cultivation practices, foods, and knowledge about the forest and its animals, plants, and spirits. Mpiemu, Kako, and Bomassa now share a common repertoire of deities who people their tales of the distant past. Mpiemu and other people of the middle and upper Sangha also employ a common set of spatial metaphors about social, cultural, political, and environmental relations that are crucial to their interpretations of the past, present, and future. Indeed, people throughout equatorial Africa use metaphors of vines and cords (domesticated vines) to talk about the connections that bound people together. Mpiemu, for instance, speak of cord families and other cords of kinship, attach special importance to the care and disposal of umbilical cords after an infant is born, and remember the ways that men once literally and figuratively tied together their dwellings. More generally, equatorial Africans have used forest vines to fashion cords for various constructions but also speak metaphorically of vines and cords to discuss changing relationships between people and their environments.[25] For Mpiemu, severed vines and cords are metaphors that refer to their historical movements over rivers within the forest and their declining participation in regional and global economies.

Such interactions and linguistic and cultural borrowing continued in the twentieth century, as Sangha basin inhabitants and neighboring savanna dwellers such as Banda and Gbaya were drawn into a French colonial economy. Both the French administration and European rubber, coffee, cacao, tobacco, and diamond enterprises facilitated the mobility and interaction of African workers, their families, and conscripted soldiers from West and Central Africa. Even after independence in 1960, diamond, timber, and coffee enterprises continued to draw workers from far-flung regions of the Central African Republic, but by the 1970s many had foundered. In their place individual farmers and miners cultivated or extracted their products alone or in small groups, selling them to Hausa, Fulbé, and other West African merchants from Cameroon, Chad, Senegal, Mauritania, and Mali.

Mpiemu participated actively in these changes. The pressure of paying colonial taxes, the lure of new opportunities and access to new consumer goods, and the desire to escape the ravages of sleeping sickness inspired many Mpiemu to take up work on plantations in Salo and Lindjombo. Some returned to their home villages to marry Mpiemu women of other *kuli ajing,* only to return to the plantations. Later, the attraction of opportunities in diamond mines near Nola and Salo and timber companies in Bayanga, south of Lindjombo, and in Cameroon drove younger generations to seek work there.

Cultural borrowing among Africans occasioned these economic changes. Forced recruitment for construction of roads, administrative buildings, and the infamous Congo-Ocean railway that linked Brazzaville to the Atlantic Ocean brought workers from Middle Congo (of which the Sangha basin was a part), Ubangi-Shari, and Chad together into administrative centers and worksites.[26] Subsequent generations of African workers crowded into plantation and mining towns, rubbing shoulders with one another, earlier inhabitants of the riverine villages, troops, and merchants. These encounters precipitated further exchanges of language, food, farming techniques, religious beliefs, healing practices, dress, and environmental knowledge.

Sangha basin people and Central Africans found a common language first through their participation in Christian missions during the late colonial period and in their citizenship in the Central African Republic after 1959. Sango, originally a language of a Ubangi riverine population, was adopted by Christian missionaries during the late colonial years. In their translations of the Bible, they simplified the language and promoted its dissemination among people in Ubangi-Shari. Following independence, the CAR adopted Sango as its national language.[27] And thus Mpiemu speakers came to share a language but also a set of metaphors to depict movement, stasis, and their changing relationships to their forest environments. Like many Sango speakers, Mpiemu people used several words connoting both movement and stasis, or "sitting." In the Mpiemu language tellers of *doli* used such terms as *ntche* (to come from) or *wimbo* (to wander or voyage) to refer to their historical movements and *dio* (to be sitting or to live or exist in a space) to refer to times of past settlement, which punctuated wanderings through forests and over rivers. In Sango they employed similar terms: *londo* (to come from), *duti* (to sit), and *ga* (to arrive), and at times *gagango,* referring to those people who had come from elsewhere.

Currently, Mpiemu speakers do not have a major presence either politically or numerically in the Central African Republic. Although one minister in the national government (and former deputy to the National Assembly) considered himself Mpiemu, neither he nor other Mpiemu sought to promote "Mpiemu politics" in a national forum. This is primarily because Mpiemu comprise a very small proportion of the CAR's population, far outnumbered—and outpowered—by Ngbaka, Yakoma, Gbaya, and most recently, "northern" ethnic groups. On the national political level, it appears that Mpiemu interests are frequently subsumed under the rubric of "southern" interests and are included within political parties that can cut across regional and ethnic affiliations.

On a regional level, though, Mpiemu speakers do form a major but not predominant ethnic group in the upper and middle Sangha basin. They dominate, both numerically and politically, in the Nola town and region; the colonially created M'Bimou, where Mpiemu live alongside their Ngombe clients and diamond workers from throughout the country, lies to the east of the town. Farther south in the Sangha basin of the Central African Republic, in the villages of Salo, Bayanga, and Lindjombo, Mpiemu are a significant ethnic group, numerically outnumbering all other ethnic groups (Pomo, Bomassa, Gbaya, Aka) in Lindjombo in 1993. During the late colonial period, they were able to translate their numerical and financial wealth and prestige into one chieftainship in Lindjombo, but they lost that position when Pomo speakers relocated their village back to Lindjombo and reassumed leadership of it. In 1994, however, a Mpiemu man became the deputy for the Lope region in the National Assembly. Mpiemu people thus remained part of a mix of ethnic groups in the upper and middle Sangha basin, able to exercise some influence at certain historical moments but, like all other ethnic groups, not a predominant presence.

All of these interactions and exchanges of language, knowledge, and practices among various people moving in and out of the Sangha River basin had important consequences for how Mpiemu created *doli*. In the long-term historical context of movement and borrowing, *doli* could never stand as a unique, monolithic way of seeing or body of knowledge, practices, and claims to truth about the past. Instead, historical interactions among diverse people have rendered *doli* a refraction of a broader Sangha basin repertoire of notions about people, their environments, and the past.

COLONIZERS AND AFRICAN SUBJECTS

Colonizers included a host of historical agents, who pursued various agendas but generally sought to assert control over African people and Sangha basin resources. In comparison to the rest of Africa, colonization came relatively late to equatorial Africa. Colonial state building was a haphazard and attenuated process. But the transformation of relations between persons and their environments lay at the very heart of European colonization. From the turn of the twentieth century, European perceptions and aims lay in transforming the Sangha basin forest through the labor of Africans into a boundless source of wealth for French and German commercial interests and later for France. Africans, in turn, would be turned into avid consumers of European goods.[28] But these processes proved far more difficult for French administrators and commercial interests; specters of scarcity and loss consistently haunted them as they anguished over the insufficiency of agricultural production; Africans' unwillingness to work; the loss of productive African workers from sleeping sickness, flight, and rebellion; and the disappearance of valued forest resources from overuse. During colonial interventions to alter patterns of human settlement and resource use, colonizers conveyed their anxieties about scarcity, loss, and dissolution to their colonial subjects.

The imposition of colonial rule in the upper and middle Sangha basin began with European discoveries and rivalries for African territories, from the mid-1880s to 1907. During the "scramble for Africa" in the 1880s, European powers saw the Sangha basin as a critical strategic outpost in the broader territorial contest for space and prestige. Imagined as a crucial way of access to West Africa, the basin became the focus of diplomatic desire, plotting, and negotiation. The French fantasized that it would link their equatorial African possessions with those in North and West Africa; a solid foothold in the Sangha basin would hamper British and German expansion in the Fulbé state of Adamawa in northern Cameroon and Belgian influence in the Congo basin. Hence, Sangha basin explorations under Pierre Savorgnan de Brazza and his associates beginning in 1886 and continuing in the 1890s were supposed to establish a safe route to Chad, to promote trade with Africans, and generally to increase French influence in the region. A solid foothold in the Sangha basin would enable the French to hamper British and German expansion. Germany, which had already made substantial inroads in northern Cameroon, followed the French lead up the Sangha basin years later. Explorers Carnapp-Quernheim, Plehn, and Stein did not reach Ouesso until 1898, continuing their movement farther north through Yokadouma and west across Djem, Djimou, Bajwe, and Maka lands.[29]

The French defeat at Fashoda in 1898 inaugurated a new set of European aims and spatial and environmental conceptions of the Sangha, for both the French and the Germans. No longer the means of claiming vast swaths of African territory, the Sangha basin forest now took on greater significance as the focus of French and German dreams of commercial exploitation. The Sangha basin was already the focus of intensive commerce among Dutch, British, German, Belgian, and other European agents. Commercial interest stemmed from perceptions that the Sangha basin forest was a boundless source of wealth. Both the French and the Germans turned their attentions to building colonial states to exploit the riches of the Sangha basin and to protect these resources from one another. And both followed the Belgian example in order to establish their authority and to claim sole access to forest resources: they granted concessions to European-owned private enterprises, which struggled to assert their control over rubber, ivory, and African laborers.[30]

European administrators were few and far between during the first decades of colonial rule, and thus their direct influence on Africans was relatively limited. Administrations found themselves besieged by rival European powers and competitive concessionary and trading companies for control of African labor to tap rubber and to transport goods. French and German administrations vied to attract Africans to their own territories on either side of the Sangha and Ndoki Rivers. Tensions escalated. Prodded by incessantly bickering concessionary companies, which claimed that African labor and forest resources were hemorrhaging to rival companies, France and Germany repeatedly negotiated the boundaries separating German Cameroon from the French Congo.[31]

Explorations were ostensibly part of French and German efforts to gather information in order to settle boundary disputes and conflicting claims to Sangha peoples and commodities. But these explorations also advanced French and German claims over the people and forests and were part of an erratic effort to establish state control. They allowed them to demonstrate their knowledge of and control over the disputed subjects and lands. Explorers sought to learn the landscape of the Sangha basin, to locate and to attach names to particular peoples living there, and to trace the historical movements of various linguistic groups. Their efforts aided the development of ethnicity in the Sangha basin. Explorers focused on riverine people, who congregated in large villages along the large navigable rivers of the northern forest, and did not encounter Mpiemu speakers until 1905. Explorers' maps of the basin and their characterizations of distinct groups had an enormous influence on contemporary and future administrators.

After an initial mapping of the upper and middle Sangha basin, the entire area was designated the Sangha region, part of the French Congo colony, in 1900. In the following year the French divided the basin into two *circonscriptions,* the Lower Sangha, with its capital in Ouesso, and the Upper Sangha, whose capital was first Carnot and later Nola. From these *circonscriptions* the French carved a series of *terrains* named for the prominent *races,* or ethnic groups (M'Bimou, Baya, and Haoussa), that supposedly reflected ethnographic and economic homogeneity and would enhance chiefly authority to tax and recruit their subjects. In 1910 France created French Equatorial Africa, made up of Middle Congo, Ubangi-Shari, and Gabon. It also reformed the M'Bimou, Baya, and Haoussa *terrains* into official *circonscriptions.*[32]

In 1911 German-French negotiations produced a redrawing of the colonial African map. France ceded its possessions in the Sangha and Lobaye regions in exchange for German possessions between the Logone and Chari Rivers in Chad and others in Morocco, evacuating the last of their Sangha posts in 1913. The French rapidly regained control of the basin during the First World War, when it became a battlefield for German-French rivalries. With the Treaty of Versailles, the previously ceded territories within the Sangha basin officially returned to French control, and it became the Kadei-Sangha *circonscription.* From then on, French colonial rule began to have a much more pervasive effect on Africans' lives and on the forests. The administration began in earnest to assert its control, to build a colonial state, and to implement the "development" (*mise en valeur*) of the basin's resources, which in practice was their rapacious extraction. It appointed chiefs where they had never existed, collected taxes, constituted and relocated villages, conscripted labor for constructing local roads and the distant Congo-Ocean railroad, compelled cassava and maize cultivation, commanded Africans to carry health passes in order to contain sleeping-sickness epidemics, and imposed a series of hunting laws.

And the colonial administration intensified these interventions after the 1928–31 Kongo-Wara rebellion. The "War of the Hoe Handle" began north of the Sangha basin, in Gbaya towns where a charismatic healer and his followers instigated an anti-European, anti-Fulbé rebellion but also created a movement of "non-violent protection and peace."[33] The rebellion spread to Cameroon, the lower Ubangi region, and the upper Sangha, but it did so unevenly. French officials, labeling every failure to support the colonial order as "dissent," ruthlessly dispatched troops to suppress the rebellion and imprison Kongo-Wara followers. But they also sent soldiers into parts of the forest apparently unaffected by Kongo-Wara, enforcing African subjects' relocation to designated villages. In 1933, in order to assert greater control over the vast administrative territory, the French divided the Kadei-Sangha *circonscription* in two (Haute-Sangha and N'Goko-Sangha), but the following year it reunited them into a single department.

For the next three decades, until independence, the French colonial administration struggled to make the Sangha basin productive and profitable, and it did so by attempting to transform relations between people and the equatorial forest. It drew from a wide repertoire of economic and environmental strategies. Elsewhere in Ubangi-Shari (the colony in French Equatorial Africa that had assumed control of the Sangha basin from the Middle Congo colony) the French administration opted for peasant production, compelling Africans to plant cotton, peanuts, cassava, and other foods. But by the 1930s in the Sangha basin, as in southeast Cameroon, the French staunchly promoted European commercial concerns, excluding Africans from any role other than as laborers.[34] European plantation owners and the Compagnie Forestière de la Sangha-Oubangui cleared vast tracts of forest and produced coffee with African labor, leaving Africans to grow lower-valued cassava, peanuts, and maize for workers.

This strategy shifted in the 1950s after the upper and middle Sangha was ceded to Ubangi-Shari. Concerned over the purportedly massive depopulation among Mpiemu people, the French colonial administration curtailed European plantation owners' monopoly over coffee. In 1953, over the vociferous objections of CFSO, the major coffee producer in the Sangha basin, it introduced the Paysannat Café-Cacao, a cooperative encouraging peasant production of coffee and cacao. French administrators envisioned the *paysannat* as a way to "stabilize" declining Mpiemu families, whose youthful productive members either had perished from sleeping-sickness epidemics or had left home because of forced conscription or the lure of plantation and diamond-mine work.[35] This new strategy developed within a broader context of decolonization in French Equatorial Africa. Throughout the 1950s France sought ways of ensuring that Ubangi-Shari and other francophone countries would remain firmly linked to French commercial and political interests.[36] French provided price supports for coffee, but the benefits only accrued to French commercial interests, and not to small coffee growers.

The French not only promoted different arrangements in exploiting the middle and upper Sangha basin forests, but they simultaneously sought to protect game from overhunting both by setting aside lands for protection and by establishing hunting laws. The earliest form of such regulation came with the creation of concessionary companies, whose rights to the soil and to other resources within their concessions limited the hunting rights of Africans. But beginning in 1916, the French administration began to introduce a host of piecemeal measures, ostensibly designed to protect big game, such as elephants, gorillas, and certain birds, from overexploitation, but also intended to earn revenues for the administration.[37] It introduced hunting permits in 1929 for different classes of hunters. And spurred by British East Africa's development of tourism and safari hunting, the French in the 1920s began to discuss the possibility of setting aside protected areas in French Equatorial Africa; in 1934 the governor-general of the AEF consented to the creation of protected areas in parts of the AEF.[38] Shortly thereafter, the administration amended the list of protected species to include rhino, buffalo, and other game but also encouraged the destruction of "harmful" species. It eventually created several hunting reserves and parks in Middle Congo, Ubangi-Shari, and Chad, regulating whether, when, which species, how many, and by what methods game could be hunted. Over time, then, the administration expanded the scope of protection, spurred by anxieties over the disappearance in particular of elephants. This disappearance of certain game (like elephants) would entail not only the loss of the species but also a serious loss of revenues for French Equatorial Africa.[39]

French attempts to harness African labor to clear the forest for the colonial administration, to promote forest exploitation through concessionary companies and other European enterprises, to encourage peasant production of cash crops, and to regulate African hunting and trapping practices helped to alter relations between Sangha basin populations and the forest. By the time that the French gave up control of Ubangi-Shari and French Equatorial Africa in 1960, they were clearly disappointed in their past efforts to tap the Sangha basin forest's wealth and to "civilize" the basin's inhabitants by settling them in stable, productive households and villages. Administrators interpreted

France's interventions in the Sangha basin as indelibly marked by a host of losses—by Mpiemu depopulation and the subsequent loss of familial life, by the excessive exploitation of some valued game, and by France's inability to transform this rich forest into wealth for the metropole. Both French environmental interventions and their anxieties provided ample fodder for the constitution of Mpiemu *doli*.

COMMERCIAL ENTERPRISES

Commercial enterprises carried on a dynamic and complex relationship with both European colonial administrations and Africans living in the Sangha basin, and they too contributed to *doli*. Two constants remained part of this colonial equation throughout the twentieth century: first, these enterprises owed their very presence in the Sangha to European colonial administrations yet frequently found themselves at odds with administrative policy over the exploitation of forest resources and people; and second, they relied on African labor to acquire valued forest resources but consistently found it impossible to control the labor of the sparse, refractory populations available. Nevertheless, their influence has pervaded Sangha basin inhabitants' environmental and historical consciousness.[40] From 1899 to 1911 France and Germany delegated the responsibility for administering the Sangha basin to private European concessionary companies.[41] Although the concessionary system eventually set the companies and states at odds with one another, it initially represented an important compromise between them. This devolution of effective rule to private concerns was part of a French and German policy to "develop" the wealth of Sangha basin territories at little or no cost to the metropole. Paying a fixed yearly rent plus an additional percentage fee based on the land area and profits, these commercial enterprises controlled ill-defined concessions that assured them monopolies to harvest rubber, ivory, and other forest resources. Companies theoretically had to contribute to the development of an administrative infrastructure, including customs posts, telegraph lines, and steamships. Sending armed guards into villages, the companies forcibly conscripted Africans to collect rubber for months at a time in the forest. They then required these workers and their families to carry rubber for considerable distances to market centers in Nola, Bania, Berbérati, Moloundou, and Bayanga and to sell it to the concessionary companies for a fraction of its world market value.[42]

Despite their coercive measures and chicanery, many companies did not prosper. They were hampered by ambiguously defined rights and small, scattered, recalcitrant African populations, who had never worked for *patrons* and did not take kindly to companies' brutal measures to coerce people to work or their efforts to cheat workers out of their earnings. Indeed, none of the three original companies receiving concessions in the French-controlled part of the Sangha basin survived beyond 1911. After Savorgnan de Brazza's damning 1905 report concerning concessionary company abuses and their failure to develop equatorial Africa, France wanted to abolish the concessionary system but was constrained by its contracts with these companies. It crafted a solution in which the diverse companies merged into a single enterprise, the Compagnie Forestière de la Sangha-Oubangui, which controlled some eleven million hectares and most of the rubber production in the Sangha region until 1935.[43] The extensive concession of the German company Gesellschaft Sud Kamerun was seriously reduced by 1905. Concessions on both sides of the European frontier faced significant competition not only from smaller European trading companies but also from the administrations themselves, jockeying for access to rubber collectors and their harvests. By the end of the First World War, most concessionary companies had gone bankrupt, although CFSO remained a powerful presence in the upper Sangha until the mid-seventies, when the company was nationalized under President, and then Emperor, Jean-Bedel Bokassa.[44]

The French administration continued to see European firms as central to the Sangha basin's *mise en valeur* during the 1920s and 1930s, but the nature of environmental exploitation changed. Up until the mid-1920s, commerce in the colonial Sangha basin was based primarily on extraction of natural resources, rubber and ivory. But after that, CFSO and other European traders began to clear vast tracts of forest for coffee plantations in Lindjombo, Salo, Bania, Nola, and Berbérati, luring workers from villages throughout the middle and upper basin. Coffee production eventually outstripped rubber production. Forest clearing for the cultivation of other crops followed, including cacao and oil palm.

The extractive industries within the forest did not entirely disappear. Although rubber died a slow death in the Sangha, experiencing a brief revival during the Second World War and disappearing thereafter, other extractive activities remained at the Sangha colonial economy's foundations. Hunting for ivory, meat, and animal skins continued in the 1940s and 1950s, and in 1945 the Compagnie Minière de l'Oubangui Oriental began to promote diamond and gold mining along the banks of the basin's streams and rivers.[45]

Following independence, these extractive industries (hunting for ivory, meat, and skins; fishing; and diamond mining) remained the mainstay of the Sangha basin's economy, and diamonds have made an important contribution to the CAR's economy as well. Safari hunting, too, was an important activity in the colonial period and is still controlled by mostly French tour operators. North American and European hunters will now pay over $26,600 for one fourteen-day safari to hunt such big game as bongo and buffalo, and from this sum come revenues (in the form of trophy taxes and other fees) for the CAR state and local treasuries.[46] The CAR's total yearly earnings from safari hunting have not been calculated, but some analysts have suggested that the CAR and other equatorial African countries could earn significant revenues from trophy taxes and various fees associated with safari hunting. In 1995, for instance, the Bayanga Commune earned an estimated $3,680 out of total annual trophy taxes paid by the sole safari company in the area, amounting to $14,720.[47]

Agricultural enterprises have fared less well. Africans assumed control of coffee production in Salo after CFSO ceded the company and its landholdings to Bokassa's state in the mid-1970s. But the M'Bimou *paysannat* ultimately failed. Most farmers abandoned coffee production in the Salo region, and eventually farmers transformed the coffee fields into plots for maize, cassava, and other food crops. The Yugoslav-owned Emona Café in Lindjombo closed its operations in 1981; for a decade African cultivators there continued to produce coffee, some earning significant revenues. But with the bankruptcy in 1992 of CAISTAB, the marketing board to whom all producers sold their coffee, Lindjombo farmers abandoned coffee cultivation, at least temporarily. Because of high-priced inputs, such as fertilizer and insecticide, and the low-quality coffee grown in the CAR, production no longer appears economically viable, except during years when big coffee-producing countries experience crop failures.[48]

The most striking postindependence development in the middle Sangha has been the development of the timber industry, which has remained under outsider control. Although timber companies had exploited the upper Sangha forests near Berbérati since the 1950s, none had even inventoried the rich Sangha forests from Salo to the CAR's border with the Republic of Congo. A 1963–64 forest inventory published by the French Centre Technique Forestier Tropical identified a wealth of valuable hardwood species, and thereafter a host of timber companies received concessions from the Central African Republic government. Logging concerns set up shop in the forest beginning in 1972, exploited their concessions, went bankrupt, and resurrected themselves, repurchasing the very same concessions from the state and recommencing timber harvesting. Others found new owners from Europe or Asia.

From the mid-1920s, all of these enterprises helped to alter ways of exploiting the Sangha forest by intensively extracting valuable resources from it or, more dramatically, clearing it entirely for coffee, oil-palm, and cacao plantations or for diamond mining. At the same time these enterprises also attracted people from diverse locations, settling them in densely populated worker quarters and facilitating the kind of cultural, agricultural, and linguistic borrowing that had occurred in the nineteenth century. Between the mid-1920s and the early 1950s, plantations and mines tended to draw people from within the Sangha basin, but after independence they attracted workers from the far corners of the CAR and financiers not only from Africa but also from the Middle East and Europe. These two changes had important consequences for how Mpiemu and other Sangha basin inhabitants perceived and acted upon the forests. Open, exploited spaces signified a proper and productive use of resources, allowing Africans to gain access to desired consumer goods, broader political economies, and networks of power. These ways of perceiving and acting on the forest's resources became embedded in *doli,* as a process of characterizing and interpreting the forest and its past and as arguments about declining Mpiemu participation in the forest's commercial exploitation.

CHRISTIAN MISSIONS

Christian missionaries made crucial contributions to *doli.* Although the missionary presence in the Sangha basin has been fairly short-lived in comparison to that elsewhere in Africa, its influence on Mpiemu ways of conceiving truths about their past, present, and future has been enormous. In 1923 Father Marc Pédron of the Congrégation du Saint-Esprit (Holy Ghost Fathers) arrived in the village of Babalati (Berbérati) to found the first Christian mission in the Sangha basin, the Mission Sainte Anne. The Capuchins of Toulouse acquired control of the mission along with the Oubangui Prefecture in 1938, ceding it to the Capuchins of Savoy in 1952. The Filles de Jésus de Massac, the Oblates of Sainte-Thérèse, and the Marist Frères, as well as lay missionaries, worked alongside the Capuchins for several decades.[49]

The Roman Catholics, however, faced serious competition for the souls of Sangha basin populations, especially in the middle Sangha forests, where many Mpiemu resided. In 1924 the Baptists of Örebro, Sweden, acquired permission from the French Equatorial African administration to build missions in the Sangha basin. Swedish Baptist missionaries first constructed mission stations in the upper and middle Sangha villages of Matele (1921) and Bania (1923). In 1927 the village of Bilolo, in the heart of *metego Mpiemu* (Mpiemu soil), also boasted a rudimentary station. From there, Brothers Aron Svensson and Reinhold Andersson began the Baptists' struggle to maintain a foothold in the Sangha basin.[50]

Both Catholic and Baptist missionaries had to contend with considerable obstacles in converting Sangha basin inhabitants, and these challenges profoundly shaped the Mpiemu narratives of loss and redemption. French colonial administrators, some of whom were notoriously anticlerical, distrusted missionary activities simply on principle. French administrative competition for African labor made matters even worse for the missionaries, even as the pool of available workers dwindled from labor conscription and repeated sleeping-sickness epidemics. Nevertheless, Spiritans, Capuchins, and Baptists fully recognized that they were in the basin only at the behest of the French and at times muted their criticisms of administrative and company brutality.[51]

Catholic and Baptist strategies for attracting converts differed in some predictable ways. In 1924 Pédron and African workers constructed a chapel in Berbérati, making that station the central post from which the fathers conducted a *mission flottante* (floating mission), traveling to far-flung villages to set up catechist posts, hold masses, and perform sacraments for believers. This centralization resulted from the two sets of hierarchies in which the mission was embedded: those of the Capuchin order and of the Roman Catholic Church itself. The Swedish Baptists did not create a single, central supervising mission station but instead built a series of stations in more-traveled (Bania, Gamboula) and less-traveled (Bilolo) population centers in the forest. In response to this strategy, the Catholics constructed additional posts to do battle directly with the Baptists. Hence Catholic and Baptist missionaries overlaid a set of marked geographies on the Sangha basin, playing out their competition for African converts by plotting and counterplotting mission posts and parishes.[52]

Catholic and Baptist missionaries adopted similar tactics in attracting followers and material resources. Both altered the physical and social environments of Sangha basin villages and towns, investing crucial resources in building chapels, missionary and catechist houses, and schools, all new places that constituted and were shaped by interactions between Sangha basin inhabitants and missionaries. In addition, in order to subsidize mission-station incomes, both Catholics and Baptists hunted game; cleared substantial forestlands to cultivate coffee, cacao, yam, cassava, and peanut plantations; and raised cattle, sheep, and goats. They distributed medical care in the middle Sangha, where Mpiemu had suffered repeated sleeping-sickness epidemics, giving food and clothing to converts. Missionaries used much the same methods to alter how Sangha basin Africans perceived their selves, their worlds, and their pasts and futures: they trained African catechists, held masses and meetings, schooled new converts, and recruited the sons and daughters of chiefs to attend mission schools. Indeed, until independence missionaries (primarily the better-endowed Catholics) took responsibility for most of the childhood schooling in the Sangha basin.

Following the Central African Republic's independence in 1960, both missions altered their strategies for accumulating followers. The Catholic Church, castigated in the years immediately after independence for failing to train or delegate authority to Central African clergy, undertook the Africanization of its ranks. In 1964 the Catholic Church could point to only six Central African priests (out of 131), one Central African brother (out of 36), and four Central African sisters (out of 131) in the CAR. By 1993 the proportions of Central African clergy had grown to eighty-three priests (out of 258), five brothers (out of 43), and sixty-three sisters (out of 304). Yet in the Berbérati diocese, this process of Africanization is far from complete. For many Catholics the most frequent contact has been with either African catechists or French priests, not African ones.[53]

The church also lost its most effective and cherished recruiting tool in the postindependence period: its monopoly on formal education. In 1963 the Central African Republic nationalized all schools, hiring Central African teachers and directors to replace Catholic missionaries. The results were catastrophic so far as the clergy were concerned. In the absence of this control over religious and secular education, the church has sought to recruit Central Africans in other ways, primarily through Action Catholique, which, beginning in the late 1950s, organized Catholic lay groups among "Workers, Employers, Functionaries and School Youth" to make them "conscious of . . . [their] religious and social duties."[54] Among the most active of such lay groups were women's groups, the Femmes Chrétiens and members of the Légion de Marie.[55]

While French Capuchins and other Roman Catholic orders retained an active, though smaller, European presence in the CAR, the Swedes withdrew altogether from the entire Sangha, handing over complete control of the Baptist churches in the Haute-Sangha and Bouar-Baboua Prefectures to Central Africans themselves. Thereafter, under the rubric of the Union of Baptist Churches of the West, CAR, Central Africans regulated the training and investiture of pastors, evangelization, the education of the faithful, and the financial conduct of the church.[56]

In the postindependence context, Mpiemu people of the middle Sangha basin have had a wealth of religious communities, cosmologies, and practices from which to draw. Both Catholics and Baptists have had to contend with a flood of competing churches since independence. Catholic missionaries have noted with alarm the growth of charismatic prayer groups, which frequently call themselves Catholic but which the Roman Catholic Church itself disavows.

The Mid-Mission Baptists, the Apostolics, and the Frères Évangéliques (Evangelical Brethren) all have active congregations throughout the region. And as West African diamond financiers and merchants have moved into the middle Sangha basin, they have facilitated the spread of Islam.[57]

Since 1924 all of these missions and religious groups have actively contributed to *doli,* promoting membership in religious communities through adherence to particular beliefs and practices but also altering the topography of Sangha basin forests and villages through environmental exploitation and building. Missionaries interpreted people, landscapes, and events in the Sangha basin with a historical vision of dearth, loss, and salvation through Jesus Christ. For both Catholic and Baptist missionaries, Mpiemu were the quintessential sufferers. But Mpiemu also actively contributed to missionary perceptions of them, just as they claimed membership in various religious communities and selectively borrowed perceptions, beliefs, and practices from their historical visions.

THE CENTRAL AFRICAN REPUBLIC

Since it achieved official independence in 1960, the Central African Republic has attempted in the Sangha basin to transform once-colonial subjects into Central African citizens and to alter human-environment relations so as to assert control over valued forest resources. But the state's agency has been fragmented and its influence piecemeal. The independent CAR has retained close political, military, and fiscal relationships with France for much of the postcolonial period but also has relied on the political influence and financial support of other entities, such as international investors, multilateral aid organizations, and at times, conservation organizations.[58]

The CAR's intimate relationship with France has its roots in de Gaulle's 1958 referendum on the soon-to-be independent African colonies. Most French colonies (with the exception of Guinea) voted then to remain in a Franco-African community, pegging their currencies to the French franc, ceding both financial and military control to France, but ostensibly retaining control over other domestic affairs. But in the CAR, France's influence went even further. After independence-movement leader Barthélémy Boganda's mysterious death, France effectively handpicked David Dacko, the CAR's first president, helping him to centralize power, subsidizing his government's operations, and facilitating his efforts to neutralize all political parties other than his own MESAN (Mouvement d'Évolution Sociale d'Afrique Noire). When Jean-Bedel Bokassa overthrew Dacko's struggling regime in 1965, he commenced highly volatile relations with France, relying heavily on its fiscal and political support but at times seeking alliances with Libya, China, the Soviet Union, and other countries to restock his depleted treasury.[59] Nevertheless, relations between Bokassa (who infamously crowned himself emperor in 1977) and French president Giscard d'Estaing were particularly close, partly because Giscard himself was a safari-hunting enthusiast, but also because French companies (including that of Giscard's father) retained significant financial interests in Central African diamonds, uranium, and ivory.[60] But by 1979 France was finally so alienated by Bokassa's excesses and outright human-rights abuses that it intervened militarily to overthrow the emperor and to reinstall David Dacko.

Dacko's tenure was brief, but again the French military and other officials kept him in power until 1981, when General André Kolingba led a military coup and ejected Dacko from office. Kolingba ruled until 1986 through a military committee and a cabinet, when he assumed the presidency after a national referendum. Ever dependent on French financial support, Kolingba concentrated all executive and legislative power in himself.[61] But by the early 1990s political pressures within and outside of the CAR made Kolingba's position increasingly tenuous. Democratization movements elsewhere in Africa were gaining strength, and some had successfully transformed single-party states into multiparty democracies. Central Africans took their inspiration from these movements, openly criticizing the Kolingba regime and resorting to riots in 1991. France under Mitterrand also made continued financial assistance contingent upon democratization. By 1993 Kolingba grudgingly relented to demands for open elections, allowing parties other than his Rassemblement Démocratique Centrafricain to form and to nominate candidates for the presidency. Thus the CAR's first democratically elected president, Ange-Félix Patassé, came to power that same year. But despite these developments, France has continued to influence CAR politics, intervening in 1996 to bolster the Patassé presidency after an attempted coup and retaining its largest military installation on the African continent in the CAR until 1998.[62]

This volatile political history and the CAR's unusually close relationship with France has had important implications for how state authority has manifested itself in the forests of the Sangha-Économique Prefecture. To be sure, the Dacko, Bokassa, and Kolingba regimes imposed state authority independent of France's influence, by collecting annual taxes, conducting censuses, and installing state police (and local gendarme) stations in all major towns and villages. Indeed, state police presence in the Sangha basin is strikingly high, primarily because of its location on the frontiers of the Republic of Congo and Cameroon, its valued economic resources, and the long history of human mobility.

The state's provision of health and educational services for Central Africans in the basin has depended on its own priorities and on French willingness to provide financial assistance. Lindjombo, Bayanga, and Salo all have state-run health clinics. The only hospitals are in Nola and Bilolo, and farther north in Berbérati and Gamboula. But during the 1990s fiscal and political crises, these clinics were very poorly funded, provisioned, and staffed, and health-care personnel were among the first civil servants not to receive their monthly pay.[63]

State-run schools have been a particularly important means of creating a shared sense of history, citizenship, and purpose among Central Africans, though again, state priorities, fiscal health, and French financial support (or the lack thereof) have profoundly shaped education.[64] The colonial and postcolonial history of education in the CAR has yet to be written, but the nationalization of schools in 1963 provided the means by which children were literally formed as Central Africans with a common history and common contemporary allegiances. But schools remain understaffed and poorly equipped; most frequently, Sangha villagers, and in some cases expatriate companies, have constructed school buildings, provided desks, benches, and blackboards, and paid for supplies. Teachers were among the last civil servants to receive their pay when the state experienced financial crises, and by the mid-1990s the state had declared two *années blanches,* when it did not have sufficient funds to run its schools. Nevertheless, state health and educational interventions have provided ample resources for the Mpiemu production of *doli.* State interventions to transform colonial subjects into Central Africans have partly subsumed Mpiemu *doli* under a more all-encompassing history of the Central African Republic and its people. But because the CAR has exercised intermittent control within its borders, its influence over Mpiemu *doli* is not nearly as influential as nationalist histories elsewhere, which have harnessed the fragmentary and multiple histories of their constituents to powerful nationalist master narratives in order to counter colonial histories.[65]

The state's most consistent interventions in the Sangha basin forest have turned on coffee, timber, and diamonds, and the shifting and uncertain course of environmental exploitation has contributed in important ways to Mpiemu conceptions of their environments and of the past, present, and future. Exploiting forest resources was a major activity in the colonial economy, and French commercial concerns retained their stakes in the CAR's forests after independence. But these same resources also provided successive regimes with much-needed exports and state revenues, which state heads and their agents have used partly to invest in diverse social and political networks. In the 1970s Bokassa promoted coffee production by encouraging the development of state-owned and smaller Central African coffee plantations. This effort was part of Opération Bokassa, a campaign to "modernize," to expand the national economy, and to achieve self-sufficiency, particularly from French capital. Although Opération Bokassa nationalized many French commercial enterprises, Bokassa was not consistently hostile to outside business interests, because the Yugoslav-owned Emona Café operated until 1981. And Bokassa's close relationship to Muammar al-Qaddhafi paved the way for Libyan businesses to operate in the empire, most notably in the middle Sangha basin, where one Libyan logging operation gained a timber concession. A rapid succession of mostly European-controlled enterprises acquired logging concessions in the region but rarely remained commercially viable for long, because they were constantly beset by poor management, high transportation costs, and shifting world prices. Yet the state's need for concession rents and stumpage fees kept it sympathetic to the plights of these logging concerns. This recent history of the state's accommodation of logging companies in the basin has helped to inculcate a perception among Mpiemu and other Sangha basin residents that economic prosperity cannot occur without the presence of expatriate enterprises and without the clearing or thinning of forests.[66]

The state's need for rents, fees, and taxes continued long after Bokassa's reign and thus encouraged further intervention into Sangha forest resources and economies. In 1986 the Kolingba regime found new reasons to support European enterprises in the Sangha. Under pressure from the World Bank and the International Monetary Fund to adhere to a structural adjustment program to reverse the growth of government spending, liberalize prices, encourage more open investment laws, and provide incentives to agriculture and forestry, the state continued to welcome foreign-owned logging companies.[67]

Financial pressures have not abated for the Patassé government but rather have increased, partly because France has steadily withdrawn its financial support from the CAR and other Communauté Franc Africain countries in recent years. Patassé inherited substantial debts from Kolingba. Desperate for funds to pay state employees and mutinous troops, Patassé negotiated more deals with international logging companies, even though in 1993–94 much of the processing of logs was done outside of the country, so that the CAR lost valuable opportunities to employ more Central African workers.

Diamonds, for both industrial and aesthetic uses, have provided crucial revenues for the CAR state since independence. The state has lured international capital to the Sangha basin since the late colonial era. Although small-scale artisanal miners have conducted much of the extraction, West African merchants financed their efforts and sold their finds to a complex hierarchy of buyers. Such small-scale mining seems to have intensified in recent years, as economic hardship has forced Sangha basin residents and other Central Africans to search for alternative sources of income. Mining, however, exacts significant ecological damage to the forest, and the state and mining interests faced considerable criticism from conservationists, particularly in the Dzanga-Sangha Special Reserve. There, the state has outlawed mining but has turned a blind eye to its widespread practice.[68]

Informally, state agents have participated in their own forms of resource exploitation in the Sangha basin.[69] More than any other industry in the early 1990s, diamonds served as effective means by which state agents could invest in social and political networks. Civil servants working in the Sangha-Économique Prefecture, for instance, reportedly invested in mining equipment and teams (sometimes with state funds), using the proceeds to increase their authority and wealth within political and social networks. Several were rumored to have been involved in illegal elephant hunting and an extensive bush-meat trade that reached from the Sangha forest to the capital, Bangui.

Other pressures in the late 1980s and 1990s limited the state's promotion of forest-resource exploitation. Although the state was beholden to international capital and had to adhere to World Bank–International Monetary Fund demands, it also experienced significant pressure from conservation groups and the World Bank to protect the Sangha basin forest.[70] So even as it encouraged logging and diamond extraction to boost exports, it also actively participated in conservation efforts in the Sangha basin forest, by creating a national park and buffer zone, providing personnel to monitor the park, and enforcing national hunting laws. Nevertheless, the Central African Republic, like many African states, remained unable or unwilling to shoulder much of the cost of protecting its resources.[71] It appropriated from an international conservationist discourse anxieties about the loss of patrimony, using the rhetoric of anxiety to consolidate state control over these resources, but also to sell them off to the highest bidder, to employ them for the benefit of the state, and to supplement the resources of particular political and social networks.

The state contributed to *doli*'s discourses of loss in contradictory ways. Because it relied in various ways on diverse external agencies, the state since independence alternately promoted the exploitation of forest resources and their protection. The state's dependence on international capital to exploit and export valued commodities rendered it vulnerable to fluctuations of world markets, particularly volatile for commodities such as timber. And that vulnerability contributed to the unpredictability and instability of the middle and upper Sangha basin economies and provided fodder for debates within Mpiemu *doli* over declining participation in these changes and loss of economic opportunities. Simultaneously, the state's promotion of conservation in the Sangha resulted from the anxieties of the World Wildlife Fund and the World Bank about the loss of the forest and their pressures for forest protection. In grappling with restrictions placed on their activities in villages, farms, and forests, Mpiemu fashioned *doli* to address concerns about depleted forests and lost economic opportunities and to understand them in terms of their pasts. But *doli* was no mere "fragment," to use Partha Chatterjee's term, of the CAR's history; Mpiemu produced it by drawing from and repudiating state efforts to create Central African citizens and to appropriate the forest resources for its varied aims.[72]

CONSERVING THE FOREST

Although the French colonial state implemented some limited measures to monitor hunting and trapping and thus conserve the Sangha basin's game resources beginning in 1916, no agency spearheaded extensive interventions to protect forest resources until the late 1980s.[73] At that time American scientific researchers conducting ecological studies on the forest, elephants, and gorillas expressed increasing concern that logging companies harvested too much timber, failed to allow sufficient time for regeneration, and opened up the forest to make hunting easier. In 1988 doctoral students Richard Carroll and J. Michael Fay, under the auspices of the World Wildlife Fund-U.S., set up a conservation project whose funding and personnel came from a wide array of sources.

The WWF, the U.S. Agency for International Development, the U.S. Fish and Wildlife Service, the World Bank, GTZ (Gesellschaft für Technische Zusammenarbeit, the German consultancy organization focusing on international development), and the Central African Ministry of Waters and Forests, Hunting, Fishing, and Tourism have all provided finances and personnel to the project. In 1990 the project worked with the Central African Republic government to establish the Dzanga-Ndoki National Park, 1,220 square kilometers of tropical rain forest allowing only approved research and regulated tourism (see fig. 1). At the same time the CAR and the project also created the Dzanga-Sangha Special Reserve, a 3,359-square-kilometer buffer zone around the park, permitting hunting with "traditional" weapons (nets, crossbows, and spears) and registered guns, as well as food and medicinal-plant gathering. Since then, the project has managed the park and reserve, seeking to promote ecologically sustainable rural development, to improve roads and construct camps, and to set up a research program to ensure sound forest management.

Most personnel came from the WWF, the Central African Republic Ministry of Waters and Forests, the Peace Corps, and Bayanga, as well as some nearby villages. Central Africans have staffed important positions within the conservation project, including that of national director. Recruits from villages in the middle Sangha also have filled the ranks of antipoaching patrols (reserve guards) and tour guides and according to one analysis serve as "mediators or brokers, moving between these worlds [of reserve inhabitants and Western donor interests] . . . and enjoying particular privileges as well as particular social burdens as a result."[74] But American and European counterparts with postgraduate training in botany, primatology, and rural development, as well as current and former Peace Corps volunteers, have exercised considerable influence in writing legislation creating the park and reserve, setting conservation priorities and policies, and formulating the project's activities. This is certainly not to say that Westerners dictated all activities. Indeed, how conservation interventions were formulated and carried out depended upon the complex and changing relations between a wide variety of players in the middle and upper Sangha: Central African civil servants assigned to the project, their respective ministries, people living in the area, guards, guides, Western researchers, and Western conservationists (who frequently doubled as botanical and primatology researchers).[75] Nevertheless, it does seem that Western employees of the project had an important influence in shaping the rhetoric and efforts of protection in the Dzanga-Sangha reserve and Dzanga-Ndoki park.

Between 1988 and 1994 the project's goals have remained relatively constant: the "long-term conservation of the natural ecosystems" in the area and the preservation of "the forest as a viable home and source of livelihood for the Aka people."[76] One Ministry of Waters and Forests agent framed the goals of the project in this way: "We need to teach you about the [forest], the treasure of our country. It is like a cashbox, one that we keep so that it improves over time."[77] In seeking to fulfill these goals, the project attempted to enforce Central African Republic national laws restricting all hunting and gathering in the park, outlawing widespread snare trapping, requiring various permits for hunting certain kinds of game with shotguns, and in 1993 substantially limiting the bush-meat trade.

Since its inception the project sought to provide some services and jobs to some people of the Dzanga-Sangha reserve's highly mixed populations, although various WWF officials disagreed over the extent to which they should promote "development" efforts. Allard Blom, the technical adviser to the project, vociferously contended that "development approaches" to conservation, in which "local people are expected to manage their own resources sustainably," have significant disadvantages, because "people almost invariably want to increase their standard of living . . . [which] clearly means an increase in the use of natural resources . . . and leads to over-exploitation."[78] It recruited antipoaching guards and clad them in standard military uniforms, but also engaged tour guides and construction workers from various ethnic groups in the region, though primarily from Bayanga, site of the project headquarters.[79] The project provided free health-care services, but primarily to "indigenous" Aka peoples.[80] In an effort to spur what it called "ecologically sustainable development," the project first organized the Association Communale Yobé Sangha, using a $5,000 MacArthur Foundation grant to support small-scale group projects developing gardening, fishing, baking, coffee growing, and other activities. Later, the Comité du Développement du Bayanga, a committee of Bayanga residents and local and regional authorities, was formed to offer small loans from tourism revenues for various projects that promoted "sustainable development" in the reserve.[81]

Influential personnel in this conservation project have justified, explained, and shaped these interventions with extensive theorizing about the Sangha basin forest's and inhabitants' pasts. Their historical theories centered on a particular loss: the overexploitation of the Sangha forest and its game and the fears that they would simply disappear in the future. Mpiemu people in Lindjombo of the middle Sangha more frequently encountered the project and its interventions than have those living in Kwapeli, near Salo. And thus Mpiemu have constituted *doli* differently in different places, some drawing from project activities and experiences of the past to incorporate into their conceptions and interpretations of the past, present, and future.

2

TRANSLATING A HISTORICAL AND
ENVIRONMENTAL CATEGORY

THIS chapter is an exercise in translation. *Doli* has no single, straight-
forward translation but rather encompasses a process of perceiving,
characterizing, and interpreting the past and present, as well as a body
of knowledge about the past through which Mpiemu people have underscored and debated significant people, events, places, natural-resource exploitation, social and political relations, social categories and self-definitions,
and environmental interventions. In all of their expressions about the past,
Mpiemu use idioms linking people and their environments, particularly
cords and vines, mobility ("wandering") and stasis ("sitting"), and fat and
hunger, to articulate *doli*'s central aim of "leaving a person behind." This
chapter analyzes *doli*'s diverse meanings. It explores *doli*'s changing significance within the Sangha basin's multiethnic, multilinguistic context and in the
context of the introduction of Western-style education, which provided new
opportunities for acquiring authority and wealth and new ways of historical
and social reproduction. The chapter elaborates *doli*'s different genres—its
formulaic advice, tales, historical narratives, and sites and objects—and it
focuses on examples that shed light on past encounters with outsiders. It simultaneously illuminates diverse Mpiemu interpretations of their twentieth-
century engagements with outsiders over persons, forest places, spaces, and
resources and their participation in broader political economies. In an analysis of one forest site of *doli,* the chapter illustrates how Mpiemu have interpreted constraints on forest use imposed by the World Wildlife Fund and
the CAR government through the prism of *doli*.[1]

DOLI AS DIDACTIC KNOWLEDGE

Elderly Mpiemu tellers used *doli* as a way of perceiving, characterizing,
and interpreting the past and environment and as a body of historical and

environmental knowledge first for didactic purposes: it situated them, their listeners, and learners in an idealized social hierarchy and in a relationship with past times and places. This idealized social hierarchy in part allowed participants to gain and to justify access to broader networks of powerful *patrons,* to dependents' labor and respect, and to such valued resources as arable land, game, fish, and edible and medicinal plants. But *doli* was only one of many categories of knowledge about the past, present, and future that multiethnic Sangha basin populations have created. It was thus a refraction of a broader repertoire of categories addressing the temporality and spatiality of human relations and authority and their implications for patterns of resource use.

In this broader Sangha basin context, *doli* bore some resemblance to what I have described elsewhere as *guiriri,* a category of knowledge among Banda people, a linguistic and ethnic group living in the central savannas of the Central African Republic. *Guiriri* is a term in Sango, the CAR's national language. Banda, as well as Central Africans throughout the country, gloss *guiriri* as the French *histoire* ("history," because they use other Sango and French terms to connote "story"), but it does not correspond exactly with that term. *Guiriri* is a body of historical knowledge that conveyed temporal and spatial interpretations of past change and present social relations through images of roads and places.[2]

Inhabitants of the Sangha basin meant something different when they used the term *guiriri.* Among networks of Mpiemu people who had moved from the Mpiemu soil (*metego Mpiemu*) in Kwapeli and Bilolo south to the Lindjombo coffee plantations in the 1920s and 1930s, people employed the term *guiriri* when speaking Sango. But what they meant by it emerged only when they spoke Mpiemu. They infused *doli* with its own unique metaphors of the social, cultural, and political connections that bound people together, giving it less well-defined temporal limits and broader aims than Banda *guiriri.* Instead of the road and place images that pervaded *guiriri,* Mpiemu people invoked idioms of forest vines and cords, which bound people together through kinship and marriage but also reflected ruptures in those relations. Their discussions of *doli* also were replete with images of movement and settlement, of wandering (*wimbo*) and sitting (*dio*) in geographical, temporal, and social spaces within the equatorial forest. And they used idioms of hunger and fat to describe various conditions of dearth and prosperity. In short, *doli* bore only a limited resemblance to the Banda category *guiriri,* and thus finding an English equivalent of the category of *doli* was a complex process.

Mpiemu contended that *doli* was advice (*meleyo*), teaching young people how to comport themselves with husbands, wives, parents, and elders, to protect themselves from the dangers of occult forces, and to exploit the forest's resources effectively. When a group of young men, for instance, described *doli* in 1993, one asserted in French that it was "tradition" conveyed from "mouth to mouth." *"Bi san bi doli* [the things of *doli*]," another continued, was "the knowledge of our ancestors that kept our fathers alive, so that we could also care for our children." "When you work," another interrupted with an example, "your father teaches you how to make a house. . . . For you white people, you write things down, but we [convey knowledge] by mouth. You can't neglect the words of your father, or else not very long from now the house will fall down."[3] Through *doli*, then, older people articulated a social charter and "tradition," the specific practices giving rise to these proper social relations.

These proper social relations and traditions were crucial dimensions of *doli*'s central aim: the creation of the person (*mori*). Mpiemu people frequently recited a proverb, *Ligo mori* (Leave a person behind), whenever I asked them about the traces they would leave of themselves after they died and how they wanted to be remembered by future generations. In invoking *doli*, tellers' central aim was to reproduce *mori*, the person, a process by which one "left behind" one's own substances, knowledge, possessions, and social relations through a child. As the father of five children observed, "People are what you possess during your life. The Mpiemu often say *Ligo mori* (Leave a person [behind]). When you have done that, you have done a great thing. If you die and you haven't given birth to children, your enemies will sleep in your house, and they'll eat your things. But if you give birth to a child, you are a person. Something of you is left [behind]."[4] Leaving a person behind reproduced a common vital force (*alembo*) that people contained in their bellies and that bound together past, present, and future lineage members. *Alembo* was transmitted from generation to generation, shaping the individual lives and deaths of people who carried it. An active *alembo* existed as a separate being, driving its host to commit acts on its part, but it also remained an integral part of its human carrier. It was one of many factors that influenced a person's agency, which "includes not only one's effects on the world, but the extent to which one controls others' actions and effects as well."[5] But leaving a person behind was more than simply a biological process of reproduction; it was also a matter of leaving a fully social person behind. It meant educating a child, drawing from knowledge, practices, and beliefs that had their roots in a distant, unchanging past, so that the child understood and contributed to valued social relations. Moreover, bequeathing material objects (houses and "things") to children enabled a person to be remembered and to become part of *doli*. Hence *doli* helped to generate *mori,* and leaving a person behind animated contemporary Mpiemu experiences and interpretations of the twentieth-century past.

This is not to imply, however, that a person's creation and development were exclusively "communal" processes, as anthropologists and philosophers once argued. Nor did Mpiemu appear to perceive persons and selves as entirely distinct from one another. Indeed, *doli* in its many forms accommodated both developing social persons and self-consciousness. Leaving a person behind was a crucial way of becoming part of *doli* in several respects. Mpiemu first understood the person as created through a cyclical process; a person was born, acquired knowledge over time, reproduced, and died, leaving behind subsequent generations to reproduce. This was part of a larger process in which a person was created by an older generation, and in some cases subsequent generations transformed that person into the recent, recollected past. Later, through the processes of forgetting, eliding, and omitting, that person became part of the knowledge, people, and practices associated with the distant past. This creation of the person did not proceed as a series of chronologically arranged events; rather, it was a cycle repeated over and over, and eventually particular cycles accreted into sediments of the distant past. Second, *mori* also was associated with accumulated knowledge based on particular past experiences. Thus, a person could acquire knowledge through the particular events, people, and places in the past that had shaped his or her life. And finally, *mori* was associated with bodily and spatial sites. These sites of remembrance enabled Mpiemu speakers to organize and to recall past persons, events, and knowledge.[6]

As in many African societies, creating persons and a sense of belonging to gender, generational, kin, and ethnic groups were intimately related. Indeed, part of leaving a person behind involved educating young people and shaping the proper relations between them and elders, spouses, and ancestors. Elders, for instance, invoked *doli* to instill among young people a necessary respect for elders, spouses, and ancestors. In exchange, they would provide junior men with bridewealth. One middle-aged Mpiemu man observed,

> Before, we young men, we would sit [with our elders]. Father would teach you how you should sit. You work, you farm, you build a house. When that was finished, you make traps for game. You must respect elders. . . . But now, we have neglected our traditions, we smoke and drink crazily. A lot of people have died. Before, people did not die easily. But now, even when you're still a child, you can die. . . . If you look around this village, you will see very few elderly left. Now, you start drinking alcohol while you're still a child. You start looking for women while you're still a child.[7]

Whether or not these changes actually occurred is irrelevant. What is important is that the speaker elaborated an idealized past characterized by fixity, in which young men "sat" (lived in the same social space) with and worked diligently for elders. In contrast, however, he described a present in which the young had lost their moorings, neglecting their traditions, smoking, drinking, and engaging in sexual activities while still young.

Women agreed that *doli* was the advice that mothers provided to their daughters about their work that would give rise to proper social relations. The elderly Foa Mabogolo leaned forward and explained:

> Work of the kitchen. A woman comes . . . to make a field. You plant peanuts . . . cassava and maize. You will plant a field. Pineapple, bananas, you will plant them. You will do your work. Water, you make food. You sweep the entire house! Water, you give it to your husband, he will wash his body. You take meat, you cut it and cook it. In the evenings you cook meat well. Cassava, you make a lot of porridge. Everyone will come to eat a big meal, their stomachs will be full, your stomach will be full. That is the work of a woman. A woman goes and fishes in the middle of the forest, she finds lots of fish. The family eats.[8]

Children, too, found *doli* useful because it allowed them to demonstrate that they possessed a kind of privileged knowledge, but also because they relished its didactic tales. But for Mpiemu men and women, the present was characterized by profound loss, one that could result in unhappy marriages and even premature death. This nostalgia for the past is far from unique to elderly Mpiemu; rather it reflects crucial consciousness of a person's relationship to the past and present—the hallmarks of historical thinking.[9]

Mpiemu understandings of *doli* as advice and "tradition" were part of a broader repertoire of knowledge about the past and proper social relations, and they shared important features with other Sangha basin inhabitants' categories of knowledge, described in Sango as *guiriri*. These people saw *guiriri* as a guide to proper behavior that rendered young people respectful and attentive to elders, and they mourned the loss of a fixed hierarchy of juniors and elders. As one older Pomo man put it, "When I think of *guiriri*, and I think of how we sit now, tears fall from my eyes. We have nothing now. And the young people don't listen, they don't sit with me. When I was young, we worked hard, and then we would sit with our father. Now I see the children so infrequently. They don't know the names of the family, they don't know the places from where our ancestors came. They know nothing."[10] A Gbaya man concurred: "Before, when you told children to do something, they would do it. Now, take a day like today, when it rained. If long ago I sent my children to go to the field to do something, they would do it. Even if it rained, they would do it." His wife cut in, "But today, these children, they will refuse."[11]

The historicity of these comments is beside the point. Rather, *guiriri* as Sangha basin inhabitants articulated it incorporated a discourse of loss similar to that of Mpiemu *doli*. For these elderly people *guiriri* invoked a past time of real prosperity, one that people no longer enjoyed. As the Gbaya man observed, "The district chief . . . would bring you goods—blankets, salt—just for free. You received an allocation for the number of children that you had, if you had six, ten, whatever. . . . *Guiriri* was good, there was a lot of money. But now our existence has become very difficult. There is no money." What is salient here is not whether colonial officials magnanimously bestowed gifts on their subjects, but that tellers of *guiriri* and *doli* interpreted their past historically, evaluating it in terms of their perceptions of their present impoverished relations and livelihoods.

For Mpiemu speakers this pervasive notion of loss and nostalgia for the colonial administrators and company bosses resulted partly from the introduction of Western-style education, which for the past eighty years has both complemented and supplanted the authority of older forms of Sangha basin knowledge. From the mid-1920s, Western education, introduced by Christian missions and later by the Central African Republic state, provided Mpiemu children with compelling alternatives to learning *doli*. This educational process occurred very slowly.

From the 1920s until 1960, Mpiemu, like many rural populations of the Sangha basin forest, had only limited and intermittent access to this education. The colonial administration generally invested little in education in the AEF and almost nothing in the Sangha basin throughout its tenure, effectively delegating this responsibility to Roman Catholic and Swedish Baptist missionaries and their catechists. Mission schools located in population centers were an important locus of such educational efforts. The Spiritan Père Pédron began his school for children in the shade of Berbérati's stately trees in 1923. In addition to his charges from neighboring villages, Pédron accumulated a dozen Mpiemu chiefs' sons, teaching them to sing hymns, to read, to count, and to learn the catechism in the Gbaya language so that they could become catechists in their home villages. In 1927 Catholic missionaries began providing rudimentary schooling for girls as well, though it focused primarily on housekeeping, hygiene, knitting, sewing, and other such activities. They also trained African followers in masonry, carpentry, brickmaking, and weaving. The Capuchins continued these activities after 1938, but they seemed to place greater emphasis on providing some French instruction than did their

Spiritan predecessors. They continued to preach in Gbaya until the 1950s, when they began to use Sango in church masses.[12]

The Swedish Baptists also educated Mpiemu and other Sangha forest populations, working primarily in their mission stations and sending trained teachers to circulate in smaller villages. After building the Bilolo mission station in 1927, they actively sought to attract both adults and children to Sunday and daily schools. By 1934 one missionary reported that some 140 children were attending school there. Instruction was in Gbaya, and eventually in Mpiemu. According to French administrative accounts, the Swedish Baptists provided some rudimentary (but "inadequate") French instruction. By the 1950s the Swedish missions began to use Sango as a language of instruction within churches and both Sango and French in the schools for children.[13]

Western education in the independent CAR saw both substantial changes and continuities once the state nationalized mission schools in 1963. Hiring primarily Central African instructors, state-run schools suppressed theological instruction and focused on instruction in mathematics, French, history, and gardening and animal husbandry. It continued the practice of using French and Sango to instruct children. And as before, state education did not reach everywhere, so that European logging and coffee companies at times funded school construction, supplies, and teacher salaries in Lindjombo, Bayanga, and Salo.

As a new form of knowledge, Western education reframed *doli* in several ways. First, it fostered new kinds of interactions between teachers and learners, altering the timing and relations of power between them. Elders taught *doli* intermittently around the hearth, under the *panjo,* in the forest while hunting or fishing. *Doli* could take a more fluid, participatory form, so that people performed activities in places to invoke past people and events, thus eliding distinctions between teachers and learners. By contrast, Western education, conferred by the missions or the state, took place according to a rigorous daily schedule and effectively solidified a hierarchy in which teachers bestowed knowledge to receptive pupils, demanded their labor in school agricultural activities, and exacted disciplinary measures on those who did not comply. Schools introduced more regimented, schedule-bound ways of learning. Indeed, in 1932 one Swedish Baptist noted that this schooling set up conflicts between missionaries and parents over the loyalties (and no doubt the labor) of enrolled children.[14]

Western education posed a striking alternative to *doli,* providing access to new networks of authority and accumulation and new ways of achieving self-realization. One elderly man even contended that he had forgotten much of *doli* because Swedish Baptists' instruction had "forced out" the knowledge of his father. Mission education supplied generations of young men with paid jobs as catechists, nurses in mission hospitals, accountants, clerks, supervisors, mechanics, carpenters, and masons. Hence, workingmen could now accumulate their own bridewealth; purchase salt, new clothing, alcohol, and cooking pots offered in the French, Portuguese, and Dutch stores; and hire their own farm laborers. And because of their understanding of expatriate *patrons* in the missions, plantations, and administration, some of these young men acquired a new kind of authority within their *panjo,* kin networks, and villages. Mission-educated women also could tap into these opportunities, but never to the extent that men could. Missionaries now deemed these women to be appropriate wives for catechists and other men trained in the missions. But even as late as the 1990s, I encountered very few Mpiemu women who had attended lycées in Berbérati or Bangui. Such opportunities for men and some women did more than permit the accumulation of authority and wealth. They provided participants with new kinds of wanderings, bringing them into contact with events, peoples, materials, and practices that they constituted as past experiences. When I asked people why they had left their homes to acquire an education and work elsewhere, countless people looked at me quizzically and responded, "I wanted to wander, to see things." Hence whereas *doli* had instructed young people to work properly and respectfully for elders, and ultimately for themselves, the new mission (and later state) education promoted alternative paths of acquiring authority and wealth and of realizing oneself.[15]

Yet this change did not entail a wholesale rejection of *doli* by the early 1990s. Mpiemu perceived *doli* as emptied of its compelling power to respect and work for seniors, and yet young and old still embraced it as a knowledge that complemented Western instruction. I once pressed the elderly Yodjala Philippe to tell me about *doli,* and he chastened me: "Slowly, slowly, you shouldn't rush. You will learn slowly. We will teach you slowly. Isn't *doli* like school? You rush around like a rat. You are trying to learn things too quickly."[16] Irritated that he had compared me to a scurrying rat, I only later realized that he was scolding me because he believed that like the young people who would not "sit" with their elders, I rushed around and did not put enough time into developing a sufficiently respectful relationship with him. I sought out his younger sibling, Modigi Casimir, to explain the parallels he had drawn between *doli* and school. Modigi pointed out that like *doli,* school was a good thing, because "you learn a little thing, you keep it in your head, and then you can tell it to your friend or a white person. You will find work, work with white people, and then you can get a little money."[17]

Although neither Yodjala nor Modigi had ever attended school, they clearly saw it as beneficial, for it could pave the way for new job opportunities, access to networks of powerful people, and broader political economies based on forest exploitation. Several of their brothers, sons, and nephews (but not female kin) had acquired Western education and then had worked as recruiters and managers for the Compagnie Forestière de la Sangha-Oubangui, which harvested rubber and later developed coffee plantations throughout the Sangha basin. Other kin-group members included the assistant mayor of Bayanga and a French-educated former government minister, who later became a deputy in the National Assembly. Still, for many elderly Mpiemu, Western education was a mixed blessing. Although they had reaped some gains from their own or their sons' education, they found that *doli* had lost its compelling force to ensure that younger generations "sat" with, provided for, and worked for their elders. This loss seemed most poignant for the aging, widowed Modigi and Yodjala, who had no one to look after them because their children lived in distant villages.

Younger Mpiemu men appeared to hedge their bets on *doli*'s efficacy and its relationship with Western education. In the villages of Adebori and Bandoka (in the Kwapeli homeplace), a group of young lycée students explained why they found both *doli* and Western learning valuable: "At the lycée we learn the research that the white people have conducted [about the past]. Some white people travel around, and they discover what things were like long ago. Their work is a science. But our fathers learned oral traditions. When you're in school, what you learn there remains in your head. When you return home, you ask your father, and then you make comparisons. . . . What you learn in the village, you must hold onto. And what you learn in school, you also must hold onto. You can't neglect either. You have to practice both."[18] In 1993 these young men faced exceedingly grim prospects in finding kin to invest in their education. Political upheaval and economic crisis in the Central African Republic had made money scarce. With limited opportunities to earn cash or to acquire alternative employment, it made sense for some to embrace *doli* to invest in relations with elder kin.

GENRES OF *DOLI*

As a historical and environmental category of knowledge, *doli* also encompassed several narrative and nonnarrative forms whose content was profoundly influenced by twentieth-century changes. Narrative genres of *doli* included tales (*saa*); recollections of important past events, people, and places, such as the movements of Mpiemu speakers in the nineteenth and twentieth centuries along rivers and streams in the equatorial forest; and advice (*meleyo*), which could take the form of proscriptions on the behavior of boys and girls, as well as that of junior men and women, or could be woven into tales and recollections. The term *nonnarrative* refers to bodily and spatial sites (and practices around them) that organized, recollected, and commented upon peoples' pasts. But these nonnarrative forms differed substantially from narratives because they located and invoked past events but did not explain or describe them. Past people, events, and social processes may be embodied in material objects around living people: a field, a tree, a fishing hole, a person's stomach.

The following examples of *doli's* range of genres and claims illustrate, first in a very broad way and then in increasingly telescoped and fragmented ways, the very questions this book explores: how Mpiemu have interpreted their twentieth-century experiences of environmental interventions, how they have woven discourses of dearth and loss into this historical category because of these interventions, and how they interpret limits imposed by the conservation project through the prism of their knowledge of past interventions.[19]

Tales

Tales recounted the actions of the deities Ntchambe Mekwombo (the deity of the forests), Ntchambe Meburi (the deity of the fallows), Ntchambe Bilon (the deity of the savannas), Ntchambe Meguwo (the deity of the sky, who reached the earth by sliding down a forest cord), their children, and a trickster figure named Bembi in a mythic, unchanging, and distant past. Both women and men recited these tales around evening fires in villages or forest camps. The best tellers skillfully wove together lurid details about rebellious young women who married into anthropophagic, limbless kin groups; arrogant young men crushed by their own game traps; jealous women who arranged the death of their co-wives and then danced on their gravesites; and young men who risked death to marry beautiful women but saved themselves by befriending helpful ducks, forest hogs, and bees. Tellers peppered their narratives with lively call-and-response songs and chants, enjoining young and old listeners to pay heed to the people and events of these distant worlds and to remark on the similarities with their own world. And they concluded their recitations with a series of didactic pronouncements about these past events and their relations to present people's behavior and circumstances.[20]

The tales had a peculiar relationship with the truth. As one elderly woman tartly observed after offering to recount a tale to me, "Tales are lies! The person who tells these tales, she hasn't ever seen with her own eyes the events about which she speaks. So isn't that a lie?"[21] And yet while the particular events within the tales may not have taken place, Mpiemu tellers and listeners of tales found other truths within these tales, about the proper relations between juniors and seniors, men and women, and clients and *patrons*. Though they ostensibly elaborated a distant and unchanging past, these tales contained poignant and compelling interpretations of twentieth-century Mpiemu encounters with white outsiders. One pithy tale described the deities whose interactions ultimately created contemporary global relations of power:

> Ntchambe Mekwombo [the deity of the forests] was the first born, and he initially commanded the other two, Ntchambe Meburi [the deity of the fallows] and Ntchambe Bilon [the deity of the savannas]. Mekwombo made the chimpanzee, the gorilla, and he made the forests. Ntchambe Meburi created Africans, and he taught them to do field work. Ntchambe Bilon was from the grasslands, and his work was to sit with writing. Me, when I sat as a child, the white people brought writing, because that was their work. The father of Ntchambe Bilon, he said, "This writing is what you do, because you are the last child, but you will be the one to command all of the big people."[22]

The tale elaborates a crucial historical and environmental cosmology of Mpiemu, in which the open savannas and their people achieved superiority over the tangled and obscuring forests, the fallowed lands, and the people who exploited them. Processes of cognition and knowledge acquisition underpinned this environmental cosmology.[23] Mpiemu frequently argued that visual perceptions and knowledge acquired by sight were "more true" that those gained by hearing. On one occasion when I asked Yodjala Philippe about *doli*, he observed: "We don't really know it, because we didn't see it with our own eyes. We only heard about it." And he continued: "White people came from the savannas. But us, we come from the forest. The forest is a pit, and there aren't any people to see you." Forest and farming people found their views of a broader world obscured by tangled fallows and forests. The ability to see, to gain knowledge and wealth through sight (reading and writing), and to be seen thus allowed white people from the savannas to overwhelm these "invisible" forest dwellers.[24]

Mpiemu frequently made allusions to this tale of the deities Mekwombo (forests), Meburi (fallows), and Bilon (grasses or savannas) in the distant past, even if they did not recite the tale in its entirety. They found in this tale critical truths about the twentieth-century changes in the Sangha basin. Ntchambe Mekwombo, Ntchambe Meburi, and Ntchambe Bilon crystallized historical processes by which white people (*peno*) moved from open European grasslands to equatorial African forests, implanting their superior visually based knowledge to exploit those forests.[25] They extracted rubber, game, and ivory, and in the villages of Lindjombo and Salo, the white company bosses began to cut down forests in the 1920s to create extensive coffee and oil-palm plantations. Their activities set off ripples of forest clearing: hundreds of plantation workers built their houses on the impeccably cleared banks of the Sangha River, and tellers of *doli* recounted that barge passengers would exclaim at the villages' impressive size; workers' wives began to cultivate their own food crops on the outskirts of the coffee and oil-palm fields. In villages near Salo the plantations precipitated even more forest clearing, because workers needed cassava, peanuts, maize, edible leaves, and other foods, so farmers now cut more fields for extra provisions. Contemporary Mpiemu recalled the forest clearings and the growth of plantations as a long period of prosperity, when as clients they gained access to the salaries, consumer goods, transport, and medical care provided by the white *patrons.*

The political and economic power that underpinned the vast cleared plantations remained in place after 1959, when the CAR received its independence. The elderly teller of the Ntchambe tale continued: "When we finally got our own president [of the CAR], he was an African, so he wouldn't supplant the white people. The white people brought money and goods. We didn't know before they arrived how to work for money. This was the work of white people, and we didn't know it."[26]

Economic and environmental interventions played out differently within the Sangha basin in the 1980s and 1990s. But Mpiemu experienced and interpreted these interventions and the changing landscapes they inhabited through the prism of this tale of Mekwombo, Meburi, and Bilon. In Lindjombo, where many Mpiemu had relocated in the 1940s, the coffee plantation bosses departed in 1981. Logging companies in Bayanga and Cameroon absorbed some younger displaced workers, but only temporarily, because most of the firms suffered repeated financial problems and bankruptcy. As Lindjombo resident Amions Anaclet observed, "The companies are dead. B-r-r-r!!! All of them are ruined. Closed. Finished."[27] And with the demise of the companies, Lindjombo Mpiemu observed that the village receded into a tangle of vines that choked the banks of the Sangha and obscured the village from outsiders. These vines are not "a fetishisation . . . imbuing a dead object with animate qualities, but . . . [are] a metaphorical assertion of the similarity and equivalence of being, of those which 'naturally' reproduce (humans, animals, plants) and of things made [and transformed] by man."[28] Unlike their predecessors, contemporary Lindjombo Mpiemu could not transform these tangled vines into cords to make them useful. The vines remained undomesticated and thus prevented Mpiemu from establishing and nurturing the social relations with new *patrons* who would link them to wider political economies. Shrouded in this tangle of forest vines, Lindjombo Mpiemu complained that they were "a dead people," disconnected from these powerful networks and stymied in their efforts to leave a person behind.[29]

Kwapeli experienced a different trajectory of economic and environmental change in the 1980s and 1990s, so that interpretations of the tales of Mekwombo, Meburi, and Bilon diverged. There the forest remained a source of wealth, and Mpiemu workers could tap into the wealth by clearing it. In Salo a French-owned logging company and sawmill, SESAM Bois, took the buildings and surrounding grounds of CFSO, luring some men and their families to the forests or to its Salo sawmill to work. Throughout Kwapeli young and old men made their way deep into the forest, clearing small tracts and diverting forest streams to mine diamonds from shallow pits. Though many Central Africans performed the labor in the diamond pits, merchants and traders from Cameroon, Chad, Mali, Mauritania, and Senegal reaped the major profits, for they financed the mining equipment and feeding of workers. Mpiemu who chose not to mine or to cut timber worked for themselves, hunting, farming, gathering forest products, and constructing baskets, mats, or other items for workers and their families. Thus in Kwapeli access to broader networks of political and economic power did not create a sense of remaining obscured by the forest, as it did in Lindjombo. Rather, the tale of Mekwombo, Meburi, and Bilon reinforced a sense of continued participation in a global political economy. But this interpretation, too, was permeated by a discourse of loss. For Lindjombo Mpiemu their contemporary situation had seen the resurgence of the forest and its obscuring vines, contributing to their inability to "be seen." For those in Kwapeli the tale of Mekwombo, Meburi, and Bilon served a different purpose: to underscore the historical processes of the entire twentieth century, in which the white people of cleared spaces had asserted their authority and sight-based knowledge over forest people. These processes also introduced new ways of accumulating wealth in people and in material goods—new ways of leaving a person behind.[30] The following two sections, which discuss *doli*'s other narrative and nonnarrative genres, elaborate further divergent interpretations of these twentieth-century changes.

Narratives of the Twentieth-Century Past

Mpiemu narratives about specific events and identifiable people and places of the past came closest to what historians understand as history. Together, the narratives detailed the processes by which Mpiemu encountered new people who sought to gain access to the resources in the forests where they resided, and ultimately how "the Mpiemu," kin groups, and persons were shaped by these struggles. Some narratives focused on the encounters with other Africans during the nineteenth century, the struggles over authority, labor, and hunting grounds, and the resulting geographical mobility. They also addressed twentieth-century encounters with missionaries, merchants, concessionaires, and colonial administrators. Many of the *doli* narratives that I heard were formulaic, in the sense that there existed a series of standard questions that learners asked and set responses that tellers recounted. I once heard a recording that Zana Henri, an archaeology student, had made of Kadele Charles discussing nineteenth-century Mpiemu migrations, and I realized that the narrative was a word-for-word recitation of what Kadele had recounted to me. When Alouba Clotere, a forty-year-old learner of such narratives, a teller of *doli* tales, and one of my research assistants, spoke with teller Nyambi Patrice, their exchange also illuminated the formulaic quality of *doli* narratives. Alouba already knew the responses to the questions he posed to Nyambi, because he had earlier recounted them to me. But he asked the same questions nonetheless, and with Nyambi's explicit approval. More than once Nyambi appreciatively remarked in response to Alouba's queries, "Your question is very correct." And when Alouba asked about late nineteenth-century wars (*dambo*) and Nyambi forgot the term for war leader, Alouba interjected, "I don't want to help you." *Doli* narratives not only conveyed information about the past and environments but also were a process of mutual training of tellers to provide the right answers and of learners to ask the right questions.

Male elders were primarily the purveyors of this genre. Most men insisted that only they could recount the truth, and that women did not know this form of *doli*. It is true that women were usually only able to provide sketchy details of significant past people and events and often deferred to men to recite these narratives.[31] Women did, however, perform songs that alluded to these narratives, and they thus provided important commentaries on the male-dominated narratives.

The following example illustrates some of the gender, generational, and regional distinctions in this narrative form of *doli*, and particularly in understandings of loss during the twentieth century. It is one of the many stories detailing how Mpiemu had come to occupy certain parts of the forest in the Sangha basin, and it reveals the loose quality to these narratives, in that listeners could interrupt and pose questions for clarification. As in other genres of *doli,* idioms of mobility and "sitting" and of cords and vines allowed tellers to evoke Mpiemu ancestors, to portray kin and client relations between Mpiemu ancestors, but also to emphasize the destruction and loss of people's kin and client relations that came with twentieth-century colonization. Kadele Charles performed this narrative under his *panjo* in the village of Bandoka, speaking to its elder men, Alouba Clotere, and me.

> Alouba Clotere: Long ago I sat under the *panjo* of my mother's brother, and someone told me, "A long time ago, the road that we live along in Kwapeli, it was once a footpath, and it went in that direction. [*He points west.*] It went up there. Then the whites came and opened up the road for our ancestors. The person who founded this village [and decided upon its name] said, "Bandi oka" (the place is finished).
>
> Kadele Charles: The place is divided.
>
> AC: And so [the chief] Bandoka came to establish the village. Would he have heard talk of this? About Bandi yoka, which is today Bandoka?
>
> KC: Yes, he could have heard about that. [A long time ago,] the family sat like this [in peace]. They were good, they were good, they were good. But then, when a problem arrived, someone would stand up and say, "Shit!" And everyone would start to say different things and to disagree. [The chiefs] Bandoka and Kobago once sat as one. Brother and brother. They were family, they sat in one place. But then, there came a hunt for bushpigs, and Bandoka went to his forest camp, and Kobago went to his village. . . . Kobago didn't find Bandoka [in the village, and he grew angry]. So Kobago went and cut down Bandoka's *panjo.* Isn't that right? [*The men seated under the* panjo *nod,* "Mmmm."] He cut down his *panjo.* Bandoka was hurt.
>
> TGV: Why did he cut down Bandoka's *panjo?*
>
> KC: Because of his nasty heart, because he was a commander. Bandoka sat under Kobago [he was a junior of Kobago].
>
> TGV: Kobago was afraid that a big man would take his place?
>
> KC: Mmm, yes. Because Bandoka was big and strong and had many followers. And so Bandoka separated from Kobago, and he stayed away. Slowly, slowly he came [toward Bandoka]. He created three villages. He ran away from Kobago three times, [settling in] Nyamitanga, Kodjimpago, Nyoue. Four with this village, Bandoka.[32]

Here Kadele described how the village of Bandoka came to exist, from a dispute that typifies the fluid relations of authority within equatorial Africa. An older war leader (*pendo*), unable to hold onto his authority, feared a younger man with a large following and an unwillingness to heed a senior's demands. He struggled openly with the younger man to destroy his authority and to scatter his followers. Many elderly in Kwapeli claimed that they or

their parents had come from a large region called Mpola, and that they had
fled the chief Kobago's wrath with Bandoka when they were children, settling later along the Nyamitanga, Kodjimpago, and Nyoue Rivers.[33]

Kadele's language describing the relationship between the two rivals echoed widely used cultural, historical, and environmental idioms of "sitting"
and mobility and of cords and vines, and they helped to highlight the losses
that particular kin groups and Mpiemu in general suffered as a result of the
dispute. Kobago and Bandoka "sat as one," sharing a social but also physical
space of kin (though tellers never specified their exact relationship) until
Kobago repudiated it and Bandoka had to flee. This idiom pervaded other
versions of this dispute, which tellers linked to the arrival of French and
German colonizers in the interior Sangha forest and to the transformation
of its topography. In the late nineteenth and early twentieth centuries, many
Mpiemu lived in the forest near the present-day border of Cameroon and
the CAR. Tellers spoke of two flights from the environs of Mpola: one of
Bandoka and his followers and the second during the First World War,
when German and French troops clashed over control of the region, driving
Mpiemu and other Sangha basin inhabitants into hiding. It is unclear whether
these two flights occurred simultaneously or at different times, but following the First World War, both the colonial and oral accounts indicate that
Mpiemu no longer lived in Mpola in such great concentrations. These
events precipitated the loss of Mpiemu autonomy and control over their
own labor and forest resources.

The idiom of cords and vines was also implicit in Kadele's account.
Kobago's destruction of Bandoka's *panjo* was not simply the destruction of
an open shelter, bound together by forest vines that men had soaked and
fashioned into cords. As a place where male kin shared food and regulated
kin-group disputes, the *panjo* also contained within it the metaphorical
"cords" of kinship. Members of a *panjo* shared the same *kuli ajing* (cord family), and those with traceable kin ties spoke of being bound together by
cords (*kuli,* or *kamba* in Sango). By destroying Bandoka's *panjo,* Kobago in
effect was repudiating the cords of kinship and patronage that bound him to
Bandoka.

This narrative of Kobago and Bandoka may have gained such promi-
nence in *doli* partly because like so many migration narratives, it detailed
how a leader and his followers came to settle in a place. But the narrative also
may crystallize several twentieth-century struggles over Mpiemu labor and
valued forest resources. There exists no colonial documentation of Kobago
and Bandoka's dispute, but there are tantalizing accounts of similar struggles
between young and old Mpiemu authorities and between Mpiemu subjects

and French colonial administrators over control of labor, the forest, and its resources. One administrative report, for instance, recounts a heated confrontation between a "youthful" and "willing" chief Messono and an "elderly" Bandoka, who put up "heavy opposition" to the former's initiatives.[34] Another, submitted in 1945, tells of a dispute between the *terre* chief Messono and his ambitious subordinate, the *capita* Metobo-Niamentshoki, who led his followers to settle in another village.[35]

Although Mpiemu tellers of *doli* spoke of only one Kobago, colonial documents mention at least two Mpiemu leaders with similar names, N'Gombako and Gobako (or Gombako). In the first case a powerful leader named N'Gombako appears in a 1905–7 report produced under the French commander Henri Moll. Moll undertook a two-year expedition to France's possessions in Congo and Cameroon bordering on German Cameroon. The expedition was part of an ongoing struggle between France and Germany to define boundaries between their equatorial African possessions and to secure control over valuable rubber, ivory, and African labor. In an effort to gain Africans' support for the French, Moll pursued a "policy of peace," concluding treaties with various "rebel chiefs" who apparently had refused to collect rubber and ivory for the concessionary companies in the region. Moll's expedition journal detailed his negotiations with one Mpiemu leader called N'Gombako, who had spent years moving through the forest with his followers, making war against company agents and challengers to his authority. Muston, a member and chronicler of the Moll expedition, contended that French intervention would "civilize" N'Gombako's and his followers' warlike and wandering nature, so that the French could gain access to their labor and to the riches of the Sangha basin forests. Hence, this early leader appeared at the very moment of the French and German imposition of colonial rule as a figure who first stymied and later acceded to Europeans' fantasies of control over this rich forest and its people.[36]

A second leader with a name similar to Kobago appears later, in a 1935 archival record, this time under the names Gobako and Gombako. Gobako was a *chef de terre* in French administrative parlance and, according to local administrators, an incompetent one. Like all chiefs, he was responsible for rounding up workers for the labor prestation levied on all adult African men. In the early 1930s most of these workers were opening up the forest to construct the region's first real roads. Administrators repeatedly complained about Gobako's inefficacy as a leader; his followers repeatedly fled to Cameroon to escape French labor demands, and villages under his control fragmented and dispersed into the middle and upper Sangha forests.[37] By 1935 a frustrated French administration temporarily abandoned work on the major road linking Ubangi-Shari and Middle Congo and lowered taxes in the hopes of luring Gobako's followers back to their officially approved villages. Just why Gobako did not deliver up his followers to fulfill administrative orders is unknown. Perhaps he simply could not wield sufficient authority to do so, or perhaps he chose not to accede to demands that many Africans perceived as onerous. If French portrayals of the early N'Gombako and Gobako radically differed, they also resembled one another in that both leaders hindered the French colonial project of transforming the middle and upper Sangha forests into useful commodities and its people into productive laborers.

Clearly, Mpiemu recollections of Kobago bear little resemblance to the French depictions of the two leaders and their struggles to retain control over Mpiemu subordinates, forest spaces, and forest resources. Nevertheless, because the broader aim here is to translate *doli* and to illuminate its genres and divergent aims in leaving a person behind, it is not necessary to reject one version of this dispute in favor of another. Rather, this narrative crystallizes many struggles that the French colonial archives document. It makes claims of truth about the generational conflicts among Mpiemu people that colonial rule precipitated, as well as the new strategies that younger Kwapeli generations used to accumulate wealth and authority. The upstart chief Bandoka embodied those who acceded to French colonial demands and in the process amassed enormous wealth in the form of wives, children, and dependents. And more than any other historical person, Bandoka most closely exemplified someone who had successfully left a person behind and had become a central figure in *doli,* the recent, remembered past.

Women did not often recite *doli* narratives, but they did help to sustain memories of these narratives through genealogies and song. Several women in Kwapeli proudly claimed to be descendants of Bandoka and elaborated, frequently in great detail, the genealogical links by which they were related to him. During one celebration of the Central African Republic's independence from France, a group of women boisterously shouted this song in the center of the village of Bandoka: "Bandoka a ligo me ri da digo / O sa ne me shou? [Bandoka left me this village / Are you going to doubt me?]" These women were not purveyors of the *doli* narrative, but they provided important commentaries on that narrative, by singing and recalling the genealogical cords binding them to Bandoka. In recalling Bandoka and the villages he founded, they ensured the dead chief's place in *doli* of the recent, remembered past.

This narrative of Kobago and Bandoka's dispute illustrates one more definition of *doli* as narrative concerning specific and named past people, events, and places. Tellers highlighted the ruptured relations of authority in the early twentieth-century middle Sangha. Young men with access to new forms of work and wealth had supplanted older leaders, whose power had lain in their abilities to lead wars and to gain additional followers. Mpiemu leaders lost their autonomy to administrators and companies. The narrative thus illuminated an ambivalence about colonial interventions that was prevalent in Kwapeli. It constituted a powerful commentary on the tale of the deities Mekwombo, Meburi, and Bilon, revealing how the implementation of European, sight-based knowledge introduced successful alternative strategies to leave a person behind but simultaneously severed the cords that bound generations of a forest and farming people to one another.

Nonnarrative Forms of *Doli*

Other forms of *doli* centered on past people, events, and places but did not entail creating a narrative. These objects and bodily and spatial sites did, however, depend on narratives for their exegesis. This form illustrates *doli*'s range but also illuminates Lindjombo Mpiemu's alternative interpretation of the twentieth-century colonial interventions contained in the tale of the deities Mekwombo, Meburi, and Bilon.

I came upon this form of *doli* as a result of several failed interviews, in which I had hoped to trace people's own and their parents' past uses and conceptions of farming lands, gardens, fishing waters, and hunting grounds. Very few provided useful glimpses into how Mpiemu people perceived their changing relationships with the Sangha basin environment. In Lindjombo I continually encountered indifference, antipathy, fear, suspicion, and expectations that I would step into a historic role as *patronne*.[38] This historic role had been created by white plantation owners and concessionaires, who gained access to extensive forest resources and arable land in exchange for jobs and access to such goods as clothing, whiskey, and cooking pots. These historical relationships powerfully influenced how and with whom I interacted, for Sangha basin residents initially perceived me as yet another white *patronne* who had come to extract yet another commodity—knowledge— from them.[39]

This fear and suspicion also stemmed from contemporary national and regional circumstances. Many people believed that I was a spy for the WWF, and that I would collect information on the locations of their snare traps and unregistered guns to report to antipoaching patrols. That I was a white woman as were many Peace Corps volunteers working for the conservation project and several biological researchers financed by the WWF did not increase my credibility. Nor did it help that I rode a Japanese-made mountain bike, as numerous project personnel did. Abandoning interviewing techniques, I took to less politically charged fields to begin studying changing farming practices, hoping for insights into changing environmental relations.

These efforts uncovered far more than a history of agricultural practices within changing regional and global political economies, for they illuminated a range of possible ways of recalling and transmitting *doli* and demonstrated the many ways in which leaving a person behind was intertwined in these objects and sites. The fields became lessons in *doli,* as older farmers pointed to food crops acquired decades or even a century earlier in trade with riverine people. Yam vines could evoke past people. Fields themselves contained genealogy lessons about how current cultivators inherited particular plots, or about who planted particular trees within those plots. Such sites also existed in the forest, where paths and trees evoked important past hunters and trappers. Dwellings, too, were also sites of *doli.* Men and women extracted small, plastic-wrapped packages of baptism cards, work identifications, and tax stubs that they had meticulously woven into the raffia roofs of their houses; they presented these documents to me as tangible expressions of their own or their parents' lives. These objects and bodily and spatial sites were also *doli,* and unlike its narrative forms, there was never any debate about the veracity of these sites and objects.[40]

Momintuwo—the child of Ntuwo—was a distant forest stream, a site of recollection that Mpiemu living in Lindjombo neglected. The stream was located within the boundaries of the Dzanga-Ndoki park, and thus access to it was illegal, forbidden by the state law governing the park that was enforced by antipoaching guards trained and paid by the WWF project. Momintuwo was more than a forest stream, truly a child left behind by a renowned trapper, Ntuwo. Sometime earlier this century he had discovered it in his movements through the forest, trapping game for European coffee plantation owners so that they could distribute the meat to their workers or sell it in company stores.

One of the great attractions of Momintuwo, the stream, was that it provided ideal fishing spots during the dry season. Over successive rainy seasons Momintuwo had carved out wide pools, so that when its waters receded, women could build dams, empty Momintuwo's waters, and collect fish from the remaining mud. One of the women who controlled access to the fish in Momintuwo was a granddaughter of Ntuwo, and she had inherited that access from her mother. Hence not only had Ntuwo left his daughters and granddaughters behind, but he had provided through Momintuwo a means of feeding them. In this respect Ntuwo and his past activities were embedded in the geography of the Sangha basin forest. Momintuwo and women's fishing activities around it made it a means of organizing and remembering Ntuwo, the inherited substances of kinship (*alembo*), and the cords of kinship that bound him, his children, and his grandchildren to one another. The women's activities also recalled his participation in a past prosperity brought about by the coffee plantation *patrons*. Ntuwo had indeed reaped the benefits of the forest clearing and the transformation of the obscuring forest into a cleared space.

For some years, however, Momintuwo remained unexploited, primarily because it lay squarely in the middle of the Dzanga-Ndoki park, where fishing was illegal. Women spoke nostalgically of the days when they had made their way to this distant location, capturing fish during the day and cooking and drying fish and telling tales of the distant and unchanging past in the evenings. This neglect of Momintuwo is best understood in the context of the tale of the deities Mekwombo, Meburi, and Bilon. Recall that Ntchambe Bilon, the white man of the savannas, asserted his authority over the deities of the forest and fallow, and that Lindjombo Mpiemu identified the departure of white plantation bosses as rendering them a "dead people," obscured from the visions of powerful white people by a tangle of forest vines. This particular notion of loss, of death and disconnection, had resulted recently from the activities of the powerful WWF conservation project, which denied Mpiemu people access to the sites by which they organized and recollected past people and events.

But later a friend told me that during the previous dry season, women had traveled to Momintuwo to fish. This outing was more than just evidence of environmental exploitation, or even a mnemonic of past movements and activities in this part of the forest. It was also a claim of truth about a past person who had successfully exploited the forest's wealth; it expressed contemporary disgruntlement with WWF conservationists, who, in conjunction with the state, had criminalized movement through and use of this part of the forest. And it echoed widespread claims that the WWF and the CAR state had deprived Mpiemu and other people living near the park of opportunities to exploit those resources and thus to gain access to the consumer goods of broader regional and global economies.

In addition, this event hints at the ways in which Mpiemu conflicts over conservation efforts, which have altered resource access and allocation, also have been struggles over the historical and cultural meanings of the person.[41] By demarcating zones in which forest use was forbidden, conservationists rendered inaccessible a fishing site at which daughters and granddaughters recollected the trapper Ntuwo and ensured that some tangible remembrance of him remained for those left behind.

CONCLUSION

Expressed in images of cords and vines and mobility and stasis, *doli* comprises a process of leaving a person behind. It is both a process of evaluation and a body of knowledge about the past and present, relations between persons and environments, and encounters between Mpiemu people and the outsiders who helped to shape those people-environment relations in the twentieth century. As a body of knowledge, *doli*'s meanings proliferate as a distant and unchanging past; as tradition and advice based upon that distant past; as tales about that distant past; as recent, recalled events, people, and places; and as bodily and spatial sites that organize and recollect the recent past.

In its themes of dearth, deprivation, and loss, *doli* bears the traces of Mpiemu encounters with powerful outsiders, who carried out political and environmental interventions in the Sangha basin during the twentieth century. Through this theme of loss, regional, generational, and gender groups have sought to explain in different ways how Mpiemu found their hold on authority, available labor, forest spaces, and valued forest resources slip away.

3

PEOPLING THE *PANJO* AND VILLAGE

AS MPIEMU people encountered and interacted with colonial administrators, concessionaires, plantation owners, and missionaries, the spatial arrangements by which they organized their social lives in domesticated spaces of villages and *panjo* (open shelters) changed dramatically. Colonial interventions also reformulated Mpiemu conceptions of the person and authority. This chapter and the next trace these processes and explore their implications for *doli*. This chapter explores how persons (*mori*) and these built environments may have constituted one another in the early twentieth century, providing a snapshot of a particular historical moment before (or at the moment of) colonization, and not an "original state" in which Mpiemu organized their *panjo* and villages and left persons behind. It also reveals some of the ways that people connected their built environments with forests and fields. This snapshot is at base speculative, premised on scant documentary and photographic descriptions of Mpiemu domestic environments of *panjo* and villages, Mpiemu linguistic terms, and *doli* tellers' characterizations of this past. The analysis in this chapter lays the foundations for exploring how *doli* changed in later decades and for examining how *doli* served as a prism through which Mpiemu people understood and engaged with conservation measures in the 1990s.

EARLY TWENTIETH-CENTURY *PANJO* AND VILLAGES

Mpiemu villages in the early twentieth century varied in size but consisted of two parallel rows of adjoined houses. Photographs from the Moll expedition (1905–7) and European commercial agents' postcards produced during the same years (figs. 2, 3, 4), as well as other explorers' descriptions, reveal that Mpiemu speakers constructed wattle-and-daub houses with roofs of forest leaves, probably *Maranthochloa* spp. (*akon, mpela,* and *kogo*) leaves. Elderly

Fig. 2. Mpiemu village, c. 1905. (© Musée de l'Homme, Mission Moll)

Fig. 3. Lindjombo, c. 1905. (From the private collection of Père Ghislain de Banville)

men and women in 1993, however, insisted that their ancestors constructed the walls of their houses with the bark of the white-wooded tree *bigwi*, or *Triplochiton scleroxylon*, and one report relying on Moll expedition information supports this claim.[1] The spatial layout of early twentieth-century Mpiemu villages resembled those of other Sangha basin peoples, including Pande, Pomo, and Ngundi.[2] Photographs show a large *panjo* at the end of the two rows

Fig. 4. Ngundi village, c. 1905. (From the private collection of Père Ghislain de Banville)

of houses, and explorer Paul Pouperon's portrayal of a Mpiemu village in 1908 describes a "boudjia"—"a meeting house open to all, a kind of shelter at the extremities of the villages."[3] This spatial arrangement of Mpiemu and other villages likely existed before the arrival of European explorers in the middle and upper Sangha. Hence the Moll report description of Mpiemu villages like Bindjo ("a line of parallel houses, like the majority of villages in this country") probably depicted many Mpiemu villages before the extensive relocations under colonial rule.[4]

VILLAGE LOCATIONS, COLONIAL VISIONS

In the early 1900s no passable roads for vehicles existed in the Sangha basin, and Mpiemu villages were located deep in the forest, far from large navigable rivers. There, according to tellers of *doli*, Mpiemu cultivated small fields of maize, sweet cassava, yams, and edible leaves for sauces. Very few raised chickens and goats, but some kept dogs for hunting. The surrounding forest, however, provided the greatest source of useful plants and animals. Women gathered edible leaves and fruits from the forest and occasionally dammed small streams during the dry season to trap fish. Men collected building materials, and they hunted and trapped game, providing the major source of protein for Mpiemu villagers. They most likely did not, however, fish in big rivers. Many elderly Mpiemu in 1993 claimed that their ancestors in the early twentieth century feared large bodies of water and avoided them entirely. Indeed, large bodies of water were reputed to be the home of Bembi, a trickster figure. This reliance on the forest for plants and game and this fear of water influenced where Mpiemu situated their villages. In this respect Mpiemu villages differed from those of Pande, Pomo, and Ngundi speakers, which were situated close to navigable rivers such as the Sangha, making them more easily accessible to encroaching explorers and traders.[5]

The situation and mobility of late nineteenth- and early twentieth-century Mpiemu villages in the forest blurred the distinctions between village and forest. To be sure, Mpiemu have had linguistic terms that divided village (*dali*) from forest (*digi*), and they used the relative terms "inside" (*to te*) and "outside" (*sin*) to make distinctions between these places and spaces. Leaving the village meant going outside. But one important factor of Mpiemu life rendered inside and outside temporary and relational spaces, in contrast with some African societies that articulated permanent and absolute differences between domestic and "wild" spaces.[6] According to tellers of *doli*, Mpiemu village inhabitants were highly mobile in the late nineteenth and early twentieth centuries, continually departing from their villages to create

several different kinds of settlements within the forest. Some left their villages temporarily to build distant forest camps to hunt or fish. A woman
married outside the *kuli ajing* (cord family) of both her father and her mother,
and she left her home village to live in her husband's village. Marriage alliances during the nineteenth century were important ways of forging and
reinforcing political alliances among *kuli ajing,* and thus mobility was embedded in the very strategies that people used to accumulate political power. By
the same token kin groups themselves could spur mobility. Men departed
from their villages to create new settlements in the forest if they had quar-
reled with members of the same *panjo.* And sometimes, all of a village's
inhabitants decided to change the village's location, perhaps because they
were harassed by rival *ajing* or other groups. They referred to abandoned
villages as *wundo.* Hence, the mobility that characterized Mpiemu lives
made their villages impermanent, movable loci of settlement. The forest
could always accommodate new villages and small settlements.[7]

Mobility not only shaped the fluidity with which Mpiemu perceived their
environments; it also influenced how early explorers wrote about Mpiemu,
compared them to other Sangha basin populations, and treated them. Riverine peoples, such as Pomo and Bomassa, who congregated in large villages
along the large navigable rivers of the northern forest were among the first
populations that explorers encountered.[8] A few explorers and administrators
collected oral testimonies illuminating the historical wars and wanderings
of riverine peoples, as well as of savanna dwellers. The Aka client hunters
of riverine people occupy a shadowy presence in the early explorers' accounts
(where they are called "Babingas") but clearly tantalized them with their
intimate knowledge of the forest and its game.[9]

By contrast, explorers encountered Mpiemu years after they first had contact with riverine populations, because these forest and farming people lived
in small, scattered villages and occupied a peripheral place along the strategic
access route of the Sangha River. How and where Mpiemu created their
villages shaped the ways in which explorers wrote about them. Indeed, these
explorers' reports marked the beginnings of writings associating Mpiemu
with conditions of dearth and deprivation. Unlike so many other contemporary French reports and articles that traced the peregrinations of riverine
peoples and the creation of their new villages in different sites, the Moll
report briefly alluded to a Mpiemu past, but it never mentioned where,
when, or why Mpiemu had moved. Mpiemu appeared in these documents
as an "inferior race," a people without history, who knew nothing of "civilization" and understood little of the riches contained in their forests.[10] Muston, on this expedition, saw them as incapable of exploiting that wealth and

therefore in need of European colonizers to "develop" forest resources and to acquire a history. Thus Mpiemu, in contrast to their neighbors, had no history until 1905 when, "ignorant of all civilization," they "came to submit themselves to the great white chief."[11]

French colonizers made these distinctions between Mpiemu and other Sangha populations in part because riverine populations were more strategically located along the banks of the Sangha River, and explorers had longer and more intensive contact with them. Early twentieth-century Mpiemu, however, lived along the peripheries of these routes of access and thus may not have been as compelling subjects of study and control. But this notion of Mpiemu as wanderers without real (large) villages or a traceable history may not be just an artifact of French observers' ignorance or lack of concern. Quite possibly, French explorers perceived riverine people as superior to those living deep in the forests. For instance, at least one early twentieth-century administrative report categorized Sangha basin populations by their "degrees of human evolution."[12] The "Bombassa" (Bomassa), who lived in larger villages along the Sangha and had access to interior peoples and European traders, ranked higher than nomadic people living in the forests and some people residing along smaller rivers. The report does not mention Mpiemu speakers at all, but later administrators may have appropriated this ranking when they complained in 1907–8 about the "indecisive, unstable and nomadic tribes" of the M'Bimou *circonscription*.[13] Nonetheless, these early exploration reports set the foundations for a discourse of dearth and deficiency about Mpiemu peoples, highlighting their lack of history and settlement and their incapacity to exploit the forest productively.

INTERVILLAGE AND INTRAVILLAGE DYNAMICS

Written sources shed only a little light on the residents of these villages or the relationships between villages. The Moll report, however, contains some brief but helpful descriptions of a few Mpiemu villages. One village consisted of only "four poor houses," although many groups scattered about the forest depended on it and its leader.[14] The leader (*wani*) N'Gombako, whose subordinate "chiefs" lived throughout the forest, resided in a much larger village, surrounded by maize plantations. Leaders like N'Gombako would rely on the advice and military strength of these lesser authorities, who settled with their wives, children, and clients in smaller, scattered forest hamlets connected by a network of paths. Oral testimonies make similar claims about the relationships between leaders like Kobago and subordinates like Bandoka. A *wani* usually wore a headdress of red feathers (*koga*). Other authorities included the *nkang*, who could serve as a diviner and healer, as a distributor of farming lands and meat, and as a *pendo* (war leader), deciding when and against whom to go to battle. Though a *nkang* could allocate access to farmlands, he did not exercise the kind of control that leaders farther south in the Congo basin wielded over the exploitation of lands and game.[15] Leaders, healers, and their subordinates lived in the same part of the forest but not necessarily in the same village and could move their settlements in tandem to new locations. These leaders, their subordinates, and subjects could be bound by relations of kinship, but not exclusively. Some shared membership in a *kuli ajing* or had concluded marriage alliances between different *ajing*.[16]

Although people in and between villages could share important kin and *ajing* connections, as well as other kinds of alliances, relations between villages were not uniformly peaceful. One teller of *doli* claimed that villages could oppose each other during wartime:

> The *pendo* would go into the enemy village, [and] . . . he started to insult people. He would insult them. "You are not men. You are not people. You see, I have come to tell you that we and you, we will engage in a war. I alone, I am going to ruin all of you, I am going to kill you all." And he would say this even though he was accompanied by many warriors [who remained hidden on the outskirts of the village]. . . . Some of the enemy would stand up, with rocks [in their hands, and counter]: "What? You've come to insult us in our village for what reason?" . . . And so, they all stood up, many of them, to throw rocks at him. . . . He would stand up and insult them and their families, "Your mother's vagina, you come here! You are not men! You come here!" He would return [to call in his troops]. . . . Then all his men would come out in the midst of the enemy, then they would come out and shield themselves and kill them all.[17]

As narratives of Kobago and Bandoka illustrate vividly, relationships between leaders and their subordinates could be fraught with tensions over authority, displays of subordination, and control over labor, a measure and generator of wealth. In a context of such friction, it is not surprising that villages often split from one another.[18]

Written sources do not, however, indicate the social and spatial dynamics within early twentieth-century Mpiemu villages, or particularly, how *panjo* functioned. But both oral historical accounts and literature about other places in the equatorial forest make it likely that these shelters linked constellations of kitchens and houses and provided a place in which male kin gathered to share food, allocate labor, and regulate disputes.

I can only hypothesize about the symbolic meanings that Mpiemu associated with the *panjo,* basing my suppositions on contemporary observations and oral histories. The *panjo,* as a shelter unifying several houses and
kitchens, was (and in many cases still is) constructed from forest resources,
such as vines (lianas), raffia mats, and building poles.[19] These materials may
have had symbolic importance, for *panjo* were collections of physical structures that brought together people related through the cords of kinship,
marriage, patronage, and friendship. Certainly the story of Bandoka and
Kobago's dispute suggests that the destruction of a *panjo* signified more to
Bandoka than the felling of a physical structure; it was an act of war, and
one that precipitated the dissolution of a village and the scattering of people from the same *ajing* (groups with putative but untraceable kin ties). If
houses and *panjo* embodied the bonds that tied people together through
their remembrances of a shared past, then the destruction of a *panjo* repudiated that shared past.

Men and women contributed differently to supporting these spatial, com-
memorative edifices and the social relations undergirding them. Men built
the frames of these structures, binding together the building poles with
stout cords made from forest vines. They then collected the bark from the
bigwi tree and fashioned bark wall material, *njowiwi,* from it, tying the bark
walls onto the structure.[20] As one Kwapeli man observed of his Mpiemu
ancestors' house construction, "Men tied the houses, the *panjo* together."
Another asserted, "The man closes the house."[21] The association of house
construction with male labor seems hardly accidental. Just as men tied together domestic structures binding them, their wives, and their children to
one another, men also conferred on their children the cords that gave them
membership in kinship groups, including broader cord families.

Houses and *panjo* were also critical sites for the conception, birth, education, marriage, and death of the person. The evidence for this linkage is
treacherous, for it is based almost entirely on *doli* accounts from 1993–94.
Mpiemu, like many other people in Africa and elsewhere, sometimes depict
practices and beliefs as old and unchanging even though they may actually
be relatively recent innovations. Nevertheless, the following are speculations about possible relationships between developing persons and their
built environments in the early twentieth century.[22]

Concepts of "inside" and "outside" were critical in these relationships
between developing persons and houses and panjo. Although a person could
be inside the built environment of a *panjo,* a house, or a village, early twentieth-
century geographical mobility rendered these places temporary and fluid
over time; people could always clear the forest to create new domesticated

spaces and edifices. The creation, death, and transformation of the person (*mori*) into *doli* may have been similarly premised on concepts of inside and outside, at least according to oral accounts. Mpiemu men and women claimed that their ancestors believed that a potential person was simply uncontained blood and vital substances inside of a woman's body. Impregnation began a process of containing the potential person within a woman's uterus. Men and women had to "sit" or remain (*dio*) within the house to achieve conception. Sexual intercourse enabled men to contribute water (*medibo*), coalescing the various substances that made up a person. Mpiemu referred to this process as "receiving pregnancy" (*togi abumi*).[23]

As tellers of *doli* described it in earlier times, a fetus confounded the distinctions between inside and outside, because it could influence people and their activities well beyond the confines of the womb. As it resided within a woman's uterus, its anger (*beno*) disrupted relationships within the house, especially between the gestating woman and her husband.[24] All human and nonhuman beings possessed and demonstrated anger, and over time a developing person learned to control his or her anger.[25] But as an inchoate nonperson, an *abumi* expressed its anger beyond the bounds of its mother's uterus, playing tricks with her moods and food preferences, fanning her anger at her husband, and even weakening sick infants or adults within the same house. Its anger spilled out beyond the house, impeding people's abilities to exploit natural resources in fields and forests. Husbands and male in-laws found that their traps no longer snared game if their pregnant wives or sisters ate meat caught in them. Nor would their fishing nets catch anything after pregnant women had consumed fish from them. New peanut, maize, and cassava fields fell barren when exposed to an embryo in its mother's womb. In the face of such disruptions, a pregnant woman marshaled cultivated and forest resources around her to contain and subdue an *abumi*'s anger. Maize, a staple food among Mpiemu until recent decades, had a critical symbolic importance in mediating the effects of a destructive pregnancy. A woman chewed on dried maize kernels (*shogo*), spitting the maize and saliva mixture on her husband's left hand and forehead (*mpombi*, the bodily site of fortune) in order to safeguard the productivity of his hunting and farming activities.[26] She could also use cords and vines to moderate the *abumi*'s anger, tying a small cord (*purokando*) around her husband's wrist to ensure a successful hunt or placing a vine at the threshold of a newborn infant's house to shelter it from the *abumi*'s harm.[27]

Childbirth (*bia*), the next stage of generating a person, involved the physical act of giving birth, the planting of the placenta and umbilical cord, and the reproduction of historical kinship ties. These practices permitted both men and women to "leave a person behind" and to incorporate that new person into broader social relations, but in different ways. Houses, embodying concepts of inside, outside, and containment, were equally important in childbirth. A woman would give birth in the home of her mother or her mother's sister. Her female kin would tie off the umbilical cord to contain the "wind" (*pubelo*) in the newborn, so as to prevent it from dying. Close female kin, preferably a mother or sister, would then plant (*mugo*) the umbilical cord and placenta behind the house, literally containing the afterbirth in the domestic space of the mother and her kin, and also protecting her from jealous outsiders who might render her infertile. Planting the afterbirth thus ensured that a woman could leave future people behind.[28]

Once this process was complete, her husband would assert his lineage's rights to the newborn, naming the child after it had lost the remainder of its umbilical cord. A crucial part of leaving a person behind, naming served as a mnemonic for past events, people, and places. Names of people born in the late nineteenth and early twentieth centuries reveal that some children received the name of their father's kin or a name that evoked a feature of their mothers' or fathers' kin groups. One informant recounted that his grandfather had been named Tombamori (big person), while another gained the name Pendo (war leader). Other names suggest that Mpiemu speakers saw developing persons as intimately connected with their forest environments: Mpiyo (rain), Bikabidigi (leaf of the forest), Balo (a forest clearing often rich in game), Modigi (child of the forest), and Mpeng (flood, inundation, year). Unlike the uncontained anger of a fetus, these naming practices seemed to bind in powerful ways a newly contained person within the house and *panjo* with the wealth of the forest. Babies and toddlers were then draped with a wealth of forest vines fashioned into cords to protect them from illness and to ensure that they grew properly.

Tellers of *doli* stressed that educating growing children was part of leaving a person behind. It transferred elders' accumulated experience and knowledge to children, teaching them to contain their innate anger, to demonstrate proper "respect" for elders, to exploit their forest environments effectively, and to realize an individual personhood through accumulated experiences. Instruction in *doli* was a crucial part of this education. Inculcating deference toward elders, it located the developing person within a generational hierarchy, but it was also strongly gendered. Girls learned a particular form of knowledge from their mothers and elder women within the house and kitchen, while boys sat with their male instructors in open shelters where male kin gathered. Both boys and girls learned about proper behavior through narratives about the past and didactic tales. They also followed elders into the forest and fields to gain knowledge of cultivation, collecting medicinal plants, trapping, and hunting. These practices of transferring knowledge (and the knowledge itself) were shared by many language groups within the Sangha basin. Mpiemu and other linguistic groups, for instance, told similar tales about deities, forest spirits, and animals, and they shared a wide repertoire of environmental practices.[29]

Marriage (to marry, *ba*) and reproduction allowed young men and women to truly achieve personhood. In the late nineteenth and early twentieth centuries, marriage may have marked a period of further education (accumulated knowledge) for young women in particular, but it also provided a socially sanctioned context in which young men and women could leave a person behind. Again, incorporation (into a new lineage, into a gender group) was a central theme in this process. According to tellers of *doli,* elder men sought to delay when their sons married so that they could retain control over their labor to clear fields and to hunt. They supplied the bridewealth (*antcholo*) in the form of flat iron disks (*luli*), chickens, and goats for their sons and, according to accounts, exercised strict control over whom they married.[30] Spousal choices could be guided by long-standing agreements between *kuli ajing.* Men from the Piantimo *ajing,* for instance, frequently married Pekwaro women, evidently as a way of preventing marriages with lineages reputed to have many witches. Among other qualities, witches possessed *alembo,* an active substance or creature (often described as crablike) that allowed them to exercise control over other people or processes outside their bodies. Male elders could also determine whether potential spouses were witches by looking for signs in slaughtered chickens, by reading the activities of caterpillars wrapped in leaves, and by applying medicines to banana trees to see whether the trees survived. Thus male elders exercised considerable control over whom and when their children married, became persons, and left persons behind, and forest and field resources were crucial media through which these elders negotiated this process.[31]

Marriages, however, were not permanent, though tellers of *doli* did not indicate how often they dissolved. Several tales (*saa*) told of brief, highly inappropriate marriages between twins or to a family of witches. And narratives about past persons recounted incidents in which men stole other men's wives. The elderly Kokameko Moise related a story that his grandfather Iya once recounted to him about his own marriage that nearly disintegrated. As a younger man, Iya discovered that his wife, Antchaburi, had left him to live with another man in a distant village. So Iya consulted his father's sister, telling her that he wanted to bring his wife back but needed advice about the obstacles he might encounter along the path that he would follow to find her. His aunt instructed him about the possible obstacles and solutions for bypassing them. Sure enough, the moment Iya left his village, he encountered seemingly insurmountable obstacles that could have prevented him from reaching Antchaburi, but for his aunt's counsel: a powerful bird associated with leaders (*wani*), a stand of sugarcane, an impassable river, a high fence. But following his aunt's advice, Iya reached Antchaburi. When he recounted the story of his difficult journey, she immediately agreed to return with him. Indeed, she returned so rapidly that nobody in Iya's village even remarked on her absence. Iya's story, then, reflected one instance in which a marriage endured.[32]

According to tellers of *doli*, a young wife became a female person through the interventions of elder women in-laws. A new wife in the early twentieth century reportedly spent at least a year cooking in her mother-in-law's kitchen, laboring in her fields, and learning how to fulfill her obligations to her husband and in-laws. She would not acquire her own kitchen or fields until the elder woman assented and kindled a cooking fire in the young wife's kitchen with the embers from her own kitchen fire. Both married men and women truly achieved personhood by leaving a person behind themselves, undergoing the processes of pregnancy, birth, and the education of their own children.[33]

Finally, it appears that in the early twentieth century, elders and ancestors (*tumba doli*) exemplified both the cyclical nature of leaving a person behind and the person as accumulated knowledge and as a site of recollecting the past. Elderly men (*ngumbi morom*) and women (*ngumbi mia*) had accumulated experiences and knowledge of their environments and of the past and thus became both producers and repositories of *doli*. They had successfully borne children and had educated them to fulfill obligations to elders and other men and women, to contain their innate anger, and to leave other persons behind.[34]

But elders' status was fleeting, because death (*-shuwi*)—the disembodiment and departure of the person—profoundly destabilized the cycle of leaving a person behind. The verb *kwangolo* was a euphemism for "to die," meaning "to make depart," and thus death seems to have been a spatial and temporal departure enforced by Ntchambe, the deity whose authority surpassed the deities of the forest and fallow. The disembodied, uncontained dead could cause great harm to the living. Like an unborn child, the deceased could transgress the boundaries of its own body, causing enormous harm to those who lived in the same house or shared food under the same *panjo*, and even to children and mourners within the village. Thus in the early twentieth century, kin of the dead took precautions to protect themselves.

They washed the body, wrapped it in bark cloth, and buried it the following morning, usually within the village.[35] Mourners would also protect their own bodies from the harmful influences of the uncontained dead and from excessive grief. Close female kin of the deceased might wear cords around their foreheads to prevent their heads from "splitting open" from grief.[36] Parents, spouses, and children of the deceased received ritual washings to prevent the deceased's uncontained spirit (*sonyoli*)[37] from harassing the living, causing them to swell up, rot, and die, much like the corpse's own body would.

Early twentieth-century Mpiemu appear to have contended with this departure by transforming a living person into a bodily and spatial site of recollection to ensure that this cycle was completed. Although death transformed a contained person into an uncontained spirit, mourners took great pains to ground that person in spatial sites of recollection, especially burial sites in the village. Village gravediggers (*ndelibori*) dug a deep L-shaped pit, burying the body in its horizontal shelf to prevent animals from scenting the deceased and disturbing the grave. Elderly men who had died were buried in the *panjo*. Wives, younger men and women, and children would receive burials next to their own houses, their parents' houses, or their mother's kitchens, echoing the planting of the placenta and umbilical cord of a newborn. By burying the deceased in the domestic space, early twentieth-century Mpiemu accomplished two aims: they contained the dangers posed by the dead and created a site that recalled and organized memories of a past person. Living kin reinforced their remembrances of the deceased by clearing and sweeping around the gravesite, which eventually would be indistinguishable from the rest of the house grounds. This practice effectively transformed the dead person into *tumba doli*, a big person of the past. Kin living near the burial site might continue to receive messages from that ancestor, through dreams warning of disastrous events or portending good fortune.[38]

Yet even this practice did not ensure that the deceased person remained contained in a place where he or she would be remembered. Burial locations, even around the house, could remain secret. One proverb, *Djeng asinga shong pabo,* translated as "An outsider does not know the burial places on the veranda of a house," and it referred to these secrets (as well as others in a house-*panjo* constellation). Kadele Charles explained, "This is knowledge that women in the house will teach a person." But knowledge of such sites did not come automatically with living in a house; older women had to actively instruct younger generations.[39] Like many Sangha basin peoples in the late nineteenth and early twentieth centuries, Mpiemu-speaking *ajing* were also highly mobile and could abandon these sites for new settlements.

CONCLUSION

The domesticated, built environments of the house and *panjo* seem to have been places that helped to generate persons, just as people helped to create the house, *panjo,* and village. The house, *panjo,* and village contained the essential spatial and social relations between husbands, wives, and the husband's kin that gave rise to a person's very existence, containment, and transformation into *doli* as a site organizing and recollecting the past. By the same token, the developing person also helped to constitute this built environment; buried bodies and placentas marked the locations of human habitation and ensured that inhabitants—both dead and alive—could leave persons behind. Yet Mpiemu mobility made this entire process a fluid and uncertain one: under the late nineteenth- and early twentieth-century pressures of resource competition, mutual slave raiding, and intra–kin group conflict, people moved, created new settlements, and over several generations abandoned the spatial sites of *doli.*

4

DEPLETING THE *PANJO* AND VILLAGE

F ROM THE early twentieth century, the French fitfully imposed their authority over inhabitants of the middle and upper Sangha basin, dramatically altering their built environments, power relations, and models of personhood through village relocations, labor recruitment, and sleeping-sickness crises and interventions. In their efforts to attract converts, Christian missions also shaped *panjo* and villages.

These practices had substantial implications not only for the locations and spatial configurations of villages and *panjo* but also for *doli* as a way of perceiving built environments and as environmental and historical knowledge. Mpiemu transformed their processes of "leaving a person behind" and the attendant social, political, and cultural relations within these built environments. In narratives of these twentieth-century changes, gender, generational, regional, and kin groups portrayed geographical mobility from flight and labor recruitment, population loss, deprivation, and reworked relations of authority differently. Moreover, in their engagement with administrators, health officials, company agents, and missionaries, they interpreted and transformed colonial discourses of dearth, deprivation, and depletion to address their own concerns about depopulation and lost authority. In the early 1990s gender, generational, and regional groups came to understand conservation interventions through the prism of their past engagements with colonial agents and in terms of this older discourse of loss and depletion.

REGROUPEMENT

Regroupement, the consolidation and relocation of villages to colonially designated roads, was a policy deployed in many parts of French Equatorial Africa. This social and spatial engineering fits well into the broad framework that James Scott has recently elaborated concerning modern state interventions:

that modern states have intervened to impose order on nature and society, convinced that their simplifying interventions will improve a disordered civil society. *Regroupement* was a keystone of French colonial state building, for it allowed France to assert military and administrative control over mobile, scattered populations in order to count, tax, and recruit colonial subjects and laborers; it continued into the early 1960s when the newly independent Central African Republic sought to assert its control over scattered villages. Christopher Gray's study of *regroupement* in colonial southern Gabon illustrates how the French first emptied this colony of its distinguishing features and then remapped it as a European space and imposed "modern territoriality" through the creation of permanent roads and fixed villages. Although the concept of territoriality is useful, the colonial state did not entirely erase and rewrite the Sangha basin and its peoples to suit its needs. Rather, the basin presented people and features (rivers, rubber) that could aid administrators in transforming a physical and social geography into a rational, exploitable, and "civilized" space.[1]

During the first thirteen years of the twentieth century, the French military administration began to map and to move populations into relocated villages at gunpoint and to clear and enlarge forest paths between these villages (fig. 5). Village relocations and consolidations began as early as 1905 in the larger Sangha villages such as Nola, where powerful leaders were most easily identifiable. Meager French military forces consolidated villages, identifying chiefs to carry out the task. By 1908 one military report happily declared:

> Today the vast region that includes the group of *circonscriptions* of the upper valleys of the Sangha can be considered pacified. . . . A certain number of villages have made notable improvements. Some have been brought closer to roads, and it has been possible to shake off the natural apathy of these populations and to push them to develop food production and plantations. The grouped villages of the upper N'Daki [N'Doki] in the Sangha have returned to the places that they once abandoned to escape from authority; the chiefs who incited them to riot and flee have offered their submission; the villages have been reconstructed and their plantations reconstituted.[2]

This assessment was unduly optimistic. In many locales French officials could make little sense of complex and fluid relations of authority, and Africans continued to flee official villages to escape recruitment and taxation, unhindered by the sparse colonial military forces until the First World War. To be sure, under the efforts of Governor Merlin from 1908, the French administration expanded its control throughout the colony and equipped all major posts with telegraph lines. But the administration remained poorly

Fig. 5. Road building to Gombako, c. 1906. (From the private collection of Père Ghislain de Banville)

staffed and equipped, and its taxation, conscription, and reorganizing efforts, as well as the labor demands of concessionary companies, the most pervasive outsider presence in the Sangha, promoted flight by coercing African workers to leave their villages.[3]

The First World War interrupted the colonial remapping efforts, as battles between French and German troops erupted, creating havoc among African people, who fled marauding armies that sought to press them into service as porters, to requisition food, or to exact vengeance on villages suspected of aiding enemy troops. In 1915 the French, who had regained control of Nola, tentatively began relocating African subjects to their official villages and conscripting workers to repair forest paths, at the same time conferring more enhanced authority on selected chiefs and suppressing the authority of recalcitrant ones. In the early 1920s *regroupement* intensified, and road construction for automobiles began, as colonial officials sought to link outlying areas with major trading centers along the Sangha River. It was during this period, for instance, that the French oversaw the construction of roads linking the village of Nakombo to Nola and the villages in the Terre Ngombako with Salo. In the mid-1920s and 1930s, the administration concentrated efforts on linking the major administrative centers to one another, particularly the North-South Road that extended into Middle Congo.[4]

Local administrators noted difficulties in the M'Bimou *circonscription,* the colonially created "home district" of many Mpiemu speakers, where inhabitants did not take kindly to being told where and how they could settle in villages. They preferred to remain mobile and to create new settlements, so that they could take advantage of new opportunities and flee the onerous demands of the colonial administration. Many appointed chiefs did little or nothing to stop them. In 1923 Vingarassamy, an administrator of the Kadei-Sangha *circonscription,* complained that residents of M'Bimou Kadei were crossing the Cameroon border to sell rubber at higher prices.[5] In the same year another administrator grumbled that the "M'Bimous" and "Kakas-Goumbes" too often practiced the "custom of easily breaking up their groups and changing the placement of their villages."[6] In the southern M'Bimou, administrator Allys reported, there lived an especially intractable subject named Kalo from the village of Adebori, a subordinate of the *canton* chief Gombako. Kalo had created a new village in the forest nearly an hour from Bayanga. And to Allys, Kalo was nothing less than an annoyance. He

> does not want to obey his village chief, nor my orders, and since he lodges all of the M'Bimous who don't want to do anything and encourages them to desert their grouped villages, his actions [have] become . . . intolerable. [I] . . . sent the militiaman Dinga with two policemen to arrest him and to bring him before the Tribunal Repressif. . . . But now I have learned that Dinga couldn't arrest him, [because] Kalo has fled into the bush. . . . During my next descent down the Sangha River, this village will be destroyed in an attempt to reintegrate all rebellious people into their village.[7]

Similar opposition, however, developed elsewhere in the Sangha, and this persistent mobility at times limited French attempts to move colonial subjects into their official villages.[8]

By the late twenties the French clearly had not succeeded in imposing a new map on the Sangha. The Kongo-Wara uprising exploded in 1928, percolating from parts of the upper Sangha to eastern Cameroon and the middle Sangha. Certain that they saw "dissidents" everywhere, the French redoubled their efforts to force all Africans out of their forest camps and into official villages. Available colonial documents indicate that Mpiemu people living in Kwapeli and Bilolo were not extensively involved in this rebellion, but they did feel the effects of the French crackdown.[9]

One grim incident reveals the ferocity of Mpiemu opposition and the brutality of French reprisals. In the early morning of July 30, 1928, four Mpiemu men, the elderly Maboli, his son N'Zao, Badambi, and Koumougo, received an unwelcome visitor to their forest camp, nearly an hour-and-a-half walk from the town of Bilolo. The militiaman Mazou, accompanied by two Mpiemu policemen, disrupted their early morning repose. The camp dwellers were acquainted with Mazou, who had visited them twice before. On those occasions he had informed them that living in their distant camp was illegal, and he had escorted N'Zao, Koumougo, and another man, Besambi, back to their official village, leaving Maboli to tend the fields. Both times, the men promptly returned to their camp. Mazou's visit this time resulted from a tip he had received from the chief Bikoula; none of the men had paid their head taxes, so they were to be arrested and imprisoned in Nola.

This visit, however, brought more than the predicted arrests. When Mazou and his men arrived in the camp, the elderly Maboli emerged from his house with an enormous spear in hand and cried, "I don't want to see militiamen here anymore! I will kill you!" He hurled the spear at Mazou, and it landed squarely in his chest. Mazou wrested the spear from his body, falling at Maboli's feet. And he turned to one of his policemen, gasping: "Listen, you. He killed me, and I'm going to kill him." With that, he drew his gun, shot Maboli in the chest, and then gunned down the younger Koumougo.

French authorities, obsessed at the time with Kongo-Wara, reassured themselves that this was an isolated incident, not the result of the uprising's spread into the M'Bimou region. Nonetheless, they resolved to use the opportunity to send troops into Mpiemu camps like that of Maboli, to destroy the camps, and to regroup people into their "regular villages." Fieschi-Vivet, the commander in charge of military operations in the Nola region, vowed to the chief of the Haute-Sangha *circonscription,* "Each time that the soldiers or I want to visit [the camps], the same murderous act could repeat itself. It is necessary, then, to visit them once and for all with a sufficient force, to make them cease this opposition."[10]

French military forces left little documentation of how they actually carried out the forced *regroupements* and administrative reorganizations from the late 1920s. But French retributions were swift, extensive, and brutal, designed to impose order on the volatile upper and middle Sangha, to turn over authority to the civil administration, to settle mobile populations, to recommence road building, and to revive flagging agricultural production. These efforts established the spatial contours of French colonial rule in the middle and upper Sangha basin for the next three decades. Each *circonscription* chief would oversee a hierarchy of *canton* chiefs in the *cantons* of Biakombo, Bikoum, Bidjoki, and Koapuli and a series of village chiefs, who were responsible for collecting taxes and recruiting laborers for colonial work projects.[11]

Regroupement was a technique of political control and extraction, a means of mapping, reorganizing, and creating modern territories, as in colonial Gabon, so eloquently described by Gray. But it also entailed the imposition of a powerful colonial vision of proper relations between people and their environments. French administrators perceived the Sangha and its people through a lens of dearth: the scattered, itinerant settlements were mired in lassitude, desperately requiring reorganization into visible, carefully delineated villages that were easily distinguished from the forest and that permitted the rational exploitation of the forest's riches. In this process French administrators drew upon the assets they found in the Sangha—the networks of forest paths and rivers, valued resources, African leaders and laborers. French administrators thus believed that they were creating an official, permanent, "civilized" landscape, where distinctions between the village (where people should live) and the forest (an exploitable but not a habitable space) were clear.[12]

But in delineating habitable from uninhabitable places and in permanently rooting once-mobile *kuli ajing* (clans or cord families) and *panjo* members in official villages and colonially demarcated and mapped lands, *regroupement* also altered the spatial configurations of Mpiemu social relations. Traces of these changes were still in evidence in the 1990s. Some Mpiemu referred to *ajing* in ways that differed from its early twentieth-century significance as a group with putative but untraceable kin ties. By the end of the century, the term connoted an area (Bilolo, Kwapeli, and Bidjogi) where Mpiemu populations were most concentrated and simultaneously served as an ethnonym. As Kadele Charles observed, "They [the French] divided all the villages, and afterwards they divided up the *ajing.* The [colonially created] *cantons* [in addition to Kwapeli] are Bikun, Bilolo, Bigene, and Zendi. All of them grouped together are Mpiemu."[13] Village relocation and consolidation during colonial rule probably helped to create for Mpiemu people closer associations between kinship, residence in a particular location, and ethnicity.[14]

Regroupement also reconfigured senior male authority within villages. Colonial officials appointed a hierarchy of African chiefs, thus undercutting the authority of the village *pendo* (war leader), *nkang* (healer), and *wani* (leader), who allocated farming lands and distributed meat, and disrupting the means by which people acquired access to such resources. Regrouped villages around Kwapeli and Bilolo brought together from various *kuli ajing* several *ja* (groups with traceable kin ties), each of which built one or more *panjo,* so that each village had multiple *panjo* rather than the one or two that had previously existed in early twentieth-century Mpiemu settlements. The loss of the *wani* and *nkang* and the proliferation of chiefs, *capita,* who carried out chiefly orders, and *panjo* heads may account for tensions over access to labor and forest and agricultural resources that colonial documents mention developing within and between regrouped villages.[15]

In reorganizing relations between people and their villages and *panjo*, *regroupement* affected *doli* and the processes of leaving a person behind. Evidence of these changes emerged in contemporary Mpiemu recollections and interpretations of the colonial past. Many informants recalling past French interventions simply subsumed *regroupement* under the broader rubric of French colonialism, making no mention at all of villages being moved and reconfigured according to a colonial design. But several older men and women discussed French relocations of villages. As Kadele recounted,

> [The leader] Adoumandjali commanded the people of Bilolo. Abogi commanded the [*ajing*] Bikoun. Djendi commanded the [*ajing*] Bidjogi. But at that time Kobago sat at Mpola. Mpola. . . . They gave birth to me there in 1914 during the First World War. It was M. Dupont, Sous-préfet Dupont, he came to take some of us from Mpola. He said, "Oh, you go there to Bilolo." Some stood up and went; they met, and they went with Abogi. . . . [Dupont] crossed [the river] here, in Salo. He went here, there was an old road . . . [to Mpola]. [He went to Mpola to relocate us and find workers] so that the road would be fixed.[16]

Moreover, several, including one Lindjombo man, recalled that during these village reorganizations, French authorities forced Mpiemu to construct wattle-and-daub houses, instead of those enclosed by the bark of the *bigwi* tree, and they burned older houses deemed "unfit" for habitation. These new constructions altered the gender division of labor in house building. Men still tied the house frame together, but they no longer enclosed it with bark; it was women's responsibility to clothe the house with protective mud walls, one more of the many burdens that they shouldered during colonial rule. This task echoed women's older practices of enclosing and containing persons in their wombs, and in Kwapeli and Bilolo it continued into the 1990s. In Lindjombo and Bayanga in the early 1970s and in Salo during the 1990s, however, this division of labor changed because of access to new house-building materials—rejected wood planks—so that men again constructed houses almost entirely by themselves. These house-building practices helped to shape the production of male and female persons through the labor that they performed (or refrained from).[17]

Further evidence of the effects of village relocation and consolidation on *doli* was embedded in the Sangha basin's landscape, through which people organized and recollected the past. The spatial locations and layouts of existing villages along roads served as mnemonics for the people and events that had contributed to their creation. One Mpiemu village name, Domisili, resembled the French word *domicile,* a testament to its colonial creation. Some villages in *metego Mpiemu,* the Mpiemu home region, had moved multiple times during French colonial rule but retained the old names to recall their founders and the events surrounding their establishment.[18]

Other villages have altered their locations and in the process lost their old names and acquired new ones. Inhabitants of the village of Bandoka claimed that their origins were in Mpola but moved three times before settling along the Kwapeli road between Salo and Bilolo. The names of these three settlements have since been forgotten. But former inhabitants' children and grandchildren recalled the rivers along which Bandoka's population settled, and some could identify abandoned village locations because human settlement indelibly marked the forest with oil palms and fruit trees that later grew up around them. Passing through these abandoned villages in the forest precipitated discussions about a village's founder or of conflicts between subordinates, chiefly authorities, and the colonial state that led to movement. But encountering abandoned villages could also prompt nostalgic recollections of Mpola. It seems that tellers of *doli* reinterpreted the colonial visions of itinerant, scattered, disorganized settlement, transforming a discourse of "lack" (of "civilized" stability and of habitable places clearly delineated from forest) into one of "loss": of the tutelage of earlier German colonizers in Mpola, whom some recalled as more generous and less brutal than the French, of Mpiemu autonomy to select where in the forest they would live, of control over their labor and forest resources, of a time when people "sat as one."[19]

RECRUITMENT

Labor recruitment also reconfigured relations between Mpiemu persons and their *panjo* and villages through depopulation, and it reshaped *doli.* Much of the historical literature in French Equatorial Africa focuses on the forced recruitment of African laborers and on their fierce resistance to it.[20] I do not want to minimize the coercive measures that concessionary companies, colonial administrations, and later other commercial enterprises used to recruit and retain African workers, at least until the end of the Second World War. But for many Mpiemu workers, colonial labor recruitment was just as much a story of their own desires to leave their *panjo* and home villages, to settle in new villages, to gain access to new opportunities and new consumer goods, and to pursue new paths to acquiring wealth and authority.

Both colonial coercion and African initiative contributed to what administrators, missionaries, and Mpiemu alike deemed an exodus of young men and
women from their home villages and a depletion of their villages and *panjo*.

For the colonial administration recruitment and *regroupement* went hand
in hand. Settling villages on or near the newly constructed roads allowed the
administration to count, tax, monitor, and conscript adult male workers for
colonial work projects. Labor recruitment by the administration remained fitful
in the very early years of French colonization, though Catherine Coquery-
Vidrovitch has indicated that the administration always intended to retain
its right to use Africans as workers, even though it faced considerable competition from concessionary companies. During their first years of the twentieth
century in occupied Sangha basin territories, administrators sought simply
to collect taxes from chiefs, and these taxes primarily took the form of ivory
and rubber, promptly sold to trading companies for revenues.[21]

But over the next decades administrative demands for African labor intensified, particularly after the First World War when the French reassumed
control of the Sangha River basin. Some conscripts remained in the Sangha
to work as porters. By the early 1920s many began laboring—unwillingly—
in the forest to build a network of roads and in the later twenties began constructing the segment of the North-South Road between Berbérati and Bayanga. Between 1921 and 1934 Mpiemu and other Sangha basin inhabitants
also were conscripted to labor on the infamous Congo-Ocean railway, and
at least one administrator sent the most refractory men who refused to do
roadwork to the railway work sites. Mpiemu proved particularly resistant to
administrative labor demands. Building roads in the dense equatorial forest
was hard work, but workers clearly feared being sent to southern Congo,
where death tolls along the railway lines were so high that many conscripts
never returned. Administrative labor demands profoundly disrupted Mpiemu
and other Sangha basin peoples' agricultural and hunting activities at home.
And even regional roadwork took them far from their villages for weeks at a
time. Efforts to link fixed villages with passable roads continued well into
the 1950s, in part because fierce tropical rainstorms made road washouts
common. The road linking Nola and Bayanga, contended one administrator, was impassable during the rainy season.[22]

Concessionary companies also contributed to Mpiemu mobility and the
exoduses from Mpiemu villages. From the beginning of their activities in the
Sangha basin, concessionary companies used the same recruitment strategies practiced elsewhere in the French Congo (later the AEF): they sent
their agents, along with armed soldiers, into villages to raid for workers.
Some workers had to labor as paddlers on boats, transporting rubber, ivory,

or manufactured goods between company warehouses. Others trooped off into the forest to collect rubber for a month or more at a time.[23] Wives frequently accompanied their husbands into the forest, where they cooked, coagulated the rubber into cakes, and carried the heavy cakes back to the market, "to the place of the white people" as one elderly man put it, where company agents would weigh the rubber and purchase it. European agents sometimes surveyed African rubber tappers' work in the forest, and even the companies themselves admitted that the agents brutalized rubber-tapping teams, causing their desertion. If the workers did not supply the requisite monthly harvest of rubber, they were whipped, beaten, and condemned to hard labor without pay, and frequently without food. And those who did supply the required harvest could find themselves cheated by company agents who weighed their rubber in the market.[24]

These abuses were common occurrences, from the earliest operations of the concessionary companies in 1899 through the mid-1920s, when André Gide documented their abuses in the Sangha basin and elsewhere in French Equatorial Africa. Although CFSO, the major concessionary company in the middle and upper Sangha from 1910, abandoned direct exploitation early on, it did buy rubber from Africans so as to pay the French administration its rent, and thus few people escaped the company's coercive measures. For the most part, the companies themselves sought to portray their practices as eminently fair, contending that Africans lacked the qualities of "civilized" peoples. The use of armed guards to recruit workers was just, the proprietor of the Compagnie de la Haute-Sangha insisted, because "the concessionaire only uses arms in case of legitimate defense. The presence of armed guards must only serve to forge relations between Europeans and Natives [Indigènes]. The latter will acquire the habit of work, and consequently commercial interactions. Everyone will benefit, and these small armed detachments will advance progressively and peacefully into the exterior, extending the zone of French influence among these people who refuse all work and all civilization."[25]

Indeed, some observers staunchly justified compulsory labor on the grounds that it would teach Africans, who had succumbed to chaos, enslavement, and a "passion for human flesh," to learn to work properly and thus to reconstitute their decimated families and depopulated villages.[26] According to Coquery-Vidrovitch, concessionaires went so far as to argue that Africans more readily accepted forced labor than long contracts because the former more closely convened to their customs.[27]

Why such brutality in their recruitment and work practices? The constraints facing concessionary companies were legion: they lacked personnel, working supplies and equipment, infrastructure, and capital, not to mention

appropriate techniques for harvesting rubber. To make a profit the companies would pay Africans only a pittance for the products they had gathered.
And concessionary companies found it unceasingly difficult to acquire and
keep workers. Company reports are replete with complaints of insufficient
numbers of laborers. By the twentieth century, population densities in the
Sangha basin forest may have declined, leaving fewer able-bodied men to
work for the companies. These dwindling densities only worsened with a
series of sleeping-sickness epidemics in the Sangha basin. In addition, for
the first decade and a half of their existence, competition among companies
for a limited pool of African laborers was fierce; not only did concessionaires in French possessions have to compete with one another, but they also
tangled with the German company in nearby Cameroon.[28]

And finally, the French colonial administration did little to regulate recruiting practices. It passed a first labor law in 1903, regulating the minimum age
for recruitment (fifteen years); requiring companies to provide lodging, food
rations, and health care in case of accidents; limiting the workday to ten
hours; providing one weekly day of rest; and demanding that employers
provide workers with a written contract detailing the duration of the labor
contract, salary, and other details concerning their employment. Neither this
law nor subsequent ones had any effect, because employers simply ignored
them. Another law in 1922 made a few minimal improvements in the lot of
African workers, requiring employers to pay their workers in money (rather
than in kind) each day or by the task and to organize medical posts in work
areas. But not until 1946 did the French, at the exhortation of African leaders, pass a labor code that outlawed coerced labor altogether.[29]

African responses to the concessionary-company activities suggest that
the companies were anything but welcome. During the first three decades
of the twentieth century, company agents (and observant administrators)
repeatedly complained about the difficulty of finding willing workers. Sangha
basin populations made the lives of company agents miserable. In Pembe
and Ikelemba (in the middle Sangha basin along the N'Doki River), representatives of the Compagnie des Produits de la Sangha found company storehouses pillaged and at least eleven employees killed, including the director of
the company and one company agent, whose body was reportedly consumed
by African subjects.[30] Africans pillaged company storehouses in Bayanga
and Lopi and stole some 140 kilos of ivory from a caravan traveling between
the two villages. Throughout the French-controlled basin, Africans refused
to sell food to company agents, even at highly elevated prices.[31]

Motivations for refusals to work, desertion, or killing company agents
must have been complex, not easily explained away as heroic resistance. But

recruitment practices likely fed Africans' hostility toward company agents, and the companies clearly saw these diverse hostilities as reflecting Africans' lack of willingness to work. They responded with even more vigorous repression. In the aftermath of several uprisings, one company director proposed draconian retaliation: "We don't need just thirty Tirailleurs [African sharpshooters] in this region. We need to take the entire group [of sharpshooters] between the Sangha and the Oubangui and sweep the entire region, especially imposing repression from the north and marching toward the south. [We must] visit all of the villages [and] impose work [on Africans]. . . . Wherever there is a vestige of a burned storehouse, we will shoot the chief and the culprits."[32]

Over the next three decades of colonial rule, the nature of environmental exploitation that companies demanded from Africans changed. From the mid-1920s, commercial enterprises in the middle and upper Sangha began to shift from monopolistic extraction of rubber to clearing forest for coffee, oil palm, tobacco, cacao, cassava, and maize plantations. CFSO, whose original activities centered on rubber exploitation, remained in the region after its concession privileges expired in 1935 as a major cultivator of oil palm and coffee and intermittently as a harvester of rubber and ivory.[33]

In coercing Africans to cultivate rather than to extract the forest's wealth, administrators and company agents sought to turn Mpiemu and other Sangha basin inhabitants from "uncivilized" people mired in activities that characterized them as "lacking": slave raiding, anthropophagy, small-scale slash-and-burn agriculture, and trapping. They would transform their subjects into modern, productive, docile workers who built roads, rationally and efficiently exploited forest resources, cleared the forest away for European profit, and acquired new consumer goods. Colonizers harnessed this transformation of mobile, docile workers to rework the landscape of the Mpiemu *terres* and the entire Sangha basin, capitalizing on generational tensions among *panjo* members to create labor reserves from regrouped villages and to transform forests into new centers of production, plantations, mining camps, and urban centers.[34] By the 1950s, however, colonial administrators' discourse of lack had transformed into one of depletion. Assessing their tenure in Ubangi-Shari, they identified labor recruitment for roads, coffee plantations, and diamond mines as a major cause of depopulation in Mpiemu villages. This excessive recruitment, they contended, would ultimately result in the demise of Mpiemu people altogether. Although demographic figures are spotty and difficult to compare, there were grounds to colonial officials' concerns. Between 1934 and 1950 Adoumandjali's population dropped 50 percent, from 615 to 304, and other villages (including Domisili, Aboghi, and Bindjo) suffered similar declines. These declines did not result from the creation of new villages; in the same period the population of the entire *terre* of Biakombo, which contained Adoumandjali, plummeted 45 percent, from 1,540 to 838. To be sure, worries about demographic loss were part of broader anxieties about depopulation in French Equatorial Africa, which some administrators and other observers believed predated French colonization. But the depopulation of the Mpiemu *terres* seemed especially dramatic.[35]

The colonial conception of a mobile, economically productive person living in populous centers and exploiting the forest effectively shaped Mpiemu notions of gendered, generational, and ethnic persons, their relationships with their built environments, and *doli* itself. Moreover, a colonial discourse of depleted Mpiemu villages emerged as a major theme in *doli*. During early decades of the twentieth century, fierce African opposition to coerced labor suggests that workers did not willingly accept the new vision of the person that administrators and company agents advanced. But notwithstanding the brutal measures to recruit workers, subsequent generations claimed that they willingly embraced a new vision of mobile male and female persons who gained access to new forms of wealth (clothes, cooking pots). According to many contemporary accounts, Mpiemu embraced these notions more willingly than some other neighboring ethnic groups.[36]

Elderly tellers of *doli* indicated that they had appropriated these conceptions of mobile, accumulating persons in their narratives of their experiences as young men and women from the 1930s to the 1960s, when they joined the ranks of mobile workers, deriving their wealth independently by leaving their home villages to cultivate plantation coffee.[37] By the Second World War, gaining access to money for clothing, taxes, and particularly for bridewealth had become a crucial means of leaving a person behind. But elderly tellers of *doli*, though they appropriated this new notion, depicted the agency of that person in complex ways, shaped by powerful colonial and company demands; expectations that young men would accumulate wealth, marry, and leave new persons behind; and their own desires for independence from *panjo* elders. Some portrayed their departures from their villages as Modigi Casimir did his: it was a quest

> for money. . . . When I first left home, I went [to the nearby coffee plantations in] Salo. I saw that it wasn't enough for me and so I looked for the road and came to this place. . . . [Salo wasn't enough] because it was close to our village. When . . . you have got some money, everyone from the village . . . [puts out a hand] like this. . . . You have to give to your mothers, your elder sister, everyone. And then all of your money is used up. . . . You see, that is why I came here. . . . People won't use up your money. Everyone came here [to the

Lindjombo coffee plantations] for that reason. If you sit with family, money will not stay in your hand.[38]

In European *patrons,* not village elders, some workers found models for accumulating wealth; a few named their children Messekotto (Monsieur Kotto, after a colonial administrator) and Lopes (after a coffee-plantation owner).[39]

But in important ways some tellers of *doli* obliquely acknowledged how colonial administrators and company agents shaped their agencies, their abilities to "produce effects on the world."[40] Mpeng Patrice presented his decision to work for the CFSO plantation in Salo as the convergence of a colonial administrator's order, pressures from fellow villagers to strike out independently, and his own desire to leave:

TGV: You couldn't refuse to go?

MP: No, I didn't refuse.

TGV: But that must have been hard for you. Everyone had to work in the fields. Did you have fields?

MP: Mmmmm.

TGV: But to leave your house and fields to go so far? You were pleased to leave?

MP: I was pleased . . . because I sat and I didn't work for money, so always people made fun of me. They made fun of me. So I said, "Mama, I am going to go. I am not going to return." I told my mother this. By then, my father had already died.

TGV: Why did people make fun of you?

MP: They made fun of me because I was a grown man, but I didn't work. Like so, like so. My heart was sore [because they made fun of me]. So I said, "I am no longer going to sit in this village."[41]

On another occasion Mpeng was more vehement about the influence of the colonial agents: "You sit in the village doing nothing??! No, no, no! If someone sat in the village doing nothing, that person would know. The chief of the village would know it. This person, they would take him and put him in a place, perhaps to do bamboo work, perhaps to do some other work, and he would do it. Each person, sitting in the village doing nothing? No, no, no!"[42]

But other tellers of *doli* recast how French administrators and company officials had once shaped workers' agencies. An elderly woman, once married to a Mpiemu man who supervised rubber tappers, contended that her husband, not European agents, coerced workers to fulfill their tasks: "[My husband] would supervise their work, and then he would return home. He would go to the rubber market, and he would inspect the work of people there. If you didn't work hard, he would scold you so that you would do good work. When you didn't work, he would beat you! Wasn't it the time of

whips? He would beat you to force you to do the work. He would force you
to work."[43] An elderly man recalled that it was the Germans, not the French,
who forcibly recruited African rubber tappers from their villages:

> The Germans came first to make villages. And then they did rubber work.
> Their work was to take our grandfathers and fathers to tap rubber. . . . [Our
> fathers and grandfathers] would climb up above [in a tree to tap the rubber].
> Then they would sell it to the Germans. This much [*he raised his arms wide*],
> and you would get a gun. A little like this [*he narrowed his arms*], and you
> would get lots of clothing. Ee-e-e-e! Lots of people [worked at rubber]. The
> Germans also were evil to some people. . . . The French saw this, and they
> came. They struggled in war with the Germans.[44]

And finally, many elderly tellers of *doli* recalled their recruitment and
work experiences in terms of a deeply personalized relationship with a *patron*,
who influenced how, where, and when they moved to work. Gomina Jean-
Marie depicted his extraordinary mobility in his younger life as part of his
relationships with a series of *patrons*, who took him to work as a secretary
and as a supervisor of nurses and of coffee workers.[45]

Women, too, appropriated new notions of female persons, propelled in
part by the changing activities and ideas of men. Leaving their home villages
to marry workers in plantation villages, women cultivated fields on the outskirts of the coffee plantations, gathered forest foods, distilled alcohol at their
houses, and performed some plantation work in these new villages. Women
like Yongo Oromain, Bessambongouri Jeannette, Abiankoe Jeannette, and
Mawindi Julienne benefited indirectly from this generation's independent
access to wealth, because they now had clothing, cooking pots, and soap
that their husbands purchased. "Before," Naro Filomene remarked, "the old
people said that they didn't have anything. It was only when the whites
arrived that we began to have things." Women began to wear imported cloth
and to use manufactured soap, not only marking new aesthetic standards but
also visually reorganizing the bodily surfaces that contained female persons.
And in embracing a new colonial model of the person as mobile laborer,
these men and women transformed generational and kin relations, rendering
younger men and women more independent of the demands of elder kin.[46]

Why did Mpiemu so easily appropriate this colonial notion of the person
as a mobile worker? This question dogged me repeatedly, especially when
elderly men wistfully recalled their experiences of leaving home to work in
the coffee fields and processing facilities. Clearly they had sought alternatives to remaining at home, where sleeping-sickness epidemics raged and
generational tensions erupted. Paid labor provided an alternative path to

submitting to the demands of elders under the *panjo;* it gave young men access to an alternative means of gaining authority, based on their ability to earn income and to rise among the ranks of coffee, diamond, and other workers. And voyaging to a new village to perform new kinds of work was simply an interesting, appealing thing to do. But this new notion of the male person may have had an older cultural logic. Leaving one's *panjo* and village and the social relations that these places framed was nothing new by 1900 or 1945. Membership in kin and residential groups was highly flexible in the nineteenth century, as people moved to cope with intragroup tensions over access to labor or women or with pressures from neighbors over access to valued resources. Although the reasons that these tellers of *doli* supplied for leaving their *panjo* and villages differed from those in the nineteenth century, the patterns of leaving probably were well established by the twentieth century.

These new notions of mobile persons translated into significant changes in the places where Mpiemu lived and reproduced persons, both biologically and socially. Most workers followed kin, in-laws, friends, or a major recruiter of Mpiemu labor, like Alouba, to work on the plantations, particularly those in Lindjombo. But although workers may have followed social networks to these new plantation settlements, they did not re-create the older spatial arrangements in which they had resided on *metego Mpiemu* (Mpiemu soil). In fact, many claimed that they abandoned *panjo* construction altogether. Some men argued that these large villages had acquired too many different *ajing* to make *panjo* construction viable; others simply contended that they wanted to escape the authoritarian demands of *panjo* elders and thus refused to build them.[47]

The new built environments in Lindjombo eventually framed different ways of reproducing persons and social relations. In 1993 Biloue Brigitte lived in one quarter of the village of Lindjombo with her husband; her mother, brother, and sister lived in their own houses scattered throughout Lindjombo's other quarter. In the absence of a *panjo* and a constellation of kitchens where kin members had once prepared and shared food, in the mid-1990s Brigitte had a wide range of options for sharing food. Of the ten meals she consumed over a three-day period in 1993, one was from her elder sister, Marcelline; one from her sister-in-law; and two from Claudine, her friend next door. She shared four of the six meals she had cooked herself with Claudine.

Another Mpiemu woman in Lindjombo, Bishiari Simone, lived with her Kako husband, Henri, two daughters, and a son.[48] Both her elder sibling and eldest daughter (married to a Mpiemu man) lived elsewhere in the village. But Simone rarely shared meals with her married daughter or her sibling, and like women in many African societies, she did not eat meals with her husband or son. Rather, she and a friend next door, Beno Julienne, exchanged meals on a daily basis. Simone ate nine out of her seventeen meals over a four-day period with her two daughters living at home and Julienne. Four of these meals Julienne provided. And only once did Simone receive meat from her son-in-law. Most other times her husband provided her with meat from his traps. These patterns of settlement and food sharing in Lindjombo differed substantially from residential and resource allocation patterns in early twentieth-century Mpiemu villages, where kin-group members shared food, allocated labor, and educated children about the past under the *panjo*.

Strikingly different arrangements and social relations developed within the built environments of the Mpiemu *terres*. One common house-kitchen-*panjo* constellation was headed by Ntchambe Marc, an elderly Mpiemu man living in the Kwapeli village of Bandoka. Marc lived in a multiroom house with his two wives, his son, his son's wife, and their daughter. His son and grandson lived across the road in their own separate houses. His daughter remained living near Ntchambe Marc, along with her husband and children. Ntchambe shared food under his *panjo* with his sons, grandsons, and son-in-law.[49] His wives, daughter, and daughter-in-law contributed to the food from their kitchens or hearths. Ntchambe Marc's *panjo* retained connections with two other constellations just west along the road to Bilolo, both belonging to the same *kuli ajing* (Pentala) as Ntchambe Marc and his kin. Ntchambe would share special foods, such as gorilla meat, with the senior men of these neighboring Pentala *panjo*.

These spatial arrangements and the social relations that inhered in them prompted some Kwapeli Mpiemu residents to claim that their *panjo*-kitchen-house constellations were spatial sites of *doli*, ones that evoked the practices and relations of the distant past. They argued, too, that Lindjombo Mpiemu had abandoned an important site associated with this distant past and thus had forsaken the important relations among kin and generational groups that those remaining in the Mpiemu *terres* enjoyed.[50]

Lindjombo Mpiemu themselves acknowledged that although labor recruitment had offered new opportunities for authority and accumulation to a generation of young men and women, those opportunities came at a cost. Children and grandchildren of recruited workers who first had left their home villages and then chose not to construct their houses around *panjo* lost both the knowledge and the protection of elder kin. Apoundjo, the son of one of these elderly workers in Lindjombo, alluded to this loss:

Our family divided. After the Second World War, in '45, the white people said that Central Africans had to pay head taxes with money. They could not pay with food anymore. But at that time there wasn't much money, although it was worth a lot. Five francs, ten francs, you could buy a beautiful outfit. Ten francs, you could get a wife. Therefore, we went to the places where the white people were so that we could earn a little money. To pay for a wife, to pay head taxes, to buy clothing. . . . And so we left our family because of the whites. We came here [to Lindjombo]. From Kwapeli, people came here. They gave birth to us here, and we grew up here. . . . We, we are the children of company work, and those people in Kwapeli, they are the children of the homeplace. Someday they will come here to ask for money or clothing [from us], and we will give it to them. It is because of the work of the whites and the head taxes that the division of our family took place. [Before] we were one family. In the past we lived in a group. In the past, when we lived during wartime, people would gather together under a *panjo* to wait for the attacks. But because we are children of company work, we don't know our family [anymore].[51]

Apoundjo underscored the losses associated with colonial recruitment practices, emphasizing his disconnection from the constellation of places (house, kitchen, *panjo*, and village) that had once organized and recollected the past and present cords of kinship that bound people together. But he also highlighted Mpiemu people's disconnection from a past time, when "we were one family."

Even more striking in these assessments of Lindjombo and Kwapeli is that spatial and social arrangements in both places were twentieth-century inventions, the result of labor recruitment and village relocations and consolidation. Ntchambe Marc's *panjo*-house-kitchen constellation reflected a significant change from the early twentieth century, when Mpiemu constructed houses in two rows with one or two *panjo*. And although Satuba Omer in Lindjombo constructed a shelter that looked much like a *panjo*, he refused to call it one, because it did not incorporate many members of the same *ajing* under it, just him and his immediate family.[52] Claims that Lindjombo workers and their families had abandoned a site of *doli*, losing their social and historical grounding, bore a resemblance to colonial laments in the early 1950s about the depletion of Mpiemu villages by coffee plantations and mine recruitment. Mpiemu thus would eventually cease to exist because they had lost their connections to spaces that defined them as Mpiemu. Colonial perceptions of population loss and Mpiemu conceptions of a lost site of both *doli* and valued social relations are not the same, of course. But the two discourses of depletion drew from interpretations of the same phenomenon of labor recruitment, concluding that it ruptured ties to spaces and places and had historical and social consequences.

It is likely that the parallels between these two discourses are more than coincidental. Though direct evidence of such an appropriation does not exist, Mpiemu appear to have borrowed from and transformed a colonial discourse about Mpiemu villages as empty, depleted of their populations, and indeed of the Sangha basin as a backwater without the capital (and tutelage) of Europeans. In 1993 many Mpiemu (speaking in both Sango and Mpiemu) divided the built environments where people lived into "hot" and "cold" places. Large population centers were highly productive, open, hot spaces, where many persons gathered to "see far" and to "be seen," particularly by powerful outsiders. Small forest villages obscured by tangled vines like Lindjombo were cold.[53] Lengi Emilienne put it as so many others did: "Lindjombo is like a ditch. You go down there, and the place is cold. Cold." And Apoundjo Rene contended: "Finding money [in Lindjombo] is incredibly difficult. . . . It's cold here." Implicit in these assessments of Lindjombo were an evaluation of and a claim to truth about the past and present. Lindjombo had once been a hot place, a focus of the activities and attentions of *patrons,* who recruited and employed workers, paid them salaries, and gave them access to consumer goods but also to alternative paths of marrying and leaving a person behind. But in the 1990s, once the outsiders had departed and labor recruitment had ceased, Mpiemu within and outside Lindjombo (as well as other Lindjombo residents) depicted the village as existing outside of past and future time, beyond the reach of the broader networks of power and political economies.[54]

RECURRENT EPIDEMICS

From the early twentieth century, colonial administrators bemoaned the recurrent epidemics of sleeping sickness (*Trypanosoma brucei gambiense*), a tsetse-fly-borne parasite that swept the Sangha basin and reduced its pool of available workers. According to both European observers and African inhabitants who experienced these repeated epidemics, the disease struck most consistently and fatally in the Mpiemu *terres.* Sleeping sickness, according to past and contemporary witnesses, depleted Mpiemu *panjo* and villages, killing its victims and prompting others to flee its ravages. Sleeping-sickness mortality, the colonial interventions to control the disease, and the depopulation of Mpiemu built environments became a touchstone of Mpiemu interpretations of their colonial past.

Sleeping-sickness epidemics occurred within the context of colonial labor

recruitment, which increased human contact with the tsetse vector and facilitated transmission from focus areas to places where the flies, but not the
disease, existed.[55] Many historians of colonial Africa have concluded that
the sleeping-sickness epidemics arose from the late nineteenth- and early
twentieth-century dislocations that European colonization wrought on African
populations and their abilities to manage their environments.[56] But Sangha
basin epidemics and the historical sources documenting them differ from
East African ones. In the first place, *T. gambiense* has no wild-animal reservoir. And though the Nola region (including what would be the Mpiemu
terres) was probably "one of the original foci of the disease" before European
colonization, it is unknown whether sleeping sickness even existed elsewhere
in the Congo before 1885, when the first few references to it appeared.[57]
Neither available documents nor Mpiemu or other informants mention
specific (land-use or other) practices that Africans used to contain sleeping
sickness before the twentieth century.

The first documented epidemic began in the early 1890s in the upper
Sangha, along the lower Congo caravan routes, and along the Congo and
Ubangi Rivers north of Brazzaville. Another erupted in 1906, and the administrator Dupont of the Haute-Sangha observed in 1908 that "sleeping sickness rages with a cruel intensity, and it is increasingly decimating the populations of the Sangha: the insects swarm throughout the countryside of
Nola, Bania, and Carnot. . . . The [human] mortality is considerable."[58] In
response to high mortality and anxieties about "the economic future of the
Congo," the Paris Geographic Society sponsored and the Pasteur Institute
supervised the Martin-Leboeuf-Roubaud Mission, a team of physicians and
entomologists who studied the disease's distribution, possible treatments,
and the ecology of the tsetse fly.[59]

Beginning in 1909, the AEF took its first steps to control sleeping sickness,
jointly financing a new Pasteur Institute in Brazzaville and an anti-sleeping-
sickness campaign with the Pasteur Institute of Paris. And in 1917, at the
initiative of the Pasteur's Dr. Eugène Jamot and Governor Merlin, the French
administration created a mobile health campaign to examine all equatorial
Africans in their villages, to diagnose the sick, and to treat those in the first
stages of the illness with atoxyl. These mobile health units, according to Rita
Headrick, were a distinctive feature of the French campaign, though they
resembled the Belgians' approach more than that of the British, who focused
instead on vector control. Over the next seventeen years the French campaign
expanded its activities into new sectors of the AEF where trypanosomiasis
infection rates were high. But inhabitants of Nola and the Mpiemu *terres*
were not treated until the creation of a Haute-Sangha sector in 1930, where

the epidemics persisted well into the 1940s, more than a decade after they subsided elsewhere in the AEF.[60]

In the Mpiemu *terres* (as in other afflicted regions of the AEF) the campaign sought to contain the disease by focusing on sick human bodies and reworking their relations with their built environments. It conducted repeated surveys of the Mpiemu *terres* to identify the sick and to send them to the Bilolo hospital (originally built by the Swedish Baptists but purchased by the Health Service in 1944) or other treatment centers each week for repeated atoxyl treatments. All travelers departing on roads and paths from the *terres* had to carry a health passport indicating that they were trypanosome-free. The Health Service ultimately assumed control of the *terres* and forbade any labor recruitment there. Though treatment of the disease, rather than vector control, predominated in the AEF, strict official controls were established over Mpiemu built environments, seeking to demarcate humanized spaces more clearly from the forest. Administrators relocated villages away from the banks of rivers but simultaneously started construction on the North-South Road in 1927 and on the M'Bimou road in 1931, which encouraged the growth of low-lying brush and thus the development of tsetse-breeding habitats. The Health Service in the late 1930s inspected villages for trash and sewage disposal and water-source maintenance, surveyed fields, and ensured that uninhabited houses were burned. Villagers had to clear the tsetse-ridden brush 500 meters behind every house and to erect bamboo enclosures around the villages to prevent tsetse flies that flourished in the bush from entering the villages.[61]

Colonial and mission reports reveal widespread perceptions that Mpiemu *terres* suffered higher infection and mortality rates and more persistent epidemics than other Sangha basin (or AEF) peoples. Their anxieties had some grounds, because the *terres* are probably an old focus of infection where multiple vectors exist. Even as infection rates dropped in much of AEF between the First World War and 1934, infection rates in the Upper Sangha near Nola were on the rise, and in the Mpiemu *terres* estimates of infection reached as high as 31.2 percent in 1936. But beginning in 1936, infection rates began to decline, increasing temporarily during the Second World War because of renewed rubber collection. The epidemics ceased altogether by 1951.[62]

But as both Waller and White have cautioned, the discourse of ecological decline and illness also merits exploration. The French Health Service and colonial administration articulated a powerful and influential vision of Mpiemu illness and depopulation. Infection rates were high, but the dire predictions that Mpiemu would eventually cease to exist seem overblown. After sleeping-sickness rates in the M'Bimou region had begun to decline, annual colonial reports were still bemoaning the devastation wrought by sleeping sickness in the *terres*. In 1950, for instance, administrator Canal of the Haute-Sangha region contended that the Mpiemu, who had once lived in populous, active villages, now resided in a "desert," victimized by the ravages of sleeping sickness and persistent mobility as a result of labor recruitment.[63] Successive administrations moderated their demands on their subjects in the Mpiemu *terres,* temporarily abandoning road construction because too few workers were available, refraining from other forms of coerced labor, and encouraging Mpiemu families to cultivate coffee and oil palms despite significant opposition from European planters. And Mpiemu greeted their reduced demands by returning to the *terres.*[64]

Missionaries shared this discourse of Mpiemu population loss, undoubtedly influenced by colonial officials, whose interest in sleeping sickness predated their own by several decades. Repeatedly the Spiritan fathers singled out the Mpiemu *terres* as particularly afflicted. "Alas! This poor country is increasingly depopulated!" one Spiritan father lamented in 1936.[65] Their Capuchin successors echoed this perception of Mpiemu population loss, criticizing the Health Service and the administration for conditions within the Mpiemu *terres* and deploring forced labor among sleeping-sickness patients and the beatings and excessive labor demands on village populations already devastated by illness and recruitment. Mgr Sintas of the Berbérati Catholic mission went so far as to estimate 90 percent infection rates among Mpiemu. He wrote of the village of Biguene: "Here there was once a big village and a large mission with a school for boys and an enclosure for young female catechumens who were to be married. Now, there remain only ten or twelve houses with a *capita* [chief's administrator]: it is from the sickness and, shortly thereafter, death. . . . In Bikula, what a spectacle of desolation. This village, once so populated, is now reduced to a few houses." "In ten or twenty years," he concluded, "there will no longer be more than a few specimens of the Mbimou race."[66]

For Sintas, though, these dire consequences resulted not simply from the presence of infected tsetse flies but from the inability of Mpiemu to exercise sufficient control over their built environments. Allowing a multitude of insects into their "dirty houses," he erroneously conjectured, permitted the transmission of sleeping sickness. And control over humanized spaces was ebbing away, as more people were dying. Elsewhere, he surveyed a landscape devastated by sleeping sickness and intoned, "For hundreds of kilometers, one encounters no other inhabitants except for gorillas and chimpanzees, who establish their habitats among the old villages and old plantations of those who were once called the Mbimous."[67]

Some Swedish Baptists' assessment of the disease was more muted. In 1936 Brother Olsson observed from his own sickbed, where he was suffering from trypanosomiasis: "This year has been a year of shadows. The Lord knows everything and He is behind everything. Praise his name."[68] Yet not all of the Baptists attributed sleeping sickness to divine intervention. Sofia Karlsson, for instance, asserted, "Since the Congo black does not understand much about hygiene and the sanitary conditions are very poor, diseases are more easily spread than they would otherwise, so when the missionary has to creep inside infected sheds and huts to help the sick, he literally puts his life on line."[69] And many depicted the Mpiemu as a sick and dying people.[70]

Missionaries drew this discourse of a depleted people with no control over their domestic spaces not only from colonial administrators and medical personnel but also from Mpiemu themselves, who found in Catholic and Baptist missionaries sympathetic advocates for some of their grievances against the colonial administration and the Health Service. They recounted to missionaries their stories of suffering at the hands of colonial administrators during the campaigns and sometimes convinced the missionaries to intervene on their behalf. Missionaries also tried, albeit unsuccessfully, to expand their activities in the Mpiemu *terres,* but colonial officials limited their efforts.[71]

It is difficult to show conclusively that Mpiemu borrowed a discourse of declining, depleted built environments from colonial officials and then used it to extract concessions from them and missionaries. Certainly they had witnessed countless kin and friends succumb to the disease and could draw their own conclusions from it. But they also must have been aware of the efforts that the Health Service expended on sleeping-sickness control, the concern that repeated epidemics elicited from colonial officials and missionaries, and the hyperbole surrounding predictions that they would soon cease to exist. By emphasizing the population losses they had suffered and by fleeing their villages, Mpiemu may have found that they could exploit the concern in order to reduce colonial labor demands, to influence how missionaries perceived them, and to gain access to missionary resources and protection from colonial labor and tax demands. This discourse became a fundamental part of Mpiemu *doli* narratives of colonial rule and sleeping-sickness epidemics.

Tellers of *doli* in the 1990s traced the epidemics not to infected tsetse but to cruel colonial officials, who sought to infect Mpiemu and other Sangha basin inhabitants with the disease. Colonial officials and Health Service personnel, they argued, had a voracious appetite for young African women. If the young women's fathers refused to give these officials access to their daughters, they and their families might find themselves either on the rolls of those infected with sleeping sickness or forcibly subjected to injections that infected them with the disease.[72] The colonial official that Mpiemu held most responsible for such abuses was one Dr. Choumara. A few people, however, argued that sleeping sickness resulted from a different imbalance of power: sexual partners of vastly different ages would fall ill with sleeping sickness.[73] The sexual power of much older men or women was simply too great for their very young partners and would cause all to fall asleep in midday, a sure sign of infection. Sleeping sickness (*mempeli*) thus came not from the bite of tsetse flies that flourished on the banks of rivers and streams or in dense underbrush. Rather, in this etiology the disease spread from the intimate social and political contexts of built environments of villages and colonial settlements, when one sexual partner exerted undue power over another.

It is doubtful that on a very wide scale colonial officials injected Mpiemu with sleeping sickness or listed recalcitrant fathers on sick rolls if they refused to give sexual access to their daughters.[74] Such activities ran contrary to colonial interests, especially during the Second World War, when the French needed every available laborer to increase food and rubber production and to continue road building. Choumara, who bore the brunt of the criticism, headed the Nola subdivision only for a short time, so he could not have been responsible for decades of trypanosomiasis infections.

Nevertheless, these remembrances do shed light on accounts that Mpiemu tellers of *doli* during the 1990s claimed to be true. Colonial health officials, soldiers, and nurses at times did use their authority to gain access to women and to exact vengeance on Mpiemu who protested their abuses. Jeanne Yambumo was one such victim. She and her friend Suzanne Ankuari paid a visit to the village of Adebori to care for Jeanne's sick mother. Upon departing Adebori, the two women encountered a soldier who, desiring the two women, arrested them and coerced them to return to Adebori. There, according to Sintas, he forced upon them a "love potion" of lemon juice and hot pepper, tied them up, and beat and tortured them until the following morning. When Jeanne Yambumo's husband, the catechist Albert Bandibeno, heard her story, he filed a complaint with Dr. Choumara, the subdivision head, and with the Haute-Sangha department chief. The soldier was disciplined. But Jeanne Yambumo paid for her husband's quest for justice. Sanitary Agent Deroziers subsequently ordered her to report to the Bilolo hospital for two weeks of sleeping-sickness treatments and forced labor, although tests showed that she had no need for the treatments. It was in that hospital that Sintas found her.[75]

But the Mpiemu 1990s etiology of sleeping sickness as colonial abuse can be read in another way. It also makes a claim about the past world of French colonialism, in which agents of the colonial administration and the Health Service inflicted a host of injustices on Mpiemu men, women, and children. Choumara has come in contemporary recollection to crystallize all French colonial authority, echoing what Mpiemu living in the *terres* told Mgr Sintas in 1944: "The whites are killing us with their whips."[76] Embedded within this causal model of the repeated epidemics was a condemnation of the excessive demands and abuses of French colonialism and a protest about the ways in which it had sapped the authority of elders, preventing them from leaving persons behind as they had previously done. French colonial rule undercut male elders' authority over their wives, daughters, and sons. They no longer could command the labor of junior men. Besieged both by the demands of the administration and by young men who independently acquired wealth, they were also deprived of the authority to shape the conditions under which their wives and daughters became pregnant and reproduced lineage members. They found themselves legally responsible for their wives, who, exempt from punishment under the colonial Code Indigénat, could refuse to cultivate fields or to help process rubber.[77] *Doli* narratives of sleeping sickness thus articulated two losses in *panjo* and villages. First, it was a cataclysmic demographic depletion of *panjo* and villages in the Mpiemu *terres*, a hollowing out of the built environments in which inhered the old measures of wealth in Sangha basin societies—wealth in persons, who were connected through kinship, marriage, alliance, and clientship. And second, it led to the depletion of senior male authority over younger men's labor and over their daughters' and wives' labor and sexuality.

REDEMPTION

In order to gain converts, Catholic missionaries and their Baptist counterparts sought to alter conceptions of the person, agency, family, and authority and in so doing reordered African built environments. Both first undertook building projects, then introduced schooling and a series of new practices surrounding birth, marriage, reproduction, and death. Missionaries evaluated Sangha basin and Mpiemu peoples in terms of lack but saw in their own interventions a promise of salvation.

The very foundations of French Catholic and Swedish Baptist efforts in the Sangha basin were both physical and symbolic. The Berbérati and Bilolo-Nola mission journals reveal that early on, missionaries spent an enormous amount of their daily energies and meager resources on building. Upon his

arrival in Berbérati, Père Pédron spent three days searching for an appropriate site for the Mission Sainte Anne and immediately set to work with conscripted Africans to build a church.

Subsequently, he and his Spiritan and Capuchin successors embarked on
a building spree throughout the Sangha basin. In addition to constructing
mission stations in Berbérati and later in Nola and Bania, the Fathers built a
series of catechists' houses, chapels, and school buildings in villages of the
Mpiemu *terres*. By 1942 the mission had created some thirty-two catechist
posts within the subdivision of Nola, fifteen of which were located in the
four Mpiemu *terres* and five of which were in the Kaka *terre*, which included
Bayanga and Lindjombo. Indeed, this strategy caused some friction in 1933
with the Haute-Sangha *circonscription* head, who perceived the catechist posts
as "a village within a village" and the catechist as "a second chief." According
to the Catholic missionaries, this administrator sought to halt the development of Catholic enclaves within regrouped villages, compelling the missionaries to agree to the following rule: "The catechist will build his house
aligned with the rest of the village, and that is all. No chapel, no house for
the priest, no house for the children visiting from other villages."[78] Clearly,
for this French administrator the Catholic mission's efforts to transform
physically and symbolically the built environments of Mpiemu villages
undercut the authority of the colonial hierarchy. The tensions between the
Catholic Church and the colonial administration over authority and the
activities of catechists continued well into the 1940s.[79]

Among the Swedish Baptists building remained more modest but was far
more concentrated in the Mpiemu *terres*. Nonetheless, the Baptists shared a
veritable obsession with building, particularly in the late 1920s when they
first arrived in Bilolo and later after 1944, once they had relocated the mission to Nola. Abandoning their well-honed carpentry skills, the missionaries chose instead to make bricks and to develop masonry skills to construct
mission-station buildings. The very first line of the Bilolo-Nola mission
journal is a biblical reference to building: "Who despises the day of small
things? Men will rejoice when they see the plumb line in the hand of
Zerubbabel." Although biblical scholars have disputed the translation of
"plumb line," Karin Sjostedt, who translated the Bilolo-Nola journal, indicated
that the Baptist missionaries assumed it referred to a mason's plumb line.
The passage in the Bible from which this excerpt came recounts the prophet
Zechariah's rebuke of the people of Judah and his efforts to motivate them
to continue rebuilding the Temple so that they would be spiritually renewed
and favored by their God. In Zechariah's prophecy, Zerubbabel received a
commandment from an angel to rebuild the temple with his own hands.

Although some saw this rebuilding as a trivial act, it promised to restore God's favor to Jerusalem. Thus, in building their first simple house and chapel in Bilolo, the missionaries saw themselves engaged in a symbolic process of reconstruction, of reworking the built environments of the Mpiemu *terres* and the upper and middle Sangha basin in order to restore them in the eyes of God. This building continued as the Baptists constructed a carpentry workshop, school buildings, a bell tower for the church, a mission workers' village, and a hospital to treat sleeping-sickness patients in Bilolo, as well as catechist houses and churches in several villages. By 1942 fourteen of the mission's eighteen catechist stations were located in Mpiemu *terres,* although it also created one in Bayanga. But the Baptists left Bilolo in 1944 because of the sleeping-sickness epidemics. After selling the Bilolo hospital to the colonial administration the same year, they recommenced their building efforts in Nola.[80]

For both Catholics and Baptists, village chapels or meetinghouses constituted a first step in transforming scattered villages into civilized Christian enclaves, distinct from the "bush" settlements of "sorcerers," "polygamists," and members of rival Christian denominations. The competition between the Catholics and Baptists was intensified not just by the existence of rival denominations but also by Africans' frequent switching of membership between Catholic and Baptist missions. These rivalries shaped the domestic space of the village. As one observer put it, "Over the years, the Baptists and the Spiritans had a thousand occasions to meet and to avoid one another. The chapel of the Protestant mission was found at one end of the village, and the Catholic chapel at the other end."[81] Nonetheless, in physically and symbolically altering the villages, the missions sought to "civilize" Mpiemu Christians by carefully delineating new distinctions between domesticated and wild spaces, between spaces for the living and the dead, and by reworking older Mpiemu notions of inside and outside. These spatial and social alterations transformed the way in which Mpiemu left a person behind by reshaping both authority and agency.[82]

In their quest to transform Mpiemu and other persons into Catholic or Baptist followers, missionaries introduced a whole series of interventions that shaped both the places and practices within which Mpiemu left a person behind. Such interventions are addressed only very briefly here.[83] Broadly speaking, missions sought to subject new Christians to the moral authority of the Catholic Church or of Baptist believers, displacing the authority of male and female elder kin and *nkang* (healer).[84] By bringing children into their schools, missionaries removed these young Christian learners from their elder kin who controlled their labor and educated them about social relations and responsibilities, farming, hunting, and gathering. Education was critically important to both missions, for it was the single most impor-tant means by which they effected these interventions. Catholic missionar-ies themselves first recruited the sons and daughters of Mpiemu and other chiefs to attend their schools in Berbérati and later Nola, leaving instruction in the villages to their catechists. Swedish Baptists, however, sought first to educate their own workers, then children and the sick, but they also preached to anyone who would listen to them.

Catholic and Baptist missions baptized persons into the Catholic Church or a community of Baptist believers, although the Baptists spent far more time schooling followers before they baptized them. Evangelizing in the Mpiemu language, Baptists taught followers of "the Creator," which they translated as *Nkomolomori* (the builder of the person), and of "the Eternal One" (*Morikendi,* or the eternal person). For both Catholic and Baptist fol-lowers, baptism could provide a new way of leaving a person behind, for it reproduced members of both churches ("the family of Christ"), allowing them to achieve new life if they fulfilled the obligations of "sitting" with Christ throughout their lives. One Baptist missionary recounted that Kounga, a young girl who "gave . . . [herself] to God," claimed after her baptism: "Now we have become God's children, all of us in our family, Daddy, my-self, and Yaki. Only Toutom is left, but he is still too little."[85] Indeed, mission-aries envisioned integrating Kounga's and other families into a broader one that they equated with a "temple," the very structure of a broader Baptist community.[86]

Like many missionaries in Africa, Catholic and Baptist missionaries sought access to a person's soul through the body. Baptist writings, for instance, fre-quently recounted stories of healing the sick with their medicines and prayers and of clothing and feeding people as a means of transforming them into Christians. These activities, they believed, enabled them to distinguish themselves from colonial officials and commercial agents, whom Africans deeply mistrusted. But like missionaries elsewhere, their sense of triumph was dampened by their encounters with "witch doctors" who sought to cure people and identify the sources of ailments and death through practices of the catch-all categories "heathenism" or "paganism." In 1930, for instance, the Baptist Brother Johansson noted in the mission journal that a Mpiemu man slashed open his stomach, killing himself, after a diviner had accused him of killing a chief in one of the villages. "Oh, God," he despaired, "when will heathenism release its grip on these poor people?"[87] His brief journal entry tells us little about the circumstances of the accusation. But it is highly likely that the killing of the chief involved *alembo,* the active substance located in the stomach that is associated with the acquisition and maintenance of political and economic power, but also with making ill, killing, consuming, or harnessing the labor power of others. Missionaries introduced a stark distinction between "witches," linking them with devilry, and those who did not participate in such practices. They dismissed the knowledge of powerful *nkang* as sheer "paganism," and they sought to counter the authoritative knowledge of ancestors about illness, witchcraft, and power with that of Ntchambe and Jesus Christ.[88]

As a means of creating true Christian marriages, both Catholic and Baptist missionaries sought to regulate relations between men and women within the house and *panjo*, outlawing the practice of marrying multiple wives, ejecting church members for participating in polygynous marriages, and prohibiting sexual relations outside of marriage.[89] Baptists, who lived in the Mpiemu *terres* and visited villages frequently until they abandoned the Bilolo mission in 1944, apparently discovered and intervened in these activities more readily than did the Catholics. Such interventions sought to demarcate an inviolable marital space between a husband and wife inside the house and to criminalize the multiple marital and sexual partners that many Mpiemu men and women were accustomed to having. These interventions held up a single appropriate way of leaving a person behind: through holy matrimony.

These interventions could also limit the numbers of people left behind, because a Christian man with only one wife could have fewer children. His house and *panjo* would then contain far fewer people, reflecting less wealth and available labor in the form of wives and children. In upholding monogamous marriage as the only legitimate context in which men and women could have sex and procreate, the missions sought, in effect, to delineate and to fix in place the highly fluid, mobile membership within houses and *panjo*.

Finally, missionaries encouraged Mpiemu to treat their dead in different ways, burying the deceased in wooden coffins outside villages in clearly designated cemeteries, rather than in village living spaces. Such practices could increase the costs of burials, because Christians would have to purchase wood planks for the coffins. It also separated sites of recollecting past people from domesticated environments where the living ate, slept, and carried on their relations with one another. Such changes in burial practices presumably were intended to alter living people's relations with their ancestors and to undercut the authority of these ancestors.

From the 1920s, Mpiemu followers responded to missionizing efforts in a variety of ways. Some rejected Christianity altogether. But many others appropriated over time not only the practices but also the faith and sense of belonging to broader communities of Catholics and Baptists, altering their conceptions of persons and integrating them into *doli*. Although many Mpiemu tellers of *doli* embraced the promise of salvation that missionaries had offered, they also transformed a discourse of lack into one of lost places and social relations. Some also characterized themselves through a borrowed theme of deprivation, invoking a Christian virtue of assistance to the needy.

The precise historical processes by which people came to understand themselves as part of these religious communities is beyond the scope of this work. But what I hope to show, through an example of burial practices and treatment of the dead, is that Christianity transformed people's relations with their domesticated environments. Such new practices also altered *doli* narratives and Mpiemu Christians' attachments to places, infusing these narratives and sites with loss and, at times, redemption. Burial practices and the treatment of the dead illustrate these points well. After missionary interventions into burial practices, many upper and middle Sangha peoples buried most of their dead in cemeteries outside of their villages, marking the sites with mounds and an occasional brown-glass beer bottle (in which people put flowers). Weed clearing in the cemeteries occurred sporadically, most often when another burial took place. This change in burial sites distanced the living from the sites in which they could recollect past people, for they were unable to sweep the burial sites each day, as they had in their own compounds. Such changes, then, may have helped to transform deceased persons into a distant, undifferentiated group of ancestors who peopled an immutable past.

But at the same time Mpiemu and other Sangha basin peoples found alternative ways of recalling past people and incorporating them into *doli*. Membership in the Catholic or Baptist Church brought new ways of documenting one's life as a "servant of God," particularly through baptism cards, marriage certificates, and other papers issued by the religious organizations that people stored in the rafters of their homes. The practice of storing old documents in the house demonstrated that even for people who could not read their personal archives, the documents reinforced the bodily and spatial memories of past persons' interactions with and experiences of the missions inside the historical space of the house. Bibles, too, were prized possessions, in which people frequently stored their rare photographs of past and present persons. All of these documents, then, provided Mpiemu Christians with new resources for remembering and commemorating their parents' and grandparents' work for their religious communities and for integrating these objects of recollection into the very structures and historical processes of their houses.[90]

Christian burial practices also helped to replace the authority of ances-tors (*tumba doli*) in living people's lives with that of another set of powerful persons. It appears that Mpiemu previously looked to these ancestors to heal the sick and to provide food and rain.[91] But in 1993 Mpiemu were supplicat-ing Ntchambe (God) and Jesus Christ (and, for Catholics, Mary) to perform these deeds. Although some Mpiemu still acquired ancestral wisdom through their dreams, many now found this wisdom in dreams about Jesus Christ. Kadele Charles once described how he experienced Jesus Christ's curative powers in a dream. In this dream he had fallen gravely ill and had lifted his hands over his head and gestured to the sky, "My Jesus, my Jesus, my Jesus." Jesus Christ cured Kadele, giving him "new life."[92] His dream thus illumi-nated how Mpiemu had appropriated and refashioned a new ancestor with whom they had developed deeply individualized relationships.

Finally, Mpiemu borrowed some features of the missionary discourse con-cerning *alembo* and heathenism, but in unexpected ways. In the Lindjombo Baptist mission in 1993, one sermon giver divided all humanity into those who were "lights of God" and those who were "followers of the devil."[93] Another in Kwapeli put it even more starkly: "There are two kinds of peo-ple: those persons with [active] *alembo* and those persons without *alembo*. *Alembo* is the devil, and people with *alembo* are people of the devil. You can read about *alembo* in the Bible. If someone with *alembo* kills you, that person can only kill the flesh [*pondo*], not the spirit [*sonyoli*]. The spirit remains."[94] Even though the use of occult powers has been an integral part of accumu-lating and sustaining political and economic authority, many spoke of these powers as if they were unambiguously, morally reprehensible.[95]

Doli as a series of narratives about the past were infused with a discourse of loss but not always the salvation that Christian missionaries had promised. The stories of Adam and Eve and original sin, of Moses and the Egyptians, and of Christ's redemption were well known to many Mpiemu Christians, for they had learned them from the vividly illustrated catechisms that mis-sionaries used. They mapped these stories of original loss, exile, journeys, and dispersal onto narratives about Mpiemu mobility. Tellers of *doli* recounted the Mpiemu journey from distant forests over a stout vine called the Mbong Alon in biblical terms of journeys, miracles, salvation, and a kind of Mpiemu diaspora after the cord broke, leaving Mpiemu clans on either side of the river. Alouba Clotere and Kadele Charles discussed this event one after-noon, recalling that their ancestors had fled their enemies:

AC: Our ancestors, they came from the Dja and Mpombo Rivers. After-wards there was something that we called, we would call it Mbong Alon.

Mbong Alon. When—I think it was a *miracle* [*he used the French word*] that they did. Is that a lie?

KC: No, it isn't a lie.

CA: This was the *miracle* that the ancestors performed to cross the river. They would climb up on the cord; when the family was finished [crossing], the cord broke. Isn't that so?

KC: Mmm hmm. . . . They crossed once. Because when they cut [the Mbong Alon], some of their family remained there [on the other side]. But some of them were saved. And so they came with the name Mpiemu and sat among many different kinds [of people].[96]

Narratives of Mpiemu departures from the town of Mpola after the First World War echo biblical themes of Edenic places and exile. Some tellers compared their ancestors to Adam and Eve. Edenic loss and disconnection from former homeplaces resonated particularly among those Mpiemu who had moved to Lindjombo and had never returned to live in the Mpiemu *terres*. Many of the former coffee and timber workers, particularly elderly ones, fantasized about returning to their homeplaces in Kwapeli and Bilolo. In the misty recollections of these elderly workers, Mpiemu soil was a place of abundant food, opportunities, and familial support.[97] But few returned, and those who did would only visit temporarily, fearing that their families would kill them. Yodjala Philippe, for instance, returned to his home village, Bandoka, in 1993, predicting a plethora of food and nonstop celebration of his return. Nothing close to a celebration resulted, and he left Bandoka little more than a week later in secret, terrified that his family "might kill me in the road. Or they might kill me here if they knew I wanted to leave. I would grow ill here and I would die."[98] Their unwillingness to return or stay made abundantly clear that these were powerful dreams but not actual intentions.

Satuba Omer was one who did return to his home village, but he did so to die. Born in Domisili in *metego* Mpiemu, he lived in Lindjombo nearly all of his life as a trusted manager on the Santini plantation, as a coffee planter, and as an active member of the Baptist mission. He never returned to his birthplace until 1993, when he fell ill and voyaged to Kowolo (a village near Domisili) to consult a well-known healer. When his condition worsened, he sought treatment at the Zendi hospital and subsequently died in Domisili. His son, Amions Anaclet, had preferred to bury his father in Nola, which was "our town, our subprefecture." But when he tried to take his father's body to Nola, his Domisili kin refused, saying, "Ntchambe sent him here. He was born here, and Ntchambe sent him here so that he could die in his birthplace. We must bury him here." In the end, Amions concluded, "Nola, Domisili, and Lindjombo, they would all be the same. It doesn't make any difference where he was buried." Nevertheless, most people with whom I spoke, including Satuba's wives, approvingly contended that he had deliberately returned to Domisili to die.[99] Perhaps, then, Satuba's death was one instance in which the lost time and place of *metego* Mpiemu were regained, even redeemed.

Those like Yodjala expressed nostalgic visions of past places like Mpola and the *metego* Mpiemu of their childhood to characterize their present deprived circumstances and to invoke an appropriated Christian virtue of providing for the needy. On his visit to Bandoka, Yodjala repeatedly mourned Lindjombo's impoverishment in comparison to its past prosperity drawn from European commerce. He voiced these complaints as he sat under numerous *panjo* in Bandoka, berating his junior male kin for failing to sit with him and attend to his needs as an elderly man. In a similar way, as he instructed me about *doli,* Mpeng Patrice frequently chose to enumerate what Mpiemu lacked in the distant past—money, clothing, the ability to write, cigarettes, distilled alcohol—and then recounted how white missionaries and colonizers introduced these commodities. And these items (with the exception of distilled alcohol, which I refused to provide) were all part of the transactions that underpinned my education as a student of *doli.* Mpeng never asked for payment for his tutelage; he simply indicated what he lacked and what I as a white woman who frequently attended Baptist and Catholic missions ought to provide. Claims of deprivation and expectations of Christian virtue had important implications for how Mpiemu people responded to conservation measures in the 1990s.[100]

THE PAST COMES HOME TO ROOST: *DOLI,* CONSERVATION, AND SETTLEMENT

The diverse influences of all of these colonial interventions into built environments emerged in contemporary conflicts over conservation during the 1990s, when Mpiemu invoked *doli* in response to state and nongovernmental organization efforts to conserve the Sangha basin forest and its wildlife. Many Mpiemu living in Lindjombo and Kwapeli recognized that the CAR and the World Wildlife Fund continued some of the same settlement policies of the colonial period. Although the aims and effects of these policies differed from their colonial predecessors, Mpiemu met the policies with reactions that echoed their earlier responses to the *regroupement,* recruitment, sleeping sickness, and missionization that had shaped colonial villages.

With the establishment of the Dzanga-Sangha Special Reserve and the Dzanga-Ndoki National Park in 1990, the state and the WWF imposed a particular map of human settlement in the middle Sangha basin. According to state laws governing the park and reserve, people could not create new places of settlement. Yet Mpiemu and other Africans did so frequently. Extensive diamond camps, which had their own markets, stores, and restaurants, sprang up in the forests near the village of Beya and in Kwapeli. Hunting camps, which the French administrators sought to dismantle in the 1930s, frequently appeared in the national park. In the 1990s antipoaching patrols combed the park and reserve for these illegal settlements and demolished some of them. Efforts to destroy illegal diamond camps have not been successful, because according to a WWF official, "Many of the enforcement officers, the local political elite, and a significant portion of the population are profiting from diamond mining, and are thus not willing to uphold the laws creating the protected area."[101] But the settlements continued to crop up in hidden—and not-so-hidden—parts of the protected forest.

Some of the personnel working for the WWF project understood this contravention of state law as the result of economic need. The WWF project technical counselor observed that inhabitants of the reserve sought to increase their standard of living. But an increase in standard of living depended on intensifying the use of natural resources, which promoted overexploitation.[102] Others added that social fragmentation exacerbated these needs. Richard Carroll, the WWF director of the Africa and Madagascar program and one of the park founders, declared:

> The attitude that the forest is an inexhaustible supermarket with free products for the taking is pervasive. . . . The forest is measured by cubic meters of timber, baskets (truckloads) of meat, and boatloads of fish. . . . People are generally individualistic: they take care of themselves and immediate family. A sense of community is lacking. Altruism is not a viable operating agenda when there are hungry mouths to feed in one's home, an attitude aggravated by the large variety of immigrants having few relations in the region. Mistrust and sorcery are the norm, hampering the establishment of community-based conservation systems.[103]

Still others like Michael Fay offered psychological explanations, attributing Mpiemu and Africans' ways of using natural resources as part of a deeper psychological propensity to overexploit the forest's resources.[104]

Each of these explanations, however, caricatures the societies inhabiting the reserve and betrays some similarities with older colonial discourses of loss. Recall that the early European explorers described Mpiemu as "indecisive, unstable," and thus "inferior," while colonial administrators lamented their failure to impose order on mobile and "disordered" Mpiemu people and settlements. For conservationists, Mpiemu and other Africans in the reserve were mired in impoverishment; seduced by their voracious, uncontrolled appetites to consume natural resources (as Fay indicated); or bereft of the social norms that fostered "a sense of community" and conservationist attitudes (as Carroll signaled). Indeed, these descriptions of "individualism," "mistrust," and "hunger" evoke stereotypes of an impersonal world fundamentally penetrated by capitalist relations—or of a competitive Darwinian world. Conservationist and colonial diagnoses of Africans' economic, social, and psychological ailments were not identical, but they resembled one another in that they both portrayed African subjects as lacking basic social qualities.

Mpiemu people's insistence on creating new villages and refusal to respect the state-WWF map of Sangha basin settlement had important dimensions rooted in leaving a person behind and in *doli* as recollections of colonial interventions into their built environments. They countered the state-conservationist map of legal settlement within the middle Sangha with these new settlements and rejected this vision of "ecologically sustainable" relations between people and their environments, adhering instead to their own historical strategies of mobility, so well honed in the years of French *regroupement* and recruitment. This historical strategy of mobility had served them well in the earlier decades, when they sought to live in places of their own choosing, far from the onerous demands of the colonial administration. In the 1990s mobility and the creation of new settlements distanced Mpiemu from project restrictions, allowing them to carry on hunting, trapping, mining, and gathering and to frequent old villages and hunting camps in the forest that served as mnemonics for past people and events.

Conservation interventions transgressed older Mpiemu, Christian, and colonial notions of the person. Many Mpiemu living near the park and reserve protested the limits on activities and settlement within the forest, and they accused the WWF of privileging the well-being of forest animals over that of people. Mpiemu speakers had long used mobility as a strategy to take advantage of new opportunities, but also to escape threats and onerous demands. The notion that people were superior to animals because they lived in villages distinct from the forest appears to have stemmed in part from *regroupement*. It also echoed Christian distinctions between the "civilized" and the "wild."[105]

Mobile Mpiemu who persisted in creating new settlements in the reserve pleaded impoverishment, illness, and hunger. These claims were part of a discourse that Mpiemu have long strategically used to elicit outsiders' support against what they perceived as heavy-handed restrictions on their mobility or as encouragement of the Christian virtue of charity in the face of insufficient food, clothing, cigarettes, or other material goods. Mpiemu people, particularly those in Lindjombo who objected to restrictions on where they could live in the forest, shrewdly calculated that they had found in project personnel, as well as in me, sympathetic and useful listeners. They continually melded their discussions of past settlement with concerns about restrictions in the present, perhaps in hopes that policies would change, or that I would openly criticize these restrictive policies to project administrators.[106]

Clearly, Mpiemu tellers demonstrated *doli's* flexibility, strategically invoking it to mobilize sympathy from outsiders. But it is crucial to note that while people could use *doli* to serve their material interests, it was not exclusively an attempt to manipulate outsiders but rather just one aspect of a complex body of knowledge and way of seeing.

CONCLUSION

This chapter has demonstrated how the built environments of villages and *panjo,* ways of leaving a person behind, and social relations changed in engagements between Mpiemu and outsiders during the twentieth century. Colonizers, commercial agents, and missionaries initially perceived the Sangha basin and Mpiemu places and people in terms of what they lacked. But over time, they came to associate Mpiemu villages with depletion and, at times, loss. Mpiemu reinterpreted and transformed colonial discourses of dearth and loss and missionary discourses of lack and redemption. Different gender, generational, and regional groups lauded new forms of wealth and authority, lamented elders' depleted authority, and mourned the depopulation of villages and the disappearance of some sites like old villages and *panjo,* even as they used new sites and objects to recall their pasts. Mpiemu responses to the new state map of settlement in the 1990s drew from these accumulated conceptions of relations between human beings and their built environments. How Mpiemu people altered *doli* in response to new forms of agricultural production constitutes the focus of the following chapter.

5

FROM FIELDS OF MAIZE TO
FIELDS OF HUNGER

THE FIELD (*pembo*) was a place of food and cash-crop production,
but as a site of *doli,* it also reflected accumulated ways of seeing the
forest, knowledge about it, and practices in it. Embedded in fields
were also recollections of the twentieth-century past and of claims of truth
about that past. Over the twentieth century, colonial administrators, company agents, missionaries, and the postcolonial state sought to expand cultivated lands in the Sangha basin forest and in turn helped to alter Mpiemu
environmental and historical perceptions, agricultural practices, and labor-
allocation patterns. The most dramatic environmental changes resulted from
the large-scale clearing of forest for coffee, oil-palm, cacao, and food-crop
plantations. In the context of these interventions, many outsiders depicted
Sangha basin farmlands and Mpiemu agriculture as insufficient, lamenting
Africans' unwillingness to produce surpluses and squandered opportunities
to develop the Sangha basin's agricultural potential, and they sought to render
farming more productive. These agricultural changes had profound effects
upon Mpiemu person-environment relations and upon *doli.* Contemporary
responses to limits on cultivation by the CAR-WWF conservation project
illustrate how Mpiemu farmers used *doli* as a prism through which they interpreted environmental interventions as they seized upon and transformed
colonial discourse of poor agricultural productivity and lost opportunities
into claims of hunger (*nja*), deprivation, and loss.

FARMING AND *DOLI* IN THE
EARLY TWENTIETH CENTURY

Early twentieth-century European explorers wrote only brief accounts of
Mpiemu and Sangha basin agriculture, but these writings reveal how Africans
farmed and how Europeans perceived that farming in terms of insufficiency.

Sangha basin agricultural production was crucial to sustaining European exploration expeditions in the region. Alfred Fourneau, exploring the middle Sangha in 1891, found "vast plantations," though many were "invaded, devastated by bands of elephants and great monkeys." In some locations he found "abundant food," but elsewhere provisions were scarce.[1] His younger brother, Lieutenant Lucien Fourneau, who explored the Sangha River in 1898 and discovered that his troops' survival depended upon a trade in foods, noted, "The natives cultivate and harvest only what they need, [and] the hunt and war and commerce assure them of a surplus." Explorer Pierre de Sallmard wrote nothing about farming during his explorations of the upper Sangha and complained repeatedly of his inability to secure provisions from hostile Sangha populations. This concern for acquiring food but inattention to how Africans produced it hardly changed when explorers encountered Mpiemu speakers. In 1905 Muston of the Moll expedition seemed far more impressed by the forest's dark and undulating terrain than he was by the few scattered, "poor" fields of maize that he encountered outside the villages. These brief, diverse observations suggest that explorers interpreted the scarcity of foods in several ways: that local populations were unwilling to trade food; that they lacked an interest in producing an agricultural surplus; and that they simply could not produce enough. All of these interpretations centered on a kind of dearth—of goodwill, of initiative, of food itself.[2]

At the beginning of the twentieth century, maize was the primary crop grown in Mpiemu fields, as it was for neighboring Pomo, Kako, some Maka, and Gbaya speakers. Although maize (*mbusa* for fresh maize and *shogo* for dried) arrived on the African continent sometime after 1500, when Mpiemu acquired it is unknown. Like Kako speakers, Mpiemu insisted that their ancestors had always cultivated and eaten hard or flint maize. Maize may have come into Mpiemu hands from the north via Kako-Bera speakers. The Mpiemu term *mbusa* is the same as that of Kako-Bera speakers, who acquired it from Hausa-speaking, Islamicized peoples occupying northern Cameroon. But in contrast with many African farmers who reduced crop diversity when they began to grow maize, Mpiemu maize farmers planted a diverse mix of intercropped foods, including cassava, yams, banana trees, peanuts, sesame, sweet potatoes, sugarcane, assorted edible greens, and squashes. Women also planted banana trees near their houses. Though widely practiced elsewhere in equatorial Africa and among some other linguistic groups within the Sangha basin, cassava cultivation was taken up belatedly by Mpiemu cultivators. Farmed by people living near Bangui as early as 1840, cassava arrived in the present-day Central African Republic via Gabon. Observations from company agents and colonial administrators support Mpiemu contentions that in the early twentieth century they relied almost primarily on maize as a staple, growing little cassava.[3]

Tellers in the 1990s asserted that *doli* has always included knowledge of agricultural practices and access to land for cultivation. Unlike societies in the lower Sangha basin, these contemporary tellers claimed that there were no "masters of the land," who allocated lands for cultivation and ensured their continued fertility. *Nkang* did distribute lands among Mpiemu speakers, but many tellers contended that their parents and grandparents chose their own plots and methods of cultivation, drawing from elders' knowledge. In the late nineteenth and early twentieth centuries, farmers practiced swidden agriculture, as they still do in food plots. In addition to maize and other food crops, farmers often planted a few oil palms, which then propagated others through seed scattering. Mpiemu fields at this time probably were small (less than one hectare) and appear to have been scattered throughout various ecological zones in the forest. Farmers reportedly selected their cultivation sites to take advantage of seasonal and vegetational diversity within the forest (fig. 6). According to tellers of *doli*, cultivation took place year-round in fields situated to profit from good drainage during the rainy season (*shogi*) and from alluvial soils during the dry season (*shio*). Marking the changing seasons by tracking shifts in the band of stars known as *nkung* (the Milky Way), Mpiemu farmers cultivated their fields accordingly.[4]

The major rainy-season farming efforts focused on *pembo akwombo,* a field in previously uncut, uncultivated forest. Men cleared these fields during the dry season and fired them after the first rains to ensure that fire did not spread to contiguous forest. After burning the field, tellers contended, a man would strip bark from a *tumbi* tree, and when he went to wash in a nearby stream, he would gently toss the bark into the water and bury it in the stream's muddy bottom to ensure that the rains would fall. Women then planted their maize, peanuts, and other food crops once the rains fell predictably. They weeded and harvested these plots for no more than two or three years. Many farmers cultivated a second rainy-season field, *nkulomani,*[5] after clearing secondary growth from fallowed lands. *Nkuli* means power, force, or strength in Mpiemu, and one elderly farmer explained that Mpiemu cultivated this field because "our strength was sapped." Men, responsible for clearing the fields, expended their strength on cutting the first rainy-season field and thus preferred to clear regrowth in fallowed fields. Once the rains had ceased, they cultivated two dry-season fields, the first called *mompeng* ("child of a flood") on rich soils that retained rainy-season moisture at the beginning of the dry season. The second field, *nto,* was a small plot located next to permanent water sources where farmers planted their maize and peanuts in the late dry season.[6]

Fig. 6. Early twentieth-century agricultural calendar

Calendar Months	Mpiemu Seasons	Agricultural Activities
January	*Shio*: dry season (*wiyele*: waters dry up) *Ampekara* (cold season)	
February	*Shogi*: rainy season begins, marked by *tolishogi*, when *nkung*, the Milky Way, shifts eastward	Plant *nto* (second dry season field) Burn first rainy season field (*pembo akwombo*) after first rain
March		Plant *pembo akwombo* (first maize and peanuts, later sweet manioc)
April		Harvest maize from *nto* field
May	*Ntchimomugi* ("planting")	
June		
July	*Kungili* (brief dry period, marked by appearance of caterpillars)	Clear *nkulomani* (second rainy season field)
August		Plant *nkulomani*
September		
October		
November	Shio (dry season begins, marked by *tolishio*, when *nkung*, the Milky Way, shifts west)	Harvest peanuts from *nkulomani*
December	*Wiyele*: waters dry up *Ampekara* (cold season)	Men cut high forest (*akwombo*) for *pembo akwombo* (first rainy season field) Plant *mompeng* (first dry season field) Burn *nto* (dry season maize field)

After harvesting the maize and other food crops, farmers left the plots to fallow for several years, perhaps seven or eight, and during that time a tangle of forest vines would render the field nearly indistinguishable from the surrounding forest. Hence, the appearance of *buri* (fallow) could vary, from scrub to a luxuriant tangle of lianas. A fallow much longer than eight years was unlikely, given Sangha basin populations' mobility in the late nineteenth and early twentieth centuries. Mpiemu migration accounts and secondary literature on the upper Sangha and contiguous areas of the equatorial forest point to very high geographical mobility and the continuous division and resettlement of villages, perhaps because, as Émile Loyre argued in 1909, people experienced wars, deaths, and the exhaustion of arable lands. More recently, Georges Dupré has argued that the mobile Nzabi people (in the present-day Republic of Congo) found their productive activities and mobility shaped by the interactions of different kinds of forest exploitation. Swidden cultivation did not precipitate their movements; rather, the competing demands for productive hunting and farming grounds propelled people to establish new places of settlement in the fertile forests, which could sustain their demands for good soil and game. Although Dupré's analysis of Nzabi mobility provides a compelling model for Mpiemu mobility, it is divorced from a broader historical context. During the late nineteenth century, upper and middle Sangha people may have moved because of environmental constraints but also because they exploited game and other products to participate in equatorial Africa's developing trade.[7]

From *doli* tellers' recollections, the late nineteenth- and early twentieth-century agricultural calendar appears to have been well suited to seasonal and vegetational changes in the Sangha basin forest. Climatic conditions, it seems, could vary significantly each year. Through varied plot locations farmers diversified the ecological zones in which they cultivated and balanced their risks of poor harvests from unpredictable floods, unproductive soils, relatively arid weather, animal predations, and the vengeance of the spirits of the deceased. Because population densities may have been increasing during the late nineteenth century, swidden cultivation may have been less productive by the early twentieth century than it had been previously, for its success depends on relatively low population densities. But more archaeological and paleobotanical research beyond the Kadei River basin is necessary, and thus the changing impact of population density and environmental change on agricultural production and soil quality is unknown.[8]

Tellers of *doli* had much to recount about how fields, farming practices, and particular food crops constituted the Mpiemu person and social groups in the early twentieth century. Fields and cultivation practices seem to have been one means by which ethnic persons were generated. In the 1990s Mpiemu conceived of themselves as originally a forest and farming people, who displayed in the distant past as much ease at hunting, trapping, and gathering forest products as at cultivating small fields of maize and other foods. Tellers asserted that Mpiemu people originated in the coupling of the offspring of the forest and fallow deities, Ntchambe Mekwombo (the deity who created and commanded the forest and its people) and Ntchambe Meburi (the deity who taught people to cultivate the land). One tale explained the introduction of agriculture into the forest through the meeting of Mekwombo and

Meburi. Wandering through the forest in search of vines to fashion into fishing traps, the two seized upon the same vine and thus met. They developed a fast friendship, arranging a series of marriages among their children, who produced the Mpiemu as forest dwellers and farmers. Through the idiom of vines, domesticated to serve as fishing traps, the tale highlighted the linkages between two ecological zones and two ways of exploiting the forest environment. The tale also distinguished Mpiemu from other Sangha basin inhabitants, recounting the creation of a dual environmentally based sense of commonality, in which Mpiemu persons derived their living from exploiting the forest and from cultivating fields.[9]

If this tale was indeed an old one, this sense of being both forest people and farmers may have provided Mpiemu with the means of differentiating themselves from other linguistic groups at historical moments in the late nineteenth century, during volatile years of warfare, enslavement, and geographical mobility. To be sure, Mpiemu speakers shared with other Sangha basin peoples common ways of exploiting the forest for its game, other products, and arable soils. But they also betrayed significant differences from linguistic groups with whom they came into contact. Ngundi, Pande, Pomo, Kako, Ngombe, and Aka peoples all lived in the forests around Nola but appear to have made their living in the Sangha basin in diverse ways. Pomo cultivated fields, fished, and hunted, whereas according to early twentieth-century accounts, Ngundi and Pande fished avidly but hunted little. Aka and Ngombe made their living primarily by hunting and then trading bush meat and other forest products for agricultural products and weapons. It seems likely, then, that Mpiemu conceptions of themselves as forest and farming people in distinction from other Sangha basin peoples existed well before the 1990s, and that these notions predated the arrival of Europeans in the Sangha basin.[10]

At the same time food-crop choices and consumption patterns were also markers of the intensive cultural exchanges between diverse clans and ethnic groups within and beyond the Sangha basin in the late nineteenth century. The Mpiemu proverb "I know other people through food" (*Me singa nyoli kolo bideyo*) may not have been uttered in the late nineteenth century (though people in the 1990s understood this proverb as counsel that expressed values of the distant past and thus was part of *doli*). But linguistic evidence suggests that food exchanges were an important dimension of nineteenth-century Sangha basin interactions. Sweet potato (*Ipomoea batatas, dangari/danbebe*), for instance, probably came from Gbaya speakers, who in turn acquired it from Hausa merchants voyaging from present-day Nigeria. Several cassava varieties, including the bitter, high-yielding variety, *njetenabongo* (Lingala for "leaves of money"), and the sweet variety, *menjelepago,* came from Mpiemu contacts with riverine peoples farther south.[11]

The practices surrounding farming enshrined a gender division of labor and thus helped to constitute male and female persons. According to tellers of *doli* in the 1990s, this division of labor created by transmitting advice (*meleyo*) was premised on values of the distant past, particularly advice given young women who cultivated fields. Recall Foa Mabogolo, who like several women contended that female forebears became women by farming: "You plant cassava and maize. You will plant a field. Pineapple, bananas, you plant them. You will do your work." Although elderly women in the early twentieth century would not have encouraged young women to plant pineapples (reportedly first grown in the twentieth century) or large quantities of cassava, women's responsibilities for cultivating food—a commonality throughout Africa—was a practice enshrined in *doli* from the early twentieth century.[12]

Within the fields themselves maize seems to have accumulated a crucial social, cultural, and historical significance among Mpiemu. It was a substance whose influences radiated from the field to the house and *panjo* and into the forest. According to some tellers of *doli* in 1993, it mediated some processes that generated different kinds of persons, as well as different parts of the process of "leaving a person behind." First, it helped to mark a woman's passage into adulthood and the transfer of her productive and reproductive abilities to the lineage of her husband. As one of the "things of *doli*" (the distant and unchanging past), *kamishogo* (literally, maize food, a thick porridge of ground maize and peanuts, steamed in banana leaves) was the first dish a young woman prepared for her husband's father when she came to live in a house associated with his *panjo.* Making this time-consuming dish marked a transition for this woman, signaling that her husband's family now controlled her labor. In addition, maize could render ineffective the dangerous influences of a fetus, an uncontained being, on a man's hunting and trapping activities in the forest, though I was never able to find out why maize possessed this ability. Over the twentieth century Mpiemu came to perceive the maize preparation, *kamishogo,* as an object of *doli,* one that contained within it a past, idealized set of relations between men, women, and in-laws and between persons and not-yet-persons.[13]

FIELDS OF CIVILIZATION: ENCOUNTERS BETWEEN FARMERS AND FRENCH ADMINISTRATORS

After 1898, France's primary interest in the Sangha basin was to extract lucrative forest products to "develop" and "civilize" its possession and to supply burgeoning French industries with a steady supply of rubber, ivory, and other raw materials. The colonial administration cherished ambitions of developing the French Congo's agricultural potential by encouraging settler cultivation of high-value cash crops, such as coffee and cacao.[14] Although it would take nearly three decades for settlers to begin planting these crops in the middle and upper Sangha basin, France's ambitions to promote agricultural production there existed well before the 1930s.[15] But initially the colonial economy of the Sangha basin remained a resolutely extractive one. Like the explorers who preceded them, early colonial officials found agricultural production in the middle and upper Sangha to be paltry and "poor" because of apathetic farmers.[16] In 1911, however, with the Sangha under military occupation (a result of increased tensions with German Cameroon), one administrator observed:

> In the *circonscriptions* of M'Bimou and of the Sangha, a certain number of villages have achieved notable improvements; some have resettled near the roads, and it has been possible to shake off the natural apathy of some of these populations and to push them to undertake and to develop food cultivation and plantations. These results, although still modest, are worth signaling because in this part of our possessions, the proximity to the frontier [with German Cameroon] obliges us to undertake a very active surveillance, while remaining very circumspect at the same time.[17]

But this assessment was premature, because France lost control of much of the Sangha basin to Germany in 1911 and then sent in troops to recover that territory during the First World War. French military officials perceived Africans living in the basin forests as crucial to the war effort, because they were to supply porters and provisions to French troops. Sangha basin inhabitants did not willingly provide the requisitioned food or porters but rather fled into the forest to escape French demands. One astute administrator contended that no real dearth of agricultural foodstuffs existed in the upper Sangha; instead cultivators were staunchly refusing to supply colonial troops with food. Most farmers, he noted, kept their plots well hidden in the forest, distant from their villages, and used that food for their own needs. The scarcity, he asserted, existed only for the sharpshooters, workers, and porters who did not come from the region and thus had no access to these sources of food.[18]

A declining world market in rubber eventually forced the French to alter their economic strategies by focusing on the Sangha basin's agricultural sectors and precipitating successive waves of forest clearing. That shift to agriculture took place very slowly. Even as other African colonies abandoned rubber exploitation because it was so unprofitable, latex extraction continued in the upper and middle Sangha well into the 1920s and revived briefly in the 1940s, fueled by French and Allied demands during the Second World War. In the mid-1920s administrators began to encourage agricultural production by undertaking a campaign among African farmers to increase food cultivation and by granting concessions to European entrepreneurs, like André Santini, Morgando Lopes, and Ajax Saint Clair, to grow foodstuffs and coffee in Berbérati, Nola, and Lindjombo.[19] The campaign surveyed African farmers' plots during the planting and growing seasons and sought to ensure that they cultivated enough to supply the growing ranks of road workers, to "satisfy more easily than in the past . . . [African subjects'] fiscal obligations, and to ameliorate the material conditions of existence."[20] In forested zones farmers had to cultivate a minimum surface area of bananas, maize, and peanuts, based upon their villages' total populations. And from December to April, when villagers cleared 500 meters of brush around villages to reduce tsetse-breeding habitats, they had to put "the zones thus cleared . . . immediately into cultivation . . . [of] potatoes, peanuts, maize, and soy near the houses, and further away, cassava and bananas."[21] However, unlike elsewhere in Africa, French agricultural policies intervened in what people cultivated and the amount of land under cultivation, not into land-management practices.[22]

The most dramatic changes in the Sangha basin forest came with the colonial administration's encouragement of European companies, merchants, and Christian missionaries to increase cash-crop and food production in the 1930s. The French administration had grandiose visions of transforming Ubangi-Shari-Chad (of which the Sangha was now a part) into an agricultural powerhouse. This effort precipitated large-scale forest clearings and led at least one administrator to claim in 1935 that the subdivision of Nola had resolved its food shortages. "Cassava, maize, potatoes, etc.," he declared, "are abundant, sufficient to assure the nourishment of the population."[23] The administration also created an Agricultural Service in 1936, designed to increase food and cash crops by improving cultivation practices among European and African farmers. Exactly what the service accomplished in the Sangha is not revealed in the archives. Administrators still complained of a scarcity of foodstuffs, particularly in urban areas where nonagriculturalists congregated, and they encouraged schools to inculcate young students with the habit of doing manual labor in the fields.[24]

During the Second World War, French demands for foods increased, encouraging further forest clearing but also increasing administrative demands of and surveillance over Sangha basin farmers. Coffee, according to Governor-General Reste of the AEF in 1938, was the colony's future.[25]

Production levels were seriously hampered by a blight of tracheomycosis in excelsa plantations between 1937 and 1939. But after European planters replaced their excelsa trees with robusta coffee, the colonial administration kept coffee growing in their hands, so that it would not interfere with Africans' abilities to fulfill other responsibilities, including food production. The war increased demand for African laborers. In 1941 coffee plantation owners sought more coffee harvesters, and administrators, fearful of the effects on food production, cautioned them to temper their demands by recruiting women and children as workers and leaving men free to clear fields during the late dry season.[26]

By the late colonial period, administrators began to observe that many parts of the Haute-Sangha *circonscription* had been transformed into food-producing areas, and that food production had reached "sufficient" levels. In some locations, such as the Terre Kaka, large forest expanses around Lindjombo were cleared by African workers to create coffee plantations and plots for food crops. The problem with Sangha basin agriculture was no longer that farmers did not produce enough food. Rather, administrators feared that Sangha basin farmers were not producing the right kinds of foods, and that these farmers "lack[ed] . . . the nutritional materials indispensable for the normal growth of the [human] organism."[27] In the last years of colonial rule, as the French relaxed their control over agricultural production, harvests of most products declined, though coffee production remained relatively stable.[28]

In the eyes of colonial administrators, agriculture in the Mpiemu *terres* took on a character distinct from that of the rest of the Sangha basin. Administrators consistently depicted Mpiemu people as wholly nonagricultural, far more interested in hunting and trapping or, if necessary, harvesting rubber in the forest. Mpiemu flights from colonially designated villages and from colonial demands for labor prestations on roads continually stymied administrative efforts to increase agricultural production. Although administrators exulted in the increased production of foodstuffs elsewhere in the thirties, they repeatedly underscored Mpiemu subjects' inability to transform the forests into centers of agricultural production. Mpiemu cultivators, administrators claimed, refused to farm plots near the roads and to live and work in their home villages. As one administrator, trying to explain Mpiemu unwillingness to cultivate foods, put it in 1931: "The natives have a tendency to live in the forest, principally in the *canton* of Gobako. This is due in large part to hunting and especially to the harvesting of rubber."[29] Of course, administrators noted some variation among the various Mpiemu *terres;* some villages contained "well-maintained fields in abundance." Nevertheless, all four of the Mpiemu *terres* consistently underproduced cassava, the staple crop that colonial officials sought in greatest quantities.[30]

Similar perceptions of Mpiemu *terres* and people as inhospitable to agricultural transformation persisted during the Second World War, because sleeping sickness and renewed demands for rubber kept inhabitants occupied with other concerns. The year 1944 was, in administrators' estimations, a particularly bad year for food production in the entire Nola district and in the Mpiemu *terres*. According to the Catholic missionary Sintas, the subdivision head Choumara accused Mpiemu of not cultivating enough food, but he simultaneously prevented them from rectifying the production deficit. In 1943, Sintas claimed, several chiefs had petitioned Choumara to allow them to clear their fields during the months of May and June, but because of the French demands for rubber, men had to leave their villages during that time to harvest rubber in the forest. Moreover, Sintas contended, colonial administrators were simply blind to Mpiemu agricultural initiative. In 1944 Choumara and his agricultural monitor inspected several villages in the Mpiemu *terres* but never strayed far enough to locate cultivated plots nestled in the thick forest. Concluding that the required plantations did not exist, the agricultural monitor whipped and imprisoned several catechists and the chief of Zankandi. It is likely that Mpiemu farmers had in fact been using the strategy of hiding fields from administrators.[31]

Administrative perceptions of Mpiemu farmers, however, shifted by the 1950s, when agriculture took on a new significance in colonial discourse concerning the Mpiemu *terres*. At this time forest clearing and family coffee cultivation began in earnest. This shift in administrative perceptions probably came about partly because forced labor had ended, and thus colonial officials did not so actively survey agricultural production and extract labor from populations already strained by labor recruitment and sleeping sickness. No longer were Mpiemu subjects castigated for their paltry agricultural production. Now agriculture, especially the production of cash crops, was the key to rescuing Mpiemu people from extinction. Administrator Canal declared, "The question of commercial production in the long term ([through] family plantations of coffee and oil palm) is a vital question . . . for the Mbimou tribe, because this question is so important from a political standpoint: [it will ensure] the stabilization of this tribe in its *terres*."[32] But the introduction of family coffee farming came over the heated protests of European planters. Europeans claimed that African coffee growers would steal their coffee or would contaminate it with parasites. These fears probably reflected more about Europeans' racial anxieties as clamors for independence intensified and had less to do with the realities of growing coffee in the Sangha basin.

Although the big planters succeeded at a 1950 conference in Bangui in temporarily preventing African farmers from growing coffee, they did not do so for long. Just a few years later, Mpiemu farmers began planting coffee and cacao, eventually selling these cash crops to the Paysannat Café-Cacao. The *paysannat* itself constituted a kind of social engineering, a cooperative that encouraged Mpiemu peasant production of coffee and cacao so as to "stabilize" families who had lost their most productive members to sleeping sickness or plantation and mine work.[33]

To fulfill colonial aims to transform the middle and upper Sangha basin forest into an agricultural region, French colonial administrators thus sought to remove forest cover, to increase land under cultivation, to alter Mpiemu agricultural strategies and crop choices, and to define Mpiemu farming as unproductive and insufficient. Despite the fact that many Mpiemu were adept at evading colonial demands to produce food, they also reshaped *doli* as a body of knowledge about farming and as a way of perceiving and characterizing farming and forest spaces.

First, partly as a consequence of colonial demands, Mpiemu slowly abandoned maize as a primary staple and as a work process and material mediating relations between persons and nonpersons, men and women, wives and in-laws, and perhaps Mpiemu and non-Mpiemu. They substituted cassava as a staple. The most dramatic shift from maize to cassava appears to have occurred after 1950. Even as late as 1944, Sintas reported that Mpiemu farmers far preferred maize over cassava. Indeed, one Mpiemu catechist told him, "You see that if I only eat cassava, my stomach becomes large, but my hands have no power; but if I eat maize, I gain power throughout my entire body, and I can cut down trees, even big ones . . . [and] my body will not become exhausted."[34] In 1950 Canal expressed regret that the administration had abandoned its efforts to commercialize maize production; he estimated that the Nola district could easily have produced one hundred tons.[35] Moreover, though many Mpiemu recall that the proportion of cassava to maize in their diets shifted over the twentieth century, the tuber was not a staple in Lindjombo or in the Mpiemu *terres* until the late 1970s. Colonial administrators helped to instigate this shift from maize to cassava by requiring Mpiemu farmers to cultivate cassava to supply workers and guards employed by the administration and by commercial enterprises. They also encouraged increased cassava cultivation through their increased demands on Mpiemu labor. Cassava, particularly the high-yielding, fast-growing bitter variety, *njetenabongo,* required far less planting and weeding time than did maize, and elderly Mpiemu in the early 1990s contended that they had altered their crop mixes because cassava was simply "less work."[36]

Cultivating cassava and decreasing quantities of maize entailed a change from early twentieth-century farming practices to different ways of exploiting agricultural terrains and new rhythms of work. In the 1990s, during the late dry season (March), farmers finished clearing and burning their fields and planted maize, peanuts, and a variety of other squashes and greens. Once these small plants emerged, they planted a few cassava cultivars. After they harvested the maize and peanuts, they then planted dense stands of cassava, simultaneously beginning a second rainy-season field with maize, peanuts, and other foodstuffs in August. After at least six months had elapsed from planting, women could harvest the cassava as they needed it. In Lindjombo, because demands for cassava were so high in the middle Sangha logging villages, farmers would weed and replant their cassava plots a year after they had first cleared and cultivated them. Farther north in *metego Mpiemu* cassava plots of one hectare lasted up to two years. Farmers fallowed the plots for only another two to three years and then returned to clear them to cultivate again—a considerably shorter fallow period than previously practiced. These practices reflected other important changes from the early twentieth century. Crop diversity in plots of certain groups of farmers declined. In a comparison of fields cultivated by older and younger generations of farmers, the fields of younger people contained far more cassava and exhibited far less crop diversity than did fields of older people, particularly in Lindjombo.[37] Moreover, Mpiemu women ultimately abandoned cultivating *nto,* the dry-season maize field located near permanent sources of water, because they contended that they had too much other work to do.[38]

This shift from maize to cassava had important consequences for the ways in which Mpiemu imagined their relations to fields, to food, to one another, and to the past. In the 1990s, though maize had been displaced as a staple, it still constituted a medium through which Mpiemu organized and recollected the past. Farmers usually grew it to eat fresh or to distill into alcohol (*menyogi*).[39] But when women prepared and served it as *kamishogo* (the steamed mixture of ground maize and peanuts), they invoked an idealized social hierarchy of the distant past, in which young men paid homage to their elders by using their wives' labor to prepare food. Alouba Clotere, for instance, insisted that a newly married women used to make it for her father-in-law and husband, particularly as the first meal that she cooked in her mother-in-law's kitchen, but, he explained with great sadness, most women refused to do it anymore. A few people on occasion prepared the dish, and when I visited Clotere and his family in Salo, he once escorted me to one house in his quarter to make sure that I sampled it. A discussion with Satuba Rose and her sisters Claudette and Caroline about *kamishogo* and working for in-laws prompted them to assert with some disdain: "Now young girls have abandoned the things of *doli*. They don't work for their in-laws, and they don't make that kind of food." But for one younger man, maize, though a staple associated with the past, had less nostalgic associations. Dogassie Salamon observed: "A long time ago, people saw great sorrow, because they only had fields of maize. Maize doesn't fill your stomach. We weren't born during the time of maize." Nevertheless, for many older people maize in the form of *kamishogo* became a nostalgic repast, a meal of elder males' lost authority over younger generations, even as it ostensibly continued to be a substance mediating relations between persons and non-persons and between gender, generational, kin, and ethnic groups.[40]

The shift from maize to cassava cultivation also altered how Mpiemu persons chose to define themselves in relation to other ethnic groups. Mpiemu in Lindjombo and Kwapeli sought out different ways of defining themselves, drawing, it seems, from the older notions of Mpiemu as a farming people (though in other contexts they also considered themselves forest people), as well as from colonial discourses on differences between ethnic groups based on their propensities for agricultural production. In Kwapeli markers of ethnic difference centered upon food varieties that farmers called "Mpiemu food" (*bideyo Mpiemu*)—maize and a wide variety of sweet cassavas—around which people organized and recollected contacts with past people, including Mpiemu ancestors and neighboring groups with whom they had exchanged foods. In Lindjombo, however, Mpiemu women articulated ethnic distinctions by emphasizing that they cultivated larger fields. Dinoramibali Martine, an older Mpiemu woman in Lindjombo, noted once that although she cultivated a field twice a year, some people did not "because they aren't Mpiemu. They don't like to work."[41] Indeed, the mean field size among Mpiemu farmers (2,173 square meters) was significantly larger than that of non-Mpiemu farmers (1,349 square meters).[42] Field sizes had increased over the past two decades, as women sought to earn income by selling bitter cassava in the logging towns of Bela and Libongo, and later as they sought to bolster household earnings when various European enterprises ceased operation.[43] Colonial interventions into agriculture thus affected Mpiemu farmers' food-crop choices, cultivation, and consumption patterns by altering labor allocation and by introducing a new staple, cassava. It was only after independence, however, with the expansion of markets for cultivated foods, that many farmers in Lindjombo began producing greater quantities of food. In this context, Mpiemu farmers did not appropriate a notion of insufficiency or dearth from these interventions but rather participated in these wider changes. Only when their efforts to participate in the changes were stymied did they respond with laments for the prosperous farming of the past and its present loss.

CONCESSIONS AND COFFEE

European commercial cultivation expanded dramatically during the twentieth century, transforming the Sangha basin forest, Mpiemu conceptions of their environmental relations, and *doli* as a way of perceiving the changing forest and farms and as knowledge of the past. Sources illuminating what European planters thought of their accomplishments in the middle and upper Sangha have been lost, so the following section documents the expansion of commercial agriculture in the middle and upper Sangha basin and traces its influence on Mpiemu conceptions of the relations between people and their environment and on *doli*.

Nearly three decades passed before European commercial cultivation took root in the middle and upper Sangha basin, primarily because the colonial economy was premised on extracting forest products such as rubber, ivory, and animal skins. Of greatest interest to these companies, then, were the populations of elephants, the rubber-producing trees, the unexploited but highly valued timber species, and nontimber forest products such as copal. Concessionary company agents wrote more about agriculture in upper and middle Sangha villages than did early colonial administrators but similarly claimed that production was "rudimentary," consisting of small plots of maize, cassava, and bananas located close to villages.[44]

During the first decade of concessionary companies, company farming was minimal and in many cases unsuccessful. The Compagnie des Produits de la Sangha-Lipa-Ouesso, for instance, was required in its contracts with France to replace each ton of collected rubber with fifty new rubber trees, but it never did so. The Compagnie de la N'Goko-Sangha took some tentative steps toward establishing rubber plantations in Bomassa, Salo, Ouesso, and N'Gali, planting thirty ares, fifteen ares, thirty ares, and eleven hectares, respectively. But the plantations in Bomassa, Salo, and Ouesso were "completely invaded by the bush and definitively abandoned" by 1911. Agricultural efforts remained on a very small scale. The Compagnie Forestière de la Sangha-Oubangui, which assumed control of several Sangha basin concessions in 1911, did create small "gardens" (ranging between one and seven hectares) of cassava to sustain workers at the Bayanga, Manvey, Banja, and Gombaco trading stations. Very little agricultural activity took place for the next decade. CFSO and other agents remained preoccupied first with France's loss of some territories in the middle and upper Sangha in 1911 and then with recouping their losses after the pillaging and burning of company properties in the basin following the First World War.[45]

That situation changed in the 1920s, however, as the French administration asserted its authority over its basin possessions, as rubber exploitation became increasingly unprofitable for CFSO and other major commercial agents, and as the number of rubber-producing trees diminished. Merchants and concessionaires began to supplement their rubber revenues with cash and food crops. In 1926 the rubber merchant André Santini had requested numerous concessions in Berbérati to grow food and industrial products, including cassava and castor-oil plants. Morgando Lopes requested a land concession to grow foods in Nola, and Ajax Saint Clair, in the same year, began growing coffee, rice, and cassava in Carnot. Similarly, CFSO sought to obtain control of a Berbérati plantation to grow cassava.[46]

Coffee, however, was the primary cash crop that transformed the middle and upper Sangha forests and populations, and it was the European commercial agents and concessionaires who effected this change. Observing that various species of coffee grew wild in the forests along the banks of the Kadei and Sangha Rivers, some merchants and administrators began to harvest it for their own profit. In 1923, for instance, Le Houx, the chief of the Nola subdivision, organized Mpiemu women to collect wild coffee in the forests near the Cameroonian border and proposed to create some plantations to grow the crop. By 1927 merchants were producing some four tons yearly of wild robusta (*Coffea canephora*), excelsa, and arabica. It did not take long, though, for them to search for ways of cultivating coffee. In 1931 several European landholders formed the Syndicat des Planteurs de Café de la Haute-Sangha, a coffee planters' association authorized by the governor-general of Middle Congo, and began to plant coffee trees and to explore ways of transporting the beans to the African coast. By 1934 the planter Santini employed a modest group of forty-two coffee workers to cultivate some 30 hectares of coffee in Lindjombo, and the Portuguese merchant Lopes followed suit, planting some 136 hectares of coffee. Within two years another merchant, Duret, began to grow 11 hectares of coffee in Nola. But by far the biggest agricultural producer in the region was CFSO, which by 1935 devoted 527½ hectares to the cultivation of arabica, robusta, niaouli, and excelsa coffees, 13 hectares to oil palm, and 31 hectares to cacao. Over the following decades acreage of coffee and other products increased. In 1950, for instance, Lopes was cultivating coffee on some 150 of the 225 hectares in his concession, and CFSO was growing coffee, oil palm, and cacao on 640 of its 2,200 hectares. Santini and Lopes also cleared forest to cultivate cacao and oil palm.[47]

Coffee precipitated further agricultural cultivation and thus more forest clearing. Because the CFSO, Santini, and Lopes plantations attracted relatively large concentrations of workers and their families, existing food production in the middle and upper Sangha did not suffice to feed everyone. The colonial administration thus sought to enforce the governor-general of French Equatorial Africa's decree requiring all employers to cultivate cassava plantations at their own cost and with their own workers. Workers' families also farmed their own plots on the edges of the coffee fields.[48]

Coffee production continued well into the postcolonial period. In the late 1960s another French planter, Kuluscu, purchased the Lopes and Santini concessions, consolidating the coffee holdings. In the early 1970s he sold the plantation to Emona Café, a Yugoslav company closely affiliated with the Slovenia Bois logging company based some thirty kilometers north in Bayanga. Although Kuluscu reportedly introduced mechanization to coffee production, Emona Café instigated some of the most dramatic environmental changes, expanding coffee acreage into the nearby forest and plowing over several coffee fields to flatten the undulating terrain. This effort to refashion the forest into flat, broad coffee fields effectively removed rich topsoil and, according to two former employees, rendered the fields less productive.[49] Emona Café continued its operations until 1981, when, bankrupt, it divided its holdings among fifteen long-standing male employees. These fifteen men subdivided their holdings, primarily because they did not control enough labor to cultivate the acreage they had received from the company. In-laws, friends, and some wives acquired coffee parcels. For the next nine years, coffee remained a primary means of earning income for men who acquired coffee parcels, as they pocketed well over $1,000 after each harvest.[50] The Central African Republic's economic decline in 1990 hit coffee growers hard. CAISTAB, the Central African marketing board responsible for purchasing coffee, went bankrupt and did not purchase growers' coffee in 1990, 1991, and 1992. The 1990 harvest decayed in abandoned storehouses for the next three years, until independent traders finally purchased it at drastically reduced prices. Coffee production temporarily resumed in 1993–94, when farmers anticipated that the incoming president, Ange-Félix Patassé, would revitalize coffee production.[51]

In Salo coffee production took a different turn in the postcolonial period. CFSO continued its operations into the 1970s but ultimately departed in the middle of that decade. Coffee and oil-palm cultivation continued fitfully, but eventually the coffee trees died. Though the west bank of the Salo still boasts a sizable plot of oil-palm trees, not a trace of the coffee plantations remains other than the vast cleared fields. Cassava farmers (mostly women) have since taken over the cleared lands on the outskirts of Salo, and the CFSO compound has been transformed into a sawmill for the French-owned logging company, SESAM Bois.

Coffee cultivation represented a striking departure from the ways in which Mpiemu perceived environmental exploitation. Swidden agriculture had depended upon an incremental, temporary clearing of the forest; careful calculations about sites, rainfall, and pests; and relations between husbands, wives, pregnancies, and ancestral spirits who could affect the fertility of a field. But with the commercial production of coffee, decisions about how, where, and when to plant, prune, combat pests, and harvest were made by plantation owners and a few subordinates, not individual farmers. It was based upon, as Dove and Kammen observe, "getting the technology 'right'"— not on the human relations that were embedded in fields and influenced their fertility.[52] Commercial agriculture also promoted substantial forest clearing around Lindjombo and Salo.

This crucial change in the Sangha basin forest cover, however, built upon an older human-centered vision of the forest, which people perceived in terms of the activities they had performed or could perform there. Plantations acquired seedlings by sending workers to forage in the forest, thus relying on older livelihood practices. But in a broader way, many Mpiemu and other Sangha basin people associated spaces cleared of forest tangle with production that linked them to broader networks of economic and political power, as the tale of Ntchambe Mekwombo, Ntchambe Meburi, and Ntchambe Bilon illustrated vividly.[53]

Similarly, cleared coffee fields came to be invoked as sites of recollection, inextricably bound up in nostalgic *doli* narratives of past persons and kin groups. Even in Lindjombo, where a generation of Mpiemu men had abandoned the rubber collecting of their fathers and moved south to work for plantation owners, these former employees and their children proudly claimed that they had constructed the plantations' facilities. Surveying the coffee fields from the veranda of her son's house one afternoon, the elderly Yongo Oromain asserted with pride, "My husband started this village." Amions Anaclet recalled passing one of the buildings for coffee processing with his father, who also observed proudly, "It was your grandfather who built that."[54]

Later these former workers used their own bodily strength (drawn from their fat, or *mbulo*) to nurture the "fatty" soils and coffee trees once Emona Café had ceased its operations. Good soils, according to many farmers, were fatty, rich ones that made high crop production possible. Some of that fattiness seemed to be simply a characteristic of the soil, but human labor, which depended on bodily fat, brought those soils to fruition. This fat of human bodies and the soil bound the two materially, and tellers of *doli* elucidated this connection through narratives of the past people from whom they had acquired the fields. Amions Anaclet, for instance, extolled the fatty soils of the coffee field that he had recently inherited from his father, and he viewed the field as a site of remembrance for his father, and ultimately himself. As he posed for a photograph by his ripening coffee, he observed that the picture would be a "great souvenir" that he would show to his children and grandchildren while explaining: "This is the coffee field that my father cultivated. When he died, he put it in my hands." These coffee fields, then, encompassed within them new ways of leaving a person behind, providing younger generations with a means of making a living (and thus leaving more persons behind) and incorporating the material remembrances of past people.[55]

But in the context of the economic decline in the 1990s, some Mpiemu in Lindjombo expressed ambivalence over the environmental changes that forest clearing and coffee cultivation had wrought, and they interwove their environmental perceptions with *doli* narratives of degraded vegetation and lost prosperity. Several farmers commented on the invasion of the aging coffee fields by an exotic species, *Ageratum conyzoides,* calling it a variety of names: *boganda* (after the leader of the CAR's independence movement), *bokassa* (after the self-crowned emperor), and *dacko* (after the deposed French-backed dictator who still had political aspirations). One man, typical of other male cultivators, associated the weed with an expanding European-run commerce linking Salo and Lindjombo and Ubangi-Shari's major towns. As we were walking through the old Santini coffee fields, he grabbed a stalk of the weed and muttered: "We don't know how this leaf got here. . . . Long ago, it wasn't here. Perhaps it came from Berbérati on the wheels of trucks, we don't know, maybe around 1956 or '57. It's a nasty plant, and it can clog up everything. It completely ruins fields. . . . When a little gets into the soil, it will take over the entire place." Another contended: "That plant came from the savannas, and it came here. And there's no more grass here. [That plant] ruined our fields, overran the grass. You can see it in the bush now." On the other hand, some women argued that the weed was not such an annoyance. After all, its growth indicated that the soils were fertile, and it had medicinal properties; after boiling it, people applied it to their skin to get rid of worms.[56]

This gendered vision of an invasive exotic, a by-product of Lindjombo's clearing and regrowth and of connections with the cleared spaces of the savannas, seemed to reflect concerns about a changing environment. But it also spoke to postcolonial politics in the CAR and the different effects that the departure of European plantation owners had on men and women. The associations of this weed with a revered but short-lived figure of the independence movement (Boganda) and two rapacious dictators supported by France (Bokassa and Dacko) are tantalizing. They suggest the promise of an independent CAR shattered by France's inability to relinquish control (many Central Africans believe that the French arranged Boganda's death) and by Dacko's and Bokassa's excessive ambitions. Men's relentlessly negative depiction of this invasive tangle of weeds in their aging coffee fields illustrates not just that it was a nuisance that sapped the soil of its nutrients. It also seems to have sparked in male farmers an assessment of their present lost prosperity, in the aftermath of European planters' departure, when many men lost their access to salaries and consumer goods and were forced to rely on forest exploitation, such as trapping and fishing.[57]

Women's more equivocal assessment may have reflected different concerns. They had certainly benefited from their husbands' access to wages and consumer goods, and some regretted the departure of the plantation owners. As the elderly Yongo Oromain bitterly told me, "M. Santini and his wife, they did a lot of work here. But they are dead. . . . My husband is dead. This village is ruined. Does anyone remain?"[58] But younger generations of women, who were the primary cultivators of food, continued to earn cash even after the departure of Emona Café. Dividing their time between their husband's coffee fields and their own fields, these women cultivated cassava, maize, and peanuts for sale in logging villages along the Sangha River. With the decline of coffee in the late 1980s and early 1990s, food cultivation and distilling remained among the few viable sources of income, and women frequently controlled the income from them. Indeed, when coffee cultivation ceased altogether in 1990, many women gained access to the large fields in which coffee trees had died and were able to expand the areas under food cultivation, thus earning even more income from the sale of food and alcohol. Disputes between married women and men erupted over the control of money generated from cassava, other foods, and alcohol, and they seem to have occurred more frequently between younger couples. It is not surprising that women viewed the spread of the weedy exotic *A. conyzoides* in a more favorable light. Emerging in many of the fields that had once grown coffee, this invasive species was easy to clear and thus did not require men's labor, as forest clearings had earlier in the century. Women thus enjoyed additional income and autonomy within their marriages.[59]

Doli as a way of seeing and as a body of knowledge changed in myriad ways through the influences of commercial agriculture, encouraging an increased value on cleared, humanized spaces and creating new places in which people could recollect past persons and events. But for some social groups these changes were occasioned by a sense of loss: of new opportunities after the departure of the Europeans, of proper behaviors and foods (like *kamishogo*) associated with a distant past.

CULTIVATING CHRISTIANS

Catholic and Baptist missionaries helped to transform the upper and middle Sangha forest into an agricultural landscape, but more important, they disseminated a new language linking cultivation and their endeavors to spread Christianity throughout the Sangha basin. During the later years of colonial rule, Mpiemu found in missionaries a sympathetic audience for their grievances, often articulated in terms of hunger, concerning onerous colonial demands for agricultural labor. But they also discovered in missionaries' language a rich vocabulary for expressing new notions about Christianized persons and *doli,* which they would later invoke in their engagements with state and World Wildlife Fund conservationists.

Missionary agriculture was part of a broader endeavor to bring a Christian civilization to the Sangha basin, and Catholics and Baptists alike referred to their religious aims in striking agricultural terms. The Capuchins, for instance, referred to the Sangha basin as "a field worked and planted."[60] Swedish Baptists also perceived their mission to the upper and middle Sangha in distinctly agricultural terms, in which they would clear the forest to create a fruitful, ordered landscape and peoples. One Swedish missionary wrote of the Örebromission's earliest activities in the "Kongofält," or "Congo field":

> It is no easy task to build a missionary compound in the midst of the wilderness. The forest had to be cleared, timber had to be sawed, and furthermore, the work had to be done with the help of completely untrained natives who were not used to any kind of organized work. The patience and endurance of the missionaries were really put to the test. But finally one day all the houses are up, and the gardens and plantations are in place, and it all begins to look like a pleasant oasis in a vast desert, an eloquent symbol for the role that the missionary endeavor wants to play for the oppressed peoples of Africa.[61]

Certainly this writer's description of the "Congo field" as a "pleasant oasis in a vast desert" seems odd, given that he was working in the equatorial rain forest. But the language of cultivation was compelling. He continued, "Our belief and trust made us sow our blessed seed, convinced that God would bring us a harvest."[62] The cultivation and harvest of Christians, Catholic or

Baptist, were not easy, hampered by sleeping sickness, fierce competition from rival denominations, "witch doctors," and insufficient personnel and funds.

In more concrete ways Swedish Baptist and French Capuchin and Spiritan farming activities were barely distinguishable from those of CFSO and the plantations of Santini and Lopes. The Spiritan, Capuchin, and Baptist missions all engaged in extensive forest clearing and cultivation of cash and food crops, grown to support mission personnel and to subsidize their activities. By 1932 the Spiritans already had engaged their converts to cultivate cassava, maize, peanuts, sweet potatoes, and bananas at the Berbérati mission, though the coffee that they had planted was ailing. They also raised poultry, cattle, and other animals. The Capuchins continued these agricultural efforts, incorporating farming into the curriculum of mission-school students. In 1929 Baptist missionaries had begun to plant coffee in Bilolo and in catechist posts, and by 1935 the mission received a twenty-hectare concession in Bilolo, hiring some thirty-three workers to cultivate its plots of coffee, potatoes, peanuts, bananas, cassava, and other foodstuffs. Baptist mission agricultural activities in Bilolo, however, ceased when the Örebro-mission departed in 1940 and recommenced their activities in Nola. But neither Catholic nor Baptist mission records mention agricultural activities after the 1940s, instead focusing almost exclusively on constructing additional buildings for schools, workshops, and dispensaries. The missions scaled back cultivation after independence; most of the Swedes left permanently in 1963, and although the Berbérati Catholic mission remained, its gardens in the early 1990s accounted for a fraction of what they had produced earlier in the century.[63]

That missionaries, commercial enterprises, and colonial administrations engaged in similar activities is not so surprising, for they all faced significant financial constraints in achieving their respective aims. But they also shared agricultural labor, products, and knowledge. In 1928, for instance, CFSO sent twenty-one of its male workers to uproot, soak, and dry the Berbérati Catholic mission's cassava. Spiritan and Capuchin missionaries sent out and received goats, ducks, bananas, various oils, and other foods from European planters, administrators, their wives, and merchants; and accompanying these exchanges, there seems to have been a considerable traffic in information about farming in the Sangha.[64]

Missionaries were somewhat more equivocal than other Europeans in their perceptions of Mpiemu and Sangha basin agriculture. Like colonial administrators, many missionaries perceived the agricultural potential of the upper and middle Sangha to be promising but at times found food production to be lacking. One Spiritan priest, for instance, contended that the M'Bimou region, and particularly Bilolo, experienced famine in 1933, the result of an unpredictable and unforgiving climate. Both Baptist and Catholic missionaries distributed food to hungry people (which also attracted followers), and some Catholics encouraged Mpiemu farmers to expand their cultivation of foods. Later, a Capuchin observer enthusiastically celebrated the middle and upper Sangha's rich soils and wealth of such foods as cassava, maize, and palm oil, in contrast to administrators who complained of a scarcity of such foods. But like some administrators, this witness also contended that "the natives in general are totally disinterested" in cultivating fruit trees, partly because their villages were so mobile but also because they lacked a "spirit" of obedience to the colonial administration.[65]

But in 1944, in contrast to simultaneous administrative claims of deficient farming in Mpiemu *terres,* Sintas composed a luminous, romanticized description of a highly domesticated agricultural landscape:

> The Sunday evening of October 20, I went down to the chapel of Njendi after the confirmation ceremony given for the Djancandi chapel. The fires of the setting sun gave a vivid, dazzling brightness to the magical colors of this corner of Africa: the red earth and the tender greens or browns of the palms, bananas, coffee trees, and cacao trees, the dark blue outlines of the forest, and the mellow cloud of mist that outlined the Banja valley, and the glowing sky; everything enchanted the hundreds of our Christians and catechumens who were overjoyed at our visit. The bananas, taro, peanuts, eggs, chickens, also a sheep from the *terre* chief, all bore witness to the sincerity of their welcome.[66]

Perhaps it was the warm welcome and the confirmation of a new chapel in this "field" of Catholic missionization that colored Sintas's vivid description. At other times he was far from consistent in his depictions of the Mpiemu agricultural landscape and farmers. He and his subordinates disparaged Mpiemu farming knowledge as "primitive," writing that women and children "always return [from the fields] with full hands; though they don't know how to plant, they know very well how to harvest in times of necessity by beating a tree to harvest its fruit."[67] In the subsequent decade one missionary reported to one of his superiors that the agricultural activities of inhabitants of the Nola region were too productive, and thus they lacked sufficient humility to make them receptive to Catholic missionaries' efforts. "The richness of the land, especially in coffee," one noted, "allows for a more intelligent, more evolved population, and thus makes them even more materialistic and more proud."[68]

Mpiemu Christian men and women also invoked a discourse of deficiency, though it was not of their willingness to work or of their agricultural knowledge, but rather of food. In missionaries Mpiemu found a receptive audience for their complaints about French administrative demands, and they voiced their grievances in terms of hunger. In October 1933, for instance, workers on the North-South Road "all complain[ed] . . . of lack of food and of never having received a visit from any administration employee."[69] In 1944 Mpiemu farmers lamented to Mgr Sintas that they were required to cultivate plantations not only to supply normal administrative needs but also to provision the hospital in Bilolo and members of the Health Service, sharpshooters, and agricultural inspectors. "More than one," Sintas sardonically observed, "complains of dying of hunger in this paradise of the sleeping sick, although in their village they have so many resources: maize, potatoes, oranges, bananas, etc."[70] These claims of hunger may have referred more to a sense of deprivation that Mpiemu felt in the face of excessive administrative demands, rather than an actual dearth of food.

Missionaries were less influential in terms of how or what Mpiemu produced than about how they conceived of their relations with their fields and *doli*. Missionaries' use of agricultural idioms for the cultivation and harvest of Christian souls profoundly influenced Mpiemu conceptions of persons and their relations to cleared, farmed lands. These notions fit well into an older cultural logic that Mpiemu marshaled to describe their origins as farming and forest people, the descendants of Ntchambe Meburi and Ntchambe Mekwombo. Evidence of this appropriation appeared in contemporary sermons, songs, and discussions among Christians. Images of clearing and cultivating, for instance, pervaded songs at various church celebrations. Among these songs were the catchy women's chants at the weekly Catholic and Baptist *ndoye,* the Sango term for "gift," connoting a lively celebration of a member's contributions to a church, in which participants brought food and firewood for the honoree and danced and sang to her in exchange for coffee and a small snack. One of the most popular of the chants was a song in Sango about farming:

> You grab, you grab [brush]
> You cut, you cut, you throw [the brush away],
> You turn around, you stop.
> You clear a field, Mother,
> You tighten your belt.

The song lauded the resolve, hard work, and sacrifice necessary to clear a field, qualities evoking the ideals of Catholics and Baptists alike.[71]

Christian notions of agriculture, cleared forest, and good and evil persons became embedded in *doli* narratives about the distant and more recent past. In 1993 the Mpiemu catechist at the Lindjombo Catholic mission read the parable of the sower (Matthew 13:1–23), concerning the fate of seeds sowed on footpaths, rocky ground, and good soil. The parable is usually interpreted to explain the ways in which different people—the uncomprehending listener, the person seduced by material wealth, the staunchly faithful convert—understand the Word when they hear it. But in his sermon the catechist elaborated an alternative interpretation:

> When the rain falls, before it evaporates, it softens the soil. And we receive food to eat. Like the evaporating rain, before Jesus returned, he softened the hearts of people. Abraham was our ancestor, long ago, when people prayed to trees and animals. But Abraham said, "No, God made all of this." In this family we follow his lead. . . . Jesus came here not to kill with guns, spears, or poison. He softened our hearts like the rain softens the soil. . . . You can toss sesame seeds in fields. Some seeds fall on the road and dry out. Some fall onto drying floors and sprout, but they don't grow. Some fall on soil, on the fields that you have cultivated well. You harvest them and put them into a granary. People need to follow God's lead. . . . Some people come here to the mission to hear the pretty songs, to look at other people. They are the ones who put the seeds on the road. There are those who think all the time about clothes and money. They use evil medicines to get [these goods] . . . or to hurt other people. [*He clucked his tongue as he said this.*] Jesus came to this soil to soften our hearts, to show us the road of God's work.

The catechist here elucidated a historical vision, first identifying the origins of Lindjombo Catholics in Abraham, their ancestor who rejected the worship of "trees and animals." Rather than equating people with rocky, thistle-choked, or rich soils, as conventional interpretations did, the catechist contended that people were different kinds of farmers, who sowed seeds in diverse soils (roads, drying floors, and rich soils). Some of these farmers obsessed about clothes and money, drank excessively, or used "evil medicines" for their own gain. Jesus, like the rain, would soften people's hearts, allowing them to do good deeds and turning them away from sowing their deeds in barren places, from investing their efforts in killing others or reaping material wealth. In so doing, though, the catechist and others who echoed him espoused a notion of the person that ran counter to both the notions of the person advanced by companies and older Mpiemu notions of the person. Rejecting people with (active) *alembo* (occult powers) and criticizing those who obsessed about material wealth, they eschewed conceptions of both powerful persons and mobile, independent laborers, who displayed their wealth in the form of Western consumer goods.[72]

Rejecting their origins as worshipers of "trees and animals" and practitioners of occult powers, Mpiemu Christians (as well as Christians of other ethnic groups) came to see the cultivated, productive plots cleared from the forest as concrete means of sustaining their churches' incomes and activities and as material evidence of God's concern.[73] Field work, according to one Mpiemu woman, was something divinely ordained: "God said . . . you work in the fields, and you will eat. You plant a lot and the field will produce a lot."[74] Though some Baptists and Catholics rejected older practices and beliefs associated with *doli,* the distant knowledge of the past, they also conflated "good Christian behavior" with a prosperous, recent past, associated with the big coffee plantations.[75] When I discussed a Sunday meeting at the Baptist mission in which the pastor publicly scolded the youth choir for being unprepared, one elderly man invoked *doli,* observing, "Before, things weren't as they are now. During the time of the white people, everyone—men, women and children—all worked. . . . Children, Beka [Aka pygmies], they were all paid. But now, there is too much drinking." But wasn't there alcohol before? I asked. "There was. You could find whiskey, cognac, and Cointreau here all the time. When people ran out in Berbérati and Nola, they would [come to Lindjombo to] buy here. But people worked and there was money. On weekends, the white man running the place would give people money so that they could go to Salo and Bilolo to buy a wife if they were single."[76]

In contrasting present youthful negligence and excessive drinking with past plantation work, proper behavior, and coffee *patrons'* magnanimity, this elderly man invoked a compelling discourse of loss, tempered by the possibility of redemption through future work. The cleared, cultivated spaces of the plantation not only provided the means for workers to gain access to consumer goods and to wives who enabled them to leave a person behind. Working on these coffee plantations also inculcated good behavior, the very behavior he saw lacking among church members now. The departure of the European plantation owners and the loss of coffee had precipitated not only significant economic problems but moral ones as well. And thus people waited for another opportunity for salvation.

AGRICULTURE IN THE POSTCOLONIAL CENTRAL AFRICAN REPUBLIC

Following the Central African Republic's independence, commercial coffee and other cash-crop fields remained a significant feature of the Sangha basin's topography and regional economy. Essentially, the state continued earlier colonial policies concerning agriculture, promoting cash-crop production, especially of coffee and tobacco, to earn export revenues. This agricultural policy was part of a broader economic aim, in which economic growth was premised on "foreign trade, foreign investment, and a . . . [steady] international demand for Central African exports."[77] But in the late 1980s and early 1990s, with this agricultural strategy failing, the state also adopted conservationist measures in the Sangha basin that affected local agricultural practices. Farmers whom I encountered interpreted and responded to these changes through a prism of *doli*.

Successive state regimes between 1960 and 1994 continued earlier colonial policies of expanding commercial agricultural production, though these efforts were part of development strategies that changed somewhat over time. From 1960 to 1965 President David Dacko allowed expatriate planters to remain in the newly independent Central African Republic but promoted cash-crop production under the rubric of inculcating a *"conscience nationale."* But despite Dacko's rhetoric about national development, this policy was designed, as one commentator put it, primarily to enrich administrators, ministers, and their subordinates.[78]

Following Dacko's overthrow, Opération Bokassa nationalized some commercial plantations to spur agricultural modernization and development. But in the Sangha basin this initiative left coffee cultivation in the hands of the big European commercial plantations for another decade and in those of individual coffee farmers, who sold their coffee to cooperatives controlled by foreign interests.[79] Both Dacko's and Bokassa's efforts fit well into the orthodoxy propounded by development experts in the 1960s and 1970s and adopted by newly independent African countries. They sought to promote economic "takeoff," leveraging the agricultural sector to fuel the development and expansion of other economic sectors.[80] Neither Dacko's nor Bokassa's efforts to use coffee as a springboard for development succeeded in the long run.

After 1981 André Kolingba continued earlier policies of promoting coffee production to earn much-needed revenues. Under the influence of French advisers, Kolingba developed a five-year plan for 1986–90 containing some of the very same assumptions that had animated previous development efforts. As Thomas O'Toole observed of Kolingba's regime,

> One theme remained constant. The leaders of Central Africa, along with their French and other foreign advisers, continued to seek economic development through a centrally controlled "productionist" approach without any attempt to consult with the agriculturalists who are the basic producers in this overwhelmingly agricultural economy. The only benefactors for this persistence

in the face of failure are the planners themselves and those who supply the spate of imported goods and technical assistance with which each new centrally planned project is launched.[81]

The success of the five-year plan was premised on the assumption that worldwide demand for coffee and other exports would increase—a highly unlikely scenario, given that the CAR faced substantial competition from coffee- and cotton-growing countries around the world.[82]

Partly in response to these national policies and to global coffee markets, coffee production in the Central African Republic fluctuated wildly in the decades after independence. During Dacko's first regime (1960–65), coffee production in the Haute-Sangha Prefecture increased and then fell, as did national coffee exports. Central African coffee growers found it difficult to compete in the world coffee market and agreed to restrict production and adhere to strict quotas. Under Bokassa, family coffee farms expanded considerably; from 1968 to 1975 the surface area that family farms worked grew from 39 percent of the total surface area of coffee culture to over 60 percent, though production still lagged. And during the Kolingba regime, coffee production fluctuated significantly. The revival of CAISTAB, the marketing board responsible for stabilizing prices and reforming customs laws, probably discouraged small family farmers from producing coffee, because coffee purchasing prices were so low in the Central African Republic. CAISTAB's bankruptcy in 1990 further depressed coffee production, because it could no longer purchase the coffee that farmers harvested.[83]

Beginning in the late 1980s, however, the Central African Republic state adopted a new strategy that ostensibly had little to do with agriculture but ultimately affected farmers in the middle Sangha basin. The state accommodated a conservationist agenda, articulated by the Ministry of Waters and Forests, the WWF, the World Bank, and various bilateral aid and nongovernmental organizations. National laws in the Dzanga-Sangha Special Reserve limited farming to areas of settlement that existed before the reserve's creation in 1990. These laws also prohibited cultivators from working fields that were more than 500 meters from the road or more than one kilometer outside village limits. The state also outlawed killing elephants, which frequently wreaked havoc in fields on the outskirts of Bayanga and Salo, though the project began to experiment with electrified fences there in 1995. Shooting marauding elephants had long constituted a means of controlling them. But the presence of the project that administered the Dzanga-Sangha Special Reserve and Dzanga-Ndoki National Park, Western researchers studying forest elephants, and antipoaching patrols curtailed elephant hunting.[84]

The state's adoption of measures to protect the Sangha basin forest and its wildlife affected Sangha basin agriculture, but in contradictory ways. Restrictions on farming were rarely if ever enforced around established villages in the early to mid-1990s; I measured fields in the reserve that extended well beyond the official limits. The project undoubtedly would have found such limits exceedingly difficult to enforce, not only because it did not have sufficient patrols to do so, but also because any attempts to limit farming would have resulted in fierce protests from farmers. In this sense, project officials accommodated farmers' perceptions of the centrality of cultivation in Mpiemu and Sangha basin inhabitants' lives.[85]

It is also possible that the WWF project, which engaged approximately 120 workers in the village of Bayanga in 1993, may have inadvertently encouraged agricultural expansion around Bayanga and elsewhere in the reserve. In the early 1990s antipoaching guards, tour guides, and construction crews receiving salaries from the project found that kin from elsewhere in the CAR, where economic circumstances were difficult, moved to Bayanga. These increasing populations boosted demands for cultivated foods. Of course, the logging company and sawmill in Bayanga also contributed to this expansion. Bayanga farmers themselves found it challenging to supply these needs because elephants from the park often frequented their fields. But Lindjombo farmers, who had to contend with far fewer elephants, benefited from Bayanga's population increases if they could afford to transport their cassava, peanuts, and other foods to its daily market.[86]

Beneficiaries of these population increases, however, hardly mentioned them. Instead, they and their families lamented through idioms of hunger that by curtailing activities that would replace the departed coffee plantations, the project stymied their attempts to "gain strength." "You have closed the road for us to go into the bush," one former coffee worker proclaimed to a Ministry of Waters and Forests representative and a Central African educator from the project. "We are eating only *potopoto* [cassava porridge]." Another lamented: "For two days there has been no food in the market. . . . What are we eating?" Another time Amions Anaclet complained, "This coffee, before we got our strength from coffee. But coffee is dead. Now how will we find our strength?" Others frequently declared, "They [project employees] would have us eating cassava leaves, that's all," implying that a diet of only food crops was deficient, for it lacked meat.[87]

American researchers downriver in Bomassa (Congo), an outpost in the Nouabalé-Ndoki National Park, had also earned the ire of Lindjombo's most ambitious women farmers and distillers, many of whom were Mpiemu. Michael Fay and Richard Ruggiero forbade the sale of *mbako* (a powerful alcoholic drink distilled from cassava and maize; *menyogi* in Mpiemu) in Bomassa where inhabitants were employees of a Wildlife Conservation Society project administering the Nouabalé-Ndoki park. To the fury of Lindjombo residents, they also ejected Central Africans trading in Bomassa. Fay and Ruggiero contended that *mbako* sent their employees into a drunken stupor and prevented them from doing their work. Although the WCS project in Nouabalé-Ndoki was entirely distinct from the WWF project in the Dzanga-Ndoki park and Dzanga-Sangha reserve, Lindjombo women and men saw important continuities between them: not only did both impose restrictions on other means of getting food and "strength" after the demise of the coffee plantations, but Fay himself was one of the researchers in the 1980s who had spearheaded the establishment of the Dzanga-Ndoki park and Dzanga-Sangha reserve, and he had once served as director of the WWF project administering them.[88] Fay's efforts to make amends with these women for their income loss foundered: he consented to purchase cassava from Lindjombo farmers but distributed sacks only to policemen, who sold him their wives' cassava. Lindjombo farmers then complained that they would derive no benefits at all from these sales; only wives of civil servants, who already earned salaries, would.[89]

What are we to make of these protests of hunger? These claims of hunger serve as a window into the changes that Mpiemu farmers and *doli* had experienced over the twentieth century. During the 1990s in villages where people could find food year-round in fields, as well as in rivers and the forest, it is unlikely that many were truly going hungry. Hunger, rather, was a shared idiom among Sangha basin inhabitants that reflected recent dearth and losses in the agricultural spaces that they had cultivated: the departure of European plantation owners and the disappearance of access to broader networks of political and economic power; the recent decline of the coffee economy; the inability to find other means of acquiring wealth in people, in knowledge, and in material possessions. For Mpiemu these changes also were occasioned by the decline of maize cultivation, which had symbolic and social consequences, especially for elder men and women. For many Mpiemu this dearth and loss had important historical dimensions. An older colonial discourse had once defined their agriculture as insufficient and Mpiemu farmers as lacking a willingness to produce food, when colonizers redoubled their efforts to extract an agricultural surplus for their own projects. In response, Mpiemu seemed to turn this diagnosis of dearth on its head; it wasn't that their agricultural production or goodwill was lacking but rather that they were "hungry." And although some missionaries (who had seen Mpiemu fields) doubted their actual hunger, their Mpiemu followers evidently borrowed a page from these missionaries, contending that since they were "hungry," they should receive assistance and protection.

Restrictions on farming in protected areas during the 1990s were not stringently enforced. But those who criticized conservation efforts invoked "hunger" as part of a historical response to perceived restrictions, turning around conservationists' claims of lack (of "community," of a willingness to exploit in sustainable ways, as a WWF director and project personnel have asserted) in Sangha basin populations. Claims of "hunger" also raised invidious comparisons between the present, defined by a dearth of opportunities and by constraints—even minimal ones—on farming, and a prosperous past in *doli,* when powerful outsiders instigated forest clearing and plantation agriculture, providing new opportunities to accumulate wealth and to leave persons behind.

6

EMPTYING THE FOREST

T HE FOREST (*digi*) is a space in which Mpiemu have long acquired food and building materials. But its importance has extended beyond the utilitarian: Mpiemu have understood ways of seeing and characterizing the forest, knowledge of the forest, practices of its exploitation, and sites within it as *doli*. Although they recognize and name many different forest forms, Mpiemu have used the term *digi* as a proximate contrast to more evidently humanized villages and fields, but also as a broader ecological, cultural, and historical space distinct from savannas. As twentieth-century colonial administrators, concessionaires, missionaries, and later, postcolonial state agents promoted new ways of perceiving and extracting valued commodities from the forest, they articulated two competing, and sometimes complementary, discourses of loss concerning its game, trees, and other resources. On one hand, they worried over the depletion of forest resources.[1] And alternatively, many outsiders expressed anxieties over lost, squandered economic and political opportunities that only intensive environmental exploitation would remedy. Mpiemu fit these interventions and particular notions of lost opportunities into *doli*, altering the knowledge, practices, and sites that forged relations between persons, social groups, and the forests and changing the interpretations of the forest's past, present, and future. Such changes are illustrated through Mpiemu responses to 1990s state-WWF conservation interventions in forest and wildlife use. They interpreted these interventions through the prism of *doli*, seeking to sustain their claims to labor, forest resources, and sites and their ability to "leave a person behind" by invoking hunger and a discourse of lost economic opportunities.

EARLY TWENTIETH-CENTURY FOREST PERCEPTION, KNOWLEDGE, AND USE

The Sangha basin forest was a central feature in Mpiemu and other Sangha basin livelihoods in the early twentieth century. It provided various foods, building materials, and other useful products. But the forest also helped to produce the person (*mori*), to differentiate gendered, generational, and *ajing* (cord family, or clan) persons from one another, and to ground these persons in specific forest locations and practices associated with *doli,* knowledge of the past. These persons, moreover, perceived, interacted with, and helped to shape the forest. Although evidence documenting these interactions in the early twentieth century is sparse, linguistic, oral, documentary evidence from the forests near Mpiemu areas of settlement, as well as the secondary literature, provides a speculative snapshot of *doli.*

At the turn of the century, Mpiemu referred to forest as *digi* but also reckoned several different forest typologies in humanized terms. Although some of their typologies corresponded to typical ecological classifications of equatorial rain forest, they based the forest forms upon what a person could see and do within a particular space. *Akwombo* referred to forest that had never been cultivated, and it took several forms. *Antchanjo,* for instance, was analogous to *Gilbertiodendron dewevrei* forest, a rare monodominant (single-species) forest with tall trees and a sparse understory. But Mpiemu defined this forest not exclusively by the presence of a single species but rather by the fact that "you [can] sit [in this forest], and you can see a person far away." They also found *antchanjo* forests rich in game.[2] *Kwashelo* was a denser forest, where "it rains a lot, [and] many trees fall in that place so that many leaves emerge. There are many animals there . . . when our fathers saw *kwashelo,* they said that they could cultivate many bananas very easily there." *Nkolongo akwombo* was a forest that contained much larger but more crowded trees than *kwashelo* forest.[3]

Other typologies were based upon how people had once used a particular forest space and the kinds of vegetation that grew there after the disturbance. *Mianga* forest, for instance, contained a more tangled understory than *kwashelo* but was defined by the past nonagricultural work that people had performed there, such as clearing a village or forest camp and, later, mining and logging. The tall leafy *akia* (*Aframomum sulcatum*) frequently grew up in these disturbed locations, producing flowering shoots at its base and attracting gorillas and other game to eat the fruits that grow inside them. *Buri* was any terrain that had previously been farmed; its vegetation could range from a dense forest tangle to low bushy growth (consisting primarily of the invasive light-seeking forest-gap plants and vines that developed soon after a field was fallowed). *Buri bikondo* forest resembled *buri* in that it contained very dense tangled undergrowth, even though it had never been farmed. Hence, late nineteenth- and early twentieth-century Mpiemu speakers premised the distinctions between forest types upon human perceptions and on potential and past activities there. Mpiemu reckoned the forest as a space defined by past human interventions or by its capacity for future human use, blurring distinctions between domesticated and wild spaces. This is a crucial point, and one that stands in stark contrast to ecologists' classifications of forest types.[4]

According to tellers of *doli*, early twentieth-century Mpiemu, like other Sangha basin inhabitants, used the forest in a multitude of ways. There Mpiemu and other Africans found edible leaves, such as *kumbi* (*Gnetum buccholzianum*), fruits (including *bombi*, or *Anonidium manii*), tubers, nuts (particularly from the bush mango endosperm, *payo*, or *Irvingia excelsa*), and palm wine; wood and forest leaves (especially *akon*, *mpela*, and *kogo*, or *Maranthochloa* spp.) and vines (lianas) for constructing houses, *panjo*, baskets, and traps (particularly *lon*, or *Ereospatha wendlandiana*, and *awu*, or *Manniophytum fulvum*); copal (*bele*) to burn for illumination; a wealth of medicines; and highly valued powder from redwood that people applied to their bodies and traded. But by all accounts the forest's most important product was food, especially meat. Tellers of *doli* asserted that in the late nineteenth and early twentieth centuries, men hunted large and small game using primarily traps and nets, but also spears. They disagreed, however, about whether Mpiemu had flintlock rifles before the arrival of European colonizers.[5] Access to firearms in the upper Sangha was highly uneven, and only populations who traded with the Hausa and Fulbé networks had firearms. Middle Sangha peoples participated in a different long-distance network extending into the Congo River basin and also had firearms. Oral histories mention nothing of nineteenth-century Mpiemu contact with Hausa or Fulbé traders, although linguistic terms for foods suggest that they had indirect contact with them. That situation changed quickly, particularly with the activities of the Compagnie de la N'Goko-Sangha, which sold guns and ammunition in exchange for rubber. By 1905, however, Muston described Mpiemu soldiers serving the *wani* N'Gombako as "armed to the teeth" with a variety of weapons, including rifles (see fig. 2).[6]

Tellers of *doli* explained that a master hunter (*tuma*) was an especially powerful and effective hunter, though unlike his counterparts elsewhere in equatorial Africa, he had no authority to limit where, when, or what other people hunted. Rather, *tuma* possessed exclusive knowledge about hunting in the forest, and "he knew the places for killing animals . . . where there were animals, that is where he would go."[7] Applying powerful medicines to his body, a *tuma* acquired arcane knowledge about the locations and behaviors of game. After receiving gifts from a village, he would take along two or three other hunters to accompany him into the forest. Once he had located fertile hunting grounds, the *tuma* might spend a week hunting large game before he sent word to the village, indicating that its inhabitants could follow and hunt where he had been. In this way *tuma* could exercise considerable influence about where, when, and what villagers hunted.[8]

But Mpiemu captured most animal protein by trapping. Although not as prestigious as hunting, trapping was also a finely honed science and art. Trappers had to evaluate a particular part of the forest's potential for yielding game, to set the appropriate traps (*pondo*), and to manipulate good fortune (*mpombi*, literally "forehead," the site of fortune) by using special medicines to capture animals. Trappers paid careful attention to the terrain in which they laid their traps and sought whenever possible to set a trapping path (*ntche ngonga*) across several ecological zones.[9] They scrutinized the forest paths that game created and tried to set their traps to take advantage of the passage of animals along these paths. They evaluated past human uses of a potential trapping ground, particularly whether too many people had used it and had already frightened animals away. And they had to deduce what animals they could expect to find in these grounds, so that they could choose appropriate traps to set. In the early 1990s elderly Mpiemu men could point out a plethora of forest vines that they, their fathers, and their grandfathers had fashioned into cords for different traps, and they described many of the trap configurations useful for capturing diverse types of game. All of this knowledge, according to tellers in the 1990s, became a crucial part of *doli,* for it taught men to make their livelihoods in the forest based on knowledge that ancestors had discovered and used.[10]

At the turn of the twentieth century, trapping also required that participants balance labor responsibilities and claims for the trapped animals, and it was through these struggles that the forest and its game helped to constitute Mpiemu kin-group, generational, and gendered persons. According to some contemporary Mpiemu, men sharing food under the same *panjo* set traps together along the same trapping path and then shared the meat. At times, however, men assumed responsibility for their own traps, though they still had to provide meat for the *panjo.* Boys, for instance, set their first traps alone, and each had to distribute his first trapped animals to his paternal kin in order to assure later success in capturing animals. The elderly Mpeng gave his first capture, a small antelope called a blue duiker (*ntchwen,* or *Cephalophus monticola*), to his grandfather. He gave his next kills, also two duikers, to his father's brothers' wives. And among *panjo* members, the allocation of particular game parts helped to constitute a hierarchy of elders and juniors and thus marked the development of persons as members of generational groups. Elder men consumed the choice parts of captured game—the liver, heart, the fatty meat just beneath the forelegs—as well as special game, such as gorilla.[11] Over time, boys were allowed to eat meat more often with older men under the *panjo*.

But allocating labor responsibilities among members of the same *panjo* appears to have been a tendentious process. Younger men may have resented shouldering the responsibilities for setting and checking traps and for having to give up control over meat allocation. Several kinds of evidence lend support to this conclusion. Historical narratives, such as that of Kobago and Bandoka, illustrated that elders' demands on younger men could generate significant tensions. Several tales also revealed these tensions between younger and older generations. One, for instance, recounted how young men had rebelled against their elders and killed them. In retribution, an elderly gravedigger systematically tracked down all of the young men in the forest's villages to bury them alive.[12] Although tellers agreed that the events within these tales did not actually happen, the tales did comment upon broader truths about conflicts between young and old men. Such conflicts are probably old; younger men became increasingly less vulnerable to their elders' demands for labor and game following the imposition of colonial rule, which expanded opportunities to accumulate wealth independently.

Hunting and trapping were also crucial ways that early twentieth-century Mpiemu produced gender distinctions and ultimately the gendered person. Eugenia Herbert has called hunting "the realm of male fertility par excellence," defined by a gender division of labor, ritual, and prescriptive behavior,[13] and trapping was no less so for Mpiemu. As in many of the African societies that Herbert described, Mpiemu defined hunting and trapping as exclusively male activities, which created gendered persons through a gradual process. Young boys left their sisters at home to accompany their fathers and grandfathers into the forest, to witness the selection of trapping grounds, traps, and special medicines that would promote good fortune, and finally, to set traps of their own. Sometimes, however, male *panjo* members continued to trap together.

Women did make critical contributions to the capture, preparation, and consumption of game, and these practices helped to produce female persons and to distinguish them from men. Although women did not venture into the forest to trap, tellers of *doli* recounted that women performed a secret dance when villages experienced a scarcity of fish or meat. Women butch-ered and prepared most meat, although new wives were never supposed to eat meat or they would earn the reputation of being a thief. Pregnant women were not to consume meat from their husbands', in-laws', siblings', or fathers' traps, for if they did so, they prevented those traps from capturing further game. Moreover, tellers of *doli* claimed, early twentieth-century women could never prepare or eat gorilla (*ntchilo*), because gorillas found women to be sexually attractive and would threaten them in the forest.[14] Women also could not eat other game, including *mpa* (possibly golden cat, *Profelis aurata*). Pregnant women consuming *mpa* would risk giving birth to girls without vaginas, and those eating *wago* (chimpanzee, *Pan troglodytes*) would have children with nasty dispositions. Nor were women permitted to eat *koi* (leopard, *Panthera pardus*), although when men trapped a leopard in the for-est or the village, both men and women celebrated with a series of dances, because, in the words of one elder, "they had killed a terrible animal. Great joy!"[15] As in many parts of equatorial Africa, leopards were associated with authority, for they were understood to be people who had marshaled occult powers to transform themselves in order to kill other people. During the day, for four days following the death of a leopard, an entire village would perform a dance called *so;* women exuberantly circled the village while men carried the leopard on two poles, dancing in loose, rhythmic motions to imitate the dangling limbs of the dead leopard. At night, however, men par-ticipated in their own dance, barring women and children from joining or even watching the dance.[16]

Finally, hunting, trapping, and meat consumption in the early twentieth century may have defined Mpiemu clans as forest dwellers, different from savanna or riverine people. Tellers of *doli* highlighted the distinctions be-tween their Mpiemu ancestors and riverine and savanna peoples. Nyambi Patrice, for instance, thanked Alouba Clotere for asking him about how their Mpiemu ancestors behaved near the rivers and observed: "In the time of my grandfather . . . [when] our grandparents had married and had given birth to many children . . . they went to see the river. But they couldn't put their feet in the river. They wouldn't do it. They were afraid. But the river people, they came and they said, 'It is just water. We kill fish there, and we move around in it. Look at how we move around in the water in a canoe, in a canoe.'"[17] Though Mpiemu understood themselves as the descendants of forest and farming deities, the distinction they drew between forest and fal-low was not exclusively one of ecology, but also of livelihood practices. In the late nineteenth century, several tellers of *doli* explained, Mpiemu *ajing* engaged in wars with other peoples, including Gbaya clans in the north and west, and consumed them. According to one *doli* teller, Gbaya discovered that when they consumed Mpiemu peoples, "we had a lot of fat [*mbulo*]," primarily because Mpiemu consumed so much forest game. Gbaya thus called them *biakombo,* meaning "animals of the forest." Fat was a substance that people both shared with and took from animals, and they used it to render their activities in fields and forests productive. Having a lot of bodily fat meant that these Mpiemu enjoyed a state of unambiguous well-being.[18]

In a story that the elderly Mpeng recounted, fat not only connoted a state of well-being but was also a marker of ethnic difference that could disrupt relations of authority and clientship. His father's cousin, Lagwe, was a slave of a Gbaya family living in Nakombo (a distant village north of Mpiemu settlement) and renamed Ngitowa, which according to Mpeng meant "rat of the house" in Gbaya. Lagwe returned to his home village, Zankandi, so that he could visit his family. During his stay he grew fat on forest game. Once he returned to his Gbaya masters in Nakombo, they found him both fat and disobedient and decided to kill and eat him. Lagwe's children, overhearing the masters' plan, warned him, and he fled into the forest with his spear so that he could pose as a hunter if he encountered anyone. The Gbaya elders pursued him, but he eluded them by hiding inside a tree. Eventually he made his way back to Zankandi, where the *wani* sent word to Nakombo that the elders of the two villages should engage in a ceremonial exchange of blood (*mpuni*), swearing never to consume one another. What is fascinating about Mpeng's account is the way that fat distinguishes Lagwe from his *patrons,* and how it confounds who is the hunter and who is the prey. Lagwe grew fatter than his captors by consuming forest game and consequently became the prey himself, but he posed as a hunter to elude capture. To be sure, it is treacherous to try to untangle the past perceptions of ethnic difference from present ones in this story. But Mpeng's recollection does suggest that the forest and the livelihoods and symbolic meanings that Mpiemu people developed in it helped to constitute Mpiemu persons as different from savanna persons.[19]

In describing late nineteenth- and early twentieth-century Mpiemu perceptions of the forest and its resources as "human-centered," I am aware that this phrase speaks directly to contemporary debates over how Africans have understood their own roles within "nature." Recently, anthropologist Richard Peterson has argued that Ubangian farmers and Ituri hunters and farmers "perceive that nature very much includes themselves, their ancestors, and their offspring." God provided the ancestors with forest game, but these ancestors respected limits on hunting in order not to spoil this "gift." Drawing on Vansina, Peterson concludes that these Central Africans, in using forest resources, sought to "optimize" rather than to "maximize" production, to use technologies that avoided waste and limited their effects on the forest and its resources. Evidence of Mpiemu ecological perceptions and use in the late nineteenth century appears far more equivocal. To be sure, some authorities like *tuma* or restrictions on consuming certain kinds of game could have helped to protect game populations from overexploitation. But there is evidence that counters this interpretation as well. In equatorial Africa, where relations of authority could shift constantly, a *tuma*'s influence could be highly limited. Many tellers of *doli* insisted that game was plentiful, indeed limitless, in the forest, and that their state of well-being depended on consuming fat from animals. Most important, tellers of *doli* explicitly denied that any real limits on forest exploitation existed during this time. I am not convinced, then, that Mpiemu could be described as "optimizers" or as necessarily embracing a kind of conservation ethic in the early twentieth century.[20]

EXPLORING THE FOREST IN THE EARLY TWENTIETH CENTURY

European explorers had rather different perceptions of the Sangha basin forest when they began to move through it in the late nineteenth and early twentieth centuries. At first they saw the Sangha basin forest as merely a strategic territory serving their ambitions to control vast swaths of the African continent. The earliest explorers confined their expeditions to the banks of the Sangha and its navigable tributaries and were mostly concerned with mapping the course of the Sangha River and people living along its banks, as well as the Fulbé empire farther north. Those who did comment on the forest found it a hostile place.[21]

But following their defeat at Fashoda in 1898, the French turned their attentions to building a colonial state to exploit the riches of the Sangha basin and to protect these resources from neighboring Germans. State-sponsored explorations gathered information to settle concessionary companies' boundary disputes and conflicting claims to Sangha peoples and commodities and actively sought to demonstrate knowledge of and control over these forested regions and their people as part of an erratic effort to establish state control. The content of Sangha exploratory reports changed as explorers shifted their sights to surveying the courses of major rivers, exploitable resources, and people within that forest.[22] Moreover, French explorers encountering Mpiemu and other peoples began to express anxieties about squandering opportunities to develop the Sangha basin by exploiting its resources, a concern that undoubtedly resulted from competition with Germans and Belgians nearby and with the British elsewhere on the continent. German explorers seemed to pay similar attention to the forest's people and resources on the other side of the border, in Cameroon, at least according to the Belgian journal *Le Mouvement Géographique*'s summaries of German news reports.[23]

Explorers paid careful attention to the forest and its people and exploitable resources once they reached locations of intensive Mpiemu settlement, which straddled the border between German Cameroon and the French Congo. In describing the "M'Bimou," the explorer Paul Pouperon blurred the distinctions between the people, game, and the forest, calling it "the country of large monkeys: chimpanzees and gorillas. The very hilly region has a clayey soil, covered with a thick forest and traversed by several rapid waterways. . . . The spirit of this population is known . . . for its ill humor and independence. In the middle of this truly superb equatorial forest, in daily contact with anthropoid monkeys and beasts . . . which they love to hunt, the M'Bimous have adopted these animals' savage character, which renders them intractable." Thus the "M'Bimous" were less than human, unduly shaped by the mammals they hunted. But at the same time the M'Bimou forest was ripe for French exploitation, "a magnificent country of production (rubber, ivory)." Concerned about German competition and the difficulties of extracting high-quality rubber and sustaining long-term production, Pouperon worried, "Will we hear it said again by the French that we are unfit for any sort of colonization and that we do not know how to develop our possessions or to make use of the resources that they offer us?" Such anxieties about losing opportunities to develop and to profit from the Sangha basin's untapped resources and about abdicating the responsibility of exploiting the forest's wealth to France's archrivals, the Germans, would surface again and again in the coming decades. French commercial interests were engaged in a crucial struggle with Germans for access to African labor and forest commodities of rubber, ivory, and animal skins. But France, Pouperon envisioned, needed to intervene in the M'Bimou's ancient and unchanging place and people so as to exploit its labor and resources.[24]

TRAFFICKING RUBBER, IVORY, AND ANIMAL HIDES: CONCESSIONAIRES AND MERCHANT-PLANTERS

In 1899 concessionary companies forcibly began to alter the activities that Africans and Mpiemu performed in the forest. Companies faced considerable challenges in their efforts to exploit their concessions' ivory, rubber, and African labor; concession boundaries were poorly defined, equipped, and financed, and competition for African workers, who moved frequently to avoid excessive labor demands, could be fierce.[25] In this context, many company administrators expressed real anxieties that they might squander opportunities to tap the Sangha basin forest's wealth, and their activities influenced Mpiemu ways of perceiving and knowledge about the forest in the past and present.

Rubber

Rubber was the most important commodity that companies extracted from the Sangha basin forest. The forest contained *Funtumia elastica,* a large tree that workers tapped to extract its latex, and several species of *Landolphia* vines, which workers cut and sapped. According to the Compagnie de la N'Goko-Sangha, the concession contained a rich reserve of rubber-producing trees, but *F. elastica* appeared most widespread, particularly in the forests between Salo and the Yobé River near Bayanga and Bomassa.[26] In the M'Bimou forest, where many Mpiemu speakers lived, company agents found greater concentrations of *Landolphia* species. Rubber exploitation was at the foundation of a broader economy of pillage that French commercial interests created in the Sangha basin and equatorial Africa. Commercial concerns extracted raw materials by paying Africans the lowest possible prices for these commodities and in turn sold high-priced manufactured goods, such as salt, sugar, wine, candles, tobacco, and cloth, and *midjokos* (a currency introduced by the administration) to them. These efforts did nothing to benefit Africans living in the Sangha basin, but companies did not always reap the profits that they expected.[27]

How the companies extracted this resource from the forest is crucial to understanding how Mpiemu peoples' conceptions of their pasts and their forests changed. Finding workers to collect and prepare the latex proved to be the companies' greatest challenge. Some concessionary companies hired workers on contract, while others simply purchased the rubber that individual tappers collected in the forest. The Compagnie de la N'Goko-Sangha, for instance, chose to purchase the hardened cakes of rubber from rubber tappers. CFSO, however, organized teams of fifteen workers, armed them with gouges, knives, machetes, and three-liter jugs, and herded them into the forest during the early morning hours under the supervision of a single foreman. In 1912 many CFSO workers had contracts ranging from six months to two years, earning ten to fifteen francs per month. But the company also forged contracts with village chiefs, who would send out their subordinates to tap rubber and to sell it to the companies. Chiefs received a fee based on the amount of rubber that their villages produced and would use this money to pay their taxes to the French administration. By 1920, however, the company had shifted to "direct exploitation," because it attained "deplorable" production levels by hiring workers on contract and paying them a monthly salary and meager daily rations.[28] "Direct exploitation" meant that permanent teams of harvesters and their wives collected and processed the rubber but were not under contract to the company. Most of the time workers lived in forest camps and traveled each month to company trading stations to sell their rubber. Both company agents and administrators at times acknowledged that such an existence could be difficult. As one agent put it, "The natives live in the forest with their families under deficient conditions; they are exposed to poor weather conditions; as a result of their frequent movements to find new, rich populations [of rubber trees], the harvesters do not cultivate plantations and content themselves with sending their wives to the village, often very far from their camps, to buy the necessary foods."[29]

The work process for collecting rubber reveals much about the ways in which companies perceived the forest's resources. The Compagnie des Produits de la Sangha, for instance, reportedly engaged workers to "slaughter tap"—to cut down rubber-producing trees and sap the felled trunks.[30] Clearly the company was not interested in managing these trees so that they would produce latex repeatedly over many years; rather, it was most concerned with maximizing immediate production, even at the cost of depleting the forest of its rubber-producing species. Subsequent concessionary companies claimed to support less destructive tapping procedures, although slaughter tapping continued. One 1912 report detailed the rubber-collection process:

> The trees are bled with "fish bones" [a cutting pattern] at a greater or lesser height, depending on whether the tree is virgin or has already been exploited. Some incisions [in the tree] start at the leaves and end at the base. Lianas are generally cut off at the height of one meter to permit the shoot to regenerate. The severed part is cut into fragments and the latex collected; it runs abundantly enough. Sometimes the liana is cut to the ground, placed on supports, and sapped circularly for its entire length. The rubber-harvesting work ordinarily ends in the morning, and at noon the workers return to camp. Under the direction of a European, they proceed to coagulating the latex. This liquid, after having been poured through a sieve (a can with holes in it), is precipitated in small amounts in boiling water. After coagulation, the rubber is in the form of cakes, which, after having been pressed beneath a solid and smooth surface, are then cut into spirals and small cubes and put under a

shelter where they wait for three months before being shipped to France. Although direct exploitation during the first years produced rubber at a more expensive price, at this moment a well-managed operation, with well-nourished, selected workers, can furnish products whose price varies from 1 franc 50 to 3 francs per kilo. . . . Depending on the richness of the exploited forest, a team of fifty workers can provide on average 600 kilos per month and sometimes a ton.[31]

In theory, sapping would not damage the tree. As one CFSO agent pointed out, after the plant was tapped, it "must suffer a great deal; a tree thus tapped becomes unproductive for four or five years, but most of the time it will not waste away."[32] Nevertheless, the trees died frequently enough to merit the attention of company agents. Predictably, most of them placed the blame squarely on African tappers' shoulders. One N'Goko-Sangha agent insisted that workers' methods of using a gouge was "defective," either because they pushed the gouge into the tree too deeply, or because they made incisions into its bark that were too long and effectively girdled the tree. Either practice could kill the tree and ultimately diminish the population of latex-producing flora in the forest. By 1920 one CFSO agent openly worried that latex-producing trees and vines were becoming scarce, but again he pinned the blame for their disappearance on African workers' greed. "The native," this agent declared, "only obeys his selfish interest, which drives him to obtain as rapidly as possible the maximum quantity of rubber."[33] Here, then, was another discourse of loss that would remain entrenched in discussions about African forest use for the rest of the century: that valued resources deteriorated and disappeared because Africans did not manage them responsibly and rationally.[34]

In response, some companies sought to prevent the depletion of rubber trees. The N'Goko-Sangha agent suggested that the company should hold the "collectivity, the village, responsible" for slaughter-tapped trees and excessively cut lianas; CFSO followed suit, establishing "repressive measures" to discourage rubber harvesters from these practices but holding responsible "the group, that is to say, the village chief, who thus supervises his own forest zone. Through this means, great progress has been realized in the course of this year."[35] In the M'Bimou *circonscription,* where high concentrations of Mpiemu speakers resided, the company resorted to stationing guards in the forest to prevent destructive rubber-gathering practices. Elsewhere, company agents advocated the prohibition of rubber tapping in zones where the number of latex-producing trees was dwindling, although there is no evidence that these measures were put into effect. Nevertheless, the use of punitive measures to check ruinous practices and to promote "rational" forest use would remain a common tactic that interveners in relations between people and their environment employed for the rest of the century.

Despite these complaints, concessionary companies did not assiduously seek to conserve rubber-producing species in the Sangha basin forests. These companies, after all, had created a context in which workers felt compelled to produce substantial quantities of rubber, even at the expense of the trees themselves. When recruitment took place at gunpoint and agents imprisoned and beat villagers for not extracting enough rubber, African harvesters did whatever was necessary to collect as much latex as possible. Moreover, according to the companies' concessionary agreements with the French state, they were supposed to plant new rubber trees for each ton of latex extracted from the forest. Most failed to plant or maintain trees that could produce even a fraction of the amount that they extracted from the forest.[36]

Rubber production itself began fitfully. The Compagnie des Produits de la Sangha-Lipa-Ouesso, which controlled a concession in the middle Sangha, as well as other commercial concerns in the region, found themselves beseiged by Pomo and Bomassa insurrections between 1901 and 1903 and had to suspend operations in several locations. And in 1905 Muston observed that the Compagnie de la N'Goko-Sangha purchased a paltry 300 to 400 kilos of rubber each month because workers found the work onerous and disruptive. But production increased thereafter. Only two years later the company exported 117 metric tons of rubber, and in the first trimester of 1908, it shipped an additional 40 tons. When CFSO took over the concessions of several companies, it too increased production. But shortly thereafter, rubber exports declined, hampered first by a global crisis in rubber prices and then by the First World War, when the company's warehouses were ransacked and burned.[37] In 1915 one administrator estimated that although Africans in the concession had only produced 3 tons in June and 6 tons in July, they could normally extract about 15 tons in a month. Following the war, CFSO, Santini, Lopes, the North British Rubber Company, and other commercial interests continued to produce rubber through the brief revival of rubber markets during the Second World War. Thereafter, however, rubber exploitation ended.[38]

The decades of colonial rubber extraction influenced people-environment relations and *doli*, both knowledge of the forest and of the past, as well as ways of perceiving the forest. But the effects of the rubber tapping are not easily detectable in the historical record. What remains clear from archival records is that some Mpiemu and other Africans refused to harvest rubber at all. Others, conscripted as workers, found rubber work onerous, deserted their teams, and took refuge in the forest, particularly if they had been cheated out of their pay or in rubber sales, found their contracts extended without their consent, or had suffered at the hands of a foreman.[39] Nevertheless, many people did harvest rubber, compelled by companies' coercive tactics, propelled by successive sleeping-sickness epidemics, and lured by the promise of new imported consumer goods from France. Exploiting the forest for its rubber may well have dovetailed with preexisting conceptions of the uses of the forest, which Mpiemu perceived as a space defined by past interventions into it or by its utility for humans.

At the same time Mpiemu perceptions of the forest and of their places within it and in the world altered dramatically, and such changes are evident in contemporary expressions of *doli*. Colonial rubber extraction transformed forest use so that its resources became a vehicle through which people could connect themselves to global networks of wealth. Many contemporary Mpiemu observed that rubber work supplied the raw materials to make automobile wheels. The very first time I spoke with Satuba Omer about *bi san bi doli* (the things of *doli*), he began to discuss rubber work: "The rubber would go only to the country [of white people] to make tires for cars and trucks. The rubber of the forest would go to make cars. You haven't heard that story yet? They [the white people] came to do [rubber work] . . . for their own needs. They made their own rubber afterwards, but [at the beginning] it was the rubber from the forest that they made into the 'feet' of cars. The people here and in Congo and in Cameroon, they did rubber work."[40] Rubber thus paved the way for Mpiemu and other Sangha basin workers to participate in this developing global economy and enabled them to acquire imported salt, cloth, iron tools, cooking implements, tinned foods, and alcohol. It is hard to overemphasize the importance that these consumer goods—or the role of the forest and its resources in gaining them—acquired for Mpiemu and other Sangha peoples over the century. To be sure, in the early years companies complained that demand for such wares was not especially strong, but later they found that workers avidly purchased their offerings at company stores. Indeed, cloth was an effective recruiting tool: when Alouba recruited workers to tap rubber for Santini in the 1920s, he reportedly gave them clothing to lure them to Lindjombo to work. The material goods gained through rubber exploitation also helped in the formation of new social relations, becoming a critical part of the bridewealth that young men paid to their wives' families. What the concessionary companies helped to establish, then, was a quid pro quo: in exchange for access to forest resources, companies provided workers with more income, limited access to consumer goods, and expanded and increasingly fruitful social relations.[41]

Rubber eventually became a generational marker that distinguished men who exploited the forest from those who did not. During the Second World War, when prospective workers believed that they could choose their work, younger men seemed to gravitate toward coffee work, which they explained was less difficult than the rubber harvesting that their fathers had performed.[42]

Remembrances of rubber made their way into *doli* in a variety of ways. In their narratives of the past, old and young alike in the 1990s recalled rubber as a resource and an activity connecting them and their forests with a global political economy. For instance, one lycée student, Mpendjo Edouard Matos, drew me a picture of the town of Bilolo during the time of *doli*.[43] Rubber figured prominently in his depiction of *doli*. Bilolo, he claimed, was surrounded by rubber trees, which his ancestors cut "to collect the sap so that people could make auto tires." Outside the village were also pits, in which people cut planks of wood from trees harvested from the forest, and in the center of the drawing were "places to sleep in the middle of the forest." The entire place was enclosed by a line which he called "the limits of the rubber," and a road ran from these limits to the regional town of Nola.

Rubber work also helped to create new notions of the person. The consumer goods that workers acquired in exchange for rubber became the material evidence of a certain kind of person, one who was connected to a broad network of powerful *patrons,* and it shaped Mpiemu perceptions of the past and present. Clothing in particular was an important marker of a well-connected person, a reflection of changing notions and values of what a person should look like.[44] These transformations were most striking when people sought to distinguish themselves from forest animals. Mpeng, for instance, described men's and women's clothing, created from forest bark and leaves, before the arrival of Western cloth: "Men wore bark. Women wore leaves. Women didn't cover their breasts. Just short skirt, covering pubic area. They would sit like the devil. Shit! [*He laughs.*] . . . They would sit like the devil, because this was during the time of Adam and Eve and they ruined themselves."[45] The acquisition of Western cloth, he later argued, marked Mpiemu persons as different from forest animals like chimpanzees, who wore nothing and had never domesticated spaces within the forest by creating villages. These notions that the person should be covered in cloth and that past Mpiemu persons had not been correctly clothed were profoundly Christianized ones, but concessionary companies' rubber-collecting activities made it possible for Mpiemu to acquire both cloth and notions of propriety and devilry. In this way concessionary company rubber exploitation had allowed Mpiemu to develop a new kind of person—a consumer of

Western goods—and to reinterpret their past practices in terms of the "civ-ilizing" influences that they embraced.

For many Mpiemu rubber retained some important continuities with the past, and they grafted rubber-collecting practices onto an older gender division of labor in the forest. The spoken recollections of men and women who harvested rubber echoed some of the same gendered activities surrounding trapping: male practices of cutting paths in the forest, climbing trees, using iron implements, and locating prey, as well as female practices of cooking and carrying.[46] Like trapping, rubber collection was "men's work," although men relied heavily on women's labor to perform it. For rubber collection a man hiked into the forest, cutting a small path through it and locating a tree to tap for latex. Satuba Omer described how his father once harvested rubber:

> Rubber is something inside the tree. You climb up the tree, cut open the tree [with a knife called a *tili*], and put a tube inside it. Long ago I made these [tubes], because children would ask how. I did blacksmithing long ago. . . . [The tube] was metal [iron]. You push it in [the tree], and it goes in straight. You make a channel inside, way up inside the tree. The water [sap] will come out straight into that channel. Then you pierce the bark and put a little leaf there. Then the water [sap] would trickle into a pot. Then you leave it and go to many trees, many trees. . . . You drain the water [sap] into the big pot. When it was heavy [with collected sap], you'd take it back to your camp.

Climbing, using an iron implement to penetrate a tree, and extracting a milky white latex were all hallmarks of masculinity. Mpeng Patrice, for instance, recounted his father's joy when the white latex began to seep from the tree: "Look when the rubber comes, chr-r-r-r! My rubber has arrived! My rubber has arrived! I am a man! Mpiemu!"

Once the men had carried the collected latex back to the camp, women would "cook" the latex to coagulate it. When it had hardened into large, heavy cakes, the women would carry it out of the forest to the market. The elderly Yongo Oromain found this porterage backbreaking work: "They made round [cakes of rubber]. When they had finished them, you could only carry three [at a time]. Very heavy loads! You carry only three. You, only one woman." Indeed, Bessari Alphonsine contended that rubber work was not simply men's work: "Rubber work was very difficult. When you didn't collect enough kilos [of rubber], they would beat you. Women and men would do that work." Women also took charge of finding food and preparing it for the harvesters.[47]

For tellers of *doli* the rubber-exploiting past was punctuated by two critical losses that echoed the twin discourses of loss expressed by Europeans.

First, they contended that latex-producing trees had been depleted. Walking through the forest, they encountered few of the lianas and trees that had once supplied their parents' and grandparents' livelihoods. But even more crucially, rubber in the 1990s marked a lost opportunity, and Mpiemu (and others) seem to have developed and transformed this discourse of loss from the relations and activities that concessionary companies created. Rubber exploitation, despite the abuses that accompanied it, ultimately fostered a set of expectations among Sangha basin Africans, in which they would participate in outsiders' forest exploitation in exchange for ready access to consumer goods. But at the end of the Second World War, the market for equatorial African rubber collapsed, and CFSO, Santini, and other commercial agents abandoned its collection and purchase altogether. Tellers of *doli* recalled this market collapse as an arbitrary ruling by white authorities. Satuba, for instance, observed: "The rubber work was stopped. A time came when it ended. [Why?] It ended because of the law. By the whites, no? . . . It was [something that happened in] the entire world. Africa had to 'close the road' of rubber. Everyone abandoned rubber. A law was passed. Before, or during the time of rubber, people started planting coffee, excelsa coffee. America didn't need rubber anymore. They said that they only needed excelsa coffee."[48]

After rubber work ended, then, white authorities replaced it with coffee and later timber. But these activities, too, collapsed, and several Mpiemu and other Sangha basin inhabitants observed in 1993, "Now we need to find something else." Indeed, the numerous arrivals and departures of various companies had taught Mpiemu and other Sangha inhabitants to profit as much as possible from their presence and activities in the forest so that they could survive in the future.[49] Rubber, then, shaped Mpiemu narratives about the past, signifying the depletion of a forest resource, the departure of powerful European bosses who gave them access to the consumer goods of a global economy, and a strategy for dealing with future outsiders who would wield considerable economic and political power.

Ivory, Skins, and Fat

Sangha basin concessionary companies and the commercial concerns that took over their concessions after 1935 also exploited their concessions for ivory and animal skins. Ivory sated the developing luxury tastes of Europe's middle classes; it supplied piano keys, billiard balls, jewelry, and elaborate carvings. Concessionaires also conducted an intermittent trade in antelope, leopard, and monkey skins, but ivory was by far the most valuable animal product.[50] Although European and African hunters had depleted elephant herds elsewhere in Africa, the Sangha basin forests provided early twentieth-century concessionaires with an apparently limitless elephant population, especially between Salo and the Yobé River, near Bucoli, Bayanga, and Lopi, in the forests around Bomassa, and along the right bank of the N'Goko River.

The companies acquired ivory primarily through the efforts of Sangha basin hunters and trappers. European elephant hunters were a rarity in the upper and middle Sangha during the first decades of the twentieth century, compared to other regions in Africa, where Europeans had already taken steps to monopolize big-game hunting. From the outset, Europeans drew stark distinctions between Sangha basin populations and the ways in which they captured elephants. Neither the "M'Bimou" nor the "Sangha Sangha" hunted elephants, except on rare occasions; instead they engaged "Babingas" (Aka and Ngombe peoples, known as "pygmies") to do the hunting for them. In a typical description the "Babingas" were "a highly primitive population found nearly everywhere in the equatorial forest, who seem to be the real natives of the forest. They live in small groups, take shelter under their simple leaf huts, travel constantly, do not cultivate fields, and devote their attentions solely to the hunt. They become clients of certain villages and exchange with these residents the products of the hunt for provisions: cassava, bananas, knifes, spearheads, etc."[51] The "Babinga" reputation as the quintessential hunters of the forest would circulate among outsiders throughout the century.

Killing an elephant could be a complex and downright dangerous process. Company agents took pains to delineate the methods of hunting and trapping elephants according to ethnic typologies. "Villagers" (that is, "M'Bimou" or "Sangha Sangha"), according to these agents, demonstrated little finesse or bravery in their trapping methods, simply driving elephants into large pits containing iron-tipped spears and covered with branches. At other times hunters would hide in trees, waiting for an unsuspecting pachyderm to pass by, and then they would spear it. But "Babingas" demonstrated their hunting prowess by reading the traces of elephants across the forest landscape, hunting one down, and carefully killing it. Poupon, agent of CFSO, described the process in which "the Babinga slips under the belly [of a sleeping elephant], which he opens with a blow of the lance. The elephant loses its blood and intestines and finishes by falling under the blows."[52] Clearly this method was far from foolproof. Hunters ran a high risk of injury, and wounded elephants could elude their trackers in the forest's tangle and swampy terrain. And although some European observers were dazzled by Aka and Ngombe hunting talents, the trapping methods of these forest dwellers differed little from those of other Sangha basin inhabitants. They too drove elephants into pits or strung up heavy spears above a path frequented by elephants, whereupon a passing pachyderm would trip a cord, causing the spears to rain down.[53]

"Babingas" did not receive payment for ivory directly from the companies. Rather, they forged client relations with various village-dwelling groups, who acquired the tusks in exchange for cassava, iron tools, or other goods. Mpiemu, for instance, had Ngombe hunter-gatherer clients who conducted elephant hunts for them. Village chiefs remunerated the Ngombe hunters for their tusks and in turn sold them to concessionaires. Chiefs received payment rarely in money and most commonly in kind, garnering the equivalent of two to fifteen francs per kilo, according to the size and weight of the ivory tusk.[54]

Ivory extraction and trade remained at far more modest levels than those of rubber, according to spotty statistics from 1900 to 1950. Early figures are not available; the company archives constitute a litany of complaints about low production, theft, and killed company agents.[55] But for the year 1909 the N'Goko-Sangha company extracted 6,625 kilos from its concession and increased its exploitation some 337 kilos in the following year. When CFSO took over its concession, ivory extraction fluctuated substantially (ranging from 2,694 kilos in 1911 to 4,105 kilos in 1917), although CFSO expended most of its efforts on rubber harvesting and not on ivory because it found rubber to be more profitable. Other commercial agents, including the Corsican planter Santini, also purchased ivory, but statistics for their activities are not available.[56]

The purchase of animal skins fluctuated substantially over the first five decades of the twentieth century. At times merchants expressed little interest in the skins. The N'Goko-Sangha company did not purchase skins at all, though by 1917 CFSO and other merchants in Nola (such as the Maison LeComte et Samot and Maison Simarro) did buy primarily antelope hides from local hunters and trappers. A decade later only the Maison Coulon et Wiart was purchasing animal skins; but later, in 1934–35, demand for antelope skins peaked, tripling the production of skins from 10,351 in the second trimester of 1934 to 33,248 in the final trimester of 1935. The Compagnie Forestière, Lopes, and Santini all purchased these skins for export. By 1950 production had dropped once more, as commercial houses run by West African Hausa merchants purchased only some 5,000 skins during that year. Concessionary companies and the merchant-planters who replaced them also helped to develop a market for game meat. Santini and Lopes both hired their own hunters and trappers to capture game and sell it to their plantation workers in company stores.[57]

·In purchasing ivory, animal skins, and meat, the companies clearly saw themselves as profiting from an opportunity to exploit the forest, an opportunity, they claimed, that "villagers" and "pygmies" alike failed to recognize. In contending that "M'Bimou" and "Babinga" killed primarily for meat, and not for ivory or skins, companies reassured themselves that they were averting earlier fears of squandering opportunities to profit from forest exploitation. Nonetheless, company agents argued that African elephant-hunting practices shaped the fortunes of elephant populations in the Sangha forest. In 1910 a N'Goko-Sangha agent contended that elephants were almost limitless. But only two years later Poupon of CFSO queried whether elephants would disappear altogether from the Sangha forests. If they did, he asserted, it was only because of African hunting practices. Africans slaughtered elephants indiscriminately, and it hardly mattered whether the prey was male, female, or young. And by 1920 company administrators contended: "Tracked for a long time by the natives, elephants disappear little by little in the region. . . . One no longer finds them in the M'Bimou forest, situated between the Cameroon frontier and the Sangha River, and where, beyond the group of villages in N'Gombako, there are no villages installed."[58]

Commercial agents thus had shifted from one discourse of lost economic opportunity to another of game depletion. Just as they had earlier upbraided Africans for failing to recognize the economic promise of elephants and other game, commercial agents later blamed the disappearance of forest elephants on African hunters and trappers, even though the companies themselves had encouraged it by creating a market for ivory.[59]

Mpiemu responses to the legal establishment of concessions and the commercial exploitation of game resulting from it are best understood in terms of *doli*. European acquisition of and commerce in ivory and animal hides fit well into older Mpiemu notions of the forest as a space of actual and potential human exploitation. Such activities also continued earlier gendered and generational patterns of game exploitation. Mpiemu had long perceived hunting and trapping as exclusively male activities, with the fruits of these activities to be apportioned by a hierarchy of elders.[60]

But in providing ready markets for ivory, skins, and meat, concessionary and merchant-planter game exploitation also intensified elephant and other game hunting in the upper and middle Sangha. Sales of ivory and animal skins brought colonial subjects much-needed money to pay colonial taxes. And meat was a crucial resource for the first five decades of the twentieth century. Certainly precolonial war leaders had bolstered their authority by distributing meat to their followers, much as other leaders had done elsewhere in Africa. But upper and middle Sangha chiefs faced considerable governmental and company demands to pay taxes and supply labor for rubber collecting, coffee and other cultivation, road building, and other projects. Administrators threatened and imprisoned the beleaguered chiefs who failed to provide sufficient numbers of workers or to fulfill tax obligations. At the same time chiefs could find it enormously difficult to compel their followers to submit to colonial demands; among Mpiemu people increased demands for taxes and labor left them little time to cultivate fields or check their traps and thus precipitated numerous flights to Cameroon. But chiefly control over meat distribution could assuage some of these difficulties. A butchered elephant, for instance, provided an enormous amount of meat and fat, which women rendered by exposing the skin to the sun and collecting the drippings in large demijohns, using them later to fry fish and other foods. It may have helped to nourish African workers who felt pressed to supply their own food needs, and it may have prevented them from fleeing colonial obligations. Although they are difficult to support with direct evidence, there were widespread recollections of "big men" who held positions of authority in the colonial hierarchy and who killed and distributed meat, especially elephant meat, to followers. Other people used hunting and trapping as a means to pay their taxes and thus to avoid other colonial labor demands. European commercial interests, then, probably intensified game exploitation.[61]

Remembrances of hunting and trapping elephants and other game for the companies did become an important part of *doli,* as a series of narratives about the past, as places that helped Mpiemu to organize and recollect the past, and as a set of morally charged demands on contemporary interveners into the relations between people and the environment in the middle and upper Sangha. It is impossible to know whether knowledge of and narratives about elephant hunting had been part of *doli* previously. But Mpiemu certainly crafted a series of narratives around hunters, trappers, and meat at the time of intensive European commercial activity between the 1900 and the 1960s. Indeed, although documents show that ivory and skins were less important to companies than rubber, obtaining these products for colonizers occupied a huge part of the narratives about the colonial past. Some animal products, like skins, were simply one among many commodities that merchants demanded, although tellers of *doli* did not know why Europeans sought them. Ntuwo, Moguji, Bokete, Alouba, Longo, and Yerema all hunted or trapped meat, ivory, and animal hides for the merchant-planter Santini and peopled heroic narratives of a past time when Mpiemu in Lindjombo lived and ate well. Tellers of *doli* associated the hunter Alouba most closely with elephant hunting and recruitment for Santini. Several tellers noted that

Alouba had eight wives and many children, clearly the fruits of his labor for the *patron,* Santini. Indeed, Alouba's name and past activities were synonymous with a prosperous past, when Mpiemu freely hunted or trapped and consumed elephants (*ntchogi*) and other game. One elderly coffee worker and trapper, for instance, sighed: "Before we could kill elephants without limits, during the time of Santini. The big man who killed the elephants, [that was] Alouba. . . . He killed many, many, many." The former coffee manager and planter Satuba also invoked Alouba's time as a comparison to the one in which he lived:

> When we came here, we knew the forest, and we went into it. We saw that the forest was good and that there were a lot of animals moving around, and we started to set traps, we planted cassava, and we began to kill animals near our fields. We started to go deeper into the forest, like Alouba, who went down to the Ndoki River. He went to Ndoki and Kenie . . . [because] there is a river there with a lot of fish, and all the women and men would go there for fish, baskets and baskets and baskets of them. Some would set their traps at Ndoki. But now people run away, because the project has forbidden it [*laughing*].

Finally, the very mention of Alouba would launch eloquent descriptions about the rich elephant meat and fat that Mpiemu once consumed, uninhibited by contemporary state and conservation-project restrictions.[62]

This nostalgia for a past prosperity, embodied in stories of Alouba and elephant meat, is certainly not unique to Mpiemu tellers of *doli*. Nostalgia for a past prosperity (real or imaginary) under colonial rule is common elsewhere in Africa. In this context, this nostalgia speaks to a discourse of lost access to forest resources and to opportunities embedded in *doli*. Again, this discourse of lost access and opportunities echoes that of earlier European commentators, but Mpiemu reshaped it to express their own concerns about participating in a global economy that would allow them to accumulate clothing, cooking pots, and other consumer goods. In this sense, the nostalgic reminiscences positioned tellers of *doli* in relation to their pasts and made claims to truth about the dearth of present-day opportunities to use elephants and other game as people had in the past.

Past hunters and trappers also were incorporated into *doli* as places within the forest that organized recollections of this past. Momintuwo, the "child of Ntuwo," was the stream and fishing basin in which the trapper Ntuwo's daughters and granddaughters could fish during the dry season. Visits to Momintuwo, even though it was within the confines of the national park where hunting, trapping, and fishing were prohibited, signaled a claim about a past person who had successfully exploited the forest's wealth. Hunters and trappers identified a host of paths, trees, and sites of former camps that they associated with past people within the forest. The *ntche mi Alouba* (path of Alouba) was another such site of recollection. It was a forest path that linked Kwapeli and Salo with Lindjombo, and many Mpiemu recalled that they had once followed that path to seek work in Lindjombo. By 1993 the path was less used for passage between Kwapeli and Lindjombo, instead providing a jumping-off point for men to set traps along animal paths in the forest. Walking along the *ntche mi Alouba* thus not only led people to their trapping paths but also elicited stories of the hunters' past activities and prosperity. In evoking that past prosperity, trappers lamented the present losses that they suffered, because they were no longer able to tap into opportunities presented by global capitalism.[63]

PILLAGING AND PROTECTING FOREST GAME

From the beginning, French colonial administrators promoted forest exploitation, extracting building materials, game, and rubber from the forest to finance their operations in the middle and upper Sangha basin. They also hunted, at least to feed themselves and workers who accompanied them on expeditions and to protect their parties against marauding hippos or other game. And they indirectly promoted game exploitation by collecting head taxes from Africans and by fostering the development of commercial enterprises in the middle and upper Sangha.[64] But after 1910, colonial officials began to express their concern over the fate of game in French Equatorial Africa. Periquet's 1912–14 exploratory expedition in Congo and Cameroon not only expressed anxieties over the depletion of valuable game but identified its causes, solutions, and a particular vision of the protected forest, in which certain species thrived under French protection while others were exterminated. Periquet claimed that a host of species (though he did not list them) required protection because Africans overhunted them. Some Africans depleted hunting grounds by using fire to chase game. Others, namely the "Babingas" ("pygmies"), hunted excessively, emptying the forest of such big species as elephants. Still others, armed with powerful firearms by Europeans, were heedlessly destroying African game. The solution, he contended, was to forbid the use of fire to hunt, to monitor "Babinga" hunting, and to prohibit all Africans from using guns. The forest was, of course, also full of dangerous or pestiferous game, particularly leopards, panthers, and crocodiles, but also hippos and rhino; in his estimation such game merited extermination.[65]

Beginning in 1916, the French administration introduced measures to protect big game from overhunting and to earn revenues for the administration, though it later amended the list of protected species to include rhino, buffalo, and other game. The AEF's first hunting permits were instituted in 1929, for different classes of hunters: commercial, small sport, medium sport, big sport, and, of course, *indigène* (native).[66] These annual permits attempted to regulate how Africans could hunt, outlawing, for example, the use of fires and poison in capturing game. Permits also restricted what African hunters could kill. A 1930 law allowed them to hunt or trap all "unprotected" animals but limited them to two antelope per day, as well as two elephants, two hippos, one black rhino, and eight buffalo for the duration of the permit. Moreover, hunting laws forbade the killing of such game as chimpanzees and pangolins, except if the hunter held a scientific permit or needed to defend himself and his party. Other game, including elephants, hippos, forest buffalo, gorillas, bongo, and sitatungas, could only be hunted by those holding big-game commercial and sporting permits, as well as selected "native" permits. Africans were required to pay yearly taxes on the firearms that they held and on ivory that they had acquired.[67] The administration also began to seek out sites of high game and low human population densities, where it could establish parks. In 1934 it put into place the framework for several hunting reserves and parks in Ubangi-Shari and Chad, significantly restricting hunting and trapping. None were created in the middle and upper Sangha basin forest. And finally, by 1944, the AEF formally recognized various protected areas and set up a system of surveillance for some. But despite these numerous restrictions, French administrators and commentators were careful to claim that they had safeguarded Africans' rights to hunt for meat and to kill animals that threatened them or wrought havoc on their fields, and they offered bounties on every leopard, panther, and lion destroyed. Not surprisingly, white commercial and sports hunters had considerably more latitude concerning what game and how much they could hunt.[68]

In instituting these measures, the government of French Equatorial Africa articulated a particular vision of the forest and its game that was underpinned by a fear of diminishing herds but also of a serious loss of revenues for the state. Game-protection laws were, of course, supposed to safeguard certain mammals and birds from excessive hunting, and administrators expressed real concern that African hunters and trappers would deplete many forest species. Indeed, in 1930 Saint Floris, the inspector of hunting in the AEF who sought out possible sites for protection, contended that elephants had already nearly disappeared, and that Africans hunters continued to track them despite the fact that elephants with the largest tusks were long gone. French officials, however, did not undertake these restrictions simply to stop game depletion from the Sangha basin's rich forests and other hunting grounds in the AEF. Significant economic motivations underpinned these legal measures: such measures not only would prevent certain species from disappearing but also upheld game's value as scientific specimens, tourist spectacles, and sportsmen's prey. Thus protected game was part of the forest's riches and could earn revenues for the French colonial state.[69]

The effects of hunting laws on relations between people and their environment in the Sangha basin were equivocal. On the one hand, hunting laws may not have had as much influence as colonial officials had hoped. By all accounts, they were notoriously difficult to enforce, and colonial officials complained incessantly that enforcement was seriously deficient. Moreover, efforts to protect game were far overshadowed by a long-term concern over the economic well-being of France's equatorial African possessions. Lost economic opportunities, then, may have been more pressing than a fear of game depletion, and as Hardin has noted, game-protection efforts were undergirded by contradictory motivations—aesthetic, scientific, and economic.[70] Hunting laws also posed a considerable expense for the vast majority of Africans, particularly those who hunted big game with firearms and had to purchase multiple permits. Colonial hunting regulations themselves probably had little effect on the techniques by which Mpiemu and other Africans hunted and trapped, on how they created gendered persons through these activities, or on the ethnic differences that Mpiemu articulated through such practices.

Nevertheless, regulations did have some important effects. Archival sources reveal that Africans in the Sangha and N'Goko-Sangha *circonscriptions* did purchase hunting permits, though not in great numbers, and they were arrested for violating colonial game laws.[71] Hence responses to the restrictions were mixed: some hunters and trappers purchased less expensive permits and pursued small game (and sometimes big, "valuable" species, like elephants), while others simply refused to purchase permits at all and risked arrest by colonial authorities.[72] Regulations also altered relations between African authorities and their followers. Like precolonial *wani* (leaders) and *tuma* (master hunters), African chiefs used the hunting and distribution of forest game to consolidate and accumulate authority. But French hunting laws displaced the authority of the *tuma,* setting up French authorities as arbiters over African access to forest game. They thus fundamentally changed the open access that Mpiemu and other Sangha basin people had enjoyed. And hunting and trapping regulations could enhance or curb the authority that Sangha basin chiefs held over their people. These regulations set up a dual system, in which most Africans were legally denied access to big game, because many probably found it difficult to afford such permits, while white administrators, merchants, and missionaries could pay for them.[73]

Colonial efforts to regulate African hunting and trapping also became part of *doli,* as narratives about the colonial past. Mpiemu and other Africans recalled the myriad colonial hunting regulations as a simple, easily eluded tax on elephants killed, to be paid to colonial officials in exchange for limitless access to forest game. Although there were many laws restricting hunting and trapping, Mpiemu recalled the ivory tax as the colonial administration's sole intervention in the forest itself. For every elephant killed, tellers claimed, the hunter had to give one tusk to the colonial state. According to Kadele,

> When the French took the land, and when you killed an elephant, the gov-
> ernment took one [tusk], and you took one. You didn't give up all [of the
> ivory]. . . . You gave them one. Some [Mpiemu] people took the Beka [Aka or
> Ngombe] and killed elephants. Some [Mpiemu] killed [elephants] with their
> own hands, because the Mpiemu of the past, they were nasty, they were
> strong, [and] they didn't flee from anything. But to kill one [elephant] wasn't
> for everyone. It wasn't for everyone. In one village, you might find one [such
> hunter]. Like Alouba, his grandfather [*points to Alouba Clotere, who was sitting
> next to him*]. He would kill them. He bought a permit . . . and he killed ele-
> phants, and he could [keep and] sell both of the tusks because he had paid the
> government.[74]

Hence in this remembrance, buying a permit exempted elephant hunters from giving the state half of the ivory, allowing them to sell both of the tusks of an elephant that they killed. Recollections of other colonial hunting and trapping regulations simply never came up. No one ever mentioned the bounties offered for killing a leopard, although people discussed at length the ceremonies following the death of a leopard. Nor did they allude to the long list of regulations concerning which species hunters could kill or during what seasons the killing of such game was forbidden. Moreover, no one associated a discourse of forest game depletion with the colonial adminis-tration, even though the French colonial administration was a primary pur-veyor of it until independence. In fact, most Mpiemu (in Lindjombo and Kwapeli) only discussed the extensive regulations on hunting and trapping that the conservation project, administered by the state and the World Wildlife Fund, had enforced in the 1990s.[75]

What are we to make of these recollections? And why did Mpiemu recall colonial hunting restrictions as relatively unobtrusive? One possibility is that hunting regulations were never assiduously enforced, so that Mpiemu hunters and trappers were simply unaware of their existence. But this is unlikely, because there is ample evidence of permit purchases and arrests of subjects who transgressed colonial game laws. Given the persistent mobility of Africans throughout the Sangha basin and beyond, it seems improbable that stories of arrests would not have spread.

Another possibility is that Mpiemu have collapsed their recollections of colonial regulations into contemporary grievances over hunting and trapping laws. The omissions in Lindjombo Mpiemu recollections about colonial laws were particularly striking; tellers made it appear as if constraints on hunting or trapping had not existed before the creation of the Dzanga-Ndoki National Park and Dzanga-Sangha Special Reserve and the state-WWF enforcement of these protected areas and hunting laws. In this sense, Mpiemu echoed one part of a colonial discourse of loss—that of lost opportunities. In the early 1990s, when hunters and trappers found their activities constrained by an alliance between the state Ministry of Waters and Forests and the "project" (run and supported by the WWF, with the assistance of other aid organizations), they recalled colonial restrictions on hunting and trapping as a lenient, easily bypassed tribute to colonial authorities. In exchange for this tribute, Mpiemu hunters and trappers recollected, they could capture as much game as they wished. And they contrasted the colonial past of free access to forest game with the present, in which "project" restrictions curtailed hunting and trapping activities, causing Mpiemu and others to lose opportunities to earn money and to pay their taxes. Tellers of *doli* spoke of a past unfettered consumption of elephant and other animal fat and bemoaned their present plight, in which they were reduced to consuming only edible leaves and porridge. Although many people overstated the severity of contemporary restrictions on hunting and trapping, the lost access to valued forest game was more than simply a question of livelihood; it also marked the loss of an attribute that had once marked Mpiemu speakers as prosperous (fat) forest persons.[76]

MISSIONS IN THE FOREST

Africans, European companies, and administrators, however, were not the only exploiters of the Sangha basin forest. Struggling with the meager resources provided by their home missions, Swedish Baptists and French Catholics at first found the forest and its game to be both a useful subsidy to their aims of converting Africans to Christianity and a threat that stymied their aims of creating a Christian civilization in the Sangha. In order to construct villages from "wilderness," the Swedes mined the forest for building materials, particularly tropical hardwoods, to erect the houses, schools, and meetinghouses. And they sent out hunting parties to provide food for mission-station inhabitants, because the Örebromission in Sweden sent little money for the creation and upkeep of the Bilolo station in the upper Sangha. As many as twenty African hunters using spears and dogs would haul to the station large and small game—including a 175-kilo gorilla in 1936. The French Spiritans also extracted wood from the forest and hunted with African trackers to assist their missionizing efforts, using the meat to provide food for workers and schoolchildren in their mission stations, as well as for the faithful and potential followers in villages where the church was active.[77]

But the forest and its game also imperiled missionaries' aims. The Swedes contended that the "wilderness" needed to be cleared, rendered healthy, and emptied of threatening animals like leopards so that true Christians, not "heathen savages," inhabited it.[78] Karl Ekroth described his first impressions of the Örebromission's Kongofält, or "Congo field," as "depressing." "The tropical forest," he lamented, "threatened to swallow and engulf any trace of warmth and generosity in our hearts. Indeed, we were eager to spread the gospel to the children of this forest—but what a country! We knew however that this is our future field even if it was going to be hard to get started."[79] And they frequently complained of forest animals' attacks. In 1928 Aron Svensson mentioned that a leopard raided the Bilolo mission poultry house, and in 1939 another leopard struck repeatedly, carrying off rabbits and goats until missionaries and their followers built a trap to catch it.[80]

Spiritan and Capuchin perceptions of the forest and its game took a metaphorical turn; some perceived the forest as a nearly insurmountable barrier that rendered its inhabitants inhuman. In 1925 the young Père Marion, who sought out followers in the Mpiemu forests and had little to do with mission construction, saw the forest less as a source of useful, exploitable resources and more as an oppressive presence that kept its inhabitants in a state of torpor. The forest was a place of decay, an impenetrable barrier to social interaction, and an obstruction to his communications with a higher power: "The forest during the rainy season: a path of red clay, coated with a gluey paste of leafy debris: blackened leaves, enormous fruits crushed in their fall, bundles of rotting orchids. On this slippery ground, bulging with roots, littered with trees felled in storms, [it is] . . . impossible to read, to recite a little of the Bible. To speak . . . [in] the tyranny of this green giant, of this thick cover that hides the sky, is too great an effort." In effect, he located Mpiemu and game "outside the ambit of 'human society,' confined to inhabiting the margins and interstices of the social world."[81] Emerging from this forest, Père Marion arrived in the Mpiemu village of Zendi and awakened the village's somnolent inhabitants, who heard for the first time "words of God who made all and who died for all." "It is really astonishing," Marion added, "to see all of these primitives listening without a sound to this magnificent, divine epic." The forest, then, cloaked its inhabitants in its decay, but Père Marion and the Catholic Church would inspire the Mpiemu to embrace the "divine epic" and its teachings.[82]

More exoticized perceptions of the forest, its riches, and its people subsequently replaced these early views, though missionaries continued to see Mpiemu as fundamentally shaped by the forest. Later missionary perceptions strikingly echoed earlier observations of French explorers like Pouperon, who blurred distinctions between the forest, its game, and people. In the 1940s, for instance, Mgr Sintas, writing a story of a "fallen" woman, Henriette Odjèmo, could not resist opening with a description of the "Mbimous" that theorized about the influence of the forest and gorillas on their appearance: "This is the country of the Mbimous, a Bantu race, short and stocky, with ape-like faces. One wonders whether their height hasn't been reduced over the centuries by the shadowy mass of the forest; one also wonders if their resemblance to monkeys hasn't persisted just a little, because of their fear of gorillas. In this region there are more gorillas than men; and these gorillas love to amuse themselves by terrorizing women and children."[83] Eliding the distinctions between forest, game, and people, Sintas and later Catholic missionaries found the Mpiemu to be somehow less than human, lacking humanity because they were overpowered by the "shadowy mass of the forest" and outnumbered by gorillas, who had distorted their relations with one another.

This missionary discourse of a lack of humanity differed from those of lost opportunities and depleted game. But it retained the blurred distinctions between forest, people, and game that earlier explorers and concessionaires articulated, and it eventually was transformed into a lyrical, nostalgic, exoticizing perception of the forest and its game that bore some resemblance to later conservationist visions. In 1954 Père Edouard Castaing, writing to lay and missionary readers, still found the forest, its game, and its people to be part of a seamless, transformative experience. "The forest," he wrote, "conceals its eternal mystery in its silence, interrupted by the thumping cry of the gorilla and the call of the panther." Castaing went on to rhapsodize about "the evenings of supplication to the spirits or the nights of rowdy exultation, the rumble of the tom-tom of the pygmies beating the giant tree trunks that reverberate monotonously these echoes of joy or of tears."[84]

Evidence for changes in these poetic descriptions and blurring of distinctions between the Sangha forest and its game and people after the 1950s is scant. It is possible that missionaries developed a growing concern about the disappearance of game. Père Umberto went on his first hunt in 1954 and acknowledged that he happily let several animals escape his sight. "I sensed in myself," he concluded, "a strong feeling for ecology, for the environment, and for . . . Franciscanism!"[85] Umberto was making a joke at his own expense, but combining the Franciscan tradition of letting God's living creatures be with a regard for ecology and environment suggests that he may have also appropriated broader concerns about the loss of wildlife. The only additional missionary description comes in 1994, when Père Martin Morel described the Mpengou clearing in the Kwapeli, calling it a "paradise"—for parrots and game. But he excised all human presence from this forest. "Leaving Mboli, on the path of the Kouapulis [Kwapelis]," he observed, "[visitors] will find in the middle of a primary forest the famous Mpengou clearing, the paradise of parrots. . . . A stone's throw away, [there is] a pool where elephants wallow. We didn't see any. [We saw] two forest hogs, though, huge bushpigs, even more rare, and the tail of a small forest buffalo."[86]

Thus these missionaries had shifted from perceiving game as a subsidy and the forest as a barrier to evangelization to perceiving both the forest and its game in highly romantic terms. They did not change how Mpiemu hunted or trapped. But they did shape Mpiemu notions of past and present relations with game. Mpiemu (and other Sangha basin inhabitants with whom I spoke) grafted a Christianized notion of the person, which held that people were inherently superior to animals, onto their human-centered ecological perceptions. Christian writings gave people "dominion over the fish in the sea, the birds of the air, the cattle, all wild animals on land, and everything that creeps on the earth" (Genesis 1:26–28). Indeed, in the story of Noah, God told him: "The fear and dread of you will fall upon all the beasts of the earth and all the birds of the air, upon every creature that moves along the ground, and upon all the fish of the sea. They are given into your hands. Everything that lives and moves will be food for you. Just as I gave you the green plants, I now give you everything" (Genesis 9:2–3).

Contemporary restrictions on hunting and trapping in the Dzanga-Ndoki park and Dzanga-Sangha reserve, though sporadically enforced, not only violated older notions of the Mpiemu person but also transgressed Christian notions of human dominion over animals. Countless Mpiemu and others spoke of not being able to gather food within park boundaries because conservationists sought to safeguard those plants for gorillas, elephants, and other protected species.[87]

TIMBER, DIAMONDS, AND THE POSTCOLONIAL STATE

Following independence in 1960, the Central African Republic state continued colonial policies of promoting the exploitation of forest resources in large part to repay its debts. Like its colonial predecessors, the CAR state has treated the Sangha basin forest as a reservoir of economically valuable resources that alternately requires exploitation and protection. It has also struggled to balance conflicting international demands concerning its economy and management of natural resources and to control the industries developing around resource extraction.

The upper and middle Sangha contains extensive diamond deposits, located in the gravel layers that line the region's numerous streams. Diamond and gold prospecting took place in the Nola region of the upper Sangha in 1935 under the auspices of the Compagnie Équatoriale des Mines, though mining elsewhere in the upper Sangha attracted many workers from Kwapeli and Nola. By 1945 the Compagnie Minière de l'Oubangui Oriental had commenced mechanized diamond mining (and a small amount of gold mining) in the Nola region, sending prospecting teams to Salo and Bayanga in 1950. Although the governor of Ubangi-Shari sought to limit the numbers of workers who could be recruited to work in the mines, armed guards recruited workers freely. An infusion of American capital into mining enterprises also boosted diamond output. Indeed, by 1950 the Haute-Sangha regional head contended that diamond mining was one of its principal economic activities, along with coffee and cassava production.[88]

Mining continued unabated throughout the postindependence period, fostered by the Central African Republic, which benefits from diamond and gold extraction because it can repay its debts to lenders while investing little in the country's infrastructure. Individual agents of the state, too, can profit from such activities. In the mid- to late 1990s, most mining operations were underwritten by large foreign companies, like DeBeers. As Zeffirin Mogba and Mark Freudenberger describe their operations, these international concerns "subcontract[ed] . . . with the National Purchase Office and work[ed] . . . through intermediaries" and thus "invest[ed] . . . in diamond 'shanties' that have been established by immigrants throughout the region."[89] But the most visible investors and workers in diamond mining drew from a huge range of people, including state agents, West African investors and merchants, and Africans who had moved from other parts of the CAR and equatorial Africa.

Workers extracted diamonds using several methods. The *plongé* method, conducted primarily during the dry season when the waters were low, entailed diving into a river, scooping up large quantities of gravel in a basket, and dumping them into the bottom of a canoe. One or two men sitting in the canoe sifted through the gravel to find diamonds. More commonly, prospectors dug pits ranging from two to five meters deep. Small pits, easily constructed in five days, were most attractive to young men earning money for school or bridewealth, enabling them to acquire money quickly. Larger operations used motorized pumps to extract water from the large trench, and then diggers sifted through a gravel layer containing diamond deposits, called the *bon coeur,* or good heart. These big operations had more complex forms of organizations, involving negotiated arrangements that entitled the pump owner, owners of various rights in the land and the pit, and workers different percentages of revenues earned from diamonds. The CAR state sought to govern the diamond industry by requiring workers and merchants to purchase permits. Diamond workers stressed, however, the importance of luck in acquiring diamonds. Apoundjo Rene, a middle-aged Mpiemu Lindjombo man later elected to the National Assembly, had spent months in diamond fields in Kwapeli and elsewhere farther north, and he explained the extent to which miners would go to cultivate good luck: "People can go for years without getting anything. Some go to *marabouts* [Muslim teachers, diviners, and healers] for medicines to get luck. Some go into the forest, far! They look for places of the ancestors so that the ancestors will give them luck to find diamonds. These traditions, these are things of the ancestors [that some people twist to get diamonds]: some sleep in cemeteries, so that their ancestors will give them luck. Crazy things like that."[90] Despite the hard work, many people (including residents of Lindjombo) continued to mine diamonds, because the promise of spectacular wealth was palpable. Many told stories of miners who had dug pits for themselves and excavated ten-carat diamonds, acquiring cars, aluminum-roofed houses, and new clothes as a result.[91]

But Mogba and Freudenberger, who worked for the World Wildlife Fund, have pointed out that the real power lay in the hands of the merchants, who supplied the pumps, fuel, food, alcohol, and credit and "control[ed] . . . the diamond economy from the mines to the Bangui Purchase Office, where they act as intermediaries. This domination of the industry by merchants and intermediaries is one of the main obstacles to the state's effective control of the diamond economy."[92] Their point is an apt one, although both the state and its agents benefited considerably from diamond extraction and appeared to exercise considerable influence in the national industry. The state has had to juggle conflicting agendas, ones that have drawn from older discourses of loss. On the one hand, the Central African Republic has remained a poor country since independence, though one blessed with significant exploitable resources like diamonds. In the 1990s it also suffered several economic crises and continually sought out opportunities to exploit its forests, so as to tap into global sources of wealth and to avert political upheaval.[93]

Diamond mining, though it earned considerable benefits for some indi-viduals, came at a cost. Although the recent violence that has accompanied diamond mining in Sierra Leone and Angola did not occur in the CAR,[94] mining did promote considerable conflict among diamond workers, their *patrons,* and their kin networks. Diamond camps were renowned for the most vitriolic struggles over diamond profits and for extraordinarily nasty and violent sorcery deaths.[95] Diamond mining exacted significant environ-mental costs. It intensified forest-resource use. Farmers in Kwapeli expanded cultivation to supply diamond workers and their families, although some workers turned to farming themselves to avoid paying high prices for cassava. Hunting and trapping also increased substantially to feed workers in the dia-mond camps. In addition, mining diverted waterways, causing them to dry up during the dry season and to flood during the rainy season, and water pumps polluted these waters with oil and other chemicals.[96] Hence diamond extraction was illegal in the Dzanga-Sangha reserve, even though the reserve had many large diamond-mining camps along the Alindjombo, Kangabe, Yobé, Belemboke, and Lipipi Rivers. The CAR thus found itself entrenched in an old dilemma. On the one hand, it needed to exploit diamond reserves or risk squandering a valuable economic opportunity. But if it did encour-age diamond excavation, it would inflict serious damage on the forest.

A similar dilemma, in which the CAR state had to balance its anxieties over lost economic opportunities and fears of depleted forests, existed in the 1990s with the harvest of tropical woods. Logging began in this part of the Sangha basin forest later than it did elsewhere in Ubangi-Shari and Congo. In 1963–64 French foresters conducted the first forest inventory, identifying several exploitable timbers, including sapele (*Entandrophragma cylindricum*) and sipo (*E. utile*) mahoganies, high-quality hardwoods used for veneers and fine furniture, and less valuable whitewoods used for plywood, such as ayous (*Triplochiton scleroxylon*) and limba (*Terminalia superba*).[97]

In 1970 the state under the leadership of Jean-Bedel Bokassa accorded logging concessions to a series of mostly European-owned enterprises in the Sangha basin. Slovenia Bois, a Yugoslav-owned company based in Bayanga, logged some 1,000 square kilometers of the forest before it went bankrupt, only to revive in 1994 under a new name, Sylvicole de Bayanga. Other com-panies acquired concessions in Salo (SESAM Bois), in the forests south of Lindjombo, in Bela (Cameroon), and Libongo (Cameroon). Logging enter-prises rarely remained commercially viable for long, constantly beset by poor management, exorbitant transportation costs, and fluctuating world timber prices.

Despite the continual failures, the state remained hospitable to logging concerns because it badly needed concession rents and stumpage fees. In 1986, under pressure from the World Bank and the International Monetary Fund to adhere to a structural adjustment program, the state continued to welcome foreign-owned logging companies so as to boost exports and to pay its remaining government functionaries.[98] And these financial pressures intensified in 1994, when France devalued the *cfa* franc and left the CAR even more desperate for cash. Although the World Wildlife Fund and GTZ attempted to purchase the logging concession to stop timber exploitation in 1993, the Central African Republic state granted Sylvicole de Bayanga a concession where previous logging enterprises had operated and failed.[99]

Nevertheless, the contributions of Slovenia Bois/Sylvicole de Bayanga to the national and local economies were significant. Although figures for previous years (the focus of this study) are not available, in 1996 the company employed 404 workers, spending some $371,998 in salaries and taxes on their employees and effectively supporting an estimated 2,000 people who were related to these workers. The number of employees apparently decreased in 1997. But the company also paid local taxes; hired a doctor, a midwife, and a nurse who were available to the entire Bayanga population; provided salaries for two teachers in Bayanga and one in Lindjombo; and maintained the Beya-Lindjombo road.[100]

But these logging activities may have come at an environmental cost, although the effects of timber extraction in the Sangha basin have been much disputed. Americans working for the WWF Dzanga Sangha project cited a catalog of loggers' offenses, evoking an older discourse about depleted forests. Loggers selectively cut species that clients want to purchase, and in theory this management system alters the forest's structure in the short term but allows it to regenerate over time. In practice, however, incidental damage to the forest canopy can range widely. In Gabon, according to White, logged forests suffered very low canopy loss (10 percent), but elsewhere in Africa's logged forests, canopy loss has exceeded 50 percent. To my knowledge, canopy loss in the Slovenia Bois/Sylvicole de Bayanga concession was never measured. But logging also could inflict other kinds of damage. To remove the enormous felled trees from the forest, loggers in the Sangha forests created skidder trails, which compacted forest soils. The result, WWF conservationists contended, was that logging encouraged human in-migration to ecologically sensitive forest, promoted erosion, opened up the previously inaccessible forest to hunting, and destroyed the habitats of primates that move only through forest canopy. They further argued that timber companies, faced with exorbitant transport costs from Central Africa's landlocked interior to cities and coasts, had every incentive to fell more than permitted by state-imposed logging restrictions. And state employees working for the Ministry of Waters and Forests, who went unpaid for several months and were desperate for cash, were no less interested in permitting these transgressions. For their part, officials of SESAM and Slovenia Bois contended that Sangha basin forest degradation resulted not from logging but from farming.[101]

Despite the ecological costs of logging and diamond mining, Mpiemu and many other Sangha basin inhabitants welcomed these enterprises because extracting timber and diamonds could contribute to wealth accumulation and could promote access to powerful people.[102] Mpiemu have interpreted these extractive interventions through the lens of *doli,* grafting their understandings of logging and diamond mining onto older Mpiemu perceptions of the forest as a space of potential or past exploitation. These extractive activities were the latest in a series of forest-exploitation practices, led by white *patrons* and carried out by African workers in exchange for wealth in material goods, in experience, and in people. Both activities fit well into the vision elaborated in the tales of Ntchambe Mekwombo, Meburi, and Bilon: logging and diamond mining helped to clear the forest terrain and thus were evidence of white outsiders' continuing power to transform tangled landscapes into cleared, productive ones. "White people," Kadele noted once, "are like a second Ntchambe. You see, if I speak, [my words] will not reach Bilolo. But they, they can speak to France! Isn't that something of Ntchambe?"[103] His words thus echoed an older perception of white people from cleared spaces who used to transcend great distances.

Logging and diamond mining also continued many familiar practices of colonial rule, particularly a gender division of labor through which men and women could become male and female persons. Men who worked in diamond mines or for the logging companies perceived that they were simply the latest generation of workers, much like their fathers and grandfathers, who had cleared the forest to extract valued commodities from it. Women had long supported men's extractive and clearing activities by farming and gathering foods. The advice of *doli* admonishing young girls to fulfill their duties to their husbands was still relevant. "A man marries a woman to do work in the house," Lengi Emilienne told her young daughter, her arm draped around her neck. "He leaves a field for you. You plant the field because you will find food. You take the food, you give it to your children."[104]

It remains highly doubtful that despite its embrace of the policy and practice of conserving its forests, the state will ever renounce timber harvesting or diamond mining in its Sangha-Économique Prefecture, in which this park and reserve lie. Diamond mining, illegal in the Dzanga-Sangha reserve, remained well entrenched in Kwapeli, although antipoaching patrols surveyed and dismantled mining sites more actively in southern zones of the reserve and park. The Kwapeli diamond camps had existed well before the creation of the reserve and, according to the project's primary technical counselor, were simply "too large to move."[105] At one moment in the early 1990s, however, the future of logging in the Dzanga-Sangha reserve seemed tentative. At that time Slovenia Bois faced serious financial problems, and workers remained uncertain whether the company would continue its operations. Logging companies in Cameroon, where Mpiemu and other Central Africans had once found jobs, would no longer hire Central Africans.

Mpiemu whom I encountered interpreted this momentary decline in timber exploitation by invoking *doli,* and particularly an older discourse of lost opportunities that they had transformed into one of deprivation, disconnection, and invisibility in the absence of European outsiders to stimulate economic activity. They voiced older expectations that "hot" productive places were ones in which white outsiders actively sought the forest's riches and provided Africans with access to consumer goods. Deprived of outsiders' attentions, which had provided them with lucrative opportunities to exploit forest timber, Mpiemu and others in Lindjombo felt consigned to invisibility, disconnected from broader networks of economic and political power. One elderly woman lamented Lindjombo's deterioration in stark terms: "There is no money, because white people aren't here any more." Bibelo Albert and Mamo Veronique complained similarly: "Now that white people aren't here, we don't sit well. We have no money." And the elderly Yodjala bitterly lamented the results of this absence of white outsiders' forest exploitation by castigating "those French." "We live like goats, and we get sick like animals. . . . Those French, they have nasty hearts, they have nasty hearts. They have a lot of things, bicycles, many, many things. And we sit here, and we try to create little things [*pointing to the basket he was weaving*], but we have nothing.[106]

Yodjala's criticisms of France echoed the thoughts of many Mpiemu and other Sangha basin peoples during 1993. At that time France was openly rethinking its relationship with francophone Africa and the Central African Republic, scaling back its financial commitments and preparing for the 1994 *cfa* devaluation. This contemporary situation evoked for many people recollections of the early twentieth century, when the French and Germans had battled for control of the Sangha basin, and they assessed the contemporary debates over which power would "sit with" the Central African Republic through the prism of the past. Yodjala continued:

> If they [the French] don't have any money, they should cede their place to Germany. The Germans can take the land. You know that the Germans once sat here. . . . They did well. We sat better with them than with the French. But the Germans took the land first. The French came, and they wanted to take the land, so they fought a war with the Germans. Some people died in Nola. . . . The Germans and the French fought in Nola, and the French pushed the Germans that way [*waving his hand in the direction of the Sangha River and Cameroon*], to Cameroon. The French came to this place and they ate all the land. Now, Patassé has told us if the French don't have any money, it's okay. The Germans can take the land.[107]

These sentiments seemed far more muted in Kwapeli and Salo, where diamond mines and SESAM, the functioning timber company, generated jobs and markets for cultivated foods, fish, and game. Many people acknowledged that such activities were important and productive, but a few Kwapeli Mpiemu, including those who had benefited from diamonds either directly or indirectly, also mourned the ways in which the riches generated from diamonds had depleted elders' authority of the past. Nyambi Patrice, for instance, argued that diamond mining had laid waste to old duties that newly married sons and their wives once performed for elders. "The child goes to do diamond work," Nyambi explained. "He finds money, and he buys his wife. He no longer knows his mother anymore. You want to open your mouth [to demand that your daughter-in-law do some work for you], and he says, "Ay! Do I have to do anything for you? Did you buy a wife for me? My wife, come here, and we will leave [my parents].'"[108] Such assertions of loss, however, came up relatively rarely.

CONSERVING AND CONSUMING THE FOREST

Mpiemu interpretations of the forest, its past and present exploitation, and the ways in which these interpretations and environmental practices generate persons and social groups within the forest are critical to understanding responses to conservation efforts in the middle Sangha forest. Animated by fears of a forest depleted of its timber and game, the personnel of the WWF conservation project in 1993 based their restrictions on hunting, trapping, mining, logging, and other forms of forest exploitation upon assumptions about the history of the region. In this historical vision the forest was an inherently fragile landscape populated by unique and charismatic mammals, including forest elephants, lowland gorillas, bongo, and chimpanzees. All had suffered intensifying threats over the twentieth century. As one Central African Ministry of Waters and Forests agent explained to a meeting of

Lindjombo inhabitants, "Trees, they are a great treasure. We have to make certain that they remain. Long ago, people didn't cut down trees. They took paths into the forest to find game. Now we have to protect our forests well, as our fathers told us, . . . [to ensure] that we remain 'sitting' well. [There-fore] nets, traditional traps, and guns are okay to use for hunting. But not wire snares. . . . You can use your guns. So long as you pay the taxes on your gun, you can go and hunt animals. You can also use old traps, like those of our fathers." Forest exploitation did not, however, begin recently but has been part of a repertoire of the livelihood and the cultural and historical practices of Sangha basin inhabitants for a very long time. Some conservationists were well aware of a longer history of forest exploitation, though they insisted that the scale of such exploitation expanded considerably over the past century. Such claims appear to have merit in some locations but not in others.[109]

Other conservationists invoked somewhat different historical interpreta-tions of the forest's past, claiming that repeated "cycles of [economic] boom and bust resulted in . . . cycles of immigration and emigration" from waxing and waning companies that exploited the forest.[110] Migrants were therefore agents of destruction in this historical vision, and as I have argued elsewhere, most WWF conservationists characterized Mpiemu people as migrants, marauders of the forest who stood in contrast to a changing cat-egory of "indigenous" people. The "migrant" label seems dubious, not only because part of the Dzanga-Sangha Special Reserve extends into Kwapeli, where Mpiemu have lived since at least the late nineteenth century, but also because mobility has been a hallmark of the Sangha basin's past. These assign-ments of blame for forest destruction paved the way for interventions by the state and nongovernmental organizations. Blaming Africans to justify such interventions uncannily echoed earlier colonial claims that Africans were despoiling their forest resources and thus required the tutelage of outsiders to exploit and manage their forest resources rationally.[111]

All of these interpretations of the forest's past were premised on the assump-tion that contemporary exploitation would ultimately deplete the forest of its game, trees, and the ecological relations that made this region such a unique one. Conservationists argued that forest loss could only be reversed by stemming "the pressures of expanding human populations, agriculture, logging, and development projects," by bolstering wildlife departments' authority, and by eradicating corruption among government officials who turned a blind eye to illegal hunting, ivory trading, and diamond mining.[112]

Establishing the park and reserve entailed restrictions on an array of environmental activities, but most relevant here are those on hunting, trap-ping, mining, and timber harvesting. Laws regulating hunting and trapping arguably had the most profound influence on inhabitants' livelihoods and perceptions of the past. Within the confines of the reserve, trappers were only permitted to use "traditional" traps, that is, those constructed from forest vines, sticks, and logs. The state outlawed snare traps, and in 1993 when the project's antipoaching patrols found trappers in the forest, they would confiscate their snare traps. Under the CAR law in 1993, hunters were required to buy a series of permits, just as they had been during colonial rule. Upon purchasing a gun, hunters had to pay a special arms tax and a stamp, which cost $100 before the 1994 devaluation. In addition, each year hunters purchased a permit to carry a gun, a permit to kill small game, and a hunting permit card, totaling $50. Loaning a gun to another hunter necessitated other permits. And those who wanted to hunt big game were required to purchase a $70 game-hunting permit. Finally, in 1993 hunters were supposed to pay a tax on each animal killed, ranging from approximately $6 for small mammals (duikers and monkeys) to $330 for bongo, leopards, and sitatungas. The enforcement of such regulations, however, appears to have varied over time as well as by location. Antipoaching guards, originally drawn from the ranks of some of the biggest hunters and trappers, could not patrol the forest everywhere at once. Moreover, guards had kin and marriage connections to many inhabitants, and thus arrests could be fraught with all sorts of conflicts. In early 1990s when I did my field research, stories of guards' abuses circulated with some regularity, though it appears that actual abuses diminished later in the decade.[113]

In 1993, however, Mpiemu interpreted and responded to these restrictions through the framework of *doli*. As their parents and grandparents had once ignored colonial restrictions on hunting and trapping, many simply disregarded state laws governing these activities, contending that they were too expensive, grossly inconvenient, or impossible to follow. Some set complex arrays of traps, so that if they were detained by antipoaching patrols, they might show some but not all of their set traps. Hunters frequently borrowed others' guns without paying fees on permits or on each animal felled. Virtually all trappers set cable snares, contending either that they did not know how to set "traditional" traps with forest cords or that it was too difficult to do so, because these traps decayed quickly in the humid forest. And many relied upon Aka to net hunt or trap meat for them. All had to balance the risks of capture by antipoaching patrols with their needs for meat and income, and frequently a complex calculus of where, how long, and when antipoaching patrols would make their rounds in the forest governed where, when, and how trappers set and checked their traps. Hardin mentioned in her study a delightful parody of the project, created by Mpiemu who frequented trapping grounds along the Mossoumba, a tributary of the Sangha. They declared these grounds the "Reserve Spéciale Nana Mossoumba," creating a complex hierarchy of command, identifying various activities, and "debating who is the third versus sixty-third in the convoluted chain of command of the 'Nana Mossoumba Very, Very Special Reserve.'"[114]

Such jocularity should not, however, mask the seriousness with which people leveled accusations about how conservation measures hampered their activities. In Lindjombo restrictions set by the state and enforced by the project were met with contentions that project personnel intended for people to go hungry. And *hunger* was a crucial term that evoked the prosperity of *doli*, juxtaposing it to a widespread contemporary sense of deprivation. In the midst of a village meeting, a Mpiemu man rolled up his trouser leg, tearing it as he did so, and dramatically pointed to his bared leg: "I am an old man. Look at my legs! Look at my legs! I have grown thin because of the work of the project in our forest. I have gone into the forest to look for food, to eat meat. But the guards are brutal. They won't let you pick *koko* [*Gnetum africanum*] leaves—that's food for the gorillas!"[115] So far as he and other hunters and trappers were concerned, the project and its employees had little regard for the welfare of reserve inhabitants, and they frequently repeated stories of antipoaching guards raiding hunting camps, beating or knifing arrested trappers and hunters, confiscating meat, and puncturing cooking pots. Restrictions on foraging and on hunting and trapping effectively transgressed Mpiemu notions of a person-centered ecology, in which they identified different types of forest in terms of past or potential uses. Many Mpiemu people living near the park and reserve accused the WWF of privileging the well-being of forest animals over people, thus violating Christian notions of the superiority of persons over animals.[116]

The state, and specifically the Kolingba regime, received its share of the blame as well. At a political rally in Lindjombo, one Mpiemu trapper and farmer accused Laurent Pampali, the Mpiemu politician and minister under then-President Kolingba: "We have heard that you and Kolingba, you have sold our forest to WWF. You have sold our forest, and you have eaten all the money. Here the [antipoaching] guards beat people in the bush brutally. They punctured our cooking pots. They eat all of our cassava at our hunting camps, and then they burn down our huts [at the camps]! We need food, and we need money."[117]

Forest-exploitation restrictions did more than disrupt older livelihood practices. For Mpiemu, they kept people from taking advantage of potentially productive opportunities—a historical pattern of resource use well established by a century of forest exploitation. In rendering certain sites off-limits, they disconnected Mpiemu in Lindjombo from activities and sites that allowed them to organize and recollect their pasts. And they prevented the transmission from elders to juniors of knowledge (about forest-exploitation practices but also about past people and events) that was central to educating young people and leaving a person behind. These lamentations of hunger were woven into narratives about past experiences of fat eating and of participation in broader economic and political networks. In past times, tellers of *doli* declared, people killed and ate elephants and other game without fear of state and project retribution. Yodjala, for instance, asserted: "We used to kill elephants a lot. Alouba killed many. We ate the meat, and we grew fat. Now, we eat cassava leaves, and that's it. We don't grow fat."[118] Although cassava leaves and palm oil made a common sauce that people ate with cassava porridge, this man was arguing that a meatless diet was woefully inadequate. According to many Mpiemu, that fat provided the critical energy that enabled people to work in their fields and to produce additional food. Hence, for Lindjombo Mpiemu commentators restrictions on hunting and trapping altered their access to prosperity that they associated with the past, to the power to transform their bodily fat into productive work and additional food.

Only rarely did a few younger Mpiemu appropriate the project's discourse of loss. In a discussion about a gendarme accused of elephant poaching, Amions Anaclet (who never lost an opportunity to disparage the project's activities, even though he worked for it from time to time) commented:

> Me, I was a poacher a long time ago. But I don't do it anymore. If people were left alone to hunt elephants as they wished, they would finish off the elephants. There wouldn't be any left. My father never hunted elephants himself. But he did help to trade the ivory in the time of Santini. He worked with Alouba. . . . [It is necessary to protect elephants] because what if your child grew up and you had to say, "In another time, there were these great animals. They were strong, robust, these elephants.' Your child could only see photos of the animal but could never see the real thing. I would be angry if there weren't any elephants anymore.

That said, Amions (who died in 1995) fairly flaunted state restrictions on hunting and trapping; he hunted without the required permits and set cable snares to trap game. A Mpiemu woman, Biloue Brigitte, simply observed that after a project vehicle had taken her with the Catholic Mission Legionnaires [a women's group] to see elephants gathered at the Dzanga clearing: "I saw the elephants, [and] I was no longer hungry to eat elephant meat. I saw their skin, dirty!! Their feet are too big! It's not appealing."[119]

School-age students, too, received environmental education each week, taught by a Peace Corps volunteer and a Central African counterpart, paid by the WWF. Forming nature clubs in Bayanga and Lindjombo, environmental educators instructed students about the forest's ecology and the ways in which human activity could damage it. In one activity children stood close together to represent trees in "a huge tract of undisturbed tropical rain forest."[120] When part of the forest was chopped down, students had to deduce the effects that the loss of forest cover would have for plants and animals accustomed to living in the middle of the forest, not on the forest edge. Other activities encouraged students to think of "local" and "global" reasons "to preserve the rain forest." In the sessions that I witnessed, students dutifully performed the exercises and seemed to enjoy them. But they faced a stark contradiction at home, where they consumed meat caught with illegal cable snares or shot with unregistered guns. I regret that I never asked these young students how they reconciled these different perspectives on the forest and its game. Nevertheless, it remains unlikely that Mpiemu would ever adopt conservationist discourse of depletion and loss in the forest wholeheartedly and unequivocally. The forest was still a place of past and potential exploitation, as well as a source of materials (game, palm wine, building materials, and foods) that not only were crucial to their livelihood but also helped them to leave behind gendered, ethnic, and generational persons and to transact social relations.

CONCLUSION

Through the lens of *doli,* the effects of forest exploitation over the twentieth century seem equivocal. On one hand, Mpiemu people in the Sangha basin fit outsiders' forest-exploitation practices into older perceptions of the forest. Into their human-centered ecology of the forest and its game, Mpiemu incorporated the activities of new colonial markets that connected them to broader political and economic networks. On the other hand, the influence of these outsiders' activities on *doli* was dramatic: many Mpiemu people came to see the forest as a space and its rubber, timber, game, and other products as valued resources for which outsider access could be exchanged for imported consumer goods and wealth in persons and accumulated knowledge. As a result of their engagements with colonial administration, commercial concerns, and missionaries, Mpiemu people grafted a colonial discourse of lost opportunities and missionary notions of deprivation, hunger, and redemption through charity onto their perceptions of the forest. Many contemporary Mpiemu responded to 1990s conservation interventions in terms of their accumulated understandings of past and present relations between persons and forest. Enforced laws on game hunting and trapping transgressed older Mpiemu notions of the person, as well as appropriated colonial and Christian notions. Complaining of the lost economic opportunities, Mpiemu bemoaned their present sense of deprivation through an idiom of hunger.

CONCLUSION

I N LATE 1993, after I asked Kadele Charles how he knew so much about *doli,* he said: "Our language hasn't changed. It is what people have seen that has changed." He explained that when he was born, elderly people living near him had seen much change during their lifetimes, and they had conveyed something about it to him. Kadele stressed the continuities in how generations communicated with one another about *doli* (although the Mpiemu language had acquired new words), and he contrasted these continuities with *doli's* changing content—its people, events, places, and environmental practices—of which elder generations spoke. Our conversation had been an amalgam of Sango and Mpiemu, interspersed with occasional French words, and Kadele's second sentence literally translates from Sango as "It is seeing things that have changed," suggesting that not only what people saw but also how they saw changed.[1] His remarks evoke a central argument of this book, that over the twentieth century the knowledge, practices, and ways of seeing the forest environment and the past changed as Mpiemu speakers encountered and interacted with powerful outsiders.

Exploring *doli* illuminates the means by which one group of people has perceived, characterized, evaluated, and imagined their environments and pasts. A complex, multifaceted process and body of knowledge, *doli* is intimately tied up with ways of perceiving the villages, *panjo,* hunting camps and paths, fields, and streams in the forest that have accumulated different meanings over the twentieth century. But *doli* is also a medium through which Mpiemu people highlighted and debated people, events, places, natural-resource exploitation, social and political relations, social categories and self-definitions, and environmental interventions that have been important to them. Surely Choumara, sleeping sickness, Alouba, Santini and Lopes, *regroupement,* coffee and cassava fields, and Christian evangelism all constitute major topics of *doli.* Moreover, these people, interventions, places, and spaces altered how people reproduced themselves socially, culturally, and historically, how they realized themselves by accumulating experiences over their lifetimes, and how they accumulated wealth in people and things.

But this study of *doli* not only reveals an alternative way that people can evaluate their environments and pasts. It also demonstrates that such processes and bodies of knowledge make a difference in how we understand struggles over access to spaces, places, and valued resources. In the late 1980s and early 1990s, many Mpiemu interpreted conservation efforts through the prism of *doli*. *Doli's* knowledge, practices, sites, interpretations, and ways of seeing underpinned Mpiemu responses to contemporary restrictions on hunting, trapping, logging, mining, gathering, farming, new settlements, and mobility (in some parts of the forest).

Two images of Mpiemu people's contemporary past have continued to haunt me over the years following my research in the middle and upper Sangha basin: an elderly man, sitting on a fallen tree in his field, recounting the death of his daughter and a group of furious men holding a WWF truck and its passengers hostage. Together, these arresting images help to make the central themes of this book come alive and reveal how *doli* emerged in contemporary land-use practices and struggles.

The first image took shape during a forest walk with Mpeng Patrice, as we searched for medicinal plants, a practice that he associated with *doli* because it was based on ancestral knowledge of the forest. On our return we emerged from the forest and entered his field, which contained a large fallen tree. Patrice sat on the tree and began to speak of how his young daughter had been crushed to death by a falling tree following a mild rainstorm in 1957. Her death, he asserted, was not accidental. He had recently come to Lindjombo to work on Santini's coffee plantation. Dreaming one night that his arms and chest were covered with blood, Patrice awoke, frightened, and he resolved not to go into the forest the next morning to check his traps. In fact, he told his wife that they should remain at home the entire day. His wife, however, dismissed his dream, and she convinced him to venture to their field to harvest peanuts. In the field a small rainstorm passed, and Patrice's family huddled under their shelter to avoid the rain. But a slight wind felled a large tree on the field's edge, and it crashed into the shelter, crushing his firstborn child, seven-year-old Sassio Marie, and causing her to die. Crazed with grief, Patrice canoed downriver to Ouesso to consult a diviner to find out who had caused his daughter's death. A distant kinswoman in Lindjombo, the diviner told Patrice, had taken a dislike for him and had killed his daughter. According to many Lindjombo inhabitants, Patrice possessed an active *alembo*, the substance or crablike creature in the belly that gave human hosts occult powers, and he had transmitted this active substance to his daughter.[2] Marie's death, then, prevented Patrice and his family from reproducing this vital substance and from "leaving a person behind."

In the field where his daughter died, Patrice claimed that for decades he had been reminded of his inability to leave his daughter behind him. He occasionally witnessed a gorilla (*ntchilo*) exhibiting peculiar behavior at the very place that she died. The gorilla would emerge from the forest, sit at the field's edge, and gaze placidly at Patrice. Patrice, in turn, would cock his head quizzically, asking, "Are you an animal? Or a person?" The gorilla, he believed, was neither a person nor an animal, but some manifestation of his dead daughter. This manifestation prevented him from abandoning that field, and he would continue to cultivate it as long as he was able. Patrice later confided that the deaths of Marie and later a second child galvanized him to travel to Nola to be baptized at the Catholic mission.

This story, its context, and the sites of recollection that it elaborated capture central themes of this book. First, they illustrate how *doli* works as a process of seeing, a set of narratives, as practices and knowledge associated the distant past, and as a site of accumulated past experiences. Patrice's insistence on continuing to cultivate the field and plots around it was part of a long-standing process in which people perceived and characterized the forest as a potentially exploitable space. Fields and forests were interrelated, both materially linked through livelihood practices and symbolically connected through idioms of vines and fat. Chapters 4, 5, and 6 have also shown the ways in which many Mpiemu imagine these sites and spaces to be linked through the presence or clearing of vines but also through idioms of vines and cords that evoke the connections of kinship (Patrice and his daughter) and patronage (of the European commercial agents who helped to create Lindjombo's plantations) that tied them to broader political economies. These sites and spaces were also bound together through the circulation of fats, as people hunted forest animals, consumed them in villages, and then marshaled their bodily fats to work fields, whose soils also contained fats that allowed food crops to flourish. Fields and forests had a significance that transcended material relations; as Patrice's story and his repeated cultivation of the field show, they were intimately related to leaving a person behind. In Patrice's case, he unsuccessfully sought to leave a child behind. But other sites (kitchens, coffee fields, forest paths, streams) were critically important in reproducing different kinds of gendered, generational, kin group, regional, and ethnic persons.

Some of the features of Patrice's narrative also attested to broader environmental, economic, and political changes in the Sangha basin in which

Mpiemu people participated, altering *doli* as a way of engaging with and making sense of those changes. Patrice's very presence in Lindjombo, for instance, reflected his participation in the recruitment of workers from Kwapeli, Bilolo, and elsewhere to expatriate-owned coffee plantations cleared from the forests of the middle Sangha. Chapters 4 and 5 elaborated this process and its effects in introducing young men and women to new ways of organizing their domestic spaces, new forms of environmental exploitation and geographical mobility, and relatedly, new ways of becoming a person, of self-realization, of accumulating wealth and leaving a person behind.

The second image, of the angry men surrounding a WWF truck, occurred one Saturday morning in May 1993, when some twenty-five men staged a protest (which they called a strike) in the village of Lindjombo and prevented the truck and its riders from leaving the village. Many, though not all, participants identified themselves as Mpiemu. The WWF truck had arrived earlier that morning to conduct a health clinic in the Aka camps on the outskirts of the village and to teach a nature class to young students at the village school. But once the project personnel had completed their business, the village men began to clamor angrily and blocked the truck's departure. The truck could not leave, the men asserted, until they had received their pay for reclearing a road farther south in the forest, where a logging company had once operated. Though the protesters contained among their ranks some of the most bitter critics of the project's activities, they had cleared the old road for the WWF project, performing two weeks of work (one during the previous month and one in the past week). Market women in Lindjombo sought to capitalize on the strike, but in vain. Several hurried their prepared foods to the marketplace when they discovered that a truckload of hungry people might spend several hours there. But when the stranded project personnel hustled to the gendarmerie to avoid an angry confrontation with the unpaid workers, the women were left with cooking pots full of stews and mounds of steamed cassava, but no money. Hours later the national director, technical counselor, and a civil servant who directed antipoaching efforts arrived in Lindjombo, seeking resolution to the standoff. Promising to pay the taxes of workers who had not yet paid them, the national director confessed that "we all have money problems" and that the project had been absorbed with other concerns. He resolved to pay the workers as soon as possible.[3] The protest ended uneventfully, with grumbling protestors wandering back to their homes, and they eventually received their pay.

This episode illustrates how histories of environmental interventions accumulated in particular places that became sites of *doli,* which in turn shaped understandings of WWF-state conservation efforts. As chapter 4 described, roadwork occupied a singular place in *doli*. Part of French colonial efforts to reshape the region's landscape, building roads had involved recruiting men from distant villages to clear a dense forest tangle of vines and trees. This very road had once been part of the French colonial effort to create the North-South Road that was to link Berbérati with French holdings in Middle Congo. The road reorganized the Sangha forest, promoting movement and a colonial communication network along a wide, cleared road in the forest between colonially created, regrouped, but also increasingly depleted villages. After independence, however, the road had acquired a different significance as a road recleared and used by SALCAPA, a Libyan-owned logging company. Hence it also evoked for the workers a prosperity that they associated with outsiders' forest exploitation, explored in chapter 6. This episode further illustrates how an environmental intervention could contribute to accumulated notions of a person (in this case gendered, but in others generational, familial, or ethnic). While roadwork reinforced older notions of the male person, who had long assumed responsibility for forest clearing, it also grafted new conceptions of men as workers for a colonial state, and later as mobile laborers for European and North African enterprises.

The strike revealed how Mpiemu understood contemporary environmental interventions through the prism of *doli*. To be sure, the protest had several proximate causes. The state was collecting its yearly tax, and the local gendarmerie had imprisoned several road workers who had not yet paid. Two funerals in the same week had further strained financial resources. Lindjombo strikers also took their inspiration from a long strike in the distant capital, Bangui, where the state had failed to pay most of its civil servants for many months.[4] And finally, the road crews believed that the WWF project's technical counselor had recently returned from Bangui with a full cashbox, and yet they had seen none of its contents.

But the strike also erupted from underlying tensions surrounding the conservation interventions, which Mpiemu interpreted in terms of *doli*. Though the project's aim was to protect the forest's biodiversity and "charismatic" mammals in the park and reserve, Lindjombo strikers saw the project and its officials as failed *patrons*. Indeed, that the men chose to use a labor strategy associated with work for coffee plantations and logging companies was no accident. For many Lindjombo Mpiemu and others, the project had engaged in practices that both resembled and inexplicably differed from previous European commercial agents. On one hand, the project, like plantations and concessionaires before them, hired workers, repaired roads, and constructed numerous buildings in which to conduct its business. And yet project officials' activities echoed repressive features of a French colonial administration that had once employed armed militiamen in the forest and implemented hunting and trapping regulations, though tellers of *doli* recalled the latter as an easily bypassed tribute. Nevertheless, according to the logic of previous environmental interventions, project restrictions on forest exploitation coupled with other activities associated with earlier *patrons* must have seemed bewildering. And in the eyes of many Mpiemu whom I encountered, such restrictions denied residents access to attractive consumer goods of an international economy, leaving places like Lindjombo obscured in a tangle of vines and impeding their ability to be seen by more powerful people.

These images, of a still-grieving father in his field and of men menacing a WWF truck, have more in common than is at first evident. Although tellers of *doli* frequently spoke nostalgically of the colonial past, both images provide a window into the ambivalence and tensions surrounding it. Patrice's story and his field illuminate the tensions that must have permeated the plantation village, as kin rivalries played themselves out in battles over occult forces and ultimately manifested themselves in the bodies of people and forest animals and in field sites. And roadwork, like many forms of forest clearing that Mpiemu speakers had undertaken in the twentieth century, was a task fraught with ambiguities, evoking at once a painful past of forced labor and a prosperity associated with cleared spaces.

Both Patrice and the strikers selectively interwove in their narratives and actions the notions of dearth, hunger, deprivation, and loss that Mpiemu had filtered through *doli*'s distinct intellectual tools and interpretations of their environments and pasts, as elucidated in previous chapters. Patrice had lost his daughter and thus had failed to leave her to the future. He identified this event as a central one in his own life, contending that the field where Marie appeared as a gorilla was a site that would remain as a testament to his life after he died. The field was both a mnemonic for his daughter's brief life and a historical place that defined and rooted the passions and losses that animated Patrice's life. The loss of his daughter and a younger son eventually propelled Patrice to seek redemption in Catholicism, a redemption that he sought not simply in church but in a field, a cultivated place that provided food and evidence of Christian faith and virtue.

The striking road workers evoked related discourses of deprivation and lost opportunities, appropriated and reshaped in past interactions with colonial administrators, commercial agents, and missionaries. To my knowledge, every one of these road workers set illegal cable snare traps in the forest, many had mined diamonds illicitly, and several had been arrested by anti-poaching guards. Even some who had not worked at all on the roads joined the protest. Although workers had been deprived of their pay, their claims of widespread dearth seemed overblown when many had already paid their state head tax and when market activities, meat sales, and informants' own admissions indicated that they did have money. Protestors appeared to be relying on an older colonial strategy, articulating claims of deprivation to more powerful outsiders with the hopes of eliciting back pay and sympathetic responses.

Strikers also perceived park and reserve restrictions, which aimed to place limits on commercial and livelihood practices, in terms of lost opportunities. But such restrictions had more than material implications for Mpiemu and other reserve inhabitants. Like the women who fished in the forest stream Momintuwo, strikers (who were also trappers, hunters, farmers, and sometimes miners) incorporated and interpreted changing historical circumstances and discourses by linking self-realization, environment, and interpretations of the past in the concept of leaving a person behind. Hence limits on new settlements, farming, marketing, and forest exploitation—whether consistently enforced or not—threatened access to spaces, sites, knowledge, and practices associated with *doli* that enabled many Mpiemu to leave a person behind.

What lessons does this study offer for conservationists and policymakers concerned with environmental protection in the Sangha basin, in Africa, or in forests and other protected spaces in the rest of the world? It should be clear that the dilemmas facing the project in the Dzanga-Ndoki park and the Dzanga Sangha reserve during the mid-1990s were exceptionally difficult. How should states, NGOs, and multilateral and bilateral aid organizations protect the forest and its fauna from the serious damage that logging, mining, farming, hunting, and trapping can inflict? And how, simultaneously, do they demonstrate respect for the historical, cultural, social, economic, and political contexts in which they operate? As this book has demonstrated, conservation efforts in the Sangha not only disrupted livelihood practices but also transgressed Mpiemu historical, cultural, and social knowledge, values, and practices concerning relations between people and environment embedded in *doli*. It should come as no surprise that when I asked Mpiemu residents in Lindjombo, Salo, and Kwapeli what the WWF-CAR conservation project in the park and reserve should do, the answer was clear. As one wizened Lindjombo hunter and farmer thoughtfully put it, "I would dismantle the project. . . . Or if we had to keep it, I would make them put fewer limits on people who live here." A middle-aged Lindjombo man belligerently recounted that *zaragina* (bandit, Sango) in the Central African Republic's North were doing good work by killing park personnel there. "They should kill all the white people in the project here," he snapped.

It is unlikely that the WWF will shut down its project in the Sangha basin, and it would be unrealistic to suggest that it do so. But given the histories of environmental exploitation and human mobility in the middle Sangha and how Mpiemu have interpreted these past events, I am not convinced that situating a park and reserve there was ever appropriate. Of course, officials working for the project would disagree vehemently. Allard Blom, the WWF technical adviser, claimed that the Sangha was an economically, politically, and strategically marginal region, and like all other protected areas, its marginality made it an ideal site for protection.[5] But the analysis in this book points to a very different interpretation of that past, one that conservationists and policymakers cannot ignore.

This study of *doli* leads me to some modest recommendations that encourage policymakers, state agents, and conservationists to embrace the messiness, complexity, and specificity of changing, porous local knowledge of environments and of the past. One of this book's aims has been to use historical analysis to shed light on one people's contemporary responses to conservation. Policymakers and conservationists need to be acutely aware of the historical lenses through which people see them and to adjust their activities accordingly. Mpiemu people perceived the state-WWF project as a latter-day European *patron* that inexplicably refused to hire people and distribute money, consumer goods, and health care but then inflicted constraints on hunting and trapping. There are, however, productive ways of grappling with these perceptions. State and project officials could have recognized the historical roles that they fulfilled and could have adopted some modest measures to reduce pressures on resources and to assuage the anger of residents, even though they would not resolve the complex tensions that characterize conservation activities and responses to them.

In the early 1990s, for instance, heavy-handed antipoaching patrols dressed in military uniforms all too easily evoked the coercion and brutality of the colonial military forces and the concessionary companies' guards. I understand that in recent years project guards have received further training and that incidents of brutality have diminished, to the point that these guards contend that their ability to patrol the forest has been significantly hampered.[6] Although military dress may usefully create a sense of group cohesion, conservation projects may want to consider alternative forms of dress for guards, particularly ones that do not evoke past recollections and interpretations of colonial military interventions.

State and project officials and guards also could have selectively embraced some of the responsibilities that came with these roles. International donors to the project could have financed, and state and project officials could have facilitated, reserve inhabitants' relocations outside reserve boundaries by investing in extractive industries and agricultural production beyond the reserve and subsidizing workers' relocations there. In this respect I agree with Oates that integrating conservation and development may not be possible in certain contexts. Developing opportunities outside the reserve would provide people with alternative livelihoods and allow them to practice older patterns of moving toward new opportunities and to achieve some measure of self-realization through mobility. It also would have the advantage of reducing demographic pressure on resources in protected areas. Oates's critique of the incompatibility of conservation and development led him to resurrect the old conservationist principle that "nature is worthy of protection for its intrinsic value and for the aesthetic pleasure it can bring to many people."[7] Such a principle is of no interest to people who perceive the forest and its past in a markedly different way.

State or project officials also could have occasionally killed an especially destructive elephant marauding in farmers' fields and distributed the meat as chiefs once had. The WWF probably would not support such a measure; it resisted clamors for culling in Zimbabwe after elephants had been listed in the Convention on International Trade in Endangered Species of Wild Flora and Fauna Appendix 1, indicating that they faced the greatest threat of extinction.[8] But this measure would have the advantage of mollifying residents of protected areas angered by elephant incursions into their fields.

This historical analysis also makes the case for paying careful attention to and crafting conservation interventions tailored to specific groups in precise locations. This book has shown that Mpiemu interpretations of past environmental change in the Sangha forest differed according to regional, gender, and generational groups, defying simple characterization. This complexity was compounded by the middle and upper Sangha's multiethnic population —to which I have not, admittedly, done justice. People shared some historical visions and idioms, kin ties, and livelihood practices but also displayed significant differences in language, cultural practices, historical perspectives, and environmental practices. My relatively narrow focus on one group living in the middle and upper Sangha underscores, though, that we cannot generalize about the problems or solutions that conservationists face in the Dzanga-Ndoki park and Dzanga Sangha reserve, or in other protected areas, for that matter. In the mid-1990s the project had adopted a "one-size-fits-all" strategy for dealing with conflicts in the reserve, based primarily on its experiences in Bayanga. This study of Mpiemu *doli* in Lindjombo and Kwapeli suggests that it would be useful to conduct historical, economic, social, and cultural studies of the reserve inhabitants living in smaller subregions and to develop different conservation (and, when appropriate, development) strategies according to the population mixes, dominant livelihood practices, and historical and environmental perspectives of each subregion. And such strategies would have to continue to be tailored to changing populations, economic conditions, and environmental perceptions and practices. Such research is no slower and certainly no more impractical or expensive than other ecological or biological studies currently supported in protected areas. And it has a role in helping to contribute to more sensitive ways of managing protected areas.

Finally, I want to make yet another pitch for "local knowledge," but not one that romantically argues for the eminent wisdom of static African land-use knowledge and practices. I do not believe that all "local knowledge" can usefully guide the proper and sustainable use of the forest and its resources. Nor do Africans harness such complex, dynamic knowledge in simple quests for material accumulation. Nevertheless, this knowledge is useful. It reveals the multitude of material values but also historical, social, and cultural values that people invest in their forests. It illuminates why people think their forests are worth fighting over. Policymakers and conservationists dismiss the historical and environmental knowledge, practices, and values that inform the life-and-death struggles over conservation at their peril, and at the peril of human beings and protected areas.

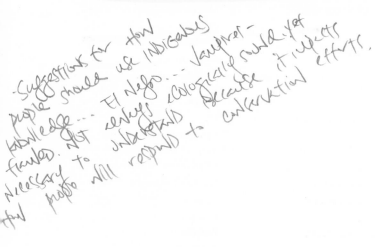

APPENDIX 1

Mpiemu Names for Selected Cultivated Plants

Common name	Scientific name	Mpiemu name
Cassava	*Manihot esculenta*	Njetenabongo (bitter)
		Mengwenje (sweet)
		Menjelepago (sweet)
		Mporo (sweet)
		Marimbong (sweet)
		Nyakoli (sweet)
		Balanyona (sweet)
		Agobo (sweet)
		Mbali (sweet)
		Ankiya (sweet)
		Koyi (sweet)
		Mongomassaman (sweet)
Yam	*Dioscorea* spp.	Mpegi mpa
		Ampino
		Akundi
		Dedeng
		Akelego
Maize	*Zea mays*	Pakwaba ("two months")
		Pakwalali ("three months")
Peanuts	*Arachis hypogaea*	Nkosi Sigisa (red variety)
		Yaounde (white variety)
Taro	*Colocasia esculenta*	Tanga
Sugarcane	*Saccharum officinarum*	Nkogo
Sweet potato	*Ipomoea batatas*	Danbebe, dangari
Tomato	*Solanum lycopersicum*	Njonjo
Tobacco	*Nicotiana* spp.	Kan
Pepper	*Capsicum* spp.	Bumba
		Tambaga
		Sekesekeantomba
		Alaga

Appendix 1 *(continued)*

Common name	Scientific name	Mpiemu name
Bitter leaves	*Solanum* spp.	Punjo
		Ntchon
		Biayi
		Kago
Squash	Cucurbitaceae	Abogi
		Kosso
Okra	*Abelmoschus esculentus*	Gbolowiyo
		Neya
Water leaf (not cultivated but found in fields)	*Talinum triangulare*	Gbogbog
Oil palm	*Elaeis guineensis*	Mebungu
		Bambu
Banana/plantain	*Musa* spp.	Kondo

APPENDIX 2

Mpiemu Names for Selected Forest Plants (identified by
Andrea Turkalo and David Harris)

Mpiemu name	Scientific name	Use
Akon, mpela, kogo	*Maranthochloa* spp.	Wrapping leaves, walls for temporary houses
Kumbi, koko	*Gnetum buccholzianum*	Edible leaf for sauces
Payo	*Irvingia excelsa*	Sauce
Awu	*Manniophytum fulvum*	Cord for construction
Abolembo	*Pallosota* sp.	Antitheft medicine in fields
Lon	*Ereospatha wendlandiana*	Cord for constructing houses and other structures
Ga	*Ancystrophyllum secundiflora*	Cord for constructing baskets, houses, and other structures
Sielo	*Sarcophrynium* spp.	Wrapping leaf
Mbaya/mpaya	*Cissus* sp.	Cord
Akia	*Aframomum sulcatum*	Edible fruit
Jembe/jimbi	*Afrostyrax lepidophyllus*	Cooking spice
Jampiyo	*Monsonia altissima*	Cord for constructing houses and other structures
Bishaga	*Albizia adianfolia*	Antitheft medicine for fields
Nkolo	*Acanthaceae* sp.	Leaves for construction (patching roofs)
Nkombosi	*Thonningia sanguineum*	Antidiarrheal medicine
Dabi	*Polyalthia saveolens*	Antidiarrheal medicine
Bombi/bambi	*Anonidium manii*	Edible fruit
Ngwale	*Dichrostachys cinera?*	Additive to alcoholic beverages (such as palm wine) for an extra "kick"
Melundju	*Fagava* sp.	Medicine for abdominal pains

Appendix 2 *(continued)*

Mpiemu name	Scientific name	Use
Tiriamori ("animal is a person")	*Anthocleista* sp.	Antifilarial medicine
Kangabele	*Mankilkara* sp.	Medicine to treat colds
Landang	*Funtumia elastica* and *Landolphia* spp.	Latex for rubber, soccer balls
Nkon	?	Fruit used for killing fish in streams
Lendo	?	Hunting medicine, applied to forehead of hunter
Ntchamyel	?	Hunting medicine to be put into trap
Ngwago	?	Medicine to keep gorillas from menacing people in the forest
Wiera	?	Cord for construction of houses and other structures
Wo/kuwo	?	Cord for construction of houses and other structures, traps

APPENDIX 3

Mpiemu Names for Selected Forest Mammals

Common name	Scientific name	Mpiemu name
Chimpanzee	*Pan trogladytes*	Wago
Gorilla	*Gorilla gorilla gorilla*	Ntchilo
Elephant	*Loxodonta africana cyclotis*	Ntchogi
Peters duiker	*Cephalophus callipygus*	Mpindi
Blue duiker	*C. monticola*	Ntchwen
Bay duiker	*C. dorsalis*	Akyemo
Yellow-backed duiker	*C. sylvicultor*	Ajemo
Bush pig	*Potamochoerus porcus*	Nkoi
Forest hog	*Hylochoerus meinertzhageni*	Nkage
Sitatunga	*Tragelaphus spekei*	Mbuli
Bongo	*Tragelaphus euryceros*	Mpongo
Hippopotamus	*Hippopotamus amphibius*	Kubi
White-bellied pangolin	*Manis tricuspis*	Ntchali
Greater white-nosed monkey	*Cercopithecus nictitans*	Tongo
Crocodile	*Crocodylus cataphractus*	Kando
Potto	*Perodicticus potto*	Jindugu
Forest buffalo	*Syncerus caffer nanus*	Ntchomo
Brush-tailed porcupine	*Atherurus africanus*	Kombo
Leopard	*Panthera pardus*	Koi

GLOSSARY

Most Mpiemu nouns consist of a root, to which prefixes are added. For the ease of readers unfamiliar with African languages, I have included only singular forms in the text and in this glossary.

abumi: pregnancy, fetus
ajing: abbreviated reference to *kuli ajing,* or cord family, patriclan but also ethnic group
akwombo: unexploited forest
alembo: vital substance. An active *alembo* is associated with witchcraft and is understood as both an integral part of and separate from its human host
alogo: women's fishing
antchanjo: monodominant forest
antcholo: bridewealth
ba: to marry
beno: anger
bia: childbirth
bideyo: food
buri: fallow, bush, forest regrowth following cultivation
buri bikondo: dense forest resembling *buri* but never exploited or cultivated
dad-: home, home village or place (*dadam* is "my home")
dali: village
dambo: war
digi: forest
dio: to be sitting
doli: a category of historical and environmental knowledge and a way of perceiving and characterizing environments and the past
ja: kin group in which people are linked through traceable genealogical connections
kam: food, porridge
kamishogo: maize porridge or maize and ground peanuts steamed in banana leaves
kanbikano: proverb
koga: headdress with feathers, worn by Mpiemu leaders
konshigo: very elderly person
kuli: cord
kuli ajing: patriclan, "cord family"
kwangolo: to make depart

kwashelo: forest form, very dense; good for farming bananas

ligo: to leave behind

lon: savanna, grass

luli: flat iron disks, used as money before French colonial rule

mbulo: fat

mbusa: fresh maize

medibo: water

meja: funeral

meleyo: advice

mempeli: sleeping sickness

menyogi: distilled alcohol made from maize and cassava

metego Mpiemu: "Mpiemu soil," the colonially designated area where Mpiemu settlement was concentrated

mianga: forest that was once exploited for nonagricultural purposes

mompeng: "child of the flood," a first dry-season field

mori: person

mpala: slave, dependent

mpindi: black person, African

mpombi: forehead, the site of fortune on the body

mpombi nyuwa: "good forehead," meaning good fortune

mpuni: ceremonial exchange of blood between men

mugo: to plant

ndelibori: gravedigger

ngumbi mia: elderly woman

ngumbi morom: elderly man

nja: hunger

njowiwi: material made from bark used to "clothe" walls of the house

nkang: healer, but also one who allocated land for cultivation, sometimes war leader

nkolongo akwombo: dense forest with large trees

nkulomani: second rainy-season field

nkung: the Milky Way

nkuno: famine, scarcity

Ntchambe: deity, also the Christian God

ntche: road, path

ntche ngonga: trapping path

ntchilo: gorilla

ntchogi: elephant

nto: second dry-season field, usually cultivated near a permanent water source

nyoli: body

panjo: an open shelter under which men and boys of a residential kin group share food, allocate labor, and regulate disputes

pembo: field

pembo akwombo: field cut from previously uncultivated forest *pendo:* war leader

peno: white person

pondo: trap

pubelo: wind

purokando: a small cord that a pregnant woman ties around her husband's wrist to ensure a successful hunt

saa: tale

sampamb-: grandparent

sho: placenta

shogi: rainy season

shio: dry season

shogo: dried maize

shumbo: pawn

-shuwi: to die

sin: outside

so: dance performed after a leopard was killed

sonyoli: "spirit," what lives after the body of a person dies

suu: friend

tili: a kind of knife used in rubber tapping

to te: inside

tuma: master hunter

tumba doli: ancestor

wago: chimpanzee; to bother

wani: leader, prior to the imposition of colonial rule

wimbo: to wander, to voyage

wundo: abandoned village

yombo: cassava

Sango Terms

duti: to sit

guiriri: category of knowledge about the past among Sango speakers

ga: to come

gagango: people who have come from elsewhere

kamba: cord

londo: to stand up

mbako: distilled alcohol from cassava and maize

ndoye: gift, a lively celebration of a church member's contribution to a church

potopoto: cassava porridge, mud

NOTES

Introduction

1. On the actual effects of forest conservation efforts, see Neumann 1998; Richards 1996; Fairhead and Leach 1994; Oates 1999; Cumming 1993; Hardin 2000; Peterson 2000. Elsewhere, see Grove 1990; Peluso 1992. Thanks to Elizabeth Meyer and Stephanie Rupp for helping me to see more clearly the complexities of Mpiemu responses to conservation interventions. More generally, I have found Stoler and Cooper's (1997) insights into the instability of categories of colonial ruler and ruled useful.

2. "Environment" can thus include but is not limited to ecology, "the study of 'nature,' 'the non-human world, the world we have not in any primary sense created'" (Arnold and Guha 1995, 2).

3. Kreike (1996, 6–13) argues that interpreting land use exclusively within a resistance paradigm forecloses other insights into land-use practices. More broadly, see Cooper 1994.

4. Although *doli* changed in distinct ways, see Foucault on an "archaeology of knowledge" (1972, 190–91; 1990, xi–xii, 345–48).

5. For notable environmental histories in Africa, see Kjekshus [1977] 1997; Beinart and Coates 1995; Feierman 1990; Ranger 1999; Giblin 1992; Moore and Vaughan 1994; McCann 1995; Maddox, Giblin, and Kimambo 1996; Mandala 1990; Anderson 1984. Elsewhere, see Guha [1989] 2000, 48–61; Gadgil and Guha [1992] 1993; Arnold and Guha 1995; Grove, Damodaran, and Sangwan 1998; Skaria 1999; McNeill 2000.

6. A few historians (Rajan 1998, Headrick 1988) have argued that some environmental interventions reflected professional concerns forged in the metropole, and not simply in the colonies.

7. See, for instance, Giles-Vernick 1996b; Hoskins 1993; Skaria 1999; Rozenzweig and Thelan 1998.

8. Prakash 1990, 391; Tonkin 1992, 2. Prakash's insistence on rooting history in Europe's post-Enlightenment helps us to understand the historical, locational specificity of historical thinking. Nevertheless, thinking and writing historically are not practices that only Western academicians undertake. Samuel (1994, 17) has usefully argued that history is "an activity rather than a profession" to which a variety of practitioners can contribute. But we should not assume that when people think, speak, and write about the past, they are producing history.

9. Klein 2000. The literature is huge, but on histories of memory, see Matsuda 1996; Geary 1994; Carruthers 1991; Yates 1966. On remembering and "realms" (or places), see Nora 1997; Roberts and Roberts 1996; Casey 1987; Fentress and Wickham 1992.

10. Mazenot 1970; Coquery-Vidrovitch 1972; Lanfranchi, Ndanga, and Zana 1998; Copet-Rougier 1998; Coquery-Vidrovitch 1998. See also Harms 1987, 1981.

11. Linden 1992; Chadwick 1995; CARPE (a U.S. Agency for International Development initiative in equatorial Africa) website at <http://carpe.gecp.virginia.edu>, although the site has been changed to address threats to this forest. See <http://carpe.umd.edu>. On the significance Eden in Western imagination, see Grove 1995; on different kinds of Edenic narratives, see Slater 1995.

12. Carroll and World Wildlife Fund 1993. See Guyer and Richards on biodiversity (1996).

13. Roach 1992, 353; Merleau-Ponty 1962; Bachelard [1964] 1994. For a recent exploration of these approaches, see Weiss 1996.

14. Merleau-Ponty 1962, 140; Hunt 1999, 11. On the process of becoming a person, see Whyte 1991, 108; Piot 1999, 15–16, 76–104; Moore 1994, 33, 36–42; Karp 1997, 392; Jackson and Karp 1991; Riesman 1986 and 1992; Beidelman 1986; Strathern 1988, 131–32; Weiner 1992, 106–7. Following Brubaker and Cooper's critique of *identity* as a term that means "too much . . . too little . . . or nothing at all," I seek to use more precise language referring to "relational connectedness" (Brubaker and Cooper 2000, 1, 20).

15. Ingold 1992, 51; Karp and Masolo 2000, 22; Watts and Peet 1996, 262–64. See Lawi 2000; Moore 1998a; Östberg 1995 on the changing ways that Africans perceive their environments. See also Slater (1994) on multifarious Amazonian narratives about dolphins.

16. Nyerges 1997, 1; Peterson 2000, 260; Douglas and Wildavsky 1982; Bourdieu 1977; Piot 1999, 76.

17. Mitchell 1994, 10. See also Cosgrove 1984; Schama 1995; White 1983; Cline-Cole 2000; McCann 1999a; Neumann 1998; Ranger 2000.

18. White 2000, 55. Environmental histories that have taken this approach include Neumann 1998; Moore 1998a; Sivaramakrishnan 1995, 25–32; Harms 1987; Fairhead and Leach 1996; Spear 1997; McCann 1995; Giblin 1992. On "access" as social, political, and economic relations guiding how people extract, use, and exchange resources, see Ribot 1998.

19. Fairhead and Leach 1996, 1998; Leach and Mearns 1996 (drawing from Roe 1991); McCann 1997, 139; Richards 1996. On "indigenous knowledge," see, for instance, Chambers 1983; Gadgil, Berkes, and Folke 1993, 151; Sillitoe 1998; Richards 1985; and more recently, Scott 1998.

20. Cf. Gadgil, Berkes, and Folke 1993.

21. Noss 1995, 176.

22. Scott 1998, 313; Giles-Vernick 1999 and 2001a; Agrawal 1995, 421–27. Cf. Sahlins 1999, vi–ix.

23. Cline-Cole 2000, 111; Giles-Vernick 1999, 169–72.

24. Ordinary people, according to Certeau (1984, xiii), interpret and subvert the laws, rituals, constraints, and representations imposed upon them, and they create new spaces and practices that rework the original intent of such laws, rituals, and representations. See Bhabha (1994, 90–91) on colonized people's ambivalence about appropriating ideas and practices from colonizers, expressing a desire both to resemble colonizers and to "radically revalue . . . the normative knowledges of the priority of race, writing, history."

25. See Burnham (1996) on "cultural logic," which guides what people borrow from others.

26. Fabian 1996, 297. Fabian has faulted anthropologists' reliance on representation, arguing, "The little word 'as' . . . was a constant marker of such an epistemological position: Movements, for instance, were studied as social change; ritual as drama; religion (but also ideology, art, and what have you) as a system of symbols."

27. Ibid., 298.

28. Tonkin (1992, 62), drawing from Morton White, distinguished narrative from nonnarrative practices, arguing that a narrative explains, describes, and locates past events.

29. This formulation owes much to Chakrabarty's and Skaria's explorations of "lack" in subaltern histories in India. Chakrabarty (1992, 18) contends that Indian history has been a "mimicry of a certain 'modern' subject of 'European' history . . . bound to represent a sad figure of lack and failure." Skaria (1999, 3–6) develops further this framework of "lack" in examining the changing meanings of, claims of, and ascriptions to wildness among the Dangi in western India. On the significance of colonialism as loss in Africa, see Fabian 1996, 280–85. On environmental interventions in Africa as a result of two "competing problematics of dearth and diversity," see Schroeder's (1999) synthesis.

30. Cooper 1997, 15–16. Cooper draws from a Foucauldian notion of discourse and power, which pervade all relations, but seeks to render a more specific and nuanced portrayal of colonial power.

31. On wealth in people and objects, see Guyer 1995; Miller 1988, 41–48; Appadurai 1986, 13. See De Waal (1989) on the metaphorical meanings of "hunger."

32. Berry 1993, 8, and 2001; Copet-Rougier 1981b; Moore 1998a, 402; Moore and Vaughan 1994; Peterson 2000. On "living the present in historical terms," see Malkki 1995. Accumulation remains a useful means of explaining struggles over power and resources, but it is not the only way of understanding these struggles. See Bassett and Crummey 1993; Mbembe 1990; Geschiere and Konings 1993; Geschiere 1997.

33. Debates over the interpretation of such sources have produced a voluminous literature, but my approach here draws its inspiration from White 2000. For critiques of the essentialized "African voice," see Moore and Vaughan 1994, xxii–xxiii; White 1995 and 2000, 89–121.

34. White 1995, 1381.

35. Vansina 1990; Geschiere 1997.

36. White 2000, 310–12.

37. American and European conceptions of environment have tended to disregard rural built environments because they do not conform to conventional distinctions between civilization and wilderness. On historical distinctions between civilization and wilderness in America and Europe, see Schama 1995.

38. See Fairhead and Leach 1996.

39. Wilson (1989, 58) applied this formulation to domestic environments, but it applies to other environments as well. I became aware of his argument after reading Köhler's (1999, 209–10) stimulating critique. On space and place as constitutive of persons and social relations, see, for instance, Massey 1994, 2–3; Moore 1986; Gray 1999; Bourdieu 1977.

1. The Sources and Contexts of *Doli*

1. For an excellent summary of the incompatibilities between environmental historians' conceptions of "environment as agent" and cultural geographers' "landscape way of seeing," see Demeritt 1994, 185.

2. Centre Technique Forestier Tropical 1989, 79; P. W. Richards 1996, 11–12; Harms 1987, 1; Franquin et al. 1988, 435; Carroll and the World Wildlife Fund 1993, 11. For these ecologists the Sangha basin forest occupies a transitional climatic zone between the moister southern Congolese equatorial climate and the drier northern subequatorial climate. Rainfall in the Congolese equatorial and the subequatorial climates averages more than 1,500 mm/year and 1,350 mm/year, respectively. In Salo rainfall averaged 1,617 mm/year between 1952 and 1979, but only eighty kilometers south, Bayanga's rainfall averaged 1,365 mm/year between 1973 and 1984.

3. Centre Technique Forestier Tropical 1967, fig. 16.

4. Centre Technique Forestier Tropical 1989, 77–82; Carroll 1988, 314; Hart, Hart, and Murphy 1989. P. W. Richards (1996, 361–62) identified five forest types in the African rain forest.

5. Ray 1997; Ray and Hutterer 1996; Ray 2001; Green and Carroll 1991; Ruggiero and Eves 1998.

6. Centre Technique Forestier Tropical 1989, 75–77; P. W. Richards 1996, 280–81; Mabberley 1992.

7. David Wilkie, personal communication, 4 Nov. 1994. According to some wildlife biologists, elephants perform similar roles in other African ecosystems (Barnes 1983; Dublin, Sinclaire, and McGlade 1990; Kordtlandt [1984], quoted in Richards 1996, 151).

8. P. W. Richards 1996, 280–83; Carroll and World Wildlife Fund 1993; Chadwick 1995; Linden 1992; Quammen 2000, 8.

9. Debates have long raged over the effects that expanding agriculture, iron production, and Bantu languages had on hunter-gatherer populations living in the Congo basin. It remains treacherous to draw definitive conclusions about early

populations in the Sangha forest, the nature of their livelihoods, or relations between pygmies and agriculturalists because so little historical research on this topic has been conducted. See Eggert 1992. On the Sangha basin, see Lanfranchi and Clist 1991; Maley 1996; Lanfranchi, Ndanga, and Zana 1998; Klieman 1999. More broadly, see Vansina 1990, 55–57, and 1985; Bailey et al., 1989; Wilkie and Curran 1993.

10. Maley 1996, 68; Copet-Rougier 1998, 56; "Rapport de M. l'administrateur Gaillard, sur son voyage dans la Haute Sangha," 10 May 1891, CAOM, Mission 24; Gouvernement Général de l'Afrique Équatoriale Française, Colonie du Moyen-Congo, "Rapport mensuel," July 1915, ibid., AEF 4(2)D17; Cholet 1890, 462; Pagnault n.d., 139–41; Headrick 1987, 185, 385, 415.

11. Leach and Fairhead (1998) have sought to revise deforestation rates in selected West African countries. Their arguments are less relevant to the Sangha forest, where historical contexts of forest use fundamentally differed from those observed in West Africa.

12. See Headrick 1994, 37–41, 132–33; "La vie des colonies, Afrique Équatoriale Française, renseignements démographiques," Oct. 1938, no. 68, CAOM, Agence des Colonies, carton 357, dossier 100 bis/1 [AEF Démographie-Recensement, Généralités AEF avant 1950, Population Indigène, Dénombrements, 1930–39]; generally, see Cordell 1987, 1994, and 1995; Laurentin 1974.

13. Headrick 1987, 911–12; Gouteaux et al. 1992, 163–66. See also Heckenroth 1909; Saragba 1994, 16; Janssens, Kivits, and Vuylsteke 1992, 1414. Specific agro-forestry practices among Mpiemu or the varied residents of Lindjombo do not appear to have increased forest cover. Cf. Fairhead and Leach, 1996.

14. Vansina 1990, 197–98, 211–37; Harms 1981, 27, 39–43, 44, 53–6; Dupré 1982, 108–10, 1985, 93–104, and 1995.

15. "Rapport de M. l'administrateur Gaillard, sur son voyage dans la Haute Sangha," CAOM, Mission 24; Harms 1981; Dupré 1985, 93–104.

16. Bahuchet 1985, 131; Vansina 1995. There are an estimated 9,700 speakers of Pande, 15,000 speakers of Aka, 10,400 speakers of Kako, and 9,000 speakers of Ngundi in the Central African Republic (Grimes 1996).

17. Hardin (2000, 159–60) has traced an unusually complex development, in which some people at times share a sense of ethnic commonality as "Sangha Sangha," a group dominated by Bantu A speakers, but speak a Bantu C.10 language and sometimes Gbaya. See also Rupp 2001.

18. Harms 1981, 7–8, 123–42; Vansina 1990, 75–81; Burnham 1996, 74, 156; Copet-Rougier 1998, 58. See Martin 1995 on regional politics in the Republic of Congo.

19. In contrast, Georges Dupré (1982, 144–45) has shown that Nzabi clans in Congo retained their political identities despite their mobility. See also Dupré 1985, 30, 78–82, 156–68; Burnham 1996, 72–75; Rupp 2001; Copet-Rougier 1998, 60; Satuba Omer, Lindjombo, 20 June 1993; Mpeng Patrice, forest, 25 June 1993; Kadele Charles, Bandoka, 4 Dec. 1993.

20. According to Rossel (1999, 108), over the past century the Ngombe have dispersed from the upper Sangha, moving westward into Cameroon and Gabon, settling near A.80 speakers, like Mpiemu, but also Bekwil speakers. In these locations they have come to be known as Baka. Both Baka and Ngombe speak Ubangian, not Bantu, languages. Baka should not be confused with BaAka, or speakers of the Aka (Bantu C.14) language.

21. Mabessimo Florent, dialogue with author, tape recording, Kodjimpago, 4 Dec. 1993 (cassette no. OA.7); Kadele Charles, dialogue with author and Alouba Clotere, tape recording, Bandoka, 5 Aug. 1993 (cassette no. OA.20). A German map from 1913 locates some of these groups along rivers that Mpiemu claim they followed to the Sangha basin (Rupp 2001).

22. Burnham, Copet-Rougier, and Noss 1986, 87. See also Burnham 1980; Copet-Rougier 1998; Dupré 1985, 53–120; Thomas 1963; Siroto 1969; Vansina 1990, 207–20.

23. Cordell 1983; Burnham 1996, 73–75; Rabut 1989; Mabessimo Florent, dialogue, 4 Dec. 1993 (OA.7); Kadele Charles, Bandoka, 29 Nov. 1993; Yodjala Philippe, Lindjombo, 26 Apr. 1993; Aka Joseph, dialogue with author, tape recording, Bayanga, 14 May 1993 (cassette no. OA.25); E. Copet-Rougier, personal communication, 22 Nov. 1994; Fourneau 1900, 1345, 1353; Bruel 1910, 9–10, 29–31; Loyre 1909, 412–13; Rupp 2001, chap. 3.

24. See Geschiere 1983, 84; Burnham 1980; Copet-Rougier 1998, 58–61; Rupp 2001.

25. Burnham 1980, 88, 188; Devisch 1993, 80–81; Rupp 2001, chap. 3. Philippe Laburthe-Tolra recounted an oral tradition among the Beti, in which their ancestors sought to cross a large river. One hit the river with the trunk of a particular tree with divinatory powers. There appeared a rainbow, which changed into a serpent, and the ancestors crossed the river on its back. Elisabeth Copet-Rougier heard a similar story from an elderly Mpiemu man in Cameroon. He, however, insisted that four of the founding families of the Mpiemu were fleeing an attack by Lingala speakers when they arrived at a river but did not know how to cross it. They then saw a huge serpent spanning the river but evidently thought it was a stout cord. Three families were able to cross until a child realized that it was not a cord but a serpent. The fourth family thus remained on one side of the river, separated from the other three (Laburthe-Tolra 1981, 104–5; Elisabeth Copet-Rougier, personal communication, 22 Nov. 1994).

26. Sautter 1967 and 1964, 626–29, 765–66.

27. On Sango's history in the CAR, see Samarin 1986.

28. For an analysis of France's *mission civilatrice* in Africa, see Conklin 1997.

29. See Burnham 1996, 48–49, 51–54; Coquery-Vidrovitch 1965 and 1972, 31–46; Rabut 1989; Anon. 1890; Clozel 1895; Ponel 1896; Maunoir 1895; Wauters 1896; Copet-Rougier 1998. Within France interest in the Congo was weak. The explorer Brazza, who laid claim to substantial parts of the Congo for France, had a unique and powerful vision of the Congo's potential as a source of wealth and commerce and as a place desperately needing the influence of French "civilization."

30. Wauters 1900; Le Capitaine Löffler, Administrateur Supérieur de la Sangha, to Monsieur le Commissaire Général du Gouvernement, Ouesso, 26 Mar. 1900, no. 171, CAOM, AEF 4(2)D1; Coquery-Vidrovitch 1972, 233–37. Rudin (1938, 76–101) insisted that in the early 1880s German traders had a critical role in the acquisition of a German colony in Cameroon. But other traders sought to keep colonial powers out of equatorial Africa.

31. Kalck 1974.

32. Sautter 1964, 177–84. See Anderson (1991, 163–64, 173) on mapping as a visual means for colonizers to imagine their possessions. See Bassett and Porter (1991) and Gray (1999, 108–18) on the relations between mapping and political control in West Africa and Gabon, respectively. On the development of ethnicity as the complex social, cultural, and political negotiations within and between historical groups, see Burnham 1996; Amselle 1998; Bravman 1998; Willis 1992; Grinker 1994; Waller and Spear 1991.

33. Burnham and Christensen 1983, 17; Nzabakomada-Yakoma 1985.

34. Geschiere (1983) traced a similar process in Makaland, Cameroon, through the late 1940s.

35. This effort was part of a broader French policy in Africa to stabilize laborers' families, especially in urban areas (Cooper 1996, 198, 262). On the *paysannat,* see Kalck 1959; Père Martin Morel-Chevillet, Couvent des Capucins, Chambéry, France, 14 May 1998.

36. Cooper 1996, 424–30. The 1956 Loi-Cadre gave francophone territories greater control over their affairs and promoted the Africanization of their civil services. Later steps toward decolonization further reinforced francophone African ties with France, including the 1958 draft constitution under de Gaulle.

37. Lieutenant Gouverneur du Moyen-Congo (Cureau) to Mgr Augouard, Évêque du Ht.-Congo Français, Brazzaville, 10 Apr. 1909, no. 340, ACGS, boîte 181, dossier A, 8 (Haut-Congo Français, Oubangui-Brazzaville, 1900–1920); 1916 laws cited in "Décret du 25 août 1929 réglementant la chasse en AEF," CAOM, AEF 5D82 (Réglementation de la Chasse en AEF, 1928–35).

38. Hardin 2000, 27.

39. "Décret du 25 août 1929 réglementant la chasse en AEF," CAOM, AEF 5D82 (Réglementation de la Chasse en AEF, 1928–35).

40. See Coquery-Vidrovitch 1972, 315–22; Samarin 1989; Zoctizoum 1983, 115–78; Kalck 1959, 154–55.

41. European commercial interests had set up trading companies in the upper Sangha as early as 1891. But this "free trade" among competitive firms gave way to concessionary companies with monopolies in 1899 (Le Commissaire Général du Gouvernement [Pierre Savorgnan de Brazza] to Monsieur le Sous-Secrétaire d'État des Colonies, 23 Nov. 1891, CAOM, Gabon-Congo III, 13; see also Coquery-Vidrovitch 1972, 25–70).

42. Coquery-Vidrovitch 1972, 266, and 1998, 75; Brégeon 1998, 41–44. What concessionary companies could exploit varied. The Compagnie Forestière de la

Sangha-Oubangui, for instance, initially acquired rights to all resources within the boundaries of its concessions but later renounced all monopoly rights except for that of rubber.

43. CFSO's concession was later reduced to five million hectares. CFSO remained in the middle and upper Sangha for decades, but it achieved its greatest notoriety in André Gide's 1927 indictment of it in *Voyage au Congo*. In his visit to villages between M'Baiki and Nola, Gide (1993, 64–68, 70–74, 75–77) described in graphic detail the fines, imprisonment, torture, and executions of Africans, all inflicted by company agents.

44. On CFSO and Gesellschaft Sud Kamerun, see Coquery-Vidrovitch 1972, 104, 198, 233–37, and 1998, 81; Geschiere 1983, 84–85. Some informants claimed that nationalization took place in 1976 (P. Martin Morel-Chevillet, Couvent des Capucins, Chambéry, France, 14 May 1998; A. Gehrick, SESAM sawmill, Salo, 10 Dec. 1993; Titley 1997, 68–69).

45. Zoctizoum 1983, 115–78; Kalck 1959, 159.

46. Wilkie and Carpenter 1999a, 339–40, 345. Trophy fees for nonresident hunters in the CAR ranged in 1998 between $US 98 for some duiker species to $1,637 for bongo and giant eland.

47. Ibid., 343; Hardin 2000, 472–83. The rest of the trophy taxes paid went to the CAR's public treasury and to a fund for Development of Tourism and Forests (Hardin 2000, 481). The Sangha forest does not appear to have been among the well-known safari destinations during the late colonial period (Rogue and Blancou, "Tourisme et chasses en A.E.F." [draft], Agence FOM, Agence des Colonies, carton 360, dossier 154 bis 1 [Tourisme AEF: Généralités Renseignement Divers avant 1950]).

48. Marc Volvert and Mustapha Zamel, Berbérati, 11 June 1993; Père Martin Morel-Chevillet, Couvent des Capucins, Chambéry, France, 14 May 1998

49. For general histories of the Roman Catholic Church in the CAR, see Toso 1994; Amaye and Soumille 1984.

50. Olsson 1946. Ultimately the Swedish Baptists created nine mission stations in the Sangha basin: Ouesso (1938), Berbérati (1939), Gamboula (1929), Carnot (1935), Doaka-Bouar (1932), and Bouar (1945).

51. "Journal de la Mission," 1 (1923–30), AGCS; Mission Sainte Anne, Berbérati, "Rapport, 1935–1936," "Statistique, juillet 1937–juillet 1938," Le Chef du Département de la Haute-Sangha (A. Courtois) to Monsieur le Révérend Père Supérieur de la Mission Sainte Anne, 13 July 1937, and "Extraits du rapport de visite pastorale de Mgr Sintas en pays Mbimou du 8 au 16 octobre 1944," personal archives of Père G. de Banville, Congrégation Spiritaine, Chevilly-la-rue; Pomodimo 1993, 143–48.

52. "Rapport du Père Pédron sur l'exploration de la Sangha-Lobay, faite par les Pères Pédron et Pedux, avril–juillet 1922," AGCS, boîte 279, dossier A, 4 (Berbérati–Haute-Sangha, 1920–1928–29, Exploration de la Sangha, P. PeduX, 1922).

53. Toso 1994, 255, 257–59, 340; Paul Zokwezo, Jean Zile, Jacques Bando, Patrice

M'Bimba, Cyrille Bando, Pierre N'Gbaounzi, "Lettre polémique sur l'Église en R.C.A.," 11 June 1964, ACS 2-Q (L'Église Centrafricaine); Père Clement Sautier, 31 Dec. 1972, ibid., 16-Q (Correspondance, 1964–78).

54. B. Baud, Évêque de Berbérati, 26 Jan. 1962, ACS 15-Q (Correspondance, 1954–63).

55. Fr. Clement Sautier, "Les écoles missionaires" (Synthèse des Réponses des Missionnaires de Berbérati), 3 Feb. 1975, ibid., 6-Q (Église de Berbérati).

56. "Constitution de l'Union des Église Baptistes de l'Ouest, RCA," ibid., 3-Q (L'Église Centrafricaine, Baptistes Suédois en RCA).

57. Père André Janoby and Père Francis Betemps, Couvent des Capucins, Annecy, France, 13 May 1998. Cf. Marshall 1991, 24.

58. Bigo 1988, 96–102, 277–83; Titley 1997, 21–22, 125–37, 152–53. On the CAR's postcolonial history in comparative context, see M'Bokolo 1998.

59. Titley 1997, 84; Faes and Smith 2000, 18, 132.

60. Titley 1997, 70–76.

61. O'Toole 1986, 66–72.

62. Titley 1997, 205; Bigo 1988, 259–76.

63. Saulnier 1997, 175–78.

64. Ibid., 178. Generally, see M'Bokolo 1983.

65. Cf. Chatterjee (1995). Mamdani's *Citizen and Subject* (1996), though it does not discuss historical production, emphasizes the inclusive power that the colonial and postcolonial states in Africa have had on their populations. He contends that colonial states (and later, postcolonial states) throughout Africa were bifurcated, ruling distinct populations of citizens and subjects and enforcing separations between urban and rural populations as well as between ethnicities. But Mamdani does not account for the multiple social groups in which his citizens could claim membership. Civil servants and chiefs in the CAR are not merely citizens; they continuously invest in kin, church, and occupational networks, so that the state's influence is never monolithic or all-subsuming.

66. Faes and Smith 2000, 115–17.

67. U.S. Department of State 1989, 5.

68. Saulnier 1997, 160–63; Mogba and Freudenberger 1998.

69. Generally, see Berry 1993, 43–66.

70. The bank does not see simultaneously encouraging commercial timber exploitation and conservation as contradictory but rather contends that timber companies can exploit sustainably. In theory, sustainable forest exploitation is possible, but conservationists are more concerned with the ways in which timber harvesting opens up the forest for hunters and farmers. Cf. Horta 1991, 145–46.

71. Wilkie and Carpenter 1999a.

72. Cf. Chatterjee 1995.

73. Cf. Neumann (forthcoming) has described how in British East Africa, game management intensified in the post-WWII period.

74. Hardin 2000, 221.

75. An analysis of relations between these various populations is beyond the scope of this book, but see Hardin 2000.

76. Fay 1993; Telesis 1991. See also Carroll 1988, 320.

77. Project-WWF meeting, Lindjombo, 18 May 1993.

78. Blom 1998, 210.

79. Some of the antipoaching guards had come from other villages but had moved to Bayanga to live close to the headquarters.

80. What populations are "indigenes" or "migrants" has remained remarkably fluid in the Sangha River basin (Giles-Vernick 1999). In some smaller villages non-Aka did receive free health care.

81. Garreau 1995, n.p.; Hardin 2000, 259, 261–73. For a critique of "community based conservation" and integrated conservation and development projects (ICDPs), see Oates 1999.

2. Translating a Historical and Environmental Category

1. This chapter appeared in a modified form as Giles-Vernick 2000. On the challenges of translating concepts of equatorial African knowledge, see Guyer and Eno Belinga 1995, 93. On genre as "the conventions of discourse through which speakers tell history and listeners understand them," see Tonkin 1992, 2, 50–55. For historical interpretations of a narrative genre, see White 2000, 92–95, and of a literary genre, see Barber 1991.

2. Giles-Vernick 1996b.

3. Four lycée students (names withheld at their request), Bandoka, 28 Nov. 1993.

4. Amions Anaclet, forest camp, 23 Nov. 1993.

5. Kratz 2000, 137.

6. Giles-Vernick 2001b. Insightful critiques of this communal model of personhood and of dichotomies between the person and the self appear in Shaw 2000 and Parkin 2000.

7. Bouloungoulou Adolphe, Bandoka, 28 Nov. 1993; Kadele Job, Bandoka, 28 Nov. 1993.

8. Foa Mabogolo, Bandoka, 8 Dec. 1993; also Mawindi Andriane, Bandoka, 30 Nov. 1993, Lengi Emilienne, Bandoka, 3 Dec. 1993.

9. Vattimo 1991, 2–4.

10. Lindjombo Etienne, Lindjombo, 7 July 1993. See also Wakama Nestor, 3 Aug. 1993; Zoassin, Lindjombo, 7 July 1993.

11. Ndi Christophe and Yawogo Monique, Lindjombo, 2 July 1993. This assessment of the French colonial administration as the magnanimous purveyor of the good life stands in sharp contrast to historians' depictions of the French Equatorial African administration as one of the more brutal and rapacious in Africa. See Coquery-Vidrovitch 1972; Zoctizoum 1983; Gide 1993.

12. Afrique Équatoriale Française, Service de l'Enseignement, "L'enseignement en AEF rapport," 1938, CAOM, Agence FOM, Agence des Colonies, carton 360, dossier 144 bis/3 (Enseignement); Agence France-Presse, "Difficultés de l'enseignement," Spécial Outre-mer, no. 578, 27 July 1948, ibid., dossier 144 bis (Enseignement AEF/ Généralités); Bois 1977, 21; Janody 1985, 20–21; Anon. (Annunciation, 1956), ACS 15-Q (Correspondance, 1954–63); A. Cobra, Chef de la Département de la Haute-Sangha, "Rapport politique," 1945, CAOM, AEF 4(3)D56. The French colonial administration did construct one poorly equipped school in Nola, probably in 1917, which educated thirty to forty-five sons of regional chiefs (Le Chef de la Circonscription de la Kadei-Sangha to Monsieur le Lieutenant-Colonel Pinet, Commandant Militaire du Moyen-Congo à Brazzaville, 18 Mar. 1917, no. 34, ibid., 4[2]D21).

13. David Johansson to Örebro Missionary Society, Jan. 1934, FAIO/AO, Ar. 1930–41, ser. E1:2. Sango, according to linguist William Samarin (1986, 379, 381), served as a lingua franca in parts of Ubangi-Shari where no Gbaya was spoken. The late adoption of Sango in the Sangha basin must have resulted, then, from the presence of Gbaya speakers. In 1958 the bishop Basile Baud observed that only three jurisdictions in Ubangi-Shari used Sango for prayer and confession. Berbérati and Nola, the mission stations of interest in this book, did not. He therefore requested that all prayer be conducted in Sango "to arrive at a uniformity that will be profitable to all" (B. Baud, 8 Apr. 1958, ACS 15-Q [Correspondance, 1954–63]).

14. Svensson 1932, 102.

15. Konga Leon, dialogue with author, tape recording, Salo, 4 Aug. 1993 (cassette no. OA.26); Langabouri Joseph, dialogue with author, tape recording, Bayanga, 23 May 1993 (cassette no. OA.5); Gomina Jean Marie, dialogue with author, tape recording, Bandoka, 30 Nov. 1993 (cassette no. OA.15); Kadele Charles, Bandoka, 4 Dec. 1993; Yongo Oromain, dialogue with author, tape recording, Lindjombo, 8 Aug. 1993 (cassette no. OA.11).

16. Yodjala Philippe, Lindjombo, 2 Nov. 1993.

17. Modigi Casimir, Lindjombo, 3 Nov. 1993. Modigi was Yodjala's father's brother's son's son (FBSS).

18. Four lycée students, Bandoka, 28 Nov. 1993.

19. People interpret and recount what happens to them through particular interpretive frameworks, and thus "experience" can never be an unmediated event that simply happens to people. See Scott (1991) on the constructedness of "experience" and on historians' inability to gain access to the unmediated event. See also White (2000, 34–35) on debates over historical interpretations of "experience."

20. Different ethnic groups in the Sangha shared some of the same characters in their tales, although the details of these tales could vary. It appears that Sangha basin peoples have shared these commonalities for at least a century. Loyre (1909, 419–20) outlined some features of Boumoali religion in 1909 that closely resembled Mpiemu tales.

21. Louko Jeannette, Lindjombo, 12 Dec. 1993.

22. Mpeng Patrice, Lindjombo, 17 Nov. 1993.

23. Vansina 1990, 71–72.

24. Yodjala Philippe, Lindjombo, 15 Nov. 1993; young lycée students, Bandoka, 28 Nov. 1993; Louko Jeannette, Lindjombo, 12 July 1993; Kadele Charles, Bandoka, 29 Nov. 1993; Amions Anaclet, Lindjombo, 13 July 1993; Yongo Oromain, Lindjombo, 22 July 1993; Yodjala Philippe, Lindjombo, 2 Nov. 1993; Bondi Charles, Bandoka, 30 Nov. 1993; Alouba Mathieu, Messadjiso, 8 Dec. 1993; Tontchoe Cecile, Salo, 5 Aug. 1993. See also Geschiere (1997, 46–47, 62) on sight and occult powers.

25. The perception that powerful people lived in cleared spaces applied to Africans as well. For many Mpiemu the 1993 election of Ange-Félix Patassé to the Central African Republic presidency confirmed that people like Patassé who came from the savannas were easily "seen" and thus had access to salaries, health care, transport, and consumer goods. Gray (1999, 105) has noted that in Gabon the equatorial forest posed "a formidable obstacle to . . . [Europeans'] visual dominance of space and effectively disoriented the European gaze." See also Richard White (1995) on white men as agents of environmental change.

26. Mpeng Patrice, Lindjombo, 17 Nov. 1993.

27. Amions Anaclet, forest hunting camp, 23 Nov. 1993.

28. Köhler 1999, 216.

29. Amions Anaclet, Lindjombo, 13 July 1993; Yongo Oromain, Lindjombo, 22 July 1993; Yodjala Philippe, Lindjombo, 2 Nov. 1993; Bondi Charles, Bandoka, 30 Nov. 1993; Alouba Mathieu, Messadjiso, 8 Dec. 1993; Tontchoe Cecile, Salo, 5 Aug. 1993. Lindjombo inhabitants betrayed a real obsession with the tangled regrowth that literally and figuratively obscured their village from outsiders' attentions. During the rainy season the chief periodically organized campaigns to clear the banks of the river, because the regrowth was "dirty" and prevented passing canoes and steamers from seeing the village's real size. Even outside of Lindjombo, Mpiemu used idioms of obscuring vines and ditches to refer to the village's isolation.

30. For a synthesis of the literature concerning the relationship between wealth in people and in things in equatorial Africa, see Guyer 1995, 88.

31. Mawindi Andriane, dialogue with author, tape recording, Bandoka, 30 Nov. 1993 (cassette no. OA.21); Mawindi Julienne, dialogue with author, tape recording, Lindjombo, 11 Nov. 1993 (cassette no. OA.10); Yongo Oromain, dialogue, 8 Aug. 1993 (OA.11).

32. Kadele Charles, dialogue, 5 Aug. 1993, (OA.20); Nyambi Patrice, dialogue with author, tape recording, Bandoka, 5 Aug. 1993 (cassette no OA.18); Yodjala Philippe, Bandoka, 30 Nov. 1993.

33. Nyambi, dialogue, 5 Aug. 1993 (OA.18); Kadele, dialogue, 5 Aug. 1993 (OA.20); Mbali Jean, dialogue with author, tape recording, Salo, 5 Aug. 1993 (cassette no. OA.27); Yodjala Philippe, Lindjombo, 19 Nov. 1993; Mawindi Andriane, dialogue, 30 Nov. 1993 (OA.21); Gomina, dialogue, 30 Nov. 1993 (OA.15); Muston 1933, 23–31. On fluid relations of authority, see Copet-Rougier 1987; Burnham 1980; Geschiere 1982; Dupré 1982.

34. Département de la Haute-Sangha, "Rapport politique," second semester, 1942, CAOM, AEF 4(2)D53.

35. A. Cobra, Chef de Département de la Haute-Sangha, "Rapport politique," 1945, ibid., 4(3)D56.

36. Muston 1933, 29; Pouperon 1908, 3–7.

37. Département de la Sangha, "Rapport trimestriel," first and second trimesters, 1935, CAOM, AEF 4(2)D66.

38. See Hunt (1999, 16–23) on the politics of doing historical research in a context where her presence evoked nostalgia for late colonialism.

39. Sarno 1993; Hardin, Rupp, and Eves 1998, 18–20.

40. Giles-Vernick 2001b.

41. Berry (1994, 1988) and many others (Peters 1994; Moore 1996, 127–28; Carney 1996) have usefully argued that resource struggles are simultaneously conflicts over social and cultural meanings.

3. Peopling the *Panjo* and Village

1. Anonymous 1906, 163; Terrier 1907, 390–91; Bruel 1923, 15; Lengi Emilienne, Bandoka, 3 Dec. 1993; Kadele Charles, Bandoka, 2 and 4 Dec. 1993; Mpeng Patrice, dialogue with author, tape recording, Lindjombo, 14 May 1993 (cassette no. OA.1); Abogi Faustin, Bandoka, 3 Dec. 1993; Konga Leon, dialogue, 4 Aug. 1993 (OA.26). The Moll expedition provided the first photographic and documentary depictions of Mpiemu people and villages in the middle Sangha basin. Alfred Fourneau's earlier forays into the upper Sangha basin did not result in contact with Mpiemu speakers. Analyses of the monthly journals documenting European explorations of Africa, *Le Mouvement Géographique* (Belgium) and *Bulletin du Comité de l'Afrique Française* (France), and a perusal of German archival materials in the Bundesarchiv (Berlin) led me to conclude that neither German nor French explorers visited these Mpiemu settlements in the Sangha basin forest before the Moll expedition. I am grateful to the late Père Ghislain de Banville for allowing me to consult and photograph his private postcard collection and to Philippe David, president of the Association des Images et Mémoires (Paris), for dating the postcards. Figure 2 shows only a fragment of a Mpiemu village, but the best photographs of Mpiemu villages were too small to reproduce clearly.

2. Fourneau 1900, 1343. Pomo and possibly Ngundi houses tended to weave raffia roofs; Mpiemu people did not adopt this practice until later in the twentieth century. In the 1960s Fang villages in Gabon and Bakwele villages in Congo revealed the same spatial layout (Fernandez 1982, 101; Siroto 1969).

3. Pouperon 1908, 5. Pouperon, who undertook a two-month journey through the Sangha, probably misheard the Mpiemu term *panjo* as "boudjia." The Mpiemu term *panjo* closely resembles the terms for similar structures in other equatorial African languages spoken nearby, including Kako, Konzimé, and Maka; "boudjia" does not. The Moll expedition report also mentioned these open shelters, calling them

"bandja," and asserted that Mpiemu villages typically contained one or two (Muston 1933, 31, 35; Loyre 1909, 417; Bruel 1910, 17–18; see also Vansina 1990, 271–72).

4. Muston 1933, 31.

5. Kadele Charles, Bandoka, 29 Nov. 1993; Kokameko Moise, dialogue with author, tape recording, Lindjombo, 15 May 1993 (cassette no. OA.8); Langabouri Joseph, dialogue, 23 May 1993 (OA.5); Mawindi Julienne, dialogue, 11 Nov. 1993 (OA.10); Konga Leon, dialogue, 4 Aug. 1993 (OA.26).

6. See, for instance, Lawi 2000.

7. Mawindi, dialogue, 11 Nov. 1993 (OA.10); Alouba Clotere, Salo, 27 Nov. 1993; Mpeng Patrice, in forest near Likembe River, 22 Nov. 1993.

8. Anonymous 1890, 459–63; Ponel 1896, 190; Anonymous 1900a, 306–8; Anonymous 1900b, 85–88; Loyre 1909, 406–20; Coquery-Vidrovitch 1972, 31. The focus on riverine peoples resulted from early explorations (until 1898), which moved along navigable rivers in the hopes of linking French equatorial possessions with Sudan and the upper Nile.

9. Giles-Vernick 1999, 179–80; Loyre 1909, 406; Cottes 1911, 99–100, 102–3; Bruel, 1910, 3–16, and 1909, 353–66; Fourneau 1900, 1341–42. On exploration as ethnographic process, see Fabian 2000.

10. Terrier 1907, 391.

11. Muston 1933, 29.

12. "The Sangha," 1900(?), CAOM, AEF 4(2)D1.

13. Congo Français et Dépendances, Colonie du Moyen-Congo, "Rapport du 2ème trimestre, 1908," 29 Aug. 1908, ibid., 4(2)D2.

14. Muston (1933, 26–30) used the Fufulde honorific title "kagama" (*kaigama*) to refer to these leaders. Among some ethnic groups in the nineteenth century, this linguistic appropriation underpinned new notions of leadership and hierarchy borrowed from the Fulbé slave-raiding empire based in Adamawa (Copet-Rougier 1998, 65). But I never heard Mpiemu speakers use the term in their references to the past. It is unclear whether Muston used the term because translators accompanying the exploration team used it or because the Mpiemu *wani* they encountered had appropriated it.

15. Authorities farther south in the Congo basin, whose titles usually contained the prefix *nga-*, exercised considerably more control over resource exploitation. See Dupré 1982 and 1995, 40–42; Laburthe-Tolra 1981; Bonnafé 1967, 13–16.

16. Mabessimo Florent, Kodjimpago diamond fields, 7 Dec. 1993; Bouloungoulou Adolphe, Bandoka, 28 Nov. 1993; Modigi Casimir, dialogue with author, tape recording, Lindjombo, 5 Nov. 1993 [cassette no. OA.9]; Gomina, dialogue, 30 Nov. 1993 [OA.15]; Kadele Charles, Bandoka, 29 Nov. 1993. The Bintuwamo *ajing* reportedly led some Mpiemu on a series of nineteenth-century geographical movements that brought them to the northern forests of the upper Sangha basin. Georges Dupré has maintained that clans enabled the Nzabi in Congo to retain their political identities during their migrations in the nineteenth century. It is unclear whether this was the case with Mpiemu *ajing* in the Sangha basin (Dupré 1982, 144–45).

17. Nyambi, dialogue, 5 Aug. 1993 (OA.18); Langabouri, dialogue, 23 May 1993 (OA.5).

18. Kadele, dialogue, 5 Aug. 1993 (OA.20); Gomina, dialogue, 30 Nov. 1993 (OA.15).

19. Some open shelters in larger villages can now incorporate a wide variety of materials, from wood planks rejected by local timber companies to aluminum roofing.

20. Mpeng, dialogue, 14 May 1993 (OA.1); Lengi Emilienne, Bandoka, 3 Dec. 1993; Mawindi, dialogue, 11 Nov. 1993 (OA.10); Kadele Charles, Bandoka, 4 Dec. 1993. The name of the bark, *njowiwi,* is derived from *njo,* which means "house," and the root *wi,* the name of the tree *Triplochiton scleroxylon.*

21. Boloungoulou Adolphe, Bandoka, 3 Dec. 1993; Kadele Charles, Bandoka, 4 Dec. 1993; Lengi Emilienne, Bandoka, 3 Dec. 1993.

22. See Hobsbawm and Ranger (1983), but also Kratz (1993). For an exploration of developing personhood among Acoli people of northern Uganda, see Odoch Pido 2000, 106–11.

23. *Togi* means "to pick up," "to gather," or "to receive." Mpiemu used the term *abumi* to refer to the embryo or fetus growing inside the uterus (*sho*). Many Bantu languages employ the root -*bumo* to connote "belly." In the related languages Konzimé and Fang, -*bum* is the root of several words relating to pregnancy (Greenberg 1973, 36; Beavon 1995; Fernandez 1982, 174, 574).

24. See also Devisch (1993, 138–39).

25. Cf. Heald (1989). Mpiemu speakers often refer simultaneously to anger (*beno*) and power (*nkuli*). Informants explained that "*abumi,* ya be mori [*abumi,* it is not a person]."

26. On symbolic relations between food and land, see Feeley-Harnik 1994; Ohnuki-Tierney 1993; Munn 1986. *Mbo amiali*—the left hand—translates as "hand of the woman."

27. Alouba Clotere, Ndoagne Micheline, Bavio Lopes, dialogue with author, tape recording, Lindjombo, 25 July 1993 (cassette no. OA.24); Gondo Jeanne, Bandoka, 2 Dec. 1993; Lengi Emilienne, Bandoka, 4 Dec. 1993. Mpiemu speakers did not give an etymology of *purokando,* but according to Vansina (1990, 293) -*kando* was the proto-Bantu term for bark cloth.

28. Ndoagne Micheline, Lindjombo, 16 Nov. 1993; Gondo Jeanne, Bandoka, 4 Dec. 1993; Yodjala Philippe, Lindjombo, 19 Nov. 1993; Ndoagne Micheline, Lindjombo, 20 Nov. 1993; Pomodimo 1993. For the significance of placenta burial in Kenya, see Cohen and Odhiambo (1989, 9).

29. Lindjombo Etienne, Lindjombo, 8 Aug. 1993; Kadele Charles, Bandoka, 28, 29 Nov. 1993; Mabessimo Florent, Kodjimpago diamond pits, 7 Dec. 1993; Burnham, Copet-Rougier, and Noss, 1986, 121; Mololi 1994, 5; Bahuchet 1979, 74–75. On educational processes in male spaces in southern Africa, see Hofmeyr 1994.

30. Nyambi, dialogue, 5 Aug. 1993 (OA.18); Mpeng Patrice, dialogue with author, tape recording, Lindjombo, 1 Aug. 1993 (cassette no. OA.2).

31. Wan-Mbissa Samuel, Lindjombo, 14 Nov. 1993; Bouloungoulou Adolphe, Bandoka, 28 Nov. 1993; Modigi Casimir, dialogue, 5 Nov. 1993 (OA.9); Gomina, dialogue, 30 Nov. 1993 (OA.15); Geschiere 1997.

32. Kokameko Moise, dialogue, 15 May 1993 (OA.8); Kouro Yvonne, dialogue with author, tape recording, Bandoka, 5 Dec. 1993 (cassette no. OA.13); Mabessimo-Angoula Levi, dialogue with author, tape recording, Adebori, 2 Dec. 1993 (cassette no. OA.30); Mawindi Andriane, dialogue, 30 Nov. 1993 (OA.21).

33. Foa Mabogolo, Bandoka, 8 Dec. 1993; Lengi Emilienne, Bandoka, 3 Dec. 1993; Satuba Rose, Lindjombo, 10 Nov. 1993.

34. Mpiemu distinguished the elderly from very old people (*konshigo* for both men and women) who were no longer able to care for themselves.

35. Cf. MacGaffey (1986, 45–49), who showed that BaKongo buried their dead at night (actually morning for the dead, who took over living people's mirrors, tools, and paths). See also Weiss (1996a, 139–44) on Haya bark-cloth funeral shrouds as linkages between the living and dead.

36. Weiss (1996a, 145) described a similar practice, though mourning Haya women use cords to prevent the "uncontrollable expansion of . . . [their] 'thoughts.'"

37. The root of this term, *-nyoli,* means "body."

38. Ntchambe Marc, dialogue with author, tape recording, Bandoka, 2 Dec. 1993 (cassette no. OA.16); Kadele Charles, Bandoka, 14 Dec. 1993.

39. Kadele Charles, Bandoka, 4 Dec. 1993.

4. Depleting the *Panjo* and Village

1. Scott 1998, 4–5. On *regroupement* in AEF, see Gray 1999; Burnham 1975; Giles-Vernick 1996b; Bonnafé 1978, 20–21; Cordell 1987. On imprisonment and enclosure in African colonial history, see Bernault 1999, 15–64.

2. "Rapport concernant la situation politique et l'organisation administrative de l'AEF," n.d. (1908?), CAOM, AEF 5D9. On the designation of chiefs, see Colonie du Moyen-Congo, Région de la Basse-Sangha, "Rapport annuel," 1908, ibid., 4(2)D2.

3. Sautter 1964, 177–84; Headrick 1994, 25–27; "Rapport du deuxième trimestre," 29 Aug. 1908, CAOM, AEF 4(2)D2; "Rapport concernant la situation politique et l'organisation administrative de l'AEF," n.d. (1908?), and Le Gouverneur Général de l'AEF to M. le Ministre des Colonies, Services Militaires, 13 Jan. 1913, ibid., 5D9; L'Agent des Douanes to Monsieur le Commissaire Général, Ouesso, 2 Jan. 1902, ibid., 4(2)D1.

4. Gouvernement Général de l'Afrique Équatoriale Française, Colonie du Moyen-Congo, "Rapport mensuel," July 1915, CAOM, AEF 4(2)D17; Le Chef de la Circonscription de la Kadei-Sangha to Monsieur le Lieutenant-Colonel Pinet, Commandant Militaire du Moyen-Congo, Brazzaville, 18 Mar. 1917, no. 34, ibid., 4(2)D21; "Rapport trimestriel de Moyen Congo," first trimester, 1915, ibid., 4(2)D17; L'Administrateur L. Vingarassamy, Chef de la Circonscription de la Kadei-

Sangha, to Monsieur le Lieutenant-Gouverneur du Moyen-Congo (Affaires Civiles), 7 June 1923, ibid., 4(2)D37; "Rapport annuel," Moyen-Congo, 1933, ibid., 4(2)D60; M. Allys (Chef de la Subdivision de Nola), "Rapport trimestriel," 1926, ibid., 4(2)D42; Le Chef de Subdivision, Subdivision de Nola, "Renseignement des villages traversés et visite des travaux de la Route nord-sud," 12 June 1933, ibid., 4(2)D60; Circonscription de la Haute-Sangha, "Rapport trimestriel," 1926, ibid., 4(2)D42; Yodjala Philippe, Lindjombo, 2 Nov. 1993; Kadele, dialogue, 5 Aug. 1993 (OA. 20).

5. L'Administrateur L. Vingarassamy, Chef de la Circonscription de la Kadei-Sangha, to Monsieur le Lieutenant-Gouverneur du Moyen-Congo (Affaires Civiles), Nola, 7 June 1923, CAOM, AEF 4(2)D37.

6. Circonscription de la Haute-Sangha, Subdivisions de Nola et Berbérati (ancienne Kadei-Sangha), "Rapport mensuel," Nov. 1923, ibid.

7. Darré, Circonscription de la Haute-Sangha, "Situation politique," first and second trimesters, 1926, ibid., 5D66 (Incidents de la Haute-Sangha, 1926–28).

8. Gouvernement Général de l'Afrique Équatoriale Française, Colonie du Moyen-Congo, Nola, "Rapport mensuel," July 1915, ibid., 4(2)D17; Circonscription de la Likouala, "Rapport d'ensemble pour 1917," ibid., 4(2)D21; Circonscription de la Haute-Sangha, Subdivisions de Nola et Berbérati (ancienne Kadei-Sangha), "Rapport mensuel," Aug. 1923, and L'Administrateur L. Vingarassamy, Chef de la Circonscription de la Kadei-Sangha, to Monsieur le Lieutenant-Gouverneur du Moyen-Congo (Affaires Civiles), Nola, 7 June 1923, ibid., 4(2)D37.

9. Fieschi-Vivet, "Rapport à Monsieur le Chef de Circonscription de la Haute Sangha," no. 1T, suite à 44 (au sujet du meurtre du Milicien Mazou), Bilolo, 31 July 1928, ibid., 5D66; Département de la Sangha, "Rapport trimestriel," first trimester, 1935, ibid., 4(2)D66; "Rapport de tournée effectuée par le Chef de la subdivision de Nola dans la région M'Bimou, du 8 au 14 Decembre," ibid., 4(2)D56 bis (Tournées 1933); cf. Nzabakomada-Yakoma 1985, 58.

10. Fieschi-Vivet, "Rapport à Monsieur le Chef de Circonscription de la Haute Sangha," no. 1T, suite à 44 (au sujet du meurtre du Milicien Mazou), Bilolo, 31 July 1928, CAOM, AEF 5D66.

11. Nzabakomada-Yakoma 1985; "Rapport de M. l'Administrateur en Chef Marchessou," Nov. 1929, CAOM, AEF 5D79 (Incidents de la Haute-Sangha; Politique Indigène (Mouvements et Troubles), Haute-Sangha, 1928–29; Tournées de l'Inspecteur des Affaires Administratives); L'Inspecteur des Affaires Administratives Marchessou to M. l'Administrateur Curet, Chef de la Circonscription de la Haute-Sangha, 24 Sept. 1929, no. 100 (Programme Politique et Économique), ibid.; "Journal de la Mission," 2 (1931–37), AGCS, entry for Feb. 1933; District de Nola, Région de la Haute-Sangha, Territoire de l'Oubangui-Chari, "Rapport économique," 1950, CAOM, AEF 4(3)D61.

12. Le Houx (Chef de la Subdivision de Nola) to Monsieur le Chef de la Circonscription de la Haute-Sangha, 30 Nov. 1923, CAOM, AEF 4(2)37; Circonscription de la Haute-Sangha, "Rapport trimestriel," 1926, ibid., 4(2)D42; Circonscription de la Haute-Sangha, "Rapport annuel," 1927, ibid., 4(2)D43; Circonscription de la

Likouala, "Rapport d'ensemble pour 1917," ibid., 4(2)D21; Pierre d'Alcantara Sintas, "Extrait du rapport de visite pastorale de Mgr Sintas en pays Mbimou du 8 au 16 octobre 1944," 1944, ACT 4R.

13. Kadele Charles, Bandoka, 4 Dec. 1993.

14. Amions Anaclet and Satuba Omer, Lindjombo, 20 June 1993. Elsewhere, see Gray 1999; Rupp 2001.

15. Département de la Haute-Sangha, "Rapport politique," second semester, 1942, CAOM, AEF 4(2)D53; A. Corbier, Chef de Département de la Haute-Sangha, "Rapport politique," 1945, ibid., 4(3)D56.

16. Kadele, dialogue, 5 Aug. 1993 (OA.20).

17. Rapport de M. L'Administrateur en Chef des Colonies de Saint Mart, Inspecteur des Affaires Administratives de l'Oubangui-Chari, Chargé de Mission dans le Département de la Haute-Sangha, 1938, CAOM, AEF 4(3)D50; Mpeng, dialogue, 14 May 1993 (OA.1); Lengi Emilienne, Bandoka, 3 Dec. 1993; Bouloungoulou Adolphe, Bandoka, 3 Dec. 1993; Mawindi Julienne, dialogue, 11 Nov. 1993 (OA.10); Kadele Charles, Bandoka, 4 Dec. 1993. See also Fernandez 1982, 122–23.

18. Département de la Sangha, "Rapport trimestriel," second trimester, 1935, CAOM, AEF 4(2)D66; Mawindi Andriane, dialogue, 30 Nov. 1993 (OA.21); Nyambi, dialogue, 5 Aug. 1993 (OA.18); Kadele, dialogue, 5 Aug. 1993 (OA.20); Kadele Charles, Bandoka, 29 Nov. 1993.

19. Département de la Sangha, "Rapport trimestriel," second trimester, 1935, CAOM, AEF 4(2)D66; Gomina, dialogue, 30 Nov. 1993 (OA.15); Nyambi, dialogue, 5 Aug. 1993 (OA.18); Kadele, dialogue, 5 Aug. 1993 (OA.20); Mabessimo Florent, Kodjimpago, 10 Dec. 1993; Yodjala Philippe, Bandoka, 30 Nov. 1993, and Lindjombo, 2, 19 Nov. 1993; Mawindi Andriane, dialogue, 30 Nov. 1993 (OA.21).

20. Coquery-Vidrovitch 1972; Samarin 1989; Bernault 1996, 22–23; Cooper 1996.

21. Coquery-Vidrovitch 1972, 488. Later the colonial administration insisted that taxes be paid in cash. By 1934 the yearly tax in the Nola subdivision amounted to twenty francs for each adult male, compared to fifteen francs in neighboring Berbérati and Carnot subdivisions. This inequity, according to one administrator, precipitated flight out of at least one Mpiemu *terre* (Administrateur Commandant la Région de la Haute-Sangha to Monsieur le Commissaire Général du Gouvernement le Congo Français, n.d., CAOM, AEF 4[2]D1; Département de la Sangha, "Rapport trimestriel," first trimester, 1935, ibid., 4[2]D66).

22. Darré, Circonscription de la Haute-Sangha, "Situation politique," first trimester, 1926, CAOM, AEF 5D66 (Incidents de la Haute-Sangha, 1926–28), dossier 1926; "Journal de la Mission," 1 (1923–30), AGCS, entry for Aug. 1925; Circonscription de la Haute-Sangha, Subdivisions de Nola et Berbérati (ancienne Kadei-Sangha), "Rapport mensuel," Dec. 1923, CAOM, AEF 4(2)D37; M. Allys (Chef de la Subdivision de Nola), "Rapport trimestriel," 1926, ibid., 4(2)D42; Cordell 1987, 147–48; Pomodimo 1993, 142.

23. In 1912 CFSO required a worker to produce about twelve kilos of rubber each month (Compagnie Forestière de la Sangha-Oubangui, "Rapport général, 1912,"

1913, CAOM, AEF 8Q31). Gide ([1927] 1993) reported in 1927 that the monthly requirement was about twenty to twenty-five kilos.

24. Manigaud to Monsieur le Commissaire Général du Gouvernement dans le Congo Français à Libreville ("Rapport sur la situation de la région," no. 373), CAOM, AEF 4(2)D1. For a discussion of concessionary company abuses in French Equatorial Africa, see Coquery-Vidrovitch 1972, 171–95; Gide [1927] 1993; Samarin 1989; [unidentified], Nieuwe Afrikaansche Handels-Vennootschap, to Monsieur le Lieutenant-Gouverneur du Congo Français, Brazzaville, 20 Aug. 1901, CAOM, Affaires Politiques, AEF Concessions, carton 14; Compagnie Forestière de la Sangha-Oubangui, "Rapport général, 1912," 1913, ibid., AEF 8Q31; Mpeng, dialogue, 1 Aug. 1993 (OA.2); Yongo, dialogue, 8 Aug. 1993 (OA.11); Satuba Omer, dialogue with author, tape recording, Lindjombo, 9 May 1993 (cassette no. OA.19).

25. Propriétaire de la Haute-Sangha to M. le Lieutenant-Gouverneur du Congo Français, Brazzaville, 27 Aug. 1901, CAOM, Affaires Politiques, AEF Concessions, carton 14/B2; "Concessions du Congo, décret," 31 Mar. 1899, ibid., Gabon-Congo III, 13; Compagnie Forestière de la Sangha-Oubangui, "Rapport annuel," 1912, ibid., AEF 8Q30; G. Mestayer, l'Administrateur Délégué de la Compagnie des Produits de la Sangha et de la Compagnie de la N'Goko-Sangha, to Monsieur le Ministre [des Colonies], 6 Aug. 1902, ibid., Gabon-Congo III, 13. Most companies had to pay for the armed forces that the French governor supplied.

26. Raymond Colrat, "Conference au cercle national et colonial," La Dépêche Coloniale, 23 Dec. 1903, ibid., Affaires Politiques, AEF Concessions, carton 25B, dossier 25A (Recrutement de la Main d'Oeuvre Indigène).

27. Coquery-Vidrovitch 1972, 105.

28. Ibid., 103; Geschiere 1983. See Martin (1983, 8–15) on violence and the "rule of the feeble" in Central Africa and, comparatively, Berry (1993, 24–25) on how British colonizers handled a similar scarcity of money and personnel.

29. Coquery-Vidrovitch 1972, 112–15; Cooper 1996, 187–89; D'Almeida-Topor 1988.

30. Sallmard to Compagnie des Produits de la Sangha, 19 Mar. 1902, no. 23, Joseph to Monsieur l'Administrateur Délégué de la C.P.S., 28 Mar. 1902, and P. de Sallmard, Compagnie des Produits de la Sangha, 6 Apr. 1902, no. 87, CAOM, Gabon-Congo III, 13.

31. Darré, Circonscription de la Haute-Sangha, "Situation politique," first tri-mester, 1926, ibid., AEF 5D66 (Incidents de la Haute-Sangha, 1926–28), dossier 1926; Compagnie Forestière de la Sangha-Oubangui, "Rapport général, 1911," 20 Jan. 1912, ibid., 8Q31; Durieux, le Directeur de la C.P.S., to Monsieur l'Administrateur de la Basse-Sangha-Ouesso, Bomassa, 21 Nov. 1901, ibid., Gabon-Congo III, 13; Gaston Mestayer, Administrateur Délégué, "Note sur la perception de l'impôt au Congo Français," 5 Oct. 1901, ibid., Affaires Politiques, AEF Concessions, carton 14/B2; Mestayer to Monsieur Grodet, Commissaire Général, Libreville, 14 Aug. 1901, Sallmard to Monsieur l'Administrateur de la [Sangha?], 23 May 1902, no. 257, M. de Sallmard to Siège Social, 21 May 1902, ibid., Gabon-Congo III, 13.

32. Sallmard to Monsieur l'Administrateur-Délégué de la C.P.S., 2 May 1902, no. 169, ibid., 12.

33. Coquery-Vidrovitch 1972, 369.

34. Catholic missionaries recognized that young men left their villages "to immediately acquire some money but also to liberate themselves from the semiservitude under the chiefs to which they must submit. This fact is especially noticeable among the Mbimus, where those who fill the role of the chief remain insatiable ogres" (Mission Ste. Anne, Berbérati, "Statistique, juillet 1937–juillet 1938," ACS 4R1 [Mission d'Afrique, Lettres, 1937–38]).

35. Chef de Subdivision de Nola, "Rapport de tournée effectuée dans la Région M'Bimou pendant la période du 11 au 21 mai 1934," 30 June 1934, CAOM, AEF 4(2)D66; District de Nola, Région de la Haute-Sangha, "Rapport économique," 1950, ibid., 4(3)D61; R. L. Briat, "La population de l'A.E.F.," Bulletin d'Information d'AEF 15 (30 Sept. 1938), ibid., Agence des Colonies, carton 357, dossier (Études Démographiques, 1930–39); R. L. Briat, "V-Documents la population de l'Afrique Équatoriale Française (I)," n.d., ibid.; Cordell 1987.

36. Amions Anaclet, Lindjombo, 20 June 1993; Dinoramibali Martine, Lindjombo, 10 May 1993; Konga Leon, dialogue, 4 Aug. 1993 (OA.26); Wakama Nestor, Salo, 3 Aug. 1993; Lindjombo Etienne, Lindjombo, 8 Aug. 1993; Mustapha Zamel, Berbérati, 10 June 1993; Bete and Angende, forest near Lindjombo, 19 July 1993.

37. Nkondja Faustin, Mekanda, 9 Dec. 1993; Satuba, dialogue, 9 May 1993 (OA.19); Mawindi Julienne, dialogue, 11 Nov. 1993 (OA.10); Mpeng Patrice, dialogue with author, tape recording, forest near Likembe, 24 Nov. 1993 (cassette no. OA.4); Gomina, dialogue, 30 Nov. 1993 (OA.15). By the time that many of these tellers of doli were old enough to work, most rubber exploitation had ended.

38. Modigi, dialogue, 5 Nov. 1993 (OA.9). This quest was not confined, of course, to Mpiemu speakers alone. See Douzimé Ambroise, dialogue with author, tape recording, Bayanga, 18 Apr. 1993 (cassette no. OA.28).

39. Alouba Clotere, Salo, 27 Nov. 1993.

40. Karp and Masolo 2000, 21.

41. Mpeng, dialogue, 24 Nov. 1993 (OA.4).

42. Mpeng, dialogue, 1 Aug. 1993 (OA.2).

43. Yongo, dialogue, 8 Aug. 1993 (OA.11).

44. Nyambi, dialogue, 5 Aug. 1993 (OA.18).

45. Gomina, dialogue, 30 Nov. 1993 (OA.15); Mustapha Zamel, Berbérati, 10 June 1993; Wakama Nestor, dialogue with author, tape recording, Salo, 3 Aug. 1993 (cassette no. OA.29); Bessari Alphonsine, Lindjombo, 15 Dec. 1993. A patron's attentions could be manifested in many ways. Former employees claimed that Santini had a red-brick "prison" measuring 1 meter by 1.5 meters where sick workers would sleep. Santini contended that isolating workers protected them from infecting their wives, but informants insisted that it really kept workers from being "lazy" and claiming illness when they did not want to come to work.

46. Mawindi Julienne, dialogue, 11 Nov. 1993 (OA.10); Yongo, dialogue, 8 Aug.

1993 (OA.11); Bessambongouri Jeannette, Lindjombo, 1 Nov. 1993; Bongolo Elisabeth, dialogue with author, tape recording, Lindjombo, 24 Apr. 1993 (OA.14); Louko Jeannette, Lindjombo, 8 Nov. 1993; Lengi Emilienne, Bandoka, 3 Dec. 1993; Dinoramibali Martine, Lindjombo, 10 Nov. 1993. On clothing, see Hendrickson 1996, 2–4.

47. Mbali Alphonsine, Lindjombo, 15 Dec. 1993; Mpeng Patrice, Lindjombo, 1 Nov. 1993; Satuba, dialogue, 9 May 1993 (OA.19); Yongo, dialogue, 8 Aug. 1993 (OA.11); Modigi Casimir, Lindjombo, 12 Nov. 1993; Satuba Omer and Amions Anaclet, Lindjombo, 20 June 1993; Kanga Dieudonne, Lindjombo, 27 May 1993; Alouba Clotere and Andoungou, Campement, 5 Aug. 1993. Although Hardin's (2000, 245) point that *panjo* could assume new forms to incorporate broader social and political networks is well-taken, my informants did not recognize these forms as true *panjo* that fulfilled their older purposes.

48. This woman's name and details of her life have been altered so as not to incriminate her husband for snare trapping.

49. Although elderly men claimed that a man never used to eat with his father-in-law out of "respect," in 1993 men rarely observed this prohibition.

50. Alouba Clotere and Andoungou, Campement, 5 Aug. 1993; Koue Clement, Bandoka, 30 Nov. 1993; Ntchambe, dialogue, 2 Dec. 1993 (OA.16). In general, *panjo* multiplied when there were too many members to eat under a single shelter.

51. Apoundjo Rene, Lindjombo, 15 Nov. 1993. Apoundjo was mistaken about the head tax requirements; the French administration had long required taxes to be paid in cash, not in kind.

52. Satuba Omer, Lindjombo, 20 June 1993.

53. Such comments were quite common, but see Tontchoe Cecile, Salo, 5 Aug. 1993; Apoundjo Rene, Lindjombo, 14 Nov. 1993; Ndoagne Micheline, Lindjombo, 26 June 1993; Lengi Emilienne, Bandoka, 1 Dec. 1993.

54. Tontchoe Cecile, Salo, 5 Aug. 1993; Apoundjo Rene, Lindjombo, 14 Nov. 1993; Louko Jeannette, Lindjombo, 5 Dec. 1993; Lengi Emilienne, Bandoka, 1 Dec. 1993.

55. Headrick 1994, 77, 337.

56. Giblin 1992; Giblin 1990; Vail 1977. Cf. Waller 1990, 100. Ford (1971, 151–66) contended, and others subsequently concurred, that late nineteenth-century colonization in East Africa reduced Africans' ability to manage their environments, leading to a growth in tsetse-fostering brush, which in turn brought about greater contact between trypanosome-carrying tsetse, wild-game reservoirs, people, and domestic animals.

57. Headrick 1994, 69, 74; Ford 1971, 453.

58. "Rapport trimestriel," first trimester, 1908, CAOM, AEF 4(2)D2 (Rapports Politiques, 1904–8).

59. Quoted in Headrick 1994, 77. See also Headrick 1987, 168–69; Anonymous 1906, 229; Heckenroth 1909, 131–46; Anonymous 1914, 243–44.

60. Headrick (1981, 9; 1987, 885–977; 1994, 345–83) offers extensive descriptions and analysis of these campaigns. For those in the Belgian Congo, see Lyons 1992; in

British East Africa, Hoppe 1997. Worboys (1994) contrasts British, German, and Belgian approaches, though Headrick (1994, 312) contends that French and Belgian campaigns resembled German Robert Koch's chemotherapeutic approach.

61. Chef du Département de la Haute-Sangha (A. Corbier) to M. le Gouverneur, Chef de Territoire de l'Oubangui-Chari, "Rapport politique," 1945, CAOM, AEF 4(3)D56; Département de la Haute-Sangha, "Rapport politique," second semester, 1941, ibid., 4(3)D52; Circonscription de la Haute-Sangha, "Rapport annuel," 1927, ibid., 4(2)D43; Headrick 1981, 9, 1987, 975, and 1994, 89–92; Jourdy 1914, 107–9.

62. Département de la Sangha, "Rapport trimestriel," first trimester, 1935, CAOM, AEF 4(2)D66; Headrick 1981, 11–12, and 1994, 380. Contemporary parasitologists identify two insect vectors, *Glossina fuscipes fuscipes* and *Glossina palpalis palpalis,* that transmit trypanosomes to human beings, although eight other trypanosome-carrying fly species live in this region (Janssens et al. 1992, 1414; Gouteaux et al. 1992, 163–66; Ford 1971, 56–57, 453).

63. Région de la Haute-Sangha, District de Nola, "Rapport économique," 1950, CAOM, AEF 4(3)D61; A. Corbier (Chef de Département de la Haute-Sangha), "Rapport politique, année 1945," 9 Feb. 1945, ibid., 4(3)D56; Département de la Sangha, "Rapport trimestriel," first and second trimesters, 1935, ibid., 4(2)D66; Département de la Sangha, "Rapport trimestriel," first and second trimesters, 1935, ibid.; Chef du Territoire de l'Oubangui-Chari (Latrille) to M. le Chef du Département de la Haute-Sangha, ibid., 4(3)D53. White (2000, 208–9) alerted me to Waller's (1990) insights and has argued for a movement away from this "paradigm" of "disaster and renewal," challenging historians to explore how sleeping sickness "was seen as a manageable disease" in parts of Africa.

64. District de Nola, Région de la Haute-Sangha, "Rapport économique," 1950, ibid., 4(3)D61; Père M. Morel-Chevillet, Chambéry, France, 14 May 1998.

65. "Journal de la Mission," 2 (1931–37), AGCS, entries for 22 May, 2 July, 28 Sept., 11 Nov. 1936, 31 Jan., 27 May 1937.

66. Préfecture Apostolique de Berbérati (Mgr Sintas) to Très Révérend Père Agathange, 1 May 1947, Fr. Pascal to [*unidentified*], 17 June 1947, ACT 4R6 (Mission d'Afrique, Lettres, 1947); Pierre d'Alcantara Sintas, "Extrait du rapport de visite pastorale de Mgr Sintas en pays Mbimou du 8 au 16 octobre 1944," 1944, ibid., 4R (Mission de Berbérati); "La maladie du sommeil," *Les Voix Franciscaines,* May 1947, 81–82, ibid.; "En visitant notre Mission d'Oubangui-Chari," Nov. 1948, ibid.

67. "La maladie de sommeil," *Les Voix Franciscaines,* May 1947, 81, ibid.; Sintas, "Extrait du rapport de visite pastorale de Mgr Sintas en pays Mbimou du 8 au 16 octobre 1944," 1944, ibid.

68. "Bilolo-Nola Dagbok, 1927–1960," FAIO/AO, Ar 1927–60, ser. F7:2, entry for 31 Dec. 1936.

69. Sofia Karlsson 1932, 108.

70. "Bilolo-Nola Dagbok, 1927–1960," FAIO/AO, Ar 1927–60, ser. F7:2, entries for 18–27 Feb. 1942, 5 July–6 Aug. 1943; Walter Olsson to John Magnusson, 13 Oct. 1936, ibid., 1930–41, ser. E1:2; Stig Andersson to Örebro Mission Board, 7 Jan. 1943,

ibid., 1940–46, ser. E1:3 (Örebromissionen Korrespondens Afrika, 1940–44); Olsson 1992, 67. The Baptists were also critical of the French administration's heavy-handed treatment of its Mpiemu subjects.

71. Karlsson 1932, 110, 113; Pierre d'Alcantara Sintas, "Extrait du rapport de visite pastorale de Mgr Sintas en pays Mbimou du 8 au 16 octobre 1944," 1944, ACT 4R; Olsson 1992, 67; Emma Svensson to John Magnusson, 3 Sept. 1938, David Johansson to John Magnusson, 11 Nov. 1935, FAIO/AO, Ar 1930–41, ser. E1:2; Larson 1997, 970–71.

72. These stories were exceedingly common. See Alouba Clotere, Lindjombo, 20 July 1993; Kadele Charles, Bandoka, 29 Nov. 1993; Amions Anaclet, Lindjombo, 17 Nov. 1993; Mpeng, dialogue, 24 Nov. 1993 (OA.4). Anna Kretsinger (personal communication, Bayanga, 27 Mar. 1993) heard similar stories repeated in the middle Sangha, as did Headrick (1987, 977–78).

73. Satuba Hortense, Lindjombo, 8 Nov. 1993; Kadele, dialogue, 5 Aug. 1993 (OA.20); Mpeng, dialogue, 24 Nov. 1993 (OA.4).

74. It is possible to transmit sleeping sickness by injecting a healthy person with the bodily fluids of an infected person (Dr. Allan Clarkson [New York University Medical School, Department of Medical and Molecular Parasitology], personal communication, 15 Mar. 1999).

75. Pierre d'Alcantara Sintas, "Extrait du rapport de visite pastorale de Mgr Sintas en pays Mbimou du 8 au 16 octobre 1944," 1944, ACT 4R. A major aim of Sintas's report was to document and to protest what he described as the "persecution" of African Catholics in the Mpiemu *terres*. According to Père Edouard Castaing, Père Emmanuel, who toured with Sintas, agreed that Choumara was a harsh taskmaster but felt that he had "saved the Mbimou" (Père Edouard Castaing, Toulouse, 18 July 1997).

76. Pierre d'Alcantara Sintas, "Extrait du rapport de visite pastorale de Mgr Sintas en pays Mbimou du 8 au 16 octobre 1944," 1944, ACT 4R; Mbali, dialogue, 5 Aug. 1993 (OA.27); Yodjala Philippe, Lindjombo, 28 July 1993; Alouba Clotere and Amions Anaclet, Lindjombo, 2 July 1993; Wakama, dialogue, 3 Aug. 1993 (OA.29).

77. Le Gouverneur des Colonies, Chef du Territoire de l'Oubangui-Chari, to M. le Gouverneur Général de l'AEF, Bangui, 5 Oct. 1938, CAOM, AEF 4(3)D51.

78. "Journal de la Mission," 2 (1931–37), AGCS, entry for Mar. 1933.

79. Ibid., 1 (1923–30), entries for 16 Feb., July 1924; Département de la Haute-Sangha, "Rapport politique," first semester, 1942, CAOM, AEF 4(3)D53; Pierre d'Alcantara Sintas, "Extrait du rapport de visite pastorale de Mgr Sintas en pays Mbimou du 8 au 16 octobre 1944," 1944, ACT 4R. Catechists' activities in villages could provoke considerable tensions with the chiefs themselves. See "Mort du catéchiste Gabriel Panjaka," 15 Dec. 1938, ibid., 4R4 (Lettres et Récits de Missionnaires).

80. "Bilolo-Nola Dagbok, 1927–1960," FAIO/AO, Ar 1927–60, ser. F7:2; Zechariah 4:10; Département de la Haute-Sangha, "Rapport politique," first semester, 1942, CAOM, AEF 4(3)D53.

81. "Notes pour les futurs historiens des missions de l'Afrique Équatoriale Notre-Dame de Buglose et sa Succursale de Carnot (R.C.A.)," ACT 3R (P. Pierre d'Alcantara [Mgr Sintas], Correspondance, Lettres, et Correspondances de Nos Pères).

82. "Journal de la Mission," 2 (1931–37), AGCS, entries for Apr. and May 1931. The question of mission influences speaks to a body of literature in African history and anthropology concerning conversion and faith. While earlier literature sought to explain why religious conversion took place, more recently the debate has centered around whether we can use the term at all. Some scholars have rejected the term altogether and instead have highlighted the agency of Africans in profoundly shaping the religious discourses that missionaries introduced and in appropriating particular Christian practices. Others have argued that scholars cannot ignore that Africans conceived of themselves as Christians, part of a religious community of the faithful, and thus did indeed convert to Christianity. This context calls for a balance between these two perspectives. Although many Mpiemu did appropriate specific practices and historically have shifted among a variety of churches in the Sangha basin, many also fundamentally thought of themselves as Christians, as members in a broader Christian community. See Horton 1975, 219–23; Landau 1995; Comaroff and Comaroff 1991 and 1997; Sanneh 1989; Hoehler-Fatton 1996.

83. Africanist scholars have produced a rich literature concerning missionary interventions into marriage, childbirth, and education, detailing complex interactions between Africans and missionaries. See, for example, Hunt 1999; Landau 1996.

84. J. Hilberth 1932, 48–58.

85. Svensson 1932, 105–6.

86. "Journal de la Mission," 1 (1923–30), AGCS, entry for 1923; Église Catholique, Lindjombo, 11 July 1993; Mission Baptiste, Lindjombo, 16 May 1993. The first baptisms did not occur until 10 Aug. 1929, two years after Brother Aron Svenson, Reinhold Andersson, and Mpiemu workers constructed the Bilolo mission station ("Bilolo-Nola Dagbok, 1927–1960," FAIO/AO, Ar 1927–60, ser. F7:2). See Larson (1997, 970) on how European missionaries altered their language "to evangelize terms, and in ways that made sense to their audiences."

87. "Bilolo-Nola Dagbok, 1927–1960," FAIO/AO, Ar 1927–60, ser. F7:2, entry for 22 July 1930.

88. Karlsson 1932, 110–13; Svensson 1932, 103; E. Hilberth 1932, 117–19; Kvist 1932. Elsewhere see Hunt 1999, though Protestant missionaries in Yakusu, despite their misunderstandings, had a far better grasp of African vocabularies of power, illness, and healing. On the association of occult powers with political authority, see Geschiere 1997.

89. "Bilolo-Nola Dagbok, 1927–1960," FAIO/AO, Ar 1927–60, ser. F7:2, entries for 22–23 Mar., 15 June 1938, 12 Jan. 1941, 26–27 May 1948.

90. Appadurai 1986, 13.

91. Pomodimo 1993; Morel 1994, 17–19; Kadele Charles and Mabessimo Florent, Bandoka, 3 Dec. 1993; Kadele Charles, Bandoka, 4 Dec. 1993.

92. Kadele Charles, Adebori, 5 Dec. 1993; also Mabessimo-Angoula Levi, Adebori, 11 Dec. 1993; Befio Georges, Lindjombo, 5 Apr. 1993.

93. Mission Baptiste, Lindjombo, 27 June 1993.

94. Kadele Charles, Bandoka, 3 Dec. 1993; Wan-Mbissa Samuel, Lindjombo, 11 Aug. 1993; Mempeli Dieudonné, Lindjombo, 9 Nov. 1993. I have translated *pondo* as "flesh" because people use the term to refer to parts of animal or human bodies that are not fur, bone, skin, or heart. *Sonyoli* is based on the root *nyoli,* meaning "body." Mpiemu speakers distinguish this term from *dimi,* which refers to a forest spirit or demon.

95. Bongmba (1998) has made the important point that discourses about "supernatural powers" can also be infused with notions of morality.

96. Kadele, dialogue, 5 Aug. 1993 (OA.20); Kokameko Moise, dialogue, 15 May 1993, (OA.8); Mpeng, dialogue, 1 Aug. 1993 (OA.2); Langabouri, dialogue, 23 May 1993, (OA.5); Yodjala Philippe, Lindjombo, 19, 21 Nov. 1993.

97. Pombo Paul, Lindjombo, 9 Aug. 1993; Bessari Alphonsine, Lindjombo, 15 Dec. 1993; Mpeng Patrice, forest near Likembe River, 23 Nov. 1993; Leon Antoinette, Lindjombo, 23 July 1993. Kin in *metego Mpiemu* also sent messages urging their Lindjombo relatives to return "home" (Alouba Clotere, dialogue with author, tape recording, Lindjombo, 21 July 1993 [cassette no. OA.23]; Alouba Mathieu, Messadjiso, 9 Dec. 1993).

98. Yodjala Philippe, on the Bilolo-Salo road, 5 Dec. 1993.

99. For instance, Naro Filomene and Dinoramibali Martine, Lindjombo, 2 Nov. 1993; Pendo David, 2 Nov. 1993; Mpeng Patrice, Lindjombo, 3 Nov. 1993; Anna Kretsinger, Bangui, 31 Oct. 1993.

100. Yodjala Philippe, Bandoka, 29 Nov., 1, 2 Dec. 1993; Mpeng, dialogue, 14 May, 1 Aug. 1993 (OA.1–2); Mpeng Patrice, Lindjombo, 1 Nov. 1993.

101. Carroll 1998, 204.

102. Blom 1998, 210, but also 209, 211; Allard Blom, Bayanga, 19 May 1993. Generally, see Vedder 1998, 171.

103. Carroll 1998, 204.

104. Fay 1993. For further discussion, see Giles-Vernick 1999, 186–87.

105. Ntchambe, dialogue, 2 Dec. 1993 (OA.16); Alouba, dialogue, 25 July 1993 (OA.24); Bandiko Albert, dialogue with author, tape recording, Bandoka, 30 Nov. 1993 (cassette no. OA.22); village meeting with project, tape recording, Lindjombo, 18 May 1993 (cassette no. OA.33); village meeting in Lindjombo, 14 July 1993; Yodjala Philippe, Lindjombo, 4 Nov. 1993; Kadele Charles, Bandoka, 4 Dec. 1993; Ampouma Charlotte, Lindjombo, 8 July 1993.

106. Village meeting with project, Lindjombo, 18 May 1993; Wanzi Lazare, Lindjombo, 22 May 1993; Pombo Paul, Lindjombo, 22 May 1993; Benkoubo Bruno, Lindjombo, 22 May 1993; Lindjombo Etienne, Lindjombo, 19 May 1993.

5. From Fields of Maize to Fields of Hunger

1. Fourneau 1932, 275, 279–80, 287.

2. Fourneau 1900, 1345; Muston, 1933, 26, 32, 35; "Rapport de M. l'Administrateur Gaillard, sur son voyage dans la Sangha," 10 May 1894, CAOM, Mission 24; M. de Sallmard to Siège Sociale (Compagnie des Produits de la Sangha-Lipa-Ouesso), 21 May 1902, ibid., Gabon-Congo III, 13, no. 53. Feeding troops throughout Middle Congo, Ubangi-Shari, and Chad was a major problem for French explorers and administrators, and the French ultimately recruited African porters to support their demands for foods and other goods (Mollion 1992, 9–13, 44).

3. Mawindi Julienne, dialogue, 11 Nov. 1993 (OA.10); Kadele Job, Bandoka, 1 Dec. 1993; Kadele Charles, Bandoka, 4 Dec. 1993; Periquet 1916, 232–37; Muston 1933, 26; Bruel 1910, 12; Burnham 1981, 129–30; Copet 1981, 515; Geschiere 1981, 528; Burnham, Copet-Rougier, and Noss 1986, 123; Rossel 1999, 112. See McCann's (1999b) history of maize in Africa. Members of the Periquet (1916, 232–33) expedition contended that cassava was unknown in the Sangha in 1900. Acreage of cultivated maize in the M'Bimou *circonscription* (comprised of the Biakombo, Bidjuki, Bikoun, and Koapuli *terrains*) was approximately 370 hectares. Cassava cultivation only occurred in the Koapuli *terrain,* amounting to 90 hectares ("Rapport de la Compagnie Forestière de la Sangha-Oubangui, 1911," CAOM, AEF 8Q30; Vansina 1990, 214; Harms 1981, 52–55; Mveng-Ayi 1981, 591; Jones 1959, 68–69).

4. Mpeng Patrice, Bafio Emmanuel, and Mami Pauline, Lindjombo, 13 July 1993; Medibodjindi Antoine, Lindjombo, 2 June 1993; Pombo Paul, Lindjombo, 9 Aug. 1993; Mempeli Didier and Borobang Georges, Lindjombo, 2 July 1993, Kadele Charles, Bandoka, 29 Nov. 1993; Muston, 1933, 26.

5. Muston's (1933) description of maize fields on the outskirts of villages that he saw in late November and early December (during the late rainy–early dry season) lends support to Mpiemu contentions that they cultivated a third field during the year.

6. Medibodjindi Antoine, Lindjombo, 2 June 1993; Pombo Paul, Lindjombo, 2 June 1993; Mempeli Didier and Borobang Georges, Lindjombo, 2 July 1993; Kadele Charles, Bandoka, 29 Nov. 1993; Alouba Clotere and Tontchoe Cecile, Salo, 27 Nov. 1993. For a general discussion of agriculture in the Congo basin, see Miracle 1967. One CFSO report detailing the Mpiemu agricultural calendar described the process somewhat differently. The first maize planting, called *kangola,* took place in March, the second (*akombo*) occurred in July, and the third (*bolomo*) was in October. During November and December, and particularly in January and February, farmers worked to prepare their fields for planting ("Rapport de la Compagnie Forestière de la Sangha-Oubangui, 1911," CAOM, AEF 8Q30; "Questionnaire: Résidence ou poste de Ouesso," 1900, ibid., 4[2]D1).

7. Loyre 1909, 417–18; Dupré 1982, 108–17; Copet-Rougier 1998, 53–56. On mobility as a land-use strategy elsewhere, see Johnson and Anderson 1988.

8. "Journal de la Mission," 2 (1931–37), AGCS, entry for July 1933. On farming-site selection in swidden agricultural systems, see Dove 1993.

9. Kokameko, dialogue, 15 May 1993 (OA.8). Elisabeth Copet-Rougier found one informant in Cameroon in 1980 who declared that the Mpiemu were the off-spring of a man named *piemo* or *jarwa,* or bushfire, and a woman named *akombo,* or forest. Because Mpiemu linked bushfires with preparing fields, I take this comment to mean that the Mpiemu people were the children of the field and the forest (E. Copet-Rougier, personal communication, 22 Nov. 1994).

10. Bruel 1910, 12–13; Anonymous 1907, 391; Cottes 1911, 104–5.

11. Burnham, Copet-Rougier, and Noss 1986, 121; Kadele Charles, Bandoka, 29 Nov. 1993; Bessari Alphonsine, Lindjombo, 15 Dec. 1993; Leon Antoinette, 28 June 1993; Biloue Raymond, Lindjombo, 18 Nov. 1993. Tisserant (1950, 71), the Catholic missionary, claimed that *mendelepako* was a variety of sweet cassava that came from Sango speakers along the Ubangi River.

12. Foa Mabogolo, Bandoka, 8 Dec. 1993; Lengi Emilienne, Bandoka, 3 Dec. 1993; Dinoramibali Martine, Lindjombo, 10 Nov. 1993.

13. Mawindi Julienne, dialogue, 11 Nov. 1993 (OA.10); Ndoagne Micheline, Lindjombo, 8 Nov. 1993; Alouba Clotere, Salo, 11 Aug. 1993. Copet-Rougier (1981, 515) maintained that Kako people also attached considerable significance to maize, even though they, like Mpiemu, no longer cultivate or eat large quantities of it.

14. Anonymous 1896, 353–54.

15. The Compagnie de la N'Goko-Sangha attempted to plant rubber in 1909 in Bomassa and Salo but abandoned these plantations when the rubber trees failed to grow ("Rapport mensuel de janvier 1911," CAOM, AEF 4[2]D7).

16. "Questionnaire: Résidence ou poste de Ouesso," 1900, ibid., 4(2)D1.

17. "Exposé sommaire des affaires survenues depuis novembre 2 juin 1911," draft, ibid., 5D9.

18. "Organisation administrative des circonscriptions, rapport annuel," 1915, and Pinelli, "Rapport mensuel (Nola)," July 1915, ibid., 4(2)D17; Le Chef de la Circonscription de la Kadei-Sangha (Pinelli) to Monsieur le Lieutenant-Colonel Pinet, Commandant Militaire du Moyen-Congo, Nola, 18 Mar. 1917, ibid., 4(2)D21.

19. Merlin (Gouverneur Général de l'Afrique Équatoriale Française) 1913. World price increases in the early 1920s and in the 1940s fueled rubber extraction in the Nola, M'Bimou, and Kaka-Goumbe subdivisions (L'Administrateur L. Vingarassamy, Chef de la Circonscription de la Kadei-Sangha, to Monsieur le Lieutenant-Gouverneur du Moyen-Congo [Affaires Civiles], Nola, 7 June 1923, CAOM, AEF 4[2]D37; Allys [Chef de la Subdivision de Nola], "Rapport trimestriel," 1926, ibid., 4[2]D42).

20. Allys (Chef de la Subdivision de Nola), "Rapport trimestriel," second trimester, 1926, CAOM, AEF 4(2)D42.

21. Circonscription de la Haute-Sangha, "Rapport annuel," 1927, ibid., 4(2)D43.

22. Beinart 1984; Feierman 1990; Mandala 1990.

23. Circonscription de la Haute-Sangha, "Rapport annuel," 1927, CAOM, AEF 4(2)D43; Département de la Sangha, "Rapport trimestriel," first trimester, 1935, ibid., 4(2)D66; Circonscription de la Haute-Sangha, Subdivision de Nola, "Rapport trimestriel," first trimester, 1931, ibid., 4(2)D52; Le Gouverneur Général P.I. de l'Afrique Équatoriale FSE (Marchessou) to Monsieur l'Inspecteur Général des Colonies, Chef de la Mission d'Inspection, 18 May 1935, ibid., 3D47 (Mission d'Inspection). Farmers in much of Ubangi-Shari had to undertake cotton cultivation. The French instituted compulsory cotton cultivation as far south as Mbaiki and Bambio, villages in the southwestern forest, but not in the middle Sangha.

24. "Rapport sur les observation recueillis au cours d'une tournée d'inspection du 14 mai au 31 juillet (Département du Moyen-Congo)," 1936, Département de la Sangha, "Rapport trimestriel," first trimester, 1936, and Le Gouverneur Général de l'Afrique Équatoriale Française to Monsieur le Ministre des Colonies (Réorganisation Administrative), 15 May 1936, no. 711, ibid., 4(2)D69.

25. Kalck 1971, 65.

26. Département de la Haute-Sangha, "Rapport politique," second trimester, 1941, CAOM, AEF 4(3)D52; Kalck 1959, 191–94.

27. A. Canal (Région de la Haute-Sangha), "Rapport économique annuel," 1950, CAOM, AEF 4(3)D61.

28. Département de la Haute-Sangha, "Rapport politique," first and second semesters, 1942, ibid., 4(3)D53; Kalck 1971, 110–11.

29. Circonscription de la Haute-Sangha, Subdivision de Nola, "Rapport trimestriel," first trimester, 1931, CAOM, AEF 4(2)D52.

30. Département de la Sangha, "Rapport trimestriel," first trimester, 1935, ibid., 4(2)D66; "Rapport du 2ème trimestre," 29 Aug. 1908, ibid., 4(2)D2; Pouperon 1908, 5; L'Administrateur L. Vingarassamy (Chef de la Circonscription de la Kadei-Sangha) to Monsieur le Lieutenant-Gouverneur du Moyen-Congo (Affaires Civiles), 7 June 1923, ibid., 4(2)D37; Circonscription de la Haute-Sangha, "Rapport trimestriel," first trimester, 1926, and Allys (Circonscription de la Haute-Sangha), "Rapport trimestriel," 1926, ibid., 4(2)D42.

31. Pierre d'Alcantara Sintas, "Extrait du rapport de visite pastorale de Mgr Sintas en pays Mbimou du 8 au 16 octobre 1944," 1944, ACT 4R; District de Nola, "Rapport économique," 1950, CAOM, AEF 4(3)D61; Subdivisions de Nola et Berbérati, ancienne Kadei-Sangha, "Rapport mensuel," Aug. 1923, ibid., 4(2)D37.

32. District de Nola, "Rapport économique," 1950, CAOM, AEF 4(3)D61.

33. Kalck 1971, 88; Père Martin Morel-Chevillet, Couvent des Capucins, Chambéry, France, 14 May 1998.

34. Pierre d'Alcantara Sintas, "Extrait du rapport de visite pastorale de Mgr Sintas en pays Mbimou du 8 au 16 octobre 1944," 1944, ACT 4R. Countless researchers in Africa have documented this sort of claim about particular foods in Africa. See especially Richards's (1939) pioneering study, as well as Moore and Vaughan's (1994) restudy. For a discussion of food and ethnicity in equatorial Africa, see Burnham 1996, 162. Elsewhere, see Weiss 1996, 27–149.

35. District de Nola, "Rapport économique," 1950, CAOM, AEF 4(3)D61.

36. Mawindi Julienne, dialogue, 11 Nov. 1993 (OA.10); Yongo, dialogue, 8 Aug. 1993 (OA.11); Alouba Clotere, dialogue, 21 July 1993 (OA.23); Mpeng, dialogue, 14 May 1993 (OA.1); Bishiari Filomene, Lindjombo, 18 Nov. 1993; Dogassie Salomon, Bandoka, 1 Dec. 1993; Kadele Charles, Bandoka, 3 Dec. 1993; Ekroth 1932, 86; Pinelli, "Rapport mensuel (Nola)," July 1915, CAOM, AEF 4(2)D17; Circonscription de la Haute-Sangha, "Rapport annuel," 1927, ibid., 4(2)D43. For analyses of the relationship between changing labor availability and cropping patterns elsewhere in Africa, see Berry 1993, 67–100; Carney 1988; Carney and Watts 1990. Cultivating cassava is indeed less time-consuming, but cassava made greater demands on women's food-preparation time. Maize could always be eaten grilled, as a snack food. And even when served as *kam* (stiff maize porridge) or *kamishogo*, it required only pounding, although that process could be an onerous one. Bitter cassava, however, needed soaking for three days, drying, pounding, and sifting in order to be consumed.

37. Giles-Vernick 1996a, 218–20. Cf. McCann 1999b.

38. Yongo, dialogue, 8 Aug. 1993 (OA.11); Poundja Monique, Lindjombo, 10 May 1993; Soum Madeleine, Lindjombo, 28 June 1993; Ndoagne Micheline, Lindjombo, 2 July 1993; Kadele Charles, Bandoka, 29 Nov. 1993; Tontchoe Cecile and Alouba Clotere, Salo, 27 Nov. 1993; Bessari Alphonsine, Lindjombo, 15 Dec. 1993; Louko Jeannette, Lindjombo, 18 June 1993; Biloue Brigitte, Lindjombo, 11 Nov. 1993; Mowe Eleya, Bandoka, 29 Nov. 1993.

39. Akyeampong (1997) has explored the important social and cultural meanings of alcohol. Kalck (1959, 137) contended that distilled alcohol was unknown in the area of the present-day CAR during the nineteenth century, although the history of distilled alcohol there has yet to be researched. It appears that *menyogi* has not gained the enduring cultural and social significance that it has in West Africa, though palm wine has (J. Hilberth 1932, 51).

40. Alouba Clotere, Salo, 8 Aug. 1993; Satuba Rose, Satuba Claudette, and Njowasowe Caroline, Lindjombo, 10 Nov. 1993; Dogassie Salomon, Bandoka, 1 Dec. 1993.

41. Dinoramibali Martine, Lindjombo, 10 May 1993.

42. I measured fields by pacing them and then calculated their areas by multiplying the size of my pace by the number of paces. The difference between the field sizes of non-Mpiemu and Mpiemu farmers was statistically significant. In calculations of 1993 field sizes, I also controlled for marital status, because married women whose husbands cleared fields could cultivate larger fields than single women. On average, however, the difference in field sizes of married and single women was not statistically significantly different.

43. Langabouri, dialogue, 23 May 1993 (OA.5); Bishiari Filomene, Lindjombo, 18 June 1993; Alouba Clotere, Salo, 27 Nov. 1993; Bessari Alphonsine, Lindjombo, 15 Dec. 1993.

44. "Rapport général sur la Société N'Goko-Sangha pour l'année 1909," 28 Feb. 1910, and "Rapport général sur la Société N'Goko-Sangha," 31 Jan. 1911, CAOM, AEF 8Q20.

45. Ibid.; "Rapport de la Compagnie Forestière de la Sangha-Oubangui, 1911," ibid., 8Q30; Pinelli, "Rapport mensuel (juillet 1915)," 31 July 1915, ibid., 4(2)D17.

46. "Concessions du Congo, Décret," 31 Mar. 1899, ibid., Gabon-Congo III, 13; "Rapport général sur la Société N'Goko-Sangha," 31 Jan. 1911, ibid., AEF 8Q20; "Rapport de la Compagnie Forestière de la Sangha-Oubangui, 1911," ibid., 8Q30; Pinelli, "Rapport mensuel (juillet 1915)," 31 July 1915, ibid., 4(2)D17; Allys (Chef de la Subdivision de Nola), "Rapport trimestriel," 1926 and second trimester, 1926, ibid., 4(2)D42.

47. Subdivision de Nola, "Rapport mensuel," Dec. 1923, ibid., 4(2)D37; Circonscription de la Haute-Sangha, "Rapport annuel," 1927, ibid., 4(2)D43; Subdivision de Nola, "Rapport trimestriel," second trimester, 1931, ibid., 4(2)D52; Département de la Sangha, "Rapport trimestriel," first and second trimesters, 1935, ibid., 4(2)D66; District de Nola, "Rapport économique," 1950, ibid., 4(3)D61. Santini acquired his concession of 150 hectares in 1932, and Lopes gained one of 225 hectares in 1933. Santini later expanded the area of his concession under cultivation, but administrators did not report by how much this area had expanded by 1950. One of Santini's former plantation managers has contended that the plantation included nearly 200 hectares of coffee by the time Santini sold it to a subsequent buyer (Mustapha Zamel, Berbérati, 10 June 1993).

48. "Rapport sur les observation recueillis au cours d'une tournée d'inspection du 14 mai au 31 juillet (Département du Moyen-Congo)," 1936, CAOM, AEF 4(2)D69; Ndi Christophe, Lindjombo, 31 July 1993; Mbonga Nicholas, Lindjombo, 29 June 1993; Louko Jeannette, Lindjombo, 18 June 1993.

49. Amions Anaclet, Lindjombo, 17 Nov. 1993; Mustapha Zamel, Berbérati, 11 June 1993.

50. La Société Emona-Commerce Lubljana, "Cession de l'exploitation d'une plantation," 25 Aug. 1981; Mamo Veronique and Bibelo Albert, Lindjombo, 29 July 1993; Mbonga Nicholas, Lindjombo, 29 June 1993; Amions Anaclet, Lindjombo, 12 Dec. 1993. Although this sum seems paltry, it far exceeds average per capita income in the Central African Republic (U.S. Department of State, Bureau of Public Affairs 1989).

51. Castro, Ngandio Antoine, and Ndi Christophe, Lindjombo, 9 Nov. 1993; Marc Volvert of Plantation Volvert, Berbérati, 11 June 1993. Farmers received between $.10 and $.12 per kilo, significantly lower than the world price of $.56 per kilo in 1993.

52. Dove and Kammen 1997, 91.

53. Amions Anaclet, Lindjombo, 13 July 1993; Yongo Oromain, Lindjombo, 22 July 1993; Yodjala Philippe, Lindjombo, 2 Nov. 1993; Bondi Charles, Bandoka, 30 July 1993; Alouba Mathieu, Messadjiso, 8 Dec. 1993; Tontchoe Cecile, Salo, 5 Aug. 1993; Kadele Charles, Bandoka, 3 Dec. 1993; Douzimé, dialogue, 18 Apr. 1993 (OA.28).

54. Yongo, dialogue, 8 Aug. 1993 (OA.11); Amions Anaclet, Lindjombo, 17 Nov. 1993; Satuba, dialogue, 9 May 1993 (OA.19); Ngandio Antoine, Lindjombo, 8 July 1993; Mbonga Nicholas, Lindjombo, 29 June 1993; Ndi Christophe, 31 July 1993.

55. Amions Anaclet, Lindjombo, 14 Dec. 1993; Yodjala Philippe, Lindjombo, 4 Nov. 1993; Castro, Ngandio Antoine, and Ndi Christophe, Lindjombo, 9 Nov. 1993; Mbonga Nicholas, Lindjombo, 29 June 1993; Ndi Christophe, Lindjombo, 31 July 1993.

56. Mbonga Nicholas, Lindjombo, 29 June 1993; Benkoubo Bruno, 8 June 1993; Yodjala Philippe, Lindjombo, 6 July 1993; Ndi Christophe, Lindjombo, 31 July 1993; Leon Antoinette, Lindjombo, 2 July 1993; Louko Jeannette, Lindjombo, 18 June 1993; Yawogo Monique, Lindjombo, 7 July 1993; Dinoramibali Martine, Lindjombo, 10 May 1993. Whether *Ageratum conyzoides* actually saps the soil's nutrients has not been studied in this region. One American biologist in the area found it aesthetically displeasing, while another researcher suggested that its dense root structure might actually protect the soil from erosion (Andrea Turkalo, Dzanga, 5 May 1993; David Wilkie, Lindjombo, 9 July 1993).

57. Bibelo Albert, Lindjombo, 29 July 1993; [name withheld], Motao, 9 Dec. 1993; Castro, Lindjombo, 9 Nov. 1993; Ndi Christophe, Lindjombo 19 July 1993.

58. Yongo, dialogue, 8 Aug. 1993 (OA.11).

59. Dinoramibali Martine, Lindjombo, 10 May 1993; Ndoagne Micheline, Lindjombo, 26 June 1993; Leon Antoinette, Lindjombo, 23 July 1993; Yawogo Monique, Lindjombo, 7 July 1993; Louko Jeannette, Lindjombo, 18 June 1993; Mahmat Kamis, Lindjombo, 22 July 1993; Soum Madeleine, Lindjombo, 28 June 1993.

60. "Notes pour les futurs historiens des missions de l'Afrique Équatoriale Notre-Dame de Buglose et sa Succursale de Carnot (R.C.A.)," ACT 3R (P. Pierre d'Alcantara [Mgr Sintas], Correspondance, Lettres, et Correspondances de Nos Pères).

61. Anonymous 1932, 25.

62. Ibid., 46.

63. "Dans cette conférence nous voulons vous montrer l'oeuvre qui s'accomplit dans notre mission d'Oubangui-Tchad," ACT 3R2c (Mission d'Afrique, Varia [Berbérati]); "Bilolo-Nola Dagbok, 1927–1960," FAIO/AO, Ar 1927–60, ser. F7:2, entries for 24 Mar., 12 July 1928, 22 June, 23 Sept., 1 Oct. 1929, 4 Mar. 1930, 30 May, 18 Sept. 1931; Département de la Sangha, "Rapport trimestriel," second trimester, 1935, CAOM, AEF 4(2)D66; ibid., first and second trimesters, 1936, 4(2)D69. Catechists produced their first coffee harvest in 1926 ("Journal de la Mission," 1 [1924–30] and 2 [1931–37], AGCS, entries for April, Dec. 1926, 3 Feb. 1929, Mar., June 1932).

64. "Journal de la Mission," 1 (1924–30) and 2 (1931–37), AGCS, entries for April 1926, 1 June 1927, 20 Feb., 21 Aug. 1928, 3 Feb. 1929, 16 Apr. 1933.

65. Ibid., entries for May 1932, July 1933; Svensson 1932, 103; untitled document, n.d., ACT 4R4 (Correspondance, 1937–52).

66. "Notes d'histoire anecdotique prises à l'occasion de la tournée pastorale de Mgr Sintas et du R. P. Emmanuel chez les Mbimous le 15 au 18 octobre 1946," 26 Oct. 1946, ACT 3R (P. Pierre d'Alcantara [Mgr Sintas], Correspondances, Lettres, et Conférences de Nos Pères).

67. R. P. Pierre d'Alcantara, "Henriette Odjèmo: Pauvre fille de la forêt," 1945(?), ibid.; "Dans cette conférence nous voulons vous montrer l'oeuvre qui s'accomplit dans notre mission d'Oubangui-Tchad," ibid., 3R2c (Mission d'Afrique, Varia [Berbérati]).

68. Baud(?) to Révérendissime Père Général, Oct. 1958, ACS 15-Q (Correspondance, 1954–63).

69. "Journal de la Mission," 2 (1931–37), AGCS, entry for Oct. 1933.

70. Pierre d'Alcantara Sintas, "Extrait du rapport de visite pastorale de Mgr Sintas en pays Mbimou du 8 au 16 octobre 1944," 1944, ACT 4R.

71. Mission Baptiste, Lindjombo, 25 July 1993; Mission Baptiste, Lindjombo, 27 June 1993; Yongo Oromain, Lindjombo, 22 July 1993.

72. Mission Catholique, Lindjombo, 11 July 1993; Mabessimo-Angoula Levi, Adebori, 1 Dec. 1993; Kadele Charles, Bandoka, 2 Dec. 1993. These were criticisms that non-Mpiemu made as well in and outside of church (Kouyabou Eugène, preaching at Mission Baptiste, Lindjombo, 9 May 1993; Mission Baptiste, Lindjombo, 27 June 1993; Mbonga Mathias, Lindjombo, 16 May 1993).

73. Mission Baptiste, Lindjombo, 9 May 1993; Mabessimo-Angoula Levi, Adebori, 1 Dec. 1993; Kadele Charles, Bandoka, 2 Dec. 1993.

74. Yongo, dialogue, 8 Aug. 1993 (OA.11).

75. Mission Baptiste, Lindjombo, 9 May 1993; Mabessimo-Angoula Levi, Adebori, 2 Dec. 1993; Kadele Charles, Adebori, 2 Dec. 1993; Amions Anaclet, Lindjombo, 12 Dec. 1993. These notions were widely shared (Mbonga Nicholas, Lindjombo, 27 June 1993; Mission Catholique, Lindjombo, 11 July 1993).

76. Mission Catholique, Lindjombo, 11 July 1993.

77. O'Toole 1986, 109.

78. Zoctizoum 1984, 9–13.

79. Ibid., 35, 86, 84. One analyst, Ngoupandé (1997, 13–14), has contended that revenues from coffee financed Bokassa's coronation in 1977, an event that cost approximately one-third of the country's annual revenue. See also Bigo 1988, 91–92, 117–18; O'Toole 1986, 53.

80. For a basic outline of this strategy, see Johnston and Mellor 1961.

81. O'Toole 1986, 108–9. Assessments of Opération Bokassa vary significantly. Ngoupandé (1997, 222) has argued that between 1966 and 1969 "cotton, diamonds, foodstuffs, and practically all sectors of production benefited from 'the Bokassa effect.'" Others have been less sanguine about its long-term effects (Faes and Smith 2000, 115–16; Titley 1997, 68–69; Père Clement Sautier [Mission Catholique Carnot], 31 Dec. 1972, ACS 16-Q [Correspondance, 1964–78]).

82. O'Toole, 1986, 109.

83. Zoctizoum 1983, 21–23, 75–76, 80–81.

84. Amions Anaclet, Lindjombo, 9 July 1993; Lindjombo Etienne, Lindjombo, 19 June 1993; [name withheld at request of informant], Bayanga, 19 June 1993; Fay 1993.

85. Ngatoua Urbain, Lindjombo, 9 Nov. 1993.

86. Allard Blom, Bayanga, 19 May 1993; [name withheld], Bayanga, 19 May 1993; Bessari Alphonsine, 12 Dec. 1993; Eyama Madeleine, Lindjombo, 28 June 1993; Louko Jeannette, 18 June 1993; Biloue Brigitte, Lindjombo, 3 June 1993; Ndoagne Micheline, Lindjombo, 20 July 1993; Mekité Sylvanus, Lindjombo, 14 May 1993. On wildlife and crop loss, see Naughton-Treves 1997.

87. Lindjombo meeting with WWF project representatives, Lindjombo, 18 May 1993; Amions Anaclet, Lindjombo and forest, 23 Nov., 15 July 1993; Lindjombo Etienne, Lindjombo, 15 July 1993; Mamo Veronique, Lindjombo, 29 July 1993; Wanzi Lazare, Lindjombo, 12 July 1993; Pendo David, Lindjombo, 2 Nov. 1993; Louko Jeannette, Lindjombo, 18 June 1993.

88. Fay had a reputation in the CAR and Congo as an exacting and unrelenting champion of the forest's wildlife, and many African informants believed he was unsympathetic to their concerns. One *National Geographic* article (Chadwick 1995, 10) compared Fay to explorer Henry Morton Stanley, "the unstoppable force whom natives called Bula Matari, 'breaker of rocks.'"

89. Yemando Suzanne, Lindjombo, 15 July 1993; Amions Anaclet, Lindjombo, 15 July 1993; Ndoagne Micheline, Lindjombo, 20 July 1993.

6. Emptying the Forest

1. Scholars such as Grove (1995, 1989), Neumann (1995, 1996), Beinart and Coates (1995, 20–27), and MacKenzie (1987) have located the historical roots of this discourse in empire, colonialism, and capitalism, as well as in Christian notions of original sin, European notions of masculinity, and elite privilege.

2. The hunting literature from several geographical contexts (Forman 1995; Leach 1994, 160; cf. Wilkie and Finn 1990) argues that hunting and trapping occur most frequently at forest clearings and edges. Mpiemu forest typologies and descriptions suggest people found game on forest edges and within the forest.

3. Biloue Brigitte and Ndoagne Micheline, Lindjombo, 11 May 1993; Kadele Charles, forest outside Bandoka, 29 Nov. 1993; Andoungou, Kwapeli road, 5 Aug. 1993; Mpeng Patrice, forest outside Lindjombo, 25 June 1993, and forest near Likembe River, 23 Nov. 1993.

4. Dibango and Amions Anaclet, Lindjombo, 30 July 1993; Leon Antoinette, forest outside Lindjombo, 23 July 1993; Mpeng Patrice, forest outside Lindjombo, 25 June 1993; Biloue Brigitte and Ndoagne Micheline, Lindjombo, 11 May 1993.

5. Kadele and Alouba, dialogue, 5 Aug. 1993 (OA.20); Nyambi, dialogue, 5 Aug. 1993 (OA.18).

6. On redwood powder, see Vansina 1990, 291; Copet-Rougier 1998, 56 and, on guns, 65; Lt. Fourneau 1900, 1349–50; A. Fourneau 1932, 284; "Rapport général sur la Société N'Goko-Sangha pour l'année 1909," 1910, CAOM, AEF 8Q20; Muston 1933, 26; Coquery-Vidrovitch 1972, 315–30; Hladik and Hladik 1990.

7. Kadele, dialogue, 5 Aug. 1993 (OA.20).

8. On equatorial African specialist hunters, see Birmingham 1983; Dupré 1985, 93–104, and 1995; Harms 1981, 27, 39–43, 44, 53–56; Koch 1968; Marks 1984, 61–64.

9. *Ntche* means "road" or "path"; *ngonga* means "to set."

10. Kadele, dialogue, 5 Aug. 1993 (OA.20); Kouro Yvonne, dialogue, 5 Dec. 1993 (OA.13); Alouba Clotere, dialogue, 21 July 1993 (OA.13); Dogassie Salomon, Bandoka, 1 Dec. 1993; Mpeng Patrice, forest outside of Lindjombo, 25 June 1993; Yodjala Philippe, forest outside of Lindjombo, 6 July 1993. See also Koch 1968; Bahuchet and Garine 1990; Herbert 1993, 166.

11. Mpeng, dialogue, 23 Nov. 1993 (OA.4); Wan-Mbissa Samuel, Lindjombo, 17 Nov. 1993.

12. Ntchambe, dialogue, 2 Dec. 1993 (OA.16); Bandiko Albert, Bandoka, 30 Nov. 1993.

13. Herbert (1993, 166) has shown that men appropriate notions of fecundity in hunting rituals. See also Leach 1994, 161–65; Beinart and Coates 1995, 17–20.

14. Leon Antoinette, forest outside of Lindjombo, 23 July 1993; Alouba Clotere, Lindjombo, 24 July 1993; Ndoagne Micheline, Lindjombo, 8 Nov. 1993; Dinoramibali Martine, Lindjombo, 8 Nov. 1993; Mpeng, dialogue, 1 Aug. 1993 (OA.2). I was never able to elicit from tellers how they or their ancestors categorized various groups within the animal kingdom. But Mpiemu tellers contended that gorillas and chimpanzees (*wago*) shared similar origins with people, although apes did not live in villages or "listen to the word of Ntchambe." The belief in gorillas' penchant for women is a widespread, long-standing one in equatorial Africa (Du Chaillu 1969; Kisliuk 1998, 159; Giles-Vernick and Rupp, 2000).

15. Nyambi, dialogue, 5 Aug. 1993 (OA.18). On pregnancy, hunting, and trapping among Badjoué and Bikélé peoples in Cameroon, see Koch 1968, 27–33.

16. Nyambi Patrice, dialogue, 5 Aug. 1993 (OA.18); Amions Anaclet and Alouba Clotere, Lindjombo, 20 July 1993; Satuba Igor, forest, 13 July 1993; J. Hilberth 1932, 57. Tellers maintained that many Sangha basin peoples performed this dance after killing a leopard. On leopards, see Vansina 1990, 74, 276–77. For an analysis of hunting and reproduction in Cameroon, see Koch 1968, 27–33.

17. Nyambi, dialogue, 5 Aug. 1993 (OA.18).

18. Mabessimo Florent, Kwapeli forest, 7 Dec. 1993; Yodjala Philippe, Lindjombo, 21, 28 July 1993; Alouba Clotere, Lindjombo, 24 July 1993. *Biakombo* closely resembles the name of the Mpiemu *kuli ajing*, Piakombo, and the root *-kombo* means "forest" in Mpiemu. For their part, Mpiemu named Gbaya *bilonbi*, or "people of the savanna." See Burnham (1996) on ethnic differences among Gbaya, Fulbé, and Mbororo peoples premised partly upon perceptions of livelihood difference.

19. Mpeng Patrice, forest south of Lindjombo, 22 Nov. 1993. Blood brotherhoods were important political strategies for creating alliances among diverse groups in the nineteenth century. Copet-Rougier (1998, 61) has written: "By mixing blood . . . [groups] became consanguineous and the same blood would henceforth run through them. . . . Violent or sexual contact with identical blood brought weakness and death."

20. Peterson 2000, 77, 94–99. See also Vansina 1990, 88–93. Peterson's work alerted me to Douglas's (1954) analysis of Lele (Congo) beliefs that human beings were superior to animals. See also Harms 1987.

21. Burnham 1996, 48–49; Anonymous 1890; Clozel 1895; Ponel 1896; Maunoir 1895; Wauters 1896; Fourneau 1932, 274–75, 279–80, 292–98.

22. Fourneau 1900; Muston 1933; Cottes 1909, 406–20. The Belgian journal *Le Mouvement Géographique* (Wauters, 18 Feb. 1900, 85–88, 4 Mar. 1900, 109–13, 11 Mar. 1900, 121–24) was particularly concerned with synthesizing the "discoveries" concerning the course of the Sangha and its tributaries.

23. Anonymous 1900, 306–8.

24. This discussion of Pouperon (1908, 4–7) draws from Giles-Vernick 1999, 181. Concessionary company representatives shared Pouperon's opinion ("Rapport de la Compagnie de la N'Goko-Sangha," 1911, CAOM, AEF 8Q20; "Rapport de la Compagnie Forestière de la Sangha-Oubangui," 1911, ibid., 8Q30).

25. Coquery-Vidrovitch 1972, 315–22.

26. "Rapport général sur la Société N'Goko-Sangha pour l'année 1909," 1910, CAOM, AEF 8Q20.

27. Coquery-Vidrovitch 1972, 315–22, 403–19; "Rapport général sur la Société N'Goko-Sangha pour l'année 1909," 1910, CAOM, AEF 8Q20.

28. "Rapport général sur la Société Forestière de la Sangha-Oubangui pour l'année 1912," 1913, "Rapport de la colonie du Nouveau Cameroun, territoires occupés de la circonscription de la Kadei-Sangha de l'année 1917," 1918, and "Rapport général sur la Société Forestière de la Sangha-Oubangui pour l'année 1920 (Secteur Nola)," 1921, CAOM, AEF 8Q31; Subdivision de Nola, "Rapport mensuel (Nola)," Dec. 1923, ibid., 4(2)D37; Coquery-Vidrovitch 1972, 112–15.

29. "Rapport général sur la Société Forestière de la Sangha-Oubangui pour l'année 1920 (Secteur Nola)," 1921, ibid., 8Q31.

30. "Rapport général sur la Société N'Goko-Sangha pour l'année 1909," 1910, ibid., 8Q20.

31. "Rapport général sur la Compagnie Forestière de la Sangha-Oubangui pour l'année 1912," 1913, ibid., 8Q31.

32. Ibid.; "Rapport général sur la Compagnie Forestière de la Sangha-Oubangui pour l'année 1911," 1912, and "Rapport de la colonie du Nouveau Cameroun, territoires occupés de la circonscription de la Kadei-Sangha de l'année 1917," 1918, ibid.

33. "Rapport sur la Société Forestière de la Sangha-Oubangui pour l'année 1920 (Nola)," 1921, ibid. See also Subdivision de Nola et Berbérati (ancienne Kadei-Sangha), "Rapport mensuel," 1923, ibid., AEF 4(2)D37. According to the CFSO report for 1920, the disappearance of rubber also accounted for the declining quality of rubber exports, because Africans frequently mixed high-value rubber with that of an inferior quality.

34. "Rapport général sur la Société N'Goko-Sangha," 1911, ibid., 8Q20; "Rapport général sur la Compagnie Forestière de la Sangha-Oubangui pour l'année

1912," 1913, ibid., 8Q31. Disputes erupted over the quality of the rubber that Africans supplied. Agents complained that rubber cakes frequently were contaminated with debris and could not bring high prices on the market.

35. "Rapport général sur la Société N'Goko-Sangha pour l'année 1909," 1910, ibid., 8Q20; "Rapport général sur la Compagnie Forestière de la Sangha-Oubangui pour l'année 1912," 1913, ibid., 8Q31.

36. "Rapport général sur la Compagnie Forestière de la Sangha-Oubangui pour l'année 1912," 1913, and "Rapport pour l'année 1917, Colonie du Nouveau Cameroun, territoires occupés de la circonscription de la Kadei-Sangha," 1918, ibid. The Compagnie des Produits de la Sangha, for instance, agreed to plant 150 new rubber trees for every ton of rubber produced by the concession ("Concessions du Congo, Cahiers des charges [Compagnie des Produits de la Sangha]," 31 Mar. 1899, ibid., Gabon-Congo III, 13).

37. Malaysian and other Asian rubber plantations flooded the world market with low-cost, high-quality rubber. Merlin (1913, 422, 428), the governor-general of AEF, contended that the crisis resulted not from actual overproduction but from a "feared and even anticipated crisis." He proposed resolving the crisis by improving the quality of wild rubber harvested in Congo and by diminishing tariffs on exported rubber. Cf. Austen and Headrick 1983, 47–53.

38. Coquery-Vidrovitch 1972, 368–69; Durieux (Directeur de la Cie des Produits de la Sangha) to Monsieur Chaffaud (Administrateur de la Basse-Sangha), 26 Oct. 1901, Sallmard to Compagnie des Produits de la Sangha, 10 Mar., 6 Apr. 1902, to Monsieur l'Administrateur-Délégué de la C.P.S., 2 May 1902, Pauwels to Monsieur l'Administrateur-Délégué, 14 Sept. 1901, CAOM, Gabon-Congo III, 13; Muston 1933, 17; "Rapport trimestriel," first trimester, 1908, CAOM, AEF 4(2)D2; "Rapport mensuel (Nola)," 1915, ibid., 4(2)D17. CFSO rubber harvests peaked in 1917 and 1925–26 but declined thereafter.

39. "Rapport général sur la Compagnie Forestière de la Sangha-Oubangui pour l'année 1912," 1913, CAOM, AEF 8Q31.

40. Satuba, dialogue, 9 May 1993 (OA.19); Mpeng, dialogue, 1 Aug. 1993 (OA.2).

41. "Rapport général sur la Société N'Goko-Sangha pour l'année 1909," 1910, CAOM, AEF 8Q20; "Rapport général sur la Compagnie Forestière de la Sangha-Oubangui pour l'année 1912," 1913, and "Rapport sur la Société de la Sangha-Oubangui pour l'année 1917," 1918, ibid., 8Q31; Yodjala Philippe, Lindjombo, 22 June 1993; Alouba Mathieu, Messadjiso, 9 Dec. 1993; Nkondja Faustin, Mekanda, 9 Dec. 1993; Yongo, dialogue, 8 Aug. 1993 (OA.11); Satuba, dialogue, 9 May 1993 (OA.19). Elisabeth Copet-Rougier (personal communication, 3 June 1996) suggested that the rapid disappearance of bark cloths, extensive tattooing, and other forms of bodily adornment after 1910 resulted from the relatively easy acquisition of imported goods. How people came to desire clothes and other goods is a crucial, and as yet unanswered, question, but see Burke 1996.

42. Satuba, dialogue, 9 May 1993 (OA.19); Modigi Casimir, dialogue, 5 Nov. 1993 (OA.9).

43. Mpendjo Edouard Matos, Lindjombo, 15 Nov. 1993.

44. Hendrickson (1996, 2–3) has argued that "bodies and dress help to express and shape ideas about the most potent kinds of political and spiritual power thought to be available to human beings."

45. Mpeng, dialogue, 1 Aug. 1993 (OA.2).

46. These activities, according to Herbert (1993, 132–34, 165, 222), are associated with men throughout Africa.

47. Satuba, dialogue, 9 May 1993 (OA.19); Mpeng, dialogue, 1 Aug. 1993 (OA.2); Yongo, dialogue, 8 Aug. 1993 (OA.11); Bessari Alphonsine, Lindjombo, 15 Dec. 1993; Kadele, dialogue, 5 Aug. 1993 (OA. 20).

48. Satuba, dialogue, 9 May 1993 (OA.19); Bessari Alphonsine, 15 Dec. 1993; Mpeng, dialogue, 1 Aug. 1993 (OA.2).

49. Amions Anaclet, forest south of Lindjombo, 23 Nov. 1993.

50. Coquery-Vidrovitch 1972, 370.

51. "Rapport général sur la Société N'Goko-Sangha pour l'année 1910," 1911, CAOM, AEF 8Q20.

52. "Rapport général sur la Compagnie Forestière de la Sangha-Oubangui pour l'année 1911," 1912, ibid., 8Q30.

53. "Rapport sur la Société Forestière de la Sangha-Oubangui pour l'année 1915" (Ikelemba), ibid., 8Q31; "Rapport général sur la Compagnie Forestière de la Sangha-Oubangui pour l'année 1911," 1912, and "Rapport général sur la Compagnie Forestière de la Sangha-Oubangui pour l'année 1910," 1911, ibid., 8Q30; "Rapport pour l'année 1917, colonie du Nouveau Cameroun, territoires occupés de la circonscription de la Kadei-Sangha," 1918, ibid., 8Q31.

54. "Rapport général sur la Compagnie Forestière de la Sangha-Oubangui pour l'année 1912," 1913, ibid., 8Q30; "Rapport général sur la Société N'Goko-Sangha pour l'année 1910," 1911, ibid., 8Q20. The Compagnie de la N'Goko-Sangha paid slightly lower prices for ivory, between two and ten francs per kilo.

55. Nieuwe Afrikaansche Handels-Venootschap to Monsieur le Lieutenant Gouverneur du Congo Français, 30 Aug. 1901, ibid., Affaires Politiques, AEF Concessions, carton 14; Durieux (Directeur de la Cie des Produits de la Sangha) to Monsieur Chaffaud, Administrateur de la Basse-Sangha, Ouesso, 26 Oct. 1901, ibid., Gabon-Congo III, 13.

56. "Rapport général sur la Société N'Goko-Sangha pour l'année 1909," 1910, and "Rapport général sur la Société N'Goko-Sangha pour l'année 1910," 1911, ibid., AEF 8Q20; "Rapport général sur la Compagnie Forestière de la Sangha-Oubangui pour l'année 1911," 1912, ibid., 8Q30; Coquery-Vidrovitch 1972, 370.

57. "Rapport général sur la Société N'Goko-Sangha pour l'année 1909," 1910, CAOM, AEF 8Q20; "Rapport général sur la Société N'Goko-Sangha pour l'année 1910," 1911, ibid.; "Rapport sur la Société Forestière de la Sangha-Oubangui pour l'année 1917, colonie du Nouveau Cameroun, territoires occupés de la Circonscription de la Kadei-Sangha," 1918, ibid., 8Q31; Circonscription de la Haute-Sangha, "Rapport économique," fourth trimester, 1927, ibid., 4(2)D43; Département de la

Sangha, "Rapport trimestriel," second trimester, 1935, ibid., 4(2)D66; "Production du département (Sangha) de janvier à mai 1936," ibid., 4(2)D69; District de Nola, "Rapport économique," 1950, ibid., 4(3)D61.

58. "Rapport général sur la Société N'Goko-Sangha pour l'année 1909," 1910, ibid., 8Q20; "Rapport général sur la Compagnie Forestière de la Sangha-Oubangui pour l'année 1911," 1912, ibid., 8Q30; "Rapport de la Compagnie Forestière de la Sangha-Oubangui (Secteur Nola)," 1921, ibid., 8Q31.

59. This point echoes that of contemporary conservationists, who according to Escobar (1996, 51) "have discovered the 'degrading' activities of the poor, but have seldom recognized that such problems were rooted in a development process that displaced indigenous communities, disrupted people's habitats and occupations, and forced many rural societies to increase their pressures on the environment. Now poor people are admonished not for their lack of industriousness but for their 'irrationality' and lack of environmental consciousness." In the Sangha the latter accusation has not displaced the former; at different historical moments, outsiders have leveled both.

60. Mpeng Patrice, Lindjombo, 23 Nov. 1993; Wan-Mbissa Samuel, Lindjombo, 17 Nov. 1993.

61. Alouba Matthieu, Messadjiso, 8 Dec. 1993; Lindjombo Etienne, Lindjombo, 8 Aug. 1993; Yongo Oromain, Lindjombo, 22 July 1993; Yodjala Philippe, Lindjombo, 22 June, 2 Nov. 1993; L'Administrateur L. Vingarassamy, Chef de la Circonscription de la Kadei-Sangha, to Monsieur le Lieutenant-Gouverneur du Moyen-Congo (Affaires Civiles), 7 June 1923, CAOM, AEF 4(2)D37; "Situation Politique," ibid., 4(2)D56 bis (Tournées); Le Chef de la Circ. de Yokadouma to M. le Chef du Département (Ouesso), 16 Mar. 1935, ibid., 4(2)D66; A. Canal (Région de la Haute-Sangha), "Rapport économique," 1950, ibid., 4(3)D61; Circonscription de la Likouala, "Rapport d'ensemble pour 1917," 1918, ibid., 4(2)D21.

62. Kadele, dialogue, 5 Aug. 1993 (OA.20); Satuba, dialogue, 9 May 1993 (OA.19); Yodjala Philippe, Lindjombo, 22 June, 20 July, 2 Nov. 1993.

63. Amions Anaclet and Satuba Igor, forest, 13 July 1993; Mpeng Patrice, forest, 25 June 1993.

64. Periquet 1916, 338.

65. Ibid., 344–45.

66. "Décret du 25 août 1929 réglementant la chasse en AEF," CAOM, AEF 5D82. Later laws amended the categories of hunters.

67. "Résumé des règlements actuellement en vigueur en AEF," ibid., Agence FOM, Agence des Colonies, carton 360, dossier 154 bis 1 (Tourisme AEF: Généralités Renseignement Divers avant 1950). In Ubangi-Shari, African and European hunters had to pay a 7.5 franc tax per kilo of ivory, in addition to a 10 percent export tax.

68. Ibid.; "Décret du 25 août 1929 réglementant la chasse en AEF," Le Gouverneur Général de l'Afrique Équatoriale Française, "Projet d'arrêté determinant les conditions de la chasse aux armes locales," 1930, and Le Lieutenant-Gouverneur

P.I. du Moyen-Congo, Chevalier de la Légion d'Honneur, to Monsieur le Gouverneur Général de l'Afrique Équatoriale Française, 13 Feb. 1930, no. 101, ibid., AEF 5D82; Direction des Affaires Économiques, "Projet de décret réglementant la chasse en Afrique Équatoriale Française," ibid., Agence FOM, carton 61, dossier 6 (Chasse, Élévage, Epizooties, 1921–46); Union Coloniale Française, "La protection de la faune coloniale," 24 Oct. 1934, ibid., Agence des Colonies, carton 360, dossier 155 bis / 1 (Chasse AEF, Généralités, Renseignements Divers avant 1950); Saint-Félix (Le Lieutenant Gouverneur du Moyen-Congo) to Monsieur le Gouverneur Général de l'Afrique Équatoriale Française, 5 Apr. 1932, no. 288, Le Gouverneur Général de l'Afrique Équatoriale Française, Commandeur de la Légion d'Honneur, to Monsieur le Lieutenant-Gouverneur du Moyen-Congo, 28 Jan. 1932, no. 164, ibid., AEF 5D82; Hardin 2000, 26–28. The protection of game and creation of parks in the AEF were motivated in large part out of intense competition with British efforts in East African colonies, although as Hardin has noted, French protection has always been more centralized than British. For southern and East Africa, see Beinart and Coates 1995, 27–31; Neumann 1995; 1998, 97–156; MacKenzie 1987.

69. Saint Floris, Inspecteur des Chasses en Afrique Équatoriale Française to Monsieur le Gouverneur Général de l'Afrique Équatoriale Française, 12 Feb. 1933, CAOM, AEF 5D82; Rogue et Blancou, "Tourisme et chasses en AEF," draft, n.d., ibid., Agence FOM, Agence des Colonies, carton 360, dossier 154 bis 1 (Tourisme AEF: Généralités Renseignement Divers avant 1950); Union Coloniale Française, "La protection de la faune coloniale," 24 Oct. 1934, and Agence France-Presse, "Dans la Presse Parisienne," no. 988, 30 Nov. 1949, ibid., dossier 155 bis / 1 (Chasse AEF, Généralités, Renseignements Divers avant 1950). See Hardin (2000, 28) on the 1938 Costermanville Conference on Colonial Tourism and the capitalist underpinnings of game protection.

70. Hardin 2000, 28; Saint Floris, Inspecteur des Chasses en Afrique Équatoriale Française, to Monsieur le Gouverneur Général de l'Afrique Équatoriale Française, 12 Feb. 1933, Saint-Félix (Le Lieutenant Gouverneur du Moyen-Congo) to Monsieur le Gouverneur Général de l'Afrique Équatoriale Française, 5 Apr. 1932, no. 288, CAOM, AEF 5D82. On France's priorities in AEF, see Coquery-Vidrovitch 1972, 25–26; Marseille 1984. Cooper (1996) proposes an alternative interpretation of French economic concerns in Africa, although he does not examine the AEF experience as distinct from that of French West Africa.

71. Affaires Politiques, Section Moyen-Congo, "Projet d'arrêté fixant le nombre des permis spéciaux de chasse & accorder aux indigènes pendant l'année 1930," draft, Le Chef de la Circonscription de la Likouala-Mossaka (Courtois) to Monsieur le Gouverneur de l'AEF, Chargé de l'Administration du Moyen-Congo, n.d. (1932 or 1933?), no. 499, and Le Chef du Bureau des Finances, Afrique Équatoriale Française, Colonie du Moyen-Congo, "Situation du rendement des permis de chasse," 1932, CAOM, AEF 5D82.

72. In 1932 only two African subjects purchased elephant-hunting permits in the Haute-Sangha and N'Goko-Sangha regions. A "native hunting permit" in

Middle Congo cost 200 francs and 1,000 francs in Ubangi-Shari in 1929 ("État et montant des permis de chasse délivrés pendant l'année 1932 dans la Colonie du Moyen-Congo" and "Listes des permis de chasse en vigueur dans les différentes colonies de l'A.E.F.," Aug. 1929, ibid.).

73. Le Chef de la Circonscription de la Likouala-Mossaka (Courtois) to Monsieur le Gouverneur de l'AEF, Chargé de l'Administration du Moyen-Congo, n.d. (1933?), no. 499, Buhot-Launay, pour le Gouverneur Général, Chargé de l'Administration du Moyen-Congo, l'Administrateur en Chef Délégué, to Chef de la Circonscription de la Likouala-Mossaka (Courtois), 23 Oct. 1933, ibid.

74. Kadele, dialogue, 5 Aug. 1993 (OA.20); Alouba Mathieu, Messadjiso, 9 Dec. 1993; Bessambongouri Jeannette, Lindjombo, 1 Nov. 1993; Lindjombo Etienne, Lindjombo, 8 Aug. 1993.

75. Nyambi, dialogue, 5 Aug. 1993 (OA.18); Alouba Clotere, Lindjombo, 20 July 1993; Alouba Clotere, Ndoagne Micheline, Satuba Rosalie, Bavio Lopes, Lindjombo, 24 July 1993.

76. Pombo Paul, Lindjombo 3 Nov. 1993; Yodjala Philippe, Lindjombo, 2 Nov. 1993; village meeting with Dzanga-Sangha project, Lindjombo, 18 May 1993; Mekite Sylvanus, Lindjombo 14 May 1993; Lindjombo Etienne, Lindjombo, 17 May 1993.

77. "Bilolo-Nola Dagbok, 1927–1960," FAIO/AO, Ar 1927–60, ser. F7:2, entries for 18 Feb. 1936, 9 Mar. 1939; John Ström to John Magnusson, 21 Oct. 1939, ibid., Ar 1930–41, ser. E1:2; "Journal de la Mission," 1 (1923–30), AGCS, entries for 1923, 13 Mar. 1928, 24 Apr. 1929; Umberto 1993, n.p. It is difficult to determine whether the Swedes themselves hunted, although they certainly possessed firearms, which the French administration confiscated during the Second World War.

78. John Hilberth to Bible School (8 Oct. 1936), FAIO/AO, Ar. 1930–41, ser. E1:2.

79. Ekroth 1932, 19.

80. "Bilolo-Nola Dagbok, 1927–1960," FAIO/AO, Ar 1927–60, ser. F7:2, entries for 14 Aug., 21 Dec. 1932, 1, 5, 25 Dec. 1939; Alouba Clotere, Lindjombo, 20 July 1993. In the Belgian Congo leopard attacks were understood as the work of Anioto, a secret society of men who donned leopard skins and iron blades to attack colonial officials, elites, chiefs, and other collaborators. I found no evidence of such a society in the Sangha basin, though leopards were frequently viewed as fearful beasts associated with powerful occult forces. On Anioto in Congo, see Likaka 1997, 130; Fabian 1996, 300–306. On animal transformations, see Hegba 1998, 275–95.

81. Whatmore and Thorne 1998, 435.

82. Anonymous 1927, 28–29.

83. "Henriette Odjèmo: Pauvre fille de la forêt," n.d., ACS 3R (P. Pierre d'Alcantara [Mgr Sintas], Correspondance, Lettres, et Conférences de Nos Pères). This tendency to perceive Mpiemu people's features as a result of the forest's influence persisted into the 1980s, although missionaries did so in less crude ways (Corbet 1981, 12).

84. Castaing 1954, n.p.

85. Umberto 1993b, n.p. I thank Elizabeth Meyer for her insights about Franciscanism.

86. Morel 1994b, 22.

87. Wanzi Lazare, Lindjombo, 26 June 1993; Yodjala Philippe, Lindjombo, 4 Nov. 1993; Mekite Sylvanus, Lindjombo, 10 July 1993. At one political meeting in Lindjombo (14 July 1993), there was an outpouring of such complaints.

88. Kalck 1974, 87; Département de la Haute-Sangha, "Rapport politique," first semester, 1942, CAOM, AEF 4(3)D53; A. Canal (Région de la Haute-Sangha), "Rapport économique," 1950, ibid., 4(3)D61. American companies made substantial loans to Ubangi-Shari mining companies, including the Compagnie Minière de l'Oubangui Oriental, in 1950.

89. Mogba and Freudenberger 1998, 111, but see also 106, 112–13.

90. Mabessimo Florent and other miners, Sokolingi diamond camp, 4 Dec. 1993; Amions Anaclet, Lindjombo, 11 Aug. 1993; Biloue Raymond, Lindjombo, 10 Aug. 1993; Andoungou, Salo, 4 Aug. 1993; Alouba Clotere, Salo, 3 Aug. 1993; Apoundjo Rene, Lindjombo, 15 Nov. 1993. Arrangements for sharing the proceeds of a diamond were complex even in theory and in practice generated considerable debates. In theory, the investor putting up the capital for the mining operation received a third of the sale value of each diamond found. The *chef de terrain* had mineral rights to the land on which the particular pit was located, and he shared his mineral rights with the one or two *chefs de trou* (the "owners" of the pit who were responsible for feeding workers). Another third of a diamond's value divided evenly between the *chefs de trou* and the *chef de terrain*. Workers (usually five to ten) dug the pit and sifted through the gravel layer containing diamond deposits but received no pay for their labor. A worker received the final third of the value of a diamond that he found.

91. Mempeli Didier, Borobang Georges, and Biodjena Zeffirin, Lindjombo, 12 July 1993; Andoungou, Salo, 4 Aug. 1993; Tontchoe Cecile, Salo, 3 Aug. 1993; Narabe Albert, Lindjombo, 13 Nov. 1993.

92. Mogba and Freudenberger 1998, 113.

93. Quoted in Faes 1994, 16.

94. Richards (1996, 138) has contended that violence has occurred in diamond villages in Sierra Leone because of the "remoteness of the state, the weakness of its infrastructure, and the lack of political imagination of its leaders that served to draw insurgency into this border region."

95. Apoundjo Rene, Lindjombo, 14, 15 Nov. 1993; Mabessimo Florent, Kodjim-pago, 6 Dec. 1993.

96. Mogba and Freudenberger 1998, 116.

97. Lanly 1966a and 1966b, 43–55. Sapele, sipo, ayous (obeche), and limba are the commercial names of these timber species (Gaston Guigonis and Jean Guillard, dialogue with author, tape recording, Paris, 18 Feb. 1993 [cassette no. OA.36]; Centre Technique Forestier Tropical 1989, 491; *Webster's Third New International Dictionary*).

98. U.S. Dept. of State 1989, 5. The structural adjustment program was designed to reverse the growth of government spending, liberalize prices, encourage a more open investment code, and provide incentives to agriculture and forestry.

99. Chris Lamora, U.S. Embassy, Bangui, 19 Dec. 1993; Faes 1994, 16.

100. Mpago 1997, 30; Hardin and Remis 1997, 79. The company assumed 75 percent of each worker's medical expenses.

101. Alphonse Gehrick (Director, SESAM), Salo, 10 Dec. 1993; M. Behra (Director, Slovenia Bois), Bayanga, 3 Apr. 1993; Mpago 1997, 30–31; Allard Blom, Yobe logging site, 23 May 1993; Carroll 1998, 202–3. See also McNeil 1999, 54–57; White 1992, 318–19.

102. Andoungou, Salo, 4 Aug. 1993; Blom 1998, 102. Employment numbers for diamond mining are difficult to establish. Men mined diamonds intermittently throughout the year but also earned income through hunting and trapping or farming. Salo and Kwapeli residents asserted that diamond mining was more lucrative than logging work.

103. Kadele Charles, Bandoka, 7 Dec. 1993.

104. Lengi Emilienne, Bandoka, 3 Dec. 1993.

105. Blom 1998, 212.

106. Mabogolo Germaine, Lindjombo, 27 June 1993; Bibelo Albert and Mamo Veronique, Lindjombo, 11 July 1993; Pombo Paul, Lindjombo, 27 June 1993; Yodjala Philippe, Lindjombo, 2 Nov. 1993; Amions Anaclet and Mpeng Patrice, forest near Likembe River, 23 Nov. 1993.

107. Yodjala Philippe, Lindjombo, 2 Nov. 1993. Later, when the German development consulting firm GTZ actively helped to set conservation priorities, policies, and activities, Hardin (2000, 285–86) found that Bayangans noted that tensions between French loggers and GTZ administrators had parallels with French-German rivalries in the early twentieth century.

108. Nyambi, dialogue, 5 Aug. 1993 (OA.18).

109. Village meeting with WWF project, Lindjombo, 18 May 1993; Fay 1993, n.p.; Richard Ruggiero, Bomassa, Apr. 1994.

110. Blom 1998, 208; Allard Blom, Bayanga, 21 May 1993; Fay 1993, n.p.

111. Giles-Vernick 1999, 187; Fay 1993; Allard Blom, Bangui, 18 May 1993; cf. Carroll 1993, 31–32.

112. Barnes, Blom, and Alers 1995, 130.

113. Noss 1995; Hardin 2000, 255.

114. Hardin 2000, 246; Noss 1997.

115. Village meeting, Lindjombo, 14 July 1993.

116. Village meeting with project, 18 May 1993; Mekite Sylvanus, Lindjombo, 14 May 1993; Wanzi Lazare, Lindjombo, 12 July 1993; Ntchambe Marc, dialogue, 2 Dec. 1993 (OA.16); Alouba Clotere, dialogue, 25 July 1993 (OA.24); Bandiko Albert, dialogue, 30 Nov. 1993 (OA.22); village meeting, tape recording, Lindjombo, 14 July 1993 (cassette no. OA.33); Amions Anaclet, forest near Lindjombo, 13 July 1993. See

also Noss, citing Kretsinger, 1997, 182. This "hunger" evokes a widespread language of political discourse that Bayart (1993) explores.

117. Village meeting, Lindjombo, 14 July 1993. Pampali responded that he and Kolingba did not sell the forest but that the United Nations decided that the encroaching desert necessitated that everyone do something to protect their forests. Projects all over the world had been developed to conserve the forest. Despite Pampali's explanation, the claims persisted.

118. Yodjala Philippe, Lindjombo, 4 Nov. 1993. Ivory trafficking was widespread in the CAR, Cameroon, and the northern Congo. See Ricciuti 1993 for an overview of elephant conservation debates.

119. Amions Anaclet, Lindjombo, 4 Nov. 1993; Biloue Brigitte, Lindjombo, 3 Nov. 1993.

120. Stromme and Hunsicker n.d.

Conclusion

1. My thanks to Justin Mongosso for confirming this translation and its alternative reading.

2. An active *alembo* could also serve as a site of recollection, a marker that demarcated members of a lineage who were "different" because they possessed an active *alembo* and thus had occult powers. Patrice's father was named Menkiya, an abbreviation of *Menki ya ya ri sangi,* which translates from Mpiemu as "My blood is different from yours."

3. Ngatoua Urbain, Lindjombo, 22 May 1993.

4. Wanzi Lazare and Souki Jacques, Lindjombo, 22 May 1993.

5. Allard Blom, Bayanga, 19 May 1993.

6. Hardin 2000, 255.

7. Oates 1999, xvi.

8. Bonner 1993, 107–8; Showers 1994, 41–46; Adams and McShane 1992, 59–84; Ricciuti 1993.

BIBLIOGRAPHY

Archival Sources

Archives des Capucins de Savoie, Annecy, France
   République Centrafricaine (reports)
   L'Église Centrafricaine (reports, correspondence)
   L'Église de Berbérati (reports, correspondence)
   Sainte Anne de Berbérati (reports, photographs)
   Correspondance, 1946–97

Archives des Capucins de Toulouse, Toulouse, France
   Mission d'Afrique: Généralités (reports)
   Mission d'Afrique: Varia: Berbérati (correspondence and reports)
   P. Pierre d'Alcantara (Mgr Sintas) (reports and correspondence)
   Mission de Berbérati (reports)

Archives Générales de la Congrégation du Saint-Esprit, Chevilly-la-Rue, France
   Journal de la Mission, Ste. Anne de Berbérati
   Berbérati–Haute-Sangha, 1920–29 (Correspondance) Bangui-Berbérati, Mgr
      Guichard (Correspondence)
   Vicariat Apostolique du Haut-Congo (summaries of letters)
   Vicariat Apostolique du Haut-Congo Français (correspondence and reports
      after 1909)
   Vicariat Apostolique de Brazzaville, Mgr Guichard, 1922–36 (correspondence
      and reports)
   Mgr Augouard, Relations avec l'Administration (correspondence)
   Haut-Congo Français, 1900–1920 (correspondence and reports)
   Vicariat Apostolique de Brazzaville, Mgr Augouard (correspondence)
   Personal archives of Père Ghislain de Banville

Bibliothèque de l'École Nationale d'Administration et de la Magistrature, Bangui,
   Central African Republic
   Délimitation Franco-Allemand

Centre des Archives d'Outre-mer, Aix-en-Provence, France
   Pénétration d'Afrique Équatoriale
   Missions d'Exploration, 1895–1912
   Missions d'Inspection
   Politiques et Administration Générale, 1889–1954 (Rapports Politiques,
      1889–1954; Dossiers Divers des Affaires Politiques)

Compagnies et Sociétés Concessionnaires
Archives Privées des Compagnies Concessionnaires
Affaires Politiques, Concessions

Centre des Hautes Études Administratives sur l'Afrique et l'Asie Modernes
(CHEAM), Paris
Reports of P. Mialhe and M. Rolland

Folksrorelsernas Arkiv I Örebro, Arkivbildaire Örebromissionen, Örebro, Sweden
Bilolo-Nola Dagbook
Bilolo-Nola Protocol
Correspondence and Reports, 1917–60

Dialogues with Informants

Some dialogues with informants were recorded on cassette; these recordings are currently in my possession. Other dialogues took place in more sensitive contexts, and thus informants indicated that they preferred not to be recorded, or I chose not to record our interactions. Notes from these dialogues are also in my possession.

Secondary Sources

Adams, Jonathan S., and Thomas O. McShane. 1992. *The Myth of Wild Africa: Conservation without Illusion.* New York: W. W. Norton.

Agrawal, Arun. 1995. "Dismantling the Divide between Indigenous and Scientific Knowledge." *Development and Change* 26:413–39.

Akyeampong, Emmanuel. 1997. *Drink, Power, and Cultural Change: A Social History of Alcohol in Ghana, c. 1800 to Recent Times.* Portsmouth, N.H.: Heinemann.

Allys, M. 1930. "Monographie de la tribu Dzem." *Bulletin de la Société des Recherches Congolaises,* no. 11:3–21.

Amanor, Kojo Sebastian. 1994. *The New Frontier: Farmer Responses to Land Degradation: A West African Study.* London: Zed Books.

Amaye, M., and P. Soumille. 1984. "De l'intérêt des sources missionaires pour l'histoire générale." In *Recherches centrafricaines: Problèmes et perspectives de la recherche historique.* Table Ronde, ASOM, CHEAM, IHPOM. No. 18:104–36. Aix-en-Provence: Institut d'Histoire des Pays d'Outre-mer, Université de Provence.

Amions, Anaclet. N.d. "L'impôt à l'époque coloniale." In author's possession.

———. N.d. "L'influence de la colonisation et de la civilisation." In author's possession.

———. N.d. "Rappel sur le premier contact Bantou et Pygmée." In author's possession.

Amselle, Jean-Loup. 1998. *Mestizo Logics.* Trans. Claudia Royal. Stanford, Calif.: Stanford Univ. Press.

Anderson, Benedict. 1991. *Imagined Communities: Reflections on the Origin and Spread of Nationalism*. Rev. ed. London: Verso.

Anderson, David M. 1984. "Depression, Dust Bowl, Demography, and Drought: The Colonial State and Soil Conservation in East Africa during the 1930s." *African Affairs* 83:321–43.

Anderson, David, and Richard Grove, eds. 1987. *Conservation in Africa: People, Policies, and Practice*. Cambridge: Cambridge Univ. Press.

Anonymous. N.d. *Bia ti OTN*. Bangui: Foyer de la Littérature, Biblique des Frères.

———. N.d. *Bia ti Sepala Nzapa*. Rev. Martin Garber. Bangui: Foyer de la Literature, Biblique des Frères.

———. 1890. "Mission Cholet-Sangha." *Compte Rendu des Séances de la Société de Géographie de Paris* 9:459–63.

———. 1896. "L'agriculture au Congo français." *Bulletin du Comité de l'Afrique Française* 6 (11 Nov.): 353–54.

———. 1900a. "L'expédition du Dr Plehn au Sud-Kamerun." *Le Mouvement Géographique*, no. 25 (24 June): 306–8.

———. 1900b. "La région des concessions dans le bassin de la Sanga." *Le Mouvement Géographique*, no. 7 (18 Feb.): 85–88.

———. 1906a. "Congo français: Les instructions de M. Gentil pour la politique générale." *Bulletin du Comité de l'Afrique Française* 16 (8 Aug.): 229–32.

———. 1906b. "La Mission Moll." *Bulletin du Comité de l'Afrique Française* 16 (6 June): 163–64.

———. 1914. "Le Moyen Congo en 1913." *Renseignements Coloniaux et Documents Publiés par le Comité de l'Afrique Française et le Comité du Maroc. Supplément à l'Afrique Française de Juin 1914* 24 (6): 243–44.

———. 1927. *Un jeune apôtre: Le Père Marion de la Congrégation du Saint-Esprit, missionaire au Congo, 1900–1926*. Moselle: Imprimerie des Missions Neufgrange par Hambach.

———. 1932. "Då stationerna anlades." In *Kongoboken: Något I ord och bild från Örebro Missionsförenings fält I Franska Kongo*, 25–47. Örebro: Örebro Missionsförening Förlag.

———. 1966. *Mbeti ti Nzapa*. Bangui: Les Sociétés Bibliques.

———. 1978. *Gnoa Toma: Matthieu, Marc, Luc, ne Jean Kueli Go*. Trans. Gilbert Ankouma, Joseph Apang, Lydia Lundström. Örebro, Sweden: Welins Tryckeri.

———. 1994. "Accord de coopération entre le Comité de Développement de Bayanga représenté par son secrétaire général, d'une part, et le Projet Dzanga-Sangha représenté par sa direction, d'autre part." Bayanga, CAR. In author's possession.

Arnold, David, and Ramachandra Guha, eds. 1995. *Nature, Culture, Imperialism: Essays on the Environmental History of South Asia*. Delhi: Oxford Univ. Press.

Appadurai, Arjun. 1986. "Introduction: Commodities and the Politics of Value." In *The Social Life of Things: Commodities in Cultural Perspective*, ed. Arjun Appadurai, 3–63. New York: Cambridge Univ. Press.

Aubreville, A. 1947. "Les brousses secondaires en Afrique équatoriale: Côte d'Ivoire–Cameroun–A.E.F." *Bois et Forêts des Tropiques* 9 (2): 24–49.

———. 1949. "Ancienneté de la destruction de la couverture forestière primitive de l'Afrique tropicale." *Bulletin Agricole de Congo Belge* 40 (2): 1347–52.

Austen, Ralph A., and Rita Headrick. 1983. "Equatorial Africa under Colonial Rule." In *History of Central Africa*, ed. David Birmingham and Phyllis M. Martin, 2:27–94. London: Longman.

Babon, Victor, Anna Kretsinger, and Jean-Marc Garreau. 1994. "Evaluation de la cellule santé." Report to the Ministère des Eaux et Forêts, Chasse, Pêche, Tourisme, et de l'Environnement and Projet WWF-US/R.C.A., Parc National Dzanga-Ndoki, Reserve Spéciale Dzanga-Sangha. In author's possession.

Bachelard, Gaston. 1994. *The Poetics of Space: The Classic Look at How We Experience Intimate Places*. Trans. Maria Jolas. Boston: Beacon Press.

Baillif, Noël. 1992. *Les Pygmées de la grande forêt*. Paris: L'Harmattan.

Bahuchet, Serge. 1978. "Les contraintes écologiques en forêt tropicale humide: L'exemple des Pygmées Aka de la Lobaye (Centrafrique)." *Journal d'Agriculture Traditionelle et de Botanie Appliquée* 25 (4): 1–29.

———. 1979. "Notes pour l'histoire de la région de Bagandou." In *Pygmées de Centrafrique: Ethnologie histoire et linguistique*, ed. Serge Bahuchet, 51–76. Paris: SELAF.

———. 1985. *Les Pygmées Aka et la forêt centrafricaine*. Paris: SELAF.

———. 1993. "L'invention des Pygmeés." *Cahiers d'Études Africaines* 129 (33): 153–81.

Bahuchet, S., and I. de Garine. 1990. "The Art of Trapping in the Rainforest." In *Food and Nutrition in the African Rainforest*, ed. C. M. Hladik, S. Bahuchet, and I. de Garine, 24–25. Paris: UNESCO.

Bailey, Robert C., et al., 1989. "Hunting and Gathering in Tropical Rain Forest: Is It Possible?" *American Anthropologist* 91:59–82.

Bakhtin, M. M. 1981. *The Dialogic Imagination*, ed. Michael Holquist. Austin: Univ. of Texas Press.

Barber, Karin. 1991. *I Could Speak until Tomorrow: Oriki, Women, and the Past in a Yoruba Town*. Washington, D.C.: Smithsonian.

Barnes, R. F. W. 1983. "Effects of Elephant Browsing on Woodlands in a Tanzanian National Park: Measurements, Models, and Management." *Journal of Applied Ecology* 20:521–39.

Barnes, R. F. W., A. Blom, and M. P. T. Alers. 1995. "A Review of the Status of Forest Elephants in Central Africa." *Biological Conservation* 71:125–32.

Bassett, Thomas J., and Donald E. Crummey, eds. 1993. *Land in African Agrarian Systems*. Madison: Univ. of Wisconsin Press.

Bassett, Thomas J., and Philip W. Porter. 1991. "'From the Best Authorities': The Mountains of Kong in the Cartography of West Africa." *Journal of African History* 32:367–413.

Bayart, Jean-François. [1989] 1993. *The State in Africa: The Politics of the Belly.* Trans. Mary Harper and Christopher and Elizabeth Harrison. London: Longman.

Beavon, Keith and Mary, eds. 1995. *Lexique konzimé-français.* Yaounde: Société Internationale de Linguistique.

Beidelman, T. O. 1986. *Moral Imagination in Kaguru Modes of Thought.* Bloomington: Indiana Univ. Press.

Beinart, William. 1984. "Soil Erosion, Conservationism, and Ideas about Development: A Southern African Exploration, 1900–1960." *Journal of Southern African Studies* 11 (1): 52–83.

Beinart, William, and Peter Coates. 1995. *Environment and History: The Taming of Nature in the USA and Africa.* London: Routledge.

Bernault, Florence. 1996. *Démocraties ambiguës en Afrique centrale: Congo-Brazzaville, Gabon, 1940–1965.* Paris: Karthala.

———. 1999. "De l'Afrique ouverte à l'Afrique fermée: Comprendre l'histoire des réclusions continentales." In *Enfermement, prison, et châtiments en Afrique, du XIXe siècle à nos jours,* ed. Florence Bernault, 15–66. Paris: Karthala.

Berny, Dr. 1933. "La lèpre en Haute Sangha." *Bulletin de la Société des Recherches Congolaises,* no. 18:13–44.

Berry, Sara. 1985. *Fathers Work for Their Sons: Accumulation, Mobility, and Class Formation in an Extended Yorùbá Community.* Berkeley: Univ. of California Press.

———. 1988. "Concentration without Privatization? Some Consequences of Changing Patterns of Rural Land Control in Africa." In *Land and Contemporary Society in Africa,* ed. R. E. Downs and S. P. Reyna, 53–75. Hanover, N.H.: Univ. Press of New England.

———. 1993. *No Condition Is Permanent: The Social Dynamics of Agrarian Change in Sub-Saharan Africa.* Madison: Univ. of Wisconsin Press.

———. 2001. *Chiefs Know Their Boundaries: Essays on Property, Power, and the Past in Asante, 1896–1996.* Portsmouth, N.H.: Heinemann.

Bhabha, Homi K. 1994. *The Location of Culture.* London: Routledge.

Bigo, Didier. 1988. *Pouvoir et obéissance en Centrafrique.* 2 vols. Paris: Karthala.

Birmingham, David. 1983. "Society and Economy before A.D. 1400." In *History of Central Africa,* ed. David Birmingham and Phyllis M. Martin, 1:1–29. London: Longman.

Blom, Allard. 1998. "A Critical Analysis of Three Approaches to Tropical Forest Conservation Based on Experiences in the Sangha Region." In *Resource Use in the Trinational Sangha River Region of Equatorial Africa: Histories, Knowledge Forms, and Institutions,* ed. Heather E. Eves, Rebecca Hardin, and Stephanie Rupp. Bulletin Series, Yale School of Forestry and Environmental Studies, no. 102:208–15.

Bois, Fr. Bernard. 1977. "Joseph Abhô, premier chrétien de Berbérati." *Alpes-Afrique* 304:20–22.

Bongmba, Elias. 1998. "Toward a Hermeneutic of Wimbum Tfu." *African Studies Review* 41 (3): 165–91.

Bonnafé, Pierre. 1978. *Nzo Lipfu, le lignage de la mort: La sorcellerie, idéologie de la lutte sociale sur le plateau Kukuya*. Nanterre: Labethno.

Bonner, Raymond. 1993. *At the Hand of Man: Peril and Hope for Africa's Wildlife*. New York: Knopf.

Bourdieu, Pierre. 1977. *Outline of a Theory of Practice*. Trans. Richard Nice. Cambridge: Cambridge Univ. Press.

Bozzoli, Belinda, with the assistance of Mmantho Nkotsoe. 1991. *Women of Phokeng: Consciousness, Life Strategy, and Migrancy in South Africa, 1900–1983*. Portsmouth, N.H.: Heinemann.

Bravman, Bill. 1998. *Making Ethnic Ways: Communities and Their Transformations in Taita, Kenya, 1800–1950*. Portsmouth, N.H.: Heinemann.

Brégeon, Jean-Joël. 1998. *Un rêve d'Afrique: Administrateurs en Oubangui-Chari, la Cendrillon de l'empire*. Paris: Denoël.

Brubaker, Rogers, and Frederick Cooper. 2000. "Beyond 'Identity.'" *Theory and Society* 29 (1): 1–49.

Bruel, Georges. 1909. "Les basses vallées de l'Oubangui et de la Sanga." *La Géographie: Bulletin de la Société de Géographie*. 19:353–66.

———. 1910. "Les populations de la Moyenne Sanga: Les Pomo et Les Boumali." *Revue d'Ethnographie et Sociologie* 1:3–16.

———. 1923. *Tableau sommaire de l'exploration et de la reconnaissance de l'Afrique Équatoriale Française*. Extrait du *Bulletin de la Société de Géographie d'Études Coloniales* 43 (1920–21). Marseille: Secrétariat de la Société de Géographie.

Brunschwig, Henri. 1966. *French Colonialism, 1871–1914: Myths and Realities*. New York: Frederick A. Praeger.

Burke, Timothy. 1996. *Lifebuoy Men, Lux Women: Commodification, Consumption, and Cleanliness in Modern Zimbabwe*. Durham, N.C.: Duke Univ. Press.

Burnham, Philip. 1975. "*Regroupement* and Mobile Societies: Two Cameroon Cases." *Journal of African History* 16 (4): 577–94.

———. 1980. *Opportunity and Constraint in a Savanna Society: The Gbaya of Meiganga, Cameroon*. London: Academic Press.

———. 1981. "Notes on Gbaya History." In *Contribution de la recherche ethnologique à l'histoire des civilisations de Cameroun*, ed. Claude Tardits, 1:121–30. Paris: CNRS.

———. 1996. *The Politics of Cultural Difference in Northern Cameroon*. Edinburgh: Edinburgh Univ. Press for the International African Institute.

———. 1997. "Political Relations on the Eastern Marches of Adamawa in the Late 19th Century: A Problem of Interpretation." In *African Crossroads: Intersections between History and Anthropology in Cameroon*, ed. Ian Fowler and David Zeitlyn, 45–62. Oxford: Berghahn Books.

Burnham, Philip, and Thomas Christenson. 1983. "Karnu's Message and the 'War of the Hoe Handle': Interpreting a Central African Resistance Movement." *Africa* 53 (4): 3–22.

Burnham, Philip, Elisabeth Copet-Rougier, and Philip Noss. 1986. "Gbaya et Mkako:

Contribution ethno-linguistique à l'histoire de l'est Cameroun." *Paideuma* 32:87–128.

Carney, Judith A. 1988. "Struggles over Crop Rights and Labour within Contract Farming Households in a Gambian Irrigated Rice Project." *Journal of Peasant Studies* 15 (3): 334–49.

———. 1996. "Converting the Wetlands, Engendering the Environment: The Intersection of Gender with Agrarian Change in Gambia." In *Liberation Ecologies,* ed. Richard Peet and Michael Watts, 165–87. London: Routledge.

Carney, Judith A., and Michael Watts. 1990. "Manufacturing Dissent: Work, Gender, and the Politics of Meaning in a Peasant Society." *Africa* 60 (2): 207–41.

Carroll, Richard W. 1986. "Status of the Lowland Gorilla and Other Wildlife in the Dzanga-Sangha Region of Southwestern Central African Republic." *Primate Conservation* 7:38–44.

———. 1988. "Relative Density, Range Extension, and Conservation Potential of the Lowland Gorilla (*Gorilla gorilla gorilla*) in the Dzanga-Sangha Region of Southwestern Central African Republic." *Mammalia* 52 (3): 309–23.

———. 1998. "World Wide Fund for Nature (WWF-US) Organizational Overview: Dzanga-Sangha, Central African Republic." In *Resource Use in the Trinational Sangha River Region of Equatorial Africa: Histories, Knowledge Forms, and Institutions,* ed. Heather E. Eves, Rebecca Hardin, and Stephanie Rupp. Bulletin Series, Yale School of Forestry and Environmental Studies, no. 102:198–207.

Carroll, Richard, and World Wildlife Fund. 1993. "The Development, Protection, and Management of the Dzanga-Sangha Dense Forest Special Reserve and the Dzanga-Ndoki National Park in Southwestern Central African Republic."

Carruthers, Mary. 1991. *The Book of Memory: A Study of Memory in Medieval Culture.* Cambridge: Cambridge Univ. Press.

Casey, Edward. 1987. *Remembering: A Phenomenological Study.* Bloomington: Indiana Univ. Press.

Castaing, Edouard. 1954. *Sur les pistes d'Oubangui: La mission de Berbérati en Oubangui-Chari.* Berbérati: n.p.

Centre Technique Forestier Tropical. 1967. *Inventaire forestier dans le secteur de Nola.* Nogent-sur-Marne: Centre Technique Forestier Tropical.

———. [1976] 1989. *Memento du forestier: Techniques rurales en Afrique.* 3d ed. Paris: Ministère de la Coopération et du Développement.

Certeau, Michel de. 1984. *The Practice of Everyday Life.* Trans. S. Rendall. Berkeley: Univ. of California Press.

Chadwick, Douglas. 1995. "Ndoki: Last Place on Earth." *National Geographic* 188 (1): 2–45.

Chakrabarty, Dipesh. 1992. "Postcoloniality and the Artifice of History: Who Speaks for 'Indian' Pasts?" *Representations* 37:1–26.

Chambers, Robert. 1983. *Rural Development: Putting the Last First.* London: Longman.

Chatterjee, Partha. 1995. *The Nation and Its Fragments: Colonial and Post-Colonial Histories.* Delhi: Oxford Univ. Press.

Cleaver, Kevin, et al., eds. 1992. *Conservation of West and Central African Rainforests.* World Bank Environment Paper no. 1. Washington, D.C.: World Bank and IUCN.

Cline-Cole, Reginald. 2000. "Knowledge Claims, Landscape, and the Fuelwood-Degradation Nexus in Dryland Nigeria." In *Producing Nature and Poverty in Africa,* ed. Vigdis Broch-Due and Richard A. Schroeder, 109–47. Uppsala: Nordiska Afrikainstitutet, 2000.

Clozel, M. F.-J. 1895. "De la Sanga à la Ouom." *Bulletin de la Société de Géographie de Paris* 17:917–31.

Cohen, David William. 1989a. "Doing History from *Pim's* Doorway." In *Reliving the Past: The Worlds of Social History,* ed. Olivier Zunz, 191–235. Chapel Hill: Univ. of North Carolina Press.

———. 1989b. "The Undefining of Oral Tradition." *Ethnohistory* 36 (1): 9–18.

———. 1994. *The Combing of History.* Chicago: Univ. of Chicago Press.

Cohen, David William, and E. S. Atieno Odhiambo. 1989. *Siaya: The Historical Anthropology of an African Landscape.* Athens: Ohio Univ. Press.

Cohen, William B. 1980. *The French Encounter with Africans: White Response to Blacks, 1530–1880.* Bloomington: Indiana Univ. Press.

Comaroff, John, and Jean Comaroff. 1991. *Of Revelation and Revolution,* vol. 1, *Christianity, Colonialism, and Consciousness in South Africa.* Chicago: Univ. of Chicago Press.

———. 1997. *Of Revelation and Revolution,* vol. 2, *The Dialectics of Modernity on a South African Frontier.* Chicago: Univ. of Chicago Press.

Conklin, Alice L. 1997. *A Mission to Civilize: The Republican Idea of Empire in France and West Africa, 1895–1930.* Stanford, Calif.: Stanford Univ. Press.

Connerton, Paul. 1989. *How Societies Remember.* Cambridge: Cambridge Univ. Press.

Cooper, Frederick. 1994. "Conflict and Connection: Rethinking Colonial African History." *American Historical Review* 99:1516–45.

———. 1996. *Decolonization and African Society: The Labor Question in French and British Africa.* Cambridge: Cambridge Univ. Press.

Copet-Rougier, Elisabeth. 1981a. "Les Kakas." *Contribution de la recherche ethnologique à l'histoire des civilisations de Cameroun,* ed. Claude Tardits, 1:511–16. Paris: CNRS.

———. 1981b. "Le petit poisson cherche l'eau froide." In *Espace et pouvoir dans les sociétés multicentrées,* ed. Jean-Claude Barbier, Jean-Pierre Doumenge, and Jacques Galinier, 29–38. Bordeaux, France: Maison des Sciences de l'Homme Aquitaine.

———. 1983. "Chasseurs, pasteurs, agriculteurs: Rencontre dans un milieu contact forêt-savane." In *Milieu naturel, techniques, rapports sociaux,* ed. Claude Raynaut, 1–20. Paris: Éditions du Centre National de la Recherche Scientifique.

———. 1985. "Contrôle masculin, exclusivité féminine." In *Femmes du Cameroun: Mères pacifiques, femmes rebelles,* ed. J. C. Barbier, 153–80. Paris: ORSTOM.

———. 1986. *"Le mal court*: Visible and Invisible Violence in an Acephalous Society —Mkako of Cameroon." In *The Anthropology of Violence,* ed. D. Riche, 50–69. London: Blackwell.

———. 1987. "Du clan à la chefferie dans l'est du Cameroun." *Africa* 57 (3): 345–63.

———. 1998. "Political-Economic History of the Upper Sangha." In *Resource Use in the Trinational Sangha River Region of Equatorial Africa: Histories, Knowledge Forms, and Institutions,* ed. Heather E. Eves, Rebecca Hardin, Stephanie Rupp. Bulletin Series, Yale School of Forestry and Environmental Studies, no. 102:41–84.

Coquelin, Charles. 1909. "Dans la Sangha." *Bulletin de la Société de Géographie Commerciale du Havre,* 72–89.

Coquery-Vidrovitch, Catherine. 1965. "Les idées économiques de Brazza et les premières tentatives de compagnies de colonisation au Congo français, 1885–1898." *Cahiers d'Études Africaines* 5 (17): 57–82.

———. 1972. *Le Congo au temps des grands compagnies concessionnaires, 1898–1930.* Paris: Mouton.

———. 1998. "The Upper-Sangha in the Time of the Concession Companies." In *Resource Use in the Trinational Sangha River Region of Equatorial Africa: Histories, Knowledge Forms, and Institutions,* ed. Heather E. Eves, Rebecca Hardin, Stephanie Rupp. Bulletin Series, Yale School of Forestry and Environmental Studies, no. 102:72–84.

Corbet, Jean-Baptiste. 1981. "20 ans de Mission: Au pays des Mbimous." *Alpes-Afrique* 321:12–15.

Cordell, Dennis. 1983. "The Savanna Belt of North-Central Africa." In *History of Central Africa,* ed. David Birmingham and Phyllis M. Martin, 1:30–74. London: Longman.

———. 1987. "Extracting People from Precapitalist Production: French Equatorial Africa from the 1890s to 1930s." In *African Population and Capitalism: Historical Perspectives,* ed. Dennis D. Cordell and Joel W. Gregory, 137–52. Boulder, Colo.: Westview.

———. 1994. "The Local Contexts of Low Fertility in the Central African Republic, 1890–1960." Paper presented at the African Studies Association meeting, Toronto, 3–6 Nov.

———. 1995. "Economic Crises and Demographic Dynamics in African History: Central and Eastern Central African Republic in the Precolonial, Colonial and Contemporary Eras." Paper presented at the Seminar "Crise économique africaine et dynamique démographique," Centre Française sur la Population et le Développement, L'Abbaye de Royaumont, 22–24 May.

Cordell, Dennis, Joel Gregory, and Victor Piché. 1994. "African Historical Demography: The Search for a Theoretical Framework." In *African Population and Capitalism: Historical Perspectives,* 2d ed., ed. Dennis Cordell and Joel Gregory, 14–32. Madison: Univ. of Wisconsin Press.

Cosgrove, Denis E. 1984. *Social Formation and Symbolic Landscape.* London: Croom Helm.

Cottes, Capitaine A. 1911. *La Mission Cottes au Sud-Cameroun (1905–1908). Exposé des résultats scientifiques d'après des travaux de divers membres de la Section française de la commission de délimitation entre le Congo français et le Cameroun (frontière méridionale) et les documents étudiés au Museum d'Histoire Naturelle.* Paris: Ernest Leroux.

Cronon, William, ed. 1995. *Uncommon Ground: Toward Reinventing Nature.* New York: W. W. Norton.

Cumming, D. H. M. 1993. "Conservation Issues and Problems in Africa." In *Voices from Africa: Local Perspectives on Conservation,* ed. Dale Lewis and Nick Carter, 23–47. Washington, D.C.: World Wildlife Fund.

Curtin, Philip D. 1964. *The Image of Africa: British Ideas and Action, 1780–1850.* Madison: Univ. of Wisconsin Press.

D'Almeida-Topor, Hélène. 1988. "La question du travail forcé." In *Brazzaville, janvier– février 1944: Aux sources de la décolonisation,* 115–20. Paris: Plon.

Davies, A. Glyn, and Paul Richards. 1991. "Rain Forest in Mende Life: Resources and Subsistence Strategies in Rural Communities around the Gola North Forest Reserve (Sierra Leone)." A report to the Economic and Social Committee on Overseas Research (ESCOR), UK Overseas Development Administration.

Demeritt, David. 1994. "The Nature of Metaphors in Cultural Geography and Environmental History." *Progress in Human Geography* 18 (2): 163–85.

Devisch, Rene. 1993. *Weaving the Threads of Life: The Khita Gyn-Eco-Logical Healing Cult among the Yaka.* Chicago: Univ. of Chicago Press.

De Waal, Alexander. 1989. *Famine That Kills: Darfur, Sudan, 1984–1985.* New York: Oxford Univ. Press.

Douglas, Mary. 1954. "The Lele of Kasai." In *African Worlds: Studies in the Cosmological Ideas and Social Values of African Peoples,* ed. Daryll Forde, 1–26. London: Oxford Univ. Press.

Douglas, Mary, and Aaron Wildavsky. 1982. *Risk and Culture: An Essay on the Selection of Technical and Environmental Danger.* Berkeley: Univ. of California Press.

Dounias, Edmond. 1998. "Discussion and Comments." In *Resource Use in the Trinational Sangha River Region of Equatorial Africa: Histories, Knowledge Forms, and Institutions,* ed. Heather E. Eves, Rebecca Hardin, and Stephanie Rupp. Bulletin Series, Yale School of Forestry and Environmental Studies, no. 102:143–44.

Dove, Michael. 1993. "Uncertainty, Humility, and Adaptation in the Tropical Forest: The Agricultural Augury of the Kantu'." *Ethnology* 32 (2): 145–67.

Dove, Michael, and Daniel M. Kammen. 1997. "The Epistemology of Sustainable Resource Use: Managing Forest Products, Swiddens, and High-Yielding Variety Crops." *Human Organization* 56 (1): 91–101.

Downs, Joan. 2001. "Untamed Africa." *Wildlife Conservation* 104 (2): 50–53.

Dublin, Holly T., A. R. E. Sinclaire, and J. McGlade. 1990. "Elephants and Fire as Causes of Multiple Stable States in the Serengeti-Mara Woodlands." *Journal of Animal Ecology* 59:1147–64.

DuChaillu, Paul. [1868] 1969. *Explorations and Adventures in Equatorial Africa.* New York: Negro Univ. Press (Greenwood Corp.).

Dupré, Georges. 1982. *Un ordre et sa destruction.* Paris: ORSTOM.

————. 1985. *Les naissances d'un société: Espace et historicité chez les Beembé du Congo.* Paris: ORSTOM.

————, ed. 1991. *Savoirs paysans et développement.* Paris: Karthala and ORSTOM.

————. 1995. "The History and Adventures of a Monetary Object of the Kwélé of the Congo: Mezong, Mondjos, and Mandjong." In *Money Matters: Instability, Values, and Social Payments in the Modern History of West African Communities,* ed. Jane I. Guyer, 77–96. Portsmouth, N.H.: Heinemann.

Dupré, Marie-Claude. 1993. "La guerre de l'impôt dans les monts du Chaillu, 1913–1920, Gabon, Moyen-Congo." *Revue Française d'Histoire d'Outre-mer* 80:409–23.

————. 1995. "Raphia Monies among the Teke: Their Origin and Control." In *Money Matters: Instability, Values, and Social Payments in the Modern History of West African Communities,* ed. Jane I. Guyer, 39–52. Portsmouth, N.H.: Heinemann.

Echenberg, Myron. 1991. *Colonial Conscripts: The Tirailleurs Sénégalais in French West Africa, 1875–1960.* Portsmouth, N.H.: Heinemann.

Eggert, Manfred K. H. 1992. "The Central African Rain Forest: Historical Speculation and Archaeological Facts." *World Archaeology* 24 (1): 1–22.

Ekroth, Helma. 1932. "Kongokvinnan och möjligheterna att vinna henne för Gud." In *Kongoboken: Något I ord och bild från Örebro Missionsförenings fält I Franska Kongo,* 86–91. Örebro: Örebro Missionsförenings Förlag.

Ekroth, Karl. 1932. "Vårt Kongofält." In *Kongoboken: Något I ord och bild från Örebro Missionsförenings fält I Franska Kongo* 17–24. Örebro: Örebro Missionsförenings Förlag.

Escobar, Arturo. 1996. "Constructing Nature: Elements for a Poststructural Political Ecology." In *Liberation Ecologies: Environment, Development, Social Movements,* ed. Richard Peet and Michael Watts, 325–44. London: Routledge.

Even, M. 1930. "Quelques coutumes des populations de la Haute Sangha." *Bulletin de la Société des Recherches Congolaises,* no. 11:23–32.

Fabian, Johannes. 2000. *Out of Our Minds: Reason and Madness in the Exploration of Central Africa.* Berkeley: Univ. of California Press.

Fabian, Johannes, with Tshibumba Kanda Matulu. 1996. *Remembering the Present: Painting and Popular History in Zaire.* Berkeley: Univ. of California Press.

Faes, Géraldine. 1994. "Le temps de la révolte." *Jeune Afrique,* no. 1730:16.

Faes, Géraldine, and Stephen Smith. 2000. *Bokassa: Un empereur français.* Paris: Calmann-Lévy.

Fairhead, James, and Melissa Leach. 1994. "Contested Forests: Modern Conservation and Historical Land Use in Guinea's Ziama Reserve." *African Affairs* 93:481–512.

————. 1996. *Misreading the African Landscape.* Cambridge: Cambridge Univ. Press.

————. 1998. *Reframing Deforestation: Global Analysis and Local Realities: Studies in West Africa.* London: Routledge.

Fardon, Richard. 1996. "The Person, Ethnicity, and the Problem of 'Identity.'" In *African Crossroads: Intersections between History and Anthropology in Cameroon,* ed. Ian Fowler and David Zeitlyn, 17–44. Oxford: Berghahn Books.

Faure, H. M. 1937. "Notes sur l'exploration de la Haute-Sangha." *Bulletin de la Société des Recherches Congolaises* 24:114–16.

Fay, J. Michael. 1989. "Partial Completion of a Census of the Western Lowland Gorilla (*Gorilla g. gorilla* (Savage and Wyman)) in Southwestern Central African Republic." *Mammalia* 53 (2): 203–15.

———. 1991. "An Elephant (*Loxodonta africana*) Survey Using Dung Counts in the Forests of the Central African Republic." *Journal of Tropical Ecology* 7:25–36.

———. 1993. "Ecological and Conservation Implications of Development Options for the Dzanga-Sangha Special Reserve and the Dzanga-Ndoki National Park, Yobe-Sangha, Central African Republic." Report to GTZ, Mission Forestière Allemande, Cooperation Technique Allemande.

Fay, J. Michael, and Marcellin Agnangna. 1991. "A Population Survey of Forest Elephants (*Loxodonta africana cyclotis*) in Northern Congo." *African Journal of Ecology* 29:177–87.

Feeley-Harnik, Gillian. 1994. *The Lord's Table: The Meaning of Food in Early Judaism and Christianity.* Washington, D.C.: Smithsonian.

Feierman, Steven. 1990. *Peasant Intellectuals: Anthropology and History in Tanzania.* Madison: Univ. of Wisconsin Press.

Fentress, James, and Chris Wickham. 1992. *Social Memory.* Oxford: Blackwell.

Fernandez, James. 1982. *Bwiti: An Ethnography of Religious Imagination in Africa.* Princeton, N.J.: Princeton Univ. Press.

Fisher, Humphrey J. 1973. "Conversion Reconsidered: Some Historical Aspects of Religious Conversion in Black Africa." *Africa* 43:27–40.

Ford, John. 1971. *The Role of Trypanosomiasis in African Ecology: A Study of the Tsetse Fly Problem.* Oxford: Clarendon Press.

Forman, Richard T. T. 1995. *Land Mosaics: The Ecology of Landscapes and Regions.* Cambridge: Cambridge Univ. Press.

Fortes, Meyer. 1987. *Religion, Morality, and the Person: Essays on Tallensi Religion.* Ed. and with an introduction by Jack Goody. Cambridge: Cambridge Univ. Press.

Foucault, Michel. [1966] 1970. *The Order of Things: An Archaeology of the Human Sciences.* New York: Vintage.

———. 1972. *The Archaeology of Knowledge.* New York: Pantheon Books.

Fourneau, Alfred. 1932. *Au vieux Congo: Notes de route, 1884–1891.* Paris: Comité de l'Afrique Française.

Fourneau, Lieutenant (Lucien). 1900. "Mission Fourneau: Rapport anecdotique." *Revue Coloniale* 6:1340–70.

Franquin, Pierre, Roland Diziain, Jean-Paul Cointepas, Yves Boulvert. 1988. *Agroclimatologie du Centrafrique.* Paris: ORSTOM.

Friedman, Kajsa Ekholm. 1991. *Catastrophe and Creation: The Transformation of an African Culture.* Chur and Philadelphia: Harwood Academic Press.

Gadgil, Madhav, Fikrel Berkes, and Carl Folke. 1993. "Indigenous Knowledge for Biodiversity Conservation." *Ambio* 22 (1): 151–56.

Gadgil, Madhav, and Ramachandra Guha. [1992] 1993. *This Fissured Land: An Ecological History of India*. Berkeley: Univ. of California Press.

Ganiage, Jean. 1968. *L'expansion coloniale de la France sous la troisième République (1871–1914)*. Paris: Payot.

Garreau, Jean-Marc. 1995. "Volet développement rural: Rapport trimestriel, octobre-decembre 1994." Report to the Ministère des Eaux et Forêts, Chasse, Pêche, Tourisme, et de l'Environnement, Parc National Dzanga-Ndoki, Reserve Spéciale Dzanga-Sangha.

Geary, Patrick J. 1994. *Phantoms of Remembrance: Memory and Oblivion at the End of the First Millenium*. Princeton, N.J.: Princeton Univ. Press.

Geschiere, Peter. 1981. "Remarques sur l'histoire des Makas." *Contribution de la recherche ethnologique à l'histoire des civilisations de Cameroun*, ed. Claude Tardits, 1:517–28. Paris: CNRS.

———. 1982. *Village Communities and the State: Changing Relations among the Maka of South-eastern Cameroon since the Colonial Conquest*. Trans. James J. Ravell. London: Kegan Paul.

———. 1983. "European Planters, African Peasants, and the Colonial State: Alternatives in the *Mise en Valeur* of Makaland, South-East Cameroun, during the Interbellum." *African Economic History* 12:83–108.

———. 1997. *The Modernity of Witchcraft: Politics and the Occult in Postcolonial Africa*. Charlottesville: Univ. Press of Virginia.

Geschiere, Peter, and Piet Konings, eds. 1993. *Les itinéraires de l'accumulation au Cameroun / Pathways to Accumulation in Cameroon*. Leiden: African Studies Center.

Giblin, James L. 1990. "Trypanosomiasis Control in African History: An Evaded Issue?" *Journal of African History* 31 (1): 59–80.

———. 1992. *The Politics of Environmental Control in Northeastern Tanzania*. Philadelphia: Univ. of Pennsylvania Press.

Gide, André. [1927] 1993. *Voyage au Congo—Le retour du Tchad—Retour de l'U.R.S.S. —Retouches à mon retour de l'U.R.S.S.—Carnets d'Égypte*. Préface de Gilles Leroy. Paris: Gallimard.

Giles-Vernick, Tamara. 1996a. "A Dead People? Migrants, Land, and History in the Rainforests of the Central African Republic." Ph.D. diss., Johns Hopkins University.

———. 1996b. "*Na lege ti guiriri* (On the Road of History): Mapping Out the Past and Present in M'Bres Region, Central African Republic." *Ethnohistory* 43 (2): 245–75.

———. 1999. "We Wander like Birds: Migration, Indigeneity, and the Fabrication of Frontiers in the Sangha River Basin of Equatorial Africa." *Environmental History* 4 (2): 168–97.

———. 2000. "*Doli*: Translating an African Environmental History of Loss in the Sangha River Basin of Equatorial Africa." *Journal of African History* 41 (3): 373–94.

————. 2001a. "Comment." *Current Anthropology* 42 (2): 185–86.

————. 2001b. "Lives, Histories, and Sites of Recollection." In *Words and Lives: The Promise and Problematics of Life History Research,* ed. Luise White, Stephan Miescher, and David William Cohen. Bloomington: Indiana Univ. Press.

Giles-Vernick, Tamara, and Stephanie Rupp. 2000. "Ape Tales: Western Equatorial Africans' Historical and Contemporary Visions of Gorillas and Chimpanzees." Paper presented at the African Studies Association meeting, Nashville.

Glassman, Jonathon. 1995. *Feasts and Riot: Revelry, Rebellion, and Popular Consciousness on the Swahili Coast, 1856–1888.* Portsmouth, N.H.: Heinemann.

Gouteaux, J. P., et al. 1992. "*Glossina fuscipes fuscipes* and *Glossina palpalis palpalis* as Joint Vectors of Sleeping Sickness in the Focus of Nola-Bilolo in the Central African Republic." *Acta Tropica* 51:163–66.

Goyémidé, Étienne. 1984. *Le silence de la forêt.* Paris: Hatier.

Gray, Christopher. 1999. "Territoriality and Colonial Enclosure in Southern Gabon." In *Enfermement, prison, et châtiments en Afrique, du XIXe siècle à nos jours,* ed. Florence Bernault, 101–32. Paris: Karthala.

Green, A. A., and R. W. Carroll. 1991. "The Avifauna of Dzanga-Ndoki National Park and Dzanga-Sangha Rainforest Reserve, Central African Republic." *Malimbus* 13:49–66.

Greenberg, Joseph H. 1973. *The Languages of Africa.* 3d ed. Bloomington: Indiana Univ. Press.

Grimes, Barbara, ed. 1996. *Ethnologue: Languages of the World,* 13th ed. Dallas: Summer Institute of Linguistics.

Grinker, Roy Richard. 1994. *Houses in the Rainforest: Ethnicity and Inequality among Farmers and Foragers in Central Africa.* Berkeley: Univ. of California Press.

Grove, Richard. 1989. "Scottish Missionaries, Evangelical Discourses, and Origins of Conservation Thinking in Southern Africa, 1820–1900." *Journal of Southern African Studies* 15 (2): 163–74.

————. 1990. "Colonial Conservation, Ecological Hegemony, and Popular Resistance: Toward a Global Synthesis." In *Imperialism and the Natural World,* ed. John Mackenzie, 15–51. Manchester: Manchester Univ. Press.

————. 1995. *Green Imperialism: Colonial Expansion, Tropical Island Edens, and the Origins of Environmentalism, 1600–1800.* Cambridge: Cambridge Univ. Press.

Grove, Richard, Vinita Damodaran, and Satpal Sangwan, eds. 1998. *Nature and the Orient: The Environmental History of South and Southeast Asia.* Delhi: Oxford Univ. Press.

Grut, Mikael, John A. Gray, and Nicolas Egli. 1991. *Forest Pricing and Concession Policies: Managing the High Forests of West and Central Africa.* World Bank Technical Paper no. 143. Washington, D.C.: World Bank.

Guha, Ramachandra. [1989] 2000. *The Unquiet Woods: Ecological Change and Peasant Resistance in the Himalaya.* Expanded ed. Berkeley: Univ. of California Press.

Guyer, Jane I. 1995. "Wealth in People, Wealth in Things—Introduction." *Journal of African History* 36:83–90.

Guyer, Jane, and Paul Richards. 1996. "The Invention of Biodiversity: Social Perspectives on the Management of Biological Variety in Africa." *Africa* 66 (1): 1–13.

Guyer, Jane I., and S. M. Eno Belinga. 1995. "Wealth in People as Wealth in Knowledge: Accumulation and Composition in Equatorial Africa." *Journal of African History* 36:91–120.

Haltenorth, Theodor, and Helmut Diller. 1980. *Mammals of Africa Including Madagascar.* Trans. Robert W. Hayman. London: Collins.

Hardin, Rebecca. 2000. "Translating the Forest: Tourism, Trophy Hunting, and the Transformation of Forest Use in Southwestern Central African Republic (CAR)." Ph.D. diss., Yale University.

Hardin, Rebecca, and Melissa Remis. 1997. "Conclusions et recommendations." In *Seminaire: Recherches scientifiques et développement rural: Reserve de Forêt Dense Dzanga Sangha, République centrafricaine, 31 juillet au 2 août, 1997,* ed. Rebecca Hardin and Melissa Remis, 77–87. New Haven: Yale Council on International and Area Studies and Sangha River Network.

Hardin, Rebecca, Stephanie Rupp, and Heather E. Eves. 1998. "Introduction." In *Resource Use in the Trinational Sangha River Region of Equatorial Africa: Histories, Knowledge Forms, and Institutions,* ed. Heather E. Eves, Rebecca Hardin, and Stephanie Rupp. Bulletin Series, Yale School of Forestry and Environmental Studies, no. 102:8–28.

Harms, Robert. 1981. *River of Wealth, River of Sorrow: The Central Zaire Basin in the Era of the Slave and Ivory Trade, 1500–1891.* New Haven: Yale Univ. Press.

———. 1987. *Games against Nature: An Eco-cultural History of the Nunu of Equatorial Africa.* Cambridge: Cambridge Univ. Press.

Harries, Patrick. 1994. *Work, Culture, and Identity: Migrant Laborers in Mozambique and South Africa, c.1860–1910.* Portsmouth, N.H.: Heinemann.

Hart, Terese B., John A. Hart, and Peter G. Murphy. 1989. "Monodominant and Species-Rich Forests of the Humid Tropics: Causes for Their Co-Occurrence." *American Naturalist* 133 (5): 613–33.

Hauser, A. N.d. "Un essai d'amélioration de la condition des Pygmées." In author's possession.

———. 1951. "Les Babingas." In author's possession.

Headrick, Daniel. 1988. *Tentacles of Progress: Technology Transfer in the Age of Imperialism, 1850–1940.* New York: Oxford Univ. Press.

Headrick, Rita. 1981. "Sleeping Sickness at Nola (Central African Republic)." Paper presented to the African Studies Association conference, Bloomington, Ind., October.

———. 1987. "The Impact of Colonialism on Health in French Equatorial Africa, 1880–1934." Ph.D. diss., University of Chicago.

———. 1994. *Colonialism, Health, and Illness in French Equatorial Africa, 1885–1935.* Ed. Daniel R. Headrick. Atlanta: African Studies Association.

Heald, Suzette. 1989. *Controlling Anger: the Sociology of Gisu Violence.* London: Manchester Univ. Press.

Heckenroth, F. 1909. "Région de la Haute-Sangha." In *Rapport de la mission d'étude de la maladie de sommeil au Congo français, 1906–1908*, ed. Gustave Martin, Alexis LeBoeuf, and Émile Roubaud, 131–46. Paris: Masson and Société de Géographie de Paris.

Hegba, Meinrad. 1998. *La rationalité d'un discours africain sur les phénomènes paranormaux*. Paris: Harmattan.

Hendrickson, Hildi. 1996. "Introduction." In *Clothing and Difference: Embodied Identities in Colonial and Post-Colonial Africa*, ed. Hildi Hendrickson, 1–16. Durham, N.C., and London: Duke Univ. Press.

Herbert, Eugenia W. 1993. *Iron, Gender, and Power: Rituals of Transformation in African Societies*. Bloomington: Indiana Univ. Press.

Hewlett, Barry. 1991. *Intimate Fathers: The Nature and Context of Aka Pygmy Paternal Infant Care*. Ann Arbor: Univ. of Michigan Press.

Hilberth, Ellen. 1932. "Vår sjukvård I Kongo." In *Kongoboken: Något I ord och bild Från Örebro Missionsförenings fält I Franska Kongo*, 115–25. Örebro: Örebro Missionsförenings.

Hilberth, J. 1932. "Gudstro och andekult i Kongo." In *Kongoboken: Något I ord och bild Från Örebro Missionsförenings fält I Franska Kongo*, 48–58. Örebro: Örebro Missionsförenings.

Hladik, Claude Marcel, and Annette Hladik. 1990. "Food Resources of the Rain Forest." In *Food and Nutrition in the African Rain Forest*, ed. C. M. Hladik, S. Bahuchet, and I. de Garine, 14–16. Paris: UNESCO/MAB.

Hobsbawm, Eric, and Terence Ranger, eds. [1983] 1992. *The Invention of Tradition*. New York: Cambridge Univ. Press.

Hoehler-Fatton, Cynthia. 1996. *Women of Fire and Spirit: History, Faith, and Gender in Roho Religion in Western Kenya*. Oxford: Oxford Univ. Press.

Hofmeyr, Isabel. 1993. *"We Spend Our Years as a Tale That Is Told": Oral Historical Narrative in a South African Chiefdom*. Portsmouth, N.H.: Heinemann.

Hoppe, Kirk Arden. 1997. "Lords of the Fly: Colonial Visions and Revisions of African Sleeping-Sickness Environments in Ugandan Lake Victoria, 1906–61." *Africa* 67 (1): 86–107.

Horta, Korinna. 1991. "The Last Big Rush for the Green Gold: The Plundering of Cameroon's Rainforests." *Ecologist* 21 (3): 145–6.

Horton, Robin. 1975. "On the Rationality of Conversion." *Africa* 45:219–23.

Hoskins, Janet. 1993. *The Play of Time: Kodi Perspectives on Calendars, History, and Exchange*. Berkeley: Univ. of California Press.

Hunt, Nancy Rose. 1999. *A Colonial Lexicon of Birth Ritual, Medicalization, and Mobility in the Congo*. Durham, N.C.: Duke Univ. Press.

Ingold, Tim. 1986. *The Appropriation of Nature: Essays on Human Ecology and Social Relations*. Manchester: Manchester Univ. Press.

———. 1992. "Culture and the Perception of the Environment." In *Bush Base: Forest Farm: Culture, Environment, and Development*, ed. Elisabeth Croll and David Parkin, 39–56. London: Routledge.

Ingold, Tim, David Riches, and James Woodburn, eds. 1991. *Hunters and Gatherers: History, Evolution, and Social Change.* Vol. 1. New York: Berg.

IUCN. 1989. "Conservation et utilisation rationelle des écosystèmes forestiers en Afrique centrale: Dossier d'execution." Gland, Switzerland: International Union for the Conservation of Nature.

Jackson, Michael, and Ivan Karp, eds. 1991. *Personhood and Agency: The Experience of Self and Other in African Cultures.* Washington, D.C.: Smithsonian.

Janody, André. 1985. "Pierre Tombo." *Alpes-Afrique* 339:20–22.

Janssens, P. G., M. Kivits, and J. Vuylsteke. 1992. *Médecine et hygiène en Afrique centrale de 1885 à nos jours.* Vol 2. Bruxelles: Fondation Roi Baudouin.

Johnson, Douglas H., and David M. Anderson, eds. 1988. *The Ecology of Survival: Case Studies from Northeast African History.* Boulder, Colo.: Westview.

Johnston, Bruce, and John Mellor. 1961. "The Role of Agriculture in Economic Development." *American Economic Review* 51:566–93.

Jones, William O. 1959. *Manioc in Africa.* Stanford, Calif.: Stanford Univ. Press.

Jourdy, H.-P. 1914. "La maladie du sommeil." *Bulletin du Comité de l'Afrique Française* 24 (3): 107–9.

Juhé-Beaulaton, Dominique. 1990. "La diffusion du maïs sur les Côtes de l'Or et des esclaves aux XVIIe et XVIIIe siècles." *Revue Français d'Histoire d'Outre-mer* 77 (287): 177–98.

Kalck, Pierre. 1959. *Réalités oubanguiennes.* Paris: Berger-Levrault.

———. 1971. *Central African Republic: A Failure in De-Colonisation.* London: Pall Mall Press.

———. 1973. *Histoire centrafricaine des origines à nos jours* (Ph.D. thesis, Université de Paris, 1970). Lille: Service de reproduction des thèses.

———. 1974. *Histoire de la République centrafricaine des origines préhistoriques à nos jours.* Paris: Berger-Levrault.

Karlsson, Sofia. 1932. "Några av Kongos sjukdomar." In *Kongoboken: Något I ord och bild från Örebro Missionsförenings fält I Franska Kongo,* 108–25. Örebro: Örebro Missionsförenings Förlag.

Karp, Ivan. 1997. "Notions of Personhood." In *Encyclopedia of Africa South of the Sahara,* ed. John Middleton, 3:392–96. New York: Charles Scribner's Sons.

Karp, Ivan, and D. S. Masolo. 2000. "Introduction to Part 1." In *African Philosophy as Cultural Inquiry,* ed. Ivan Karp and D. S. Masolo, 21–24. Bloomington: Indiana Univ. Press.

Kasenene, John M. 1984. "The Influence of Selective Logging on Rodent Populations and the Regeneration of Selected Tree Species in the Kibale Forest, Uganda." *Tropical Ecology* 25:179–95.

Kisliuk, Michelle Robin. 1991. "Confronting the Quintessential: Singing, Dancing, and Everyday Life among Biaka (Central African Republic)." Ph.D. diss., New York University.

———. 1999. *Seize the Dance! BaAka Musical Life and the Ethnography of Performance.* Oxford: Oxford Univ. Press.

Kjekshus, Helge. [1977] 1997. *Ecology, Control, and Economic Development in East African History: The Case of Tanganyika, 1850–1950.* Athens: Ohio Univ. Press.

Klein, Kerwin Lee. 2000. "On the Emergence of *Memory* in Historical Discourse." *Representations* 69:127–50.

Klieman, Kairn. 1999. "Hunter-Gatherer Participation in Rainforest Trade Systems: A Comparative History of Forest v. Ecotone Societies in Gabon and Congo, c. 1000–1800 A.D." In *Central African Hunter-Gatherers in a Multidisciplinary Perspective: Challenging Elusiveness,* ed. Karin Biesbrouck, Stefan Elders, and Gerda Rossel, 89–104. Leiden: CNWS, Universiteit Leiden.

Koch, Henri. 1968. *Magie et chasse dans la forêt camerounaise.* Paris: Berger-Levrault.

Köhler, Axel. 1999. "The Forest as Home." In *Central African Hunter-Gatherers in a Multidisciplinary Perspective: Challenging Elusiveness,* ed. Karen Biesbrouck, Stefan Elders, and Gerda Rossel, 207–20. Leiden: CNWS, Universiteit Leiden.

Kratz, Corinne A. 1993. "'We've Always Done It Like This . . . Except for a Few Details': 'Tradition' and 'Innovation' in Okiek Ceremonies." *Comparative Studies in Society and History* 35:30–65.

———. 2000. "Forging Unions and Negotiating Ambivalence: Personhood and Complex Agency in Okiek Marriage Arrangements." In *African Philosophy and Cultural Inquiry,* ed. Ivan Karp and D. S. Masolo, 136–71. Bloomington: Indiana Univ. Press.

Kreike, Emmanuel H. 1996. "Recreating Eden: Agro-Ecological Change, Food Security, and Environmental Diversity in Southern Angola and Northern Namibia, 1890–1960." Ph.D. diss., Yale University.

Kretsinger, Anna. N.d. *Quelques plantes utiles des BaAka.* Washington, D.C.: World Wildlife Fund.

———. 1993. "Recommendations for Further Integration of BaAka Interests in Project Policy, Dzanga-Sangha Dense Forest Reserve." Report for Projet Reserve Dzanga-Sangha.

Kretsinger, Anna, and Henri Zana. 1996. *Quelques souvenirs de Bayanga.* Bangui: GTZ.

Kvist, Axel W. 1932. "På resor till byarna." In *Kongoboken: Något I ord och bild från Örebro Missionsförenings fält I Franska Kongo,* 78–85. Örebro: Örebro Missionsförenings Förlag.

Laburthe-Tolra, Philippe. 1981. *Les seigneurs de la forêt: Essai sur le passé, l'organisation sociale, et les normes éthiques des anciens Beti du Cameroun.* Paris: Publications de la Sorbonne.

Landau, Paul Stuart. 1995. *The Realm of the Word: Language, Gender, and Christianity in a Southern African Kingdom.* Portsmouth, N.H.: Heinemann.

———. 1996. "Explaining Surgical Evangelism in Colonial Southern Africa: Teeth, Pain, and Faith." *Journal of African History* 37 (2): 261–82.

Lanfranchi, Raymond, and Bernard Clist, eds. 1991. *Aux origines de l'Afrique centrale.* Libreville: Ministère de la Coopération et du Développement and Centres Culturels Français d'Afrique.

Lanfranchi, Raymond, and Dominique Schwartz, eds. 1990. *Paysages quaternaires de l'Afrique centrale atlantique.* Paris: ORSTOM.

Lanfranchi, Raymond, Jean Ndanga, and Henri Zana. 1998. "New Carbon 14C Datings of Iron Metallurgy in the Central African Dense Forest." In *Resource Use in the Trinational Sangha River Region of Equatorial Africa: Histories, Knowledge Forms, and Institutions,* ed. Heather E. Eves, Rebecca Hardin, Stephanie Rupp. Bulletin Series, Yale School of Forestry and Environmental Studies, no. 102:41–50.

Lanly, J. P. 1966a. "Inventaire forestier en République centrafricaine." *Revue Bois et Forêts des Tropiques,* no. 105:33–56.

———. 1966b. "La forêt dense centrafricaine." *Revue Bois et Forêts des Tropiques,* no. 108:43–55.

Larson, Pier. 1997. "'Capacities and Modes of Thinking': Intellectual Engagements and Subaltern Hegemony in the Early History of Malagasy Christianity." *American Historical Review* 102 (4): 969–1002.

Lawi, Yusefu Q. 2000. "May the Spider Web Blind Witches and Wild Animals: Local Knowledge and the Political Ecology of Natural Resource Use in the Iraqwland, Tanzania, 1900–1985." Ph.D. diss., Boston University.

Leach, Melissa. 1994. *Rainforest Relations: Gender and Resource Use among the Mende of Gola, Sierra Leone.* Washington, D.C.: Smithsonian.

Leach, Melissa, and Robin Mearns, eds. 1996. *The Lie of the Land: Challenging Received Wisdom on the African Environment.* Portsmouth, N.H.: Heinemann.

Le Kham. 1969. *Au coeur de l'Afrique: La mission de Berbérati.* St. Joriot-Lac d'Annecy: Les Presses de la STIP.

Likaka, Osumaka. 1997. *Rural Society and Cotton in Colonial Zaire.* Madison: Univ. of Wisconsin Press.

Linden, Eugene. 1992. "The Last Eden." *Time* 140 (2): 42–48.

Loyre, Émile. 1909. "Les populations de la Moyenne-Sangha." *Questions Diplomatiques et Coloniales* 28:406–20.

Mabberley, D. J. 1987. *The Plant-Book: A Portable Dictionary of the Higher Plants.* Cambridge: Cambridge Univ. Press.

———. 1992. *Tropical Rain Forest Ecology.* New York: Blackman and Hall.

MacGaffey, Wyatt. 1986. *Religion and Society in Central Africa: The BaKongo of Lower Zaire.* Chicago: Univ. of Chicago Press.

———. 2000. *Kongo Political Culture.* Bloomington: Indiana Univ. Press.

MacKenzie, John. 1987. "Chivalry, Social Darwinism, and Ritualised Killing: The Hunting Ethos in Central Africa up to 1914." In *Conservation in Africa: People, Policies, and Practice,* ed. David Anderson and Richard Grove, 41–61. Cambridge: Cambridge Univ. Press.

Maddox, Gregory, James L. Giblin, and Isaria N. Kimambo, eds. 1995. *Custodians of the Land: Ecology and Culture in the History of Tanzania.* London: James Currey.

Maley, Jean. 1996. "Fluctuations majeures de la forêt dense humide africaine au cours des vingts derniers millénaires." In *L'alimentation en forêt tropicale: Interactions bioculturelles et perspectives de développement: Les ressources alimentaires: Production et consommation,* ed. Claude Marcel Hladik et al., vol. 1. UNESCO.

Malkki, Liisa H. 1995. *Purity and Exile: Violence, Memory, and National Cosmology among Hutu Refugees in Tanzania.* Chicago: Univ. of Chicago Press.

Mamdani, Mahmood. 1996. *Citizen and Subject: Contemporary Africa and the Legacy of Late Colonialism.* Princeton, N.J.: Princeton Univ. Press.

Mandala, Elias. 1990. *Work and Control in a Peasant Economy: A History of the Lower Tchiri Valley in Malawi, 1859–1960.* Madison: Univ. of Wisconsin Press.

Manning, Patrick. [1988] 1998. *Francophone Sub-Saharan Africa, 1880–1985.* Cambridge: Cambridge Univ. Press.

Marks, Stuart A. 1976. *Large Mammals and a Brave People: Subsistence Hunters in Zambia.* Seattle: Univ. of Washington Press.

———. 1984. *The Imperial Lion: Human Dimensions of Wildlife Management in Central Africa.* Boulder, Colo.: Westview Press.

Marseille, Jacques. 1984. *Empire colonial et capitalisme française: Histoire d'un divorce.* Paris: Albins Michel.

Marshall, Ruth. 1991. "Power in the Name of Jesus." *Review of African Political Economy* 52:21–38.

Martin, Phyllis M. 1983. "The Violence of Empire." In *History of Central Africa,* ed. David Birmingham and Phyllis M. Martin, 2:1–26. London: Longman.

———. 1995. *Leisure and Society in Colonial Brazzaville.* Cambridge: Cambridge Univ. Press.

Massey, Doreen. 1994. *Space, Place, and Gender.* Minneapolis: Univ. of Minnesota Press.

Matsuda, Matt. 1996. *The Memory of the Modern.* Oxford: Oxford Univ. Press.

Maunoir, M. Ch. 1895. "M. Edmond Ponel, Medaille d'or.—Prix Léon Dewez." *Bulletin de la Société de Géographie de Paris,* ser. 7, 16:295–300.

Mauss, Marcel. 1985. "A Category of the Human Mind: The Notion of Person, the Notion of Self," trans. W. D. Halls. In *The Category of the Person: Anthropology, Philosophy, History,* ed. Michael Carrithers, Steven Collins, Steven Lukes, 1–25. Cambridge: Cambridge Univ. Press.

Mazenot, Georges. 1970. *La Likouala-Mossaka: Histoire de la pénétration du Haut Congo, 1878–1920.* Paris: Mouton.

Mbalanga, Adrien. 1994. "Rapport sur les enquêtes historiques effectuées dans la sous-préfecture de Bayanga du 30 mars au 30 mai 1994."

Mbembe, Achille. 1990. "Pouvoir, violence, et accumulation." *Politique Africaine* 39:7–24.

M'Bokolo, Elikia. 1981. "Forces sociales et idéologies dans la décolonisation de l'A.E.F." *Journal of African History* 22 (3): 393–407.

———. 1983. "Historicité et pouvoir d'État en Afrique noire: Réflexions sur les pratiques d'État et les idéologies dominantes." *Relations Internationales* 34:197–213.

———. 1998. "Comparisons and Contrasts in Equatorial Africa: Gabon, Congo, and the Central African Republic." In *History of Central Africa: The Contemporary Years since 1960,* ed. David Birmingham and Phyllis M. Martin, 67–96. London: Longman.

McCann, James C. 1995. *People of the Plow: An Agricultural History of Ethiopia.* Madison: Univ. of Wisconsin Press.

———. 1997. "The Plow and the Forest: Narratives of Deforestation in Ethiopia, 1840–1990." *Environmental History* 2 (2): 138–59.

———. 1999a. *Green Land, Brown Land, Black Land: An Environmental History of Africa, 1800–1990.* Portsmouth, N.H.: Heinemann.

———. 1999b. "Maize and Grace: History, Corn, and Africa's New Landscapes, 1500–1999." Working Papers in African Studies, no. 223, Boston University.

McNeely, Jeffrey A., et al. 1991. *Conserving the World's Biological Diversity.* Gland, Switzerland, and Washington, D.C.: International Union for Conservation of Nature and Natural Resources, World Resources Institute, Conservation International, World Wildlife Fund-US, and World Bank.

McNeil, Donald G., Jr. 1999. "The Great Ape Massacre." *New York Times Magazine,* 9 May, 54–57.

McNeill, J. R. 2000. *Something New under the Sun: An Environmental History of the Twentieth-Century World.* New York: W. W. Norton.

Merleau-Ponty, M. 1962. *Phenomenology of Perception.* Trans. Colin Smith. New York: Humanities Press.

Merlin, M. 1913. "La crise du caoutchouc." *Bulletin du Comité de l'Afrique Française* 23 (12): 420–28.

Miller, Joseph C., ed. 1980. *The African Past Speaks: Essays on Oral Tradition and History.* Hamden, Conn.: Archon.

———. 1988. *Way of Death: Merchant Capitalism and the Angolan Slave Trade, 1730–1830.* Madison: Univ. of Wisconsin.

Ministère des Eaux et Forêts, Chasses, Pêche, et du Tourisme. 1992. Arrêté no. 007 portant réglement intérieur de la Reserve Spéciale de Forêt Dense Dzanga-Sangha. 25 March.

Miracle, Marvin P. 1967. *Agriculture in the Congo Basin.* Madison: Univ. of Wisconsin Press.

Mitchell, W. J. T., ed. 1994. *Landscape and Power.* Chicago: Univ. of Chicago Press.

Mogba, Zéphirin, and Mark Freudenberger. 1998. "Human Migration in the Protected Zones of Central Africa: The Case of the Dzanga-Sangha Special Reserve." In *Resource Use in the Trinational Sangha River Region of Equatorial Africa: Histories, Knowledge Forms, and Institutions,* ed. Heather E. Eves, Rebecca Hardin, and Stephanie Rupp. Bulletin Series, Yale School of Forestry and Environmental Studies, no. 102:104–29.

Moll, Commandant. 1908. "Forêts et savanes congolais." *Bulletin de la Société de Géographie Commerciale du Havre,* 201–19.

Mollion, Pierre. 1992. *Sur les pistes de l'Oubangui-Chari au Tchad, 1890–1930: Le drame du portage en Afrique centrale.* Paris: Harmattan.

Mololi, André. 1994. "Rapport de l'étude sociolinguistique comparée de deux langues minoritaires Bantu: Le Kaka ou Linzali et le Mpiemo." In author's possession.

Moore, Donald S. 1996. "Marxism, Culture, and Political Ecology: Environmental Struggles in Zimbabwe's Eastern Highlands." In *Liberation Ecologies: Environment,*

Development, Social Movements, ed. R. Peet and M. Watts, 125–47. London: Rout-ledge.

———. 1998a. "Clear Waters and Muddied Histories: Environmental History and the Politics of Community in Zimbabwe's Eastern Highlands." *Journal of Southern African Historical Studies* 24 (2): 385–403.

———. 1998b. "Subaltern Struggles and the Politics of Place: Remapping Resistance in Zimbabwe's Eastern Highlands." *Cultural Anthropology* 13 (3): 344–81.

Moore, Henrietta L. 1986. *Space, Text, and Gender: An Anthropological Study of the Marakwet of Kenya.* Cambridge: Cambridge Univ. Press.

———. 1994. *A Passion for Difference.* Bloomington: Indiana Univ. Press.

Moore, Henrietta, and Megan Vaughan. 1994. *Cutting Down Trees: Gender, Nutrition, and Agricultural Change in the Northern Province of Zambia, 1890–1990.* Portsmouth, N.H.: Heinemann.

Morel, Père Martin. 1994a. "Le culte des ancêtres." *Alpes-Afrique* 374:17–19.

———. 1994b. "Le temps des fondations: Souvenirs d'un Broussard." *Alpes-Afrique* 375:18–22.

Morphy, Howard, and Frances Morphy. 1984. "Myths of Ngalakan History: Ideology and Images of the Past in Northern Australia." *Man* 19:459–75.

Mpago, M. 1997. "Presentation 15." In *Seminaire: Recherches scientifiques et développement rural: Reserve de Forêt Dense Dzanga Sangha, République centrafricaine, 31 juillet au 2 août 1997,* ed. Rebecca Hardin and Melissa Remis, 30–32. New Haven: Yale Council on International and Area Studies and Sangha River Network.

Munn, Nancy. 1986. *The Fame of Gawa: A Symbolic Study of Value Transformation in a Massim (Papua New Guinea) Society.* Cambridge: Cambridge Univ. Press.

Muston, Étienne. 1933. "Petit journal de la mission de délimitation Congo-Cameroun, 1905–1907." *Bulletin de la Société des Recherches Congolaises* 19:1–155.

Mveng Ayi, M. 1981. "Rapport de synthèse: Échanges précoloniaux et diffusion des plantes au Sud-Cameroun." In *Contribution de la recherche ethnologique à l'histoire des civilisations de Cameroun,* ed. Claude Tardits, 1:587–91. Paris: CNRS.

Naughton-Treves, Lisa. 1997. "Farming the Forest Edge: Vulnerable Places and People around Kibale National Park, Uganda." *Geographical Review* 87 (1): 27–47.

Neumann, Roderick E. 1995. "Ways of Seeing Africa: Colonial Recasting of African Society and Landscape in Serengeti National Park." *Ecumene* 2:149–69.

———. 1996. "Dukes, Earls, and Ersatz Edens: Aristocratic Nature Preservationists in Colonial Africa." *Environment and Planning D: Society and Space* 14:79–98.

———. 1998. *Imposing Wilderness: Struggles over Livelihood and Nature Preservation in Africa.* Berkeley: Univ. of California Press.

———. Forthcoming. "The Postwar Conservation Boom in British Colonial Africa." *Environmental History.*

Ngoupandé, Jean-Paul. 1997. *Chronique de la crise centrafricaine, 1996–1997: Le syndrome Barracuda.* Paris: Harmattan.

Nora, Pierre. [1984] 1997. "Entre mémoire et histoire: La problématique des lieux." In *Les lieux de mémoire,* ed. Pierre Nora, 23–43. Paris: Gallimard.

Noss, Andrew J. 1995. "Duikers, Cables, and Nets: A Cultural Ecology of Hunting in a Central African Forest." Ph.D. diss., University of Florida-Gainesville.

———. 1997a. "Challenges to Nature Conservation with Community Development in Central African Rainforests." *Oryx* 31 (3): 180–88.

———. 1997b. "The Economic Importance of Communal Net Hunting among the BaAka of the Central African Republic." *Human Ecology* 25 (1): 71–90.

Nummelin, Matti. 1990. "Relative Habitat Use of Duikers, Bush Pigs, and Elephants in Virgin and Selectively Logged Areas of the Kibale Forest, Uganda." *Tropical Zoology* 3:111–20.

Nyerges, A. Endre. 1997. "Introduction—The Ecology of Practice." In *The Ecology of Practice: Studies of Food Crop Production in Sub-Saharan West Africa,* ed. A. Endre Nyerges, 1–38. Amsterdam: Overseas Publishers Association and Gordon and Breach.

Nzabakomada-Yakoma, Raphael. 1986. *L'Afrique centrale insurgée: La guerre du Kongo-Wara, 1928–1931.* Paris: Harmattan.

Oates, John F. 1999. *Myth and Reality in the Rain Forest: How Conservation Strategies Are Failing in West Africa.* Berkeley: Univ. of California Press.

Odoch Pido, J. P. 2000. "Personhood and Art: Social Change and Commentary among the Acoli." In *African Philosophy as Cultural Inquiry,* ed. Ivan Karp and D. A. Masolo, 105–35. Bloomington: Indiana Univ. Press.

Ohnuki-Tierney, Emiko. 1993. *Rice as Self: Japanese Identities through Time.* Princeton, N.J.: Princeton Univ. Press.

Olsson, Walter. 1946. "Våra Missions Stationer." In *Vildmarken Vaknar: Skildringar av Örebro Missionsförenings Kongomission,* ed. John Magnusson, 306–14. Örebro: Örebro Missions Förenings Forlag.

———. 1992. "I Dödsskuggans Dal." In *100 ÅR I Ord och Bild Örebro Missionary Society, 1892–1992.* Örebro: Bokförlaget Libris.

Östberg, Wilhelm. 1995. *Land Is Coming Up: The Burunge of Central Tanzania and Their Environments.* Stockholm Studies in Anthropology, no. 34. Stockholm: Stockholm University.

O'Toole, Thomas. 1986. *The Central African Republic: The Continent's Hidden Heart.* Boulder, Colo.: Westview.

Pagnault, Étienne. N.d. "En tournée chez les Mbimous de la Sangha." In *Itinéraire d'un missionaire: Le Père Marc Pédron,* ed. Père G. de Banville, 139–50. Bangui: Maison St-Charles.

Parkin, David. 2000. "Islam among the Humors: Destiny and Agency among the Swahili." In *African Philosophy as Cultural Inquiry,* ed. Ivan Karp and D. A. Masolo, 50–65. Bloomington: Indiana Univ. Press.

Peel, J. D. Y. 1977. "Conversion and Tradition in Two African Societies: Ijebu and Uganda." *Past and Present,* no. 77:108–41.

———. 1990. "The Pastor and the Babalawo: The Interaction of Religions in Nineteenth-Century Yorubaland." *Africa* 60 (3): 338–69.

Peet, Richard, and Michael Watts, eds. 1996. *Liberation Ecologies: Environment, Development, Social Movements.* London: Routledge.

Peluso, Nancy. 1992. *Rich Forests, Poor People: Resource Control and Resistance in Java.* Berkeley: Univ. of California Press.

Periquet, L. 1916. *Rapport général sur la mission de délimitation Afrique équatoriale française—Cameroun (1912–13–14)*, vol. 3, *La flore et la faune en Afrique équatoriale française—Cultures et animaux domestique.* Paris: Imprimerie Chapelot.

Peters, Pauline. 1994. *Dividing the Commons: Politics, Policy, and Culture in Botswana.* Charlottesville: University Press of Virginia.

Peterson, Richard B. 2000. *Conversations in the Rain Forest: Culture, Values, and the Environment in Central Africa.* Boulder, Colo.: Westview.

Piot, Charles. 1999. *Remotely Global: Village Modernity in West Africa.* Chicago: Univ. of Chicago Press.

Pomodimo, Paulin. 1993. "Évangile, force de défatalisation chez les Mpiemons." Ph.D. diss., Université Catholique de Lyon.

Ponel, E. 1896. "La Haute Sangha (Congo français)." *Bulletin de la Société de Géographie de Paris*, ser. 7, 17:188–211.

Pouperon, Paul. 1908. *Deuxième mission de P. Pouperon dans la Sangha.* Alger: IMP, Typo-Lithographique S. Léon.

Prakash, Gyan. 1990. "Writing Post-Orientalist Histories of the Third World: Perspectives from Indian Historiography." *Comparative Studies in Society and History* 32 (2): 383–408.

Prins, H. H. T., and J. M. Reitsma. 1989. "Mammalian Biomass in an African Equatorial Rain Forest." *Journal of Animal Ecology* 58:851–61.

Quammen, David. 2000. "Megatransect: Across 1,200 Miles of Untamed Africa on Foot." *National Geographic* 193:2–29.

Rabut, Elisabeth. 1989. *Brazza commissaire général: Le Congo français, 1886–1897.* Paris: École des Hautes Études en Sciences Sociales.

Rajan, Ravi. 1998. "Imperial Environmentalism or Environmental Imperialism? European Forestry, Colonial Foresters, and the Agendas of Forest Management in British India, 1800–1900." In *Nature and the Orient: The Environmental History of South and Southeast Asia*, ed. Richard Grove, Vinita Damodaran, and Satpal Sangwan, 324–72. Delhi: Oxford Univ. Press.

Ranger, Terence. 1999. *Voices from the Rocks: Nature, Culture, and History in the Matopos Hills of Zimbabwe.* Bloomington: Indiana Univ. Press.

Ray, Justina C. 1997. "Comparative Ecology of Two African Forest Mongooses, *Herpestes naso* and *Atilax paludinosus.*" *African Journal of Ecology* 35:237–53.

———. 2001. "Carnivore Biogeography and Conservation in the African Forest: A Community Perspective." In *African Rainforest Ecology and Conservation*, ed. W. Weber, L. White, A. Vedder, and L. Naughton-Treves, 214–32. New Haven: Yale Univ. Press.

Ray, Justina C., and Rainer Hutterer. 1996. "Structure of a Shrew Community in the Central African Republic Based on the Analysis of Carnivore Scats, with the Description of a New Sylvisorex (Mammalia: *Soricidae*)." *Ecotropica* 1:85–97.

Reinelt, Janelle G., and Joseph R. Roach, eds. 1992. *Critical Theory and Performance.* Ann Arbor: Univ. of Michigan Press.

République Centrafricaine. 1987. *Recensement général de la population—1975 analyse abregée*. Bangui: République Centrafricaine.

———, Ministère de l'Interieur. 1964. *Recensement général de la population de la République centrafricaine*, pt. 1, *Resultats pour la région de Lobaye Haute-Sangha, 1961–1963*. Paris: INSEE Service de Coopération.

Retel-Laurentin, Anne. 1974. *Infécondité en Afrique noire: Maladies et conséquences sociales*. Paris: Masson.

Ricciuti, Edward. 1993. "The Elephant Wars." *Wildlife Conservation* 96 (2): 14–35.

Richards, Audrey. 1939. *Land, Labor, and Diet in Northern Rhodesia: An Economic Study of the Bemba Tribe*. London: Oxford Univ. Press.

Richards, Paul. 1985. *Indigenous Agricultural Revolution: Ecology and Food Production in West Africa*. London: Unwin Hyman.

———. 1993. "Natural Symbols and Natural History: Chimpanzees, Elephants, and Experiments in Mende Thought." In *Environmentalism: The View from Anthropology*, ed. Kay Milton, 144–59. London: Routledge.

———. 1996. *Fighting for the Forest: War, Youth, and Resources in Sierra Leone*. Portsmouth, N.H.: Heinemann.

Richards, Paul W. [1952] 1996. *The Tropical Rain Forest: An Ecological Study*. 2d ed. (with contributions by R. P. D. Walsh, I. C. Baillie, and P. Greig-Smith). New York and Cambridge: Cambridge Univ. Press.

Riesman, Paul. 1986. "The Person and the Life Cycle in African Social Life and Thought." *African Studies Review* 29 (2): 71–138.

———. 1992. *First Find Your Child a Good Mother: The Construction of Self in Two African Communities*. New Brunswick, N.J.: Rutgers Univ. Press.

Roach, Joseph R. 1992. "Introduction." In *Critical Theory and Performance*, ed. Janelle G. Reinelt and Joseph R. Roach. Ann Arbor: Univ. of Michigan Press.

Roberts, Mary Nooter, and Allen F. Roberts, eds. 1996. *Memory: Luba Art and the Making of History*. New York: Museum for African Art.

Roe, E. 1991. "'Development Narratives,' or Making the Best of Blueprint Development." *World Development* 19 (4): 287–300.

Rossel, Gerda. 1999. "Crop Names and the History of Hunter-Gatherers." In *Central African Hunter-Gatherers in a Multidisciplinary Perspective: Challenging Elusiveness*, ed. Karen Biesbrouck, Stefan Elders, and Gerda Rossel, 105–16. Leiden: CNWS, Universiteit Leiden.

Rozenzweig, Roy, and David Thelen. *The Presence of the Past: Popular Uses of History in American Life*. New York: Columbia Univ. Press.

Rudin, Harry. 1938. *Germans in the Cameroons, 1884–1914: A Case Study in Modern Imperialism*. London: Jonathan Cape.

Ruggiero, Richard G., and Heather E. Eves. 1998. "Bird-Mammal Associations in Forest Openings of Northern Congo (Brazzaville)." *African Journal of Ecology* 36:183–93.

Rupp, Stephanie. 2001. "I, You, We, They: Forests of Identity in Southeastern Cameroon." Ph.D. diss., Yale University.

Sahlins, Marshall. 1999. "What Is Anthropological Enlightenment? Some Lessons of the Twentieth Century." *Annual Review of Anthropology* 28:i–xxiii.

Samarin, William J. 1986. "French and Sango in the Central African Republic." *Anthropological Linguistics* 28 (3): 379–87.

———. 1989. *The Black Man's Burden: African Colonial Labor on the Congo and Ubangi Rivers, 1880–1900.* Boulder, Colo.: Westview.

Samuel, Raphael. 1994. *Theatres of Memory*, vol. 1, *Past and Present in Contemporary Culture.* London: Verso.

Saragba, Maurice. 1994. "La trypanosomiase humaine en Oubangui-Chari: Son extension pendant la période coloniale." *Ultramarines* 9:11–18.

Sanneh, Lamin. 1989. *Translating the Message: The Missionary Impact on Culture.* Maryknoll, N.Y.: Orbis.

Sarno, Louis. 1993. *Song from the Forest: My Life among the Ba-Benjellé Pygmies.* Boston: Houghton Mifflin.

Saulnier, Pierre. 1997. *Le Centrafrique: Entre mythe et réalité.* Paris: Harmattan.

Sautter, Gilles. 1964. *De l'Atlantique au fleuve Congo: Un géographie du sous-peuplement.* Paris: Mouton.

———. 1967. "Notes sur la construction du chemin de fer Congo-Océan (1922–1934)." *Cahiers d'Études Africaines* 7 (26): 219–99.

Schama, Simon. 1995. *Landscape and Memory.* New York: Alfred A. Knopf.

Schmink, Marianne, and Charles H. Wood. 1992. *Contested Frontiers in Amazonia.* New York: Columbia Univ. Press.

Schroeder, Richard. 1999. "Geographies of Environmental Intervention in Africa." *Progress in Human Geography* 23 (3): 359–78.

Scott, James C. 1998. *Seeing like a State: How Certain Schemes to Improve the Human Condition Have Failed.* New Haven: Yale Univ. Press.

Scott, Joan W. 1991. "The Evidence of Experience." *Critical Inquiry* 17:773–97.

Shaw, Rosalind. 2000. "'Tok Af, Lef Af': A Political Economy of Temne Techniques of Secrecy and Self." In *African Philosophy as Cultural Inquiry*, ed. Ivan Karp and D. A. Masolo, 25–49. Bloomington: Indiana Univ. Press.

Showers, Kate. 1994. "The Ivory Story, Africans and Africanists." *Issue: A Journal of Opinion* 22:41–46.

Shrader-Frechette, Kristin S., and Earl D. McCoy. 1995. "Natural Landscapes, Natural Communities, and Natural Ecosystems." *Forest and Conservation History* 39 (3): 138–42.

Sillitoe, Paul. 1998. "The Development of Indigenous Knowledge: A New Applied Anthropology." *Current Anthropology* 39 (3): 223–35.

Siroto, Leon. 1969. "Masks and Social Organization among the Bakwele People of Western Equatorial Africa." Ph.D. diss., Columbia University.

Sivaramakrishnan, K. 1995. "Colonialism and Forestry in India: Imagining the Past in Present Politics." *Comparative Studies in Society and History* 37 (1): 3–40.

Skaria, Ajay. 1999. *Hybrid Histories: Forests, Frontiers, and Wildness in Western India.* Delhi: Oxford Univ. Press.

Slater, Candace. 1994. *Dance of the Dolphin: Transformation and Disenchantment in the Amazonian Imagination*. Chicago: Univ. of Chicago Press.

———. 1995. "Amazonia as Edenic Narrative." In *Uncommon Ground: Toward Reinventing Nature*, ed. William Cronon, 114–31. New York: W. W. Norton.

Société Emona-Commerce Lubljana. 1981. "Cession de l'exploitation d'une plantation." In author's possession.

Soumille, Pierre. N.d. "Entre Oubangui et Chari dans les années 1925: Quelques aspects historiques de l'Afrique centrale au temps du *Voyage au Congo* d'André Gide." In author's possession.

Spear, Thomas. 1997. *Mountain Farmers: Moral Economics of Land and Agricultural Development in Arusha and Meru*. Berkeley: Univ. of California Press.

Steenthoft, Margaret. 1988. *Flowering Plants in West Africa*. Cambridge: Cambridge Univ. Press.

Stoler, Ann Laura, and Frederick Cooper. 1997. "Between Metropole and Colony: Rethinking a Research Agenda." In *Tensions of Empire: Colonial Cultures in a Bourgeois World*, ed. Frederick Cooper and Ann Laura Stoler, 1–56. Berkeley: Univ. of California Press.

Strathern, Marilyn. 1988. *The Gender of the Gift: Problems with Women and Problems with Society in Melanesia*. Berkeley: Univ. of California Press.

Stromme, Denise M., and Philip M. Hunsicker. N.d. "Let's Play Rain Forest! Nature Games." Washington, D.C.: World Wildlife Fund-US.

Svensson, Emma. 1932. "Kultskolan." In *Kongoboken: Något I ord och bild från Örebro Missionsförenings fält I Franska Kongo*, 100–107. Örebro: Örebro Missionsförening Förlag.

Tardits, Claude, ed. 1981. *Contribution de la recherche ethnologique à l'histoire des civilisations de Cameroun*, vol. 1. Paris: CNRS.

Taylor, Peter, and Raúl García-Barrios. 1995. "The Social Analysis of Ecological Change: From Systems to Intersecting Processes." *Social Science Information* 34 (1): 5–30.

Telesis USA, Inc. 1991. "Sustainable Economic Development Options for the Dzanga-Sangha Reserve Central African Republic." Final Report Prepared for World Wildlife Fund and PVO-NGO/NRMS Project. Washington, D.C.

Terrier, Auguste. 1907. "La Mission Moll." *Bulletin du Comité de l'Afrique Française* 17 (11 Nov.): 387–93.

Thomas, Jacqueline M. C. 1963. *Les Ngbakas de la Lobaye: Le dépeuplement rural chez une population forestière de la République centrafricaine*. Paris: École Pratiques des Hautes Études.

Thomas, Jacqueline M. C., Serge Bahuchet, and Alain Epelboin, eds. 1993. *Encyclopédie des Pygmées Aka*. vol. 2. Paris: Peeters.

Tisserant, R. P. 1950. *Sango Oubangui-Chari*. Issy les Molineaux: Les Presses Missionnaires.

Titley, Brian. 1997. *Dark Age: The Political Odyssey of Emperor Bokassa*. Liverpool: Liverpool Univ. Press.

Tonkin, Elizabeth. 1992. *Narrating Our Pasts: The Social Construction of Oral History.* Cambridge: Cambridge Univ. Press.

Toso, Carlo. 1994. *Centrafrique, un siècle d'évangélisation.* Bangui: Conférence Épiscopale Centrafricaine.

Umberto, P. 1993a. "En vue du centenaire: La confrontation, et bien souvent les accrochages avec les administrateurs coloniaux." *À l'Écoute de l'Église Berbérati,* no. 2 (14 Sept.): n.p.

———. 1993b. ". . . il y a *40* ans." *À l'Écoute de l'Église Berbérati,* no. 2 (14 Sept.): n.p.

U.S. Department of State, Bureau of Public Affairs. 1989. *Background Notes, Central African Republic.* Washington, D.C.: U.S. Government Printing Office.

Vansina, Jan. 1968. *Kingdoms of the Savanna.* Madison: Univ. of Wisconsin Press.

———. 1984. "Western Bantu Expansion." *Journal of African History* 25 (1): 133–41.

———. 1985a. "Esquisse historique de l'agriculture en milieu forestier (Afrique équatoriale)." *Muntu* 2:5–34.

———. 1985b. *Oral Tradition as History.* Madison: Univ. of Wisconsin Press.

———. 1990. *Paths in the Rainforest: Toward a History of Political Tradition in Equatorial Africa.* Madison: Univ. of Wisconsin Press.

———. 1994. *Living with Africa.* Madison: Univ. of Wisconsin Press.

———. 1995. "New Linguistic Evidence and 'The Bantu Expansion.'" *Journal of African History* 36:173–95.

Vedder, Amy. 1998. "Wildlife Conservation Society (WCS) Organization Overview: Central Africa Programs." In *Resource Use in the Trinational Sangha River Region of Equatorial Africa: Histories, Knowledge Forms, and Institutions,* ed. Heather E. Eves, Rebecca Hardin, and Stephanie Rupp. Bulletin Series, Yale School of Forestry and Environmental Studies, no. 102:169–75.

Waller, Richard D. 1990. "Tsetse Fly in Western Narok, Kenya." *Journal of African History* 31:81–101.

Waller, Richard D. and Thomas Spear. 1991. *Becoming Maasai: Ethnicity and Identity in East Africa.* London: James Currey.

Watts, Michael, and Richard Peet. 1996. "Conclusion: Toward a Theory of Liberation Ecology." In *Liberation Ecologies: Environment, Development, Social Movements,* ed. R. Peet and M. Watts, 260–69. London: Routledge.

Wauters, A. J. 1900a. "Carte de la rivière Sangha." *Supplément au Movement Géographique,* no. 5 (2 Feb.): n.p.

———. 1900b. "La région des concessions dans le bassin de la Sanga." *Le Mouvement Géographique,* no. 7 (18 Feb.): 85–88.

———. 1900c. "La région des concessions dans le bassin de la Sanga." *Le Mouvement Géographique,* no. 9 (4 Mar.): 109–13.

———. 1900d. "La Sanga." *Le Mouvement Géographique,* no. 10 (11 Mar.): 121–24.

Weiner, Annette B. 1992. *Inalienable Possessions: The Paradox of Keeping-While-Giving.* Berkeley: Univ. of California Press.

Weiss, Brad. 1996a. "Dressing at Death: Clothing, Time, and Memory in Buhaya,

Tanzania." In *Clothing and Difference: Embodied Identities in Colonial and Post-Colonial Africa,* ed. Hildi Hendrickson, 133–54. Durham, N.C.: Duke Univ. Press.

———. 1996b. *The Making and Unmaking of the Haya Lived World.* Durham, N.C.: Duke Univ. Press.

Wells, Michael, and Katrina Brandon, with Lee Hannah. 1992. *People and Parks: Linking Protected Area Management with Local Communities.* Washington, D.C.: International Bank for Reconstruction and Development and World Bank.

Whatmore, Sarah, and Lorraine Thorne. 1998. "Wild(er)ness: Reconfiguring the Geographies of Wildlife." *Transactions of the Institute of British Geographers* 23:435–54.

White, Lee J. T. 1992. "Effects of Commercial Mechanised Selective Logging on a Transect in Lowland Rainforest in the Lopé Reserve, Gabon." *Journal of Tropical Ecology* 10 (3): 313–22.

White, Luise. 1993. "Cars Out of Place: Vampires, Technology, and Labor in East and Central Africa." *Representations* 43:27–50.

———. 1995. "'They Could Make Their Victims Dull': Genders and Genres, Fantasies and Cures in Colonial Southern Uganda." *American Historical Review* 100:1379–1402.

———. 2000. *Speaking with Vampires: Rumor and History in East and Central Africa.* Berkeley: Univ. of California Press.

White, Richard. 1983. *The Roots of Dependency: Subsistence, Environment, and Social Change among the Choctaws, Pawnees, and Navajos.* Lincoln: Univ. of Nebraska.

———. 1995. "'Are You an Environmentalist or Do You Work for a Living?': Work and Nature." In *Uncommon Ground: Toward Reinventing Nature,* ed. William Cronon, 171–85. New York: W. W. Norton.

Whyte, Susan Reynolds. 1991. "The Widow's Dream: Sex and Death in Western Kenya." In *Personhood and Agency: The Experience of Self and Other in African Cultures,* ed. Michael Jackson and Ivan Karp, 95–114. Washington, D.C.: Smithsonian.

Wilkie, David S., and Bryan Curran. 1993. "Historical Trends in Forager and Farmer Exchange in the Ituri Rain Forest of Northeastern Zaire." *Human Ecology* 21 (4): 389–417.

Wilkie, David S., and John T. Finn. 1990. "Slash-burn Cultivation and Mammal Abundance in the Ituri Forest, Zaire." *Biotropica* 22 (1): 90–99.

Wilkie, David S., and Julia F. Carpenter. 1999a. "Can Nature Tourism Help Finance Protected Areas in the Congo Basin?" *Oryx* 33 (4): 333–39.

———. 1999b. "The Potential Role of Safari Hunting as a Source of Revenue for Protected Areas in the Congo Basin." *Oryx* 33 (4): 340–46.

Willis, Justin. 1992. "The Makings of a Tribe: Bondei Identities and Histories." *Journal of African History* 33:191–208.

Wilson, Peter J. 1989. *The Domestication of the Human Species.* New Haven: Yale Univ. Press.

Worboys, Michael. 1994. "The Comparative History of Sleeping Sickness in East and Central Africa, 1900–1914." *History of Science* 32:89–102.

World Wildlife Fund and Wildlife Conservation International. 1991. "Program Proposal: An Integrated Plan for Regional Forest Conservation and Management in Southeastern Cameroon, Southwestern Central African Republic and Northern Congo." Submitted to U.S. Agency for International Development, Bureau for Africa, Technical Resources Division, Agriculture and Natural Resources, 19 April.

Yates, Frances A. 1966. *The Art of Memory.* London: Pimlico.

Zoctizoum, Yarisse. 1983. *Histoire de la Centrafrique: Violence du développement, domination, et inégalités.* 2 vols. Paris: Harmattan.

INDEX

Note: italicized page numbers indicate illustrations.

Abumi (embryo, fetus, pregnancy), 77, 78, 125, 136, 155, 227 n. 23

Accumulation, 10, 15, 53–54, 59, 64, 90, 95–96, 113, 149, 193–94, 196, 215 n. 32

Adamawa, 24, 29

Advice (*meleyo*). See *Doli*, as advice and teaching

Ageratum conyzoides, 137–38, 151–52, 243 n. 56

Agriculture Service (French colonial), 127

Ajing. See *Kuli ajing*

Aka (peoples), 11, 24, 27, 45, 73, 124, 144, 167–68, 196

Alcohol, 16, 115, 131, 144, 147–48, 181, 241 n. 39

Alembo (vital or occult substance), 49, 50, 79, 110–11, 113, 143, 194, 255 n. 2. *See also* Person; Occult powers

Alouba (Joseph), 98, 163, 170–72, 175

American Museum of Natural History. *See* Hall of Biodiversity

Ancestors, 51, 81, 111, 112, 113, 181

Andersson, Brother Reinhold, 36

Anthropophagy, 56, 92, 94

Apoundjo, Rene, 99–100, 181

Atoxyl, 102

"Babingas," 73, 167–68, 169, 172. *See* Aka; Ngombe

Bajwe (people), 24, 29; language, 22

Bakwele (people), 25

Bananas, 120, 125, 127, 151

Banda (people), 26, 48

Bandoka, 61–65, 74, 75, 76, 90, 99, 114, 115

Bangando (people), 25

Bangui, 11, 43, 54, 120, 197

Bania, 33, 36, 37

Bantu languages, 22, 216–17 n. 9, 218 n. 20. *See also individual Bantu languages*

Bayanga, 11, 26, 27, 45, 46, 89, 91, 133, 147, 159, 183

Belgian colonialism, 102, 158

Berbérati, 21, 33, 41, 53, 54, 107, 127, 197

Bible, 27, 108–9, 112, 113, 179

Big men, 23, 61, 170, 171

Bilolo, 11, 21, 41, 87, 90, 106, 107, 140, 141, 177, 196; hospital in, 103, 106, 109

Biodiversity, 4, 8, 18–20

Blom, Allard, 45–46, 200

Blood, 77, 194, 255 n. 2; brotherhoods, 24, 156, 246 n. 19

Body (and sites on), 5, 8, 14, 77, 97, 136–37, 153

Boganda, Barthélémy, 39, 137–38

Bokassa, Jean-Bedel, 39–40, 41, 137–38, 145, 146, 182; *see also* Opération Bokassa

Bomassa (people, language, village), 25, 27, 73, 74, 159, 162

Bongo (*Tragelaphus eurycerus*), 19, 20, 35

Brazza, Pierre Savorgnan de, 29, 34, 218 n. 29

Brazzaville, 26

Bridewealth, 50, 79, 95, 181

British colonialism, 29, 158

Burnham, Philip, 23, 240 n. 34, 246 n. 18

Bush mango (*Irvingia excelsa*), 19, 152

Bushpigs (*Potamochoerus porcus*), 19, 61

Cable snare traps, 7, 45, 65, 187–88, 189, 191

Cacao, 26, 35, 37, 94, 130, 134

CAISTAB, 35, 135, 146

Cameroon, 12, 22, 23, 24, 26, 40, 58, 63, 86, 134, 163, 182, 185, 186

Cannibalism. *See* Anthropophagy

Cantons, 87, 88, 128. *See also* Chiefs and chieftaincy

Capuchin order: archives, 11; missionaries, 52–53, 104, 105, 139, 140, 141, 177; relations with Central African Republic state, 38–39; of Savoy, 36; of Toulouse, 36. *See also* Catholic missionaries

Carnapp-Quernheim (explorer), 29

Carroll, Richard, 44, 116–17

Cassava (manioc, *Manihot esculenta*), 22, 24, 72, 120–21, 124–25, 127, 129, 130–33, 134, 189, 239 n. 11, 241 n. 36

- Doli - a process. Way of perceiving, characterizing, interpreting past, present. Body of knowledge. △.
- Supplicate response to conservation interventions.
- Organized knowledge around deeply centered ecology. Grafted European influence → Flexibility. Ability to adjust and absorb. (Resilience)
- Concerned w/ questions, of temporal placement, origin, dearth, & loss.
- Way of interpreting the past and environments and as a composite historical category (17)
- Doli - diverse, not monolithic (28)
- Nationalism - influences doli (40) (gov't exploitation of the env't)
- Economic prosperity must accompany clearing/thinning of forests. (42)
- Debt-problems. More investment in logging companies.
- State contributed to doli's discourse of loss. (43)
- Doli produced by drawing from & repudiating state efforts to create CA citizens... (44) *.
- Doli - guides social relations- norms. (45)
- Doli - leaving a person behind... a legacy - developed social persona & self-consciousness (50)
- Past interpreted in terms of the present (52)
- Western education reshaped doli (53) * No true Indigenous knowledge. Mixed w/ European influence.
- Saw education as beneficial for getting jobs. → economies based on forest exploitation. (55)
- Everything - deeply ritualistic (80) * - Last week.
- Witchcraft (110-114)
- Associated conservation w/ loss & deprivation? (115) (125)
- Mpiemu perceived themselves as forest & farming people enforced gender roles.
- French portrayed Mpiemu prod. as being unprod. (130) ←
- Fattiness of the soil (136-137)
- IK-Not stagnant. Blame diff. things depending on conditions (137)
- △ Due to commercial agriculture (138)
- Deprivation associated w/ administration (142) (148)-claims of hunger.